Failure, Nationalism, and Literature

Failure, Nationalism, and Literature

The Making of Modern Chinese Identity, 1895–1937

JING TSU

Stanford University Press

Stanford, California

2005

Stanford University Press
Stanford, California

Printed in the United States of America on acid-free, archival-quality paper

Library of Congress Cataloging-in-Publication Data
Tsu, Jing.
    Failure, nationalism, and literature : the making of modern Chinese identity,
1895–1937 / Jing Tsu.
        p. cm.
    Includes bibliographical references and index.
    ISBN 0-8047-5176-5 (cloth : alk. paper)
        1. Nationalism—China.   2. National characteristics—China.   3. China—
Politics and government—20th century.   I. Title.
    JC311.T785   2006
    320.54'0951—dc22   2005019156

Typeset by G&S Book Services in 10.5/12.5 Bembo

Original Printing 2006

Last figure below indicates year of this printing:
15   14   13   12   11   10   09   08   07   06

In memory of my mother and father

徐蘇 *Caroline Hsu*   石亞藩 *Ya-Fan Tsu*
(1937−2004)   *(1923−1991)*

They gave me a drug that slowed the healing of wounds.

—Adrienne Rich, *"A Valediction Forbidding Mourning"*

Contents

Illustrations

Acknowledgments

FOR THEIR ASSISTANCE in the creation of this book, I am indebted to many teachers, institutions, and friends. I thank the following institutions for research support during the course of this project: Woodrow Wilson Foundation; Alexander von Humboldt Foundation (Bundeskanzler Fellowship); University of California, Berkeley; and Harvard University. I am particularly grateful to those who offered time and invaluable insight regarding earlier versions of this manuscript: Leo Lee, Patrick Hanan, Barbara Johnson, Steve Owen, David Wang, Lydia Liu, David Cohen, and Michael Gordin. Many have commented on parts of it in various forms and conversations, further helping to sharpen my ideas: Bill Callahan, Paul Cohen, Peter Bol, Frank Dikötter, Joan Judge, Juliette Chung, Emma Teng, Ted Huters, Wilt Idema, Li Wai-yee, Bill Todd, Nur Yalman, Oren Bar-Gill, Adriaan Lanni, Johnathan Bolton, and Dan Aaron. I would also like to express my thanks to the following libraries for facilitating my research: Harvard University libraries, Hoover Institution Library and Archives, UC Berkeley libraries, Shanghai Municipal Library, Beijing University Library, Beijing Capital Library, and Stadtbibliothek in Munich. Special thanks go to Gus Espada, Susan Kashiwa, and the librarians at the Harvard Yenching Library for their tireless assistance. I thank as well my editors at Stanford University Press and the helpful comments from two anonymous readers.

My deepest gratitude, of course, goes to my teachers at Harvard: Leo Lee, Patrick Hanan, Steve Owen, and Barbara Johnson. Their generosity, rigor, and intellectual visions inspired me to attempt my own. Each of them showed me the value of erudition and originality by exemplifying it in themselves and the different literary and cultural worlds they cross. I thank my adviser, Leo, in particular, for always probing me with his endless curiosity. Pat's willingness to share his time and knowledge single-handedly ushered me into the world of the late Qing. I am also indebted to my teachers from Berkeley and San Francisco: Judith Butler, Ralph Rader, Maxine

Hong Kingston, Avital Ronell, Fred Dolan, and Mack McCray. During the course of this project, the following people offered support, humor, and distractions, all of which contributed to its eventual completion: Josh Bloom, Anna Bellomo, Allan Adams, Kevin Eggan, Nadya Mason, Morgan Liu, Adriaan Lanni, Sigal Bar-Gill, Tania Smoliarova, Andy Strominger, Naomi Pierce, Maureen McLane, Eileen Chow, Robert Chi, Kenny Ng, Tamara Chin, Jan Kiely, Yu Jing, Zhang Jingfei, Chen Jianhua, Peter Shen, Jay Astle, Jack Chen, Natasha Keller, Chris Nugent, Sarah Allen, Alison Grappe, and Jay Fisher. I am particularly grateful to Diana Morse for her warmth and kindness.

Finally, to Ming, Lorenz, Alina, and David, I continue to accrue my debt in gratitude and indulgence.

Failure, Nationalism, and Literature

Failure and Identity

HOW OFTEN DO WE think of cultural humiliation and failure as strengths? What is our commitment to ideality such that we are continually bound to the desire for sovereignty in theories of culture, agency, colonial history, and nationalism? To examine what this ideality actually forgoes in consideration of cultural differences and history, this book is about failure, and the insistence and vicissitudes of its articulation. It places failure in a cultural context that gave rise to nationalism, race, and literary modernity in late nineteenth- and twentieth-century China, a period of struggle for cultural survival and attempted revitalization.

Despite the rich cultural history of nationalism, it has often been divided in focus between literature, history, political science, and international studies. Generally more attuned to the political culture mobilized by nationalism, political scientists emphasize its state and ideological formations as shaped by institutions and international conflicts. Literary scholars, on the other hand, reinvest the category of nationalism with the broader significance of cultural agency and prefer to examine "nation," its ideological suffix suspended, as a nexus for competing narratives of culture, power, and discourse.

An understanding of not only the historicity but also the figurations of nationalism, however, demands a new, interdisciplinary approach toward how we conceptualize the relationship between nationalism and cultural identities. In many ways, this requires a greater conceptual spectrum for analyzing how individuals operate contrary to their professed motives and how that in itself may be the desired goal. The central issues underlying this project span theories and studies of elite and popular literature, cultural and intellectual history, nationalism, race, and sexuality. To begin, I turn to two political incidents that have constituted the main focus for interpreting nationalism in modern China in recent times.

Perceiving National Injury

Shortly before America's war in Iraq began in 2003, the Chinese government made a less dramatic gesture to the U.S. ambassador to Beijing: The address of the Chinese embassy in Baghdad was provided to prevent another unexpected bombing, as happened in Belgrade in 1999.[1] This recalled one of the most contentious events in Sino-American relations in recent years. The "tragic accident" during the NATO-led war in former Yugoslavia brought on a new wave of nationalism and anti-Americanism in China. It sparked protests and demonstrations across the country as well as in Hong Kong and Taiwan. In what was the largest protest after the Tiananmen Square incident in 1989, protesters wearing white headbands—used in mourning—wept as they held up the photos of three Chinese killed in the bombing. Slogans such as "Down with U.S. imperialism," "Stop American aggression," "Abolish NATO," and "NATO Nazis" were uttered in anger and outrage. Student banners called for "the descendants of the (legendary) Yellow Emperor" to rally to China's defense. Another banner read, "The Chinese People Cannot Be Bullied." The scale of the incident, perceived as a "barbaric act" perpetrated by the American imperialists, finds its culminating expression in the protesters' retaliatory demand: "Blood debts must be paid in blood."

The sentiments behind these slogans are not unfamiliar to us and, as we will see, go back to the emergence of nationalistic culture in the late nineteenth century. In the precarious balance between domination and victimization, the perceived first- and third-world divide in the contemporary world often invokes the equation of hegemony with military might. Claims of injustice and national sovereignty impinge directly on feelings of outrage touched off by acts of injury. The appeal to the "Yellow Emperor," the mythical founder of Chinese civilization invented by twentieth-century nationalistic rhetoric, underscores the utility of cultural and racial origins in bolstering an injured national identity. In a similar way, the idea of blood retaliation, inciting a more primordial sense of ethnic strife, brings honor into the picture as a true stake, as the Chinese are seen as being pushed and "bullied" into a position of self-defense. Whereas civilization lays claim to superiority, and barbarism to inferiority, here the dichotomy is reversed to shame the superior party with barbarism and honor the inferior with civility.[2]

In the polarized verbal arena of winners and losers, it is difficult to say which runs deeper: an already deep-seated skepticism toward a perceived Western colonial power or an inherently passionate allegiance to China's sovereignty. The difficulty, indeed, lies in the fact that the two are often not distinguishable. Antiforeignism has always served as a sure catalyst in consolidating national and ethnic communities. Professions of national sovereignty occur most passionately with injuries done by perceived outsiders. The familiar political castigation of "traitor to the Han people" (*hanjian*), for example, a figure prominently despised in twentieth-century China as a name for those who collaborated with foreigners or the Manchu and Japanese governments against the Han Chinese, reflects a relatively recent choice of ethnicized national identity. It emphasizes the greater crime of betraying an inner unity over that committed by foreign perpetrators. An earlier figuration can be found in the more general idea of "fawning to the outside" (*meiwai*), a frequent description in the late nineteenth century of obsequious behavior toward Westerners. The shift from an unspecified "outside" to an inside "traitor" corresponds to the turn of nationalism from general xenophobia to conscientious citizenship based on a shared allegiance.

Often, rhetorical recourse to the sanctity of national sovereignty indicates an identity already in distress rather than a self-image of invincibility. Even though official propagations of nationalism usually present a robust picture of innate legitimacy naturalized by great destinies and favored by teleological world systems, they are often extrapolated from a cultural milieu of despair and turmoil. In this way, claimed national injuries, rather than the atrocities committed by foreign perpetrators, have much to reveal about the complex problem of nationalism itself: its intents, passions, and embeddedness in an operating cultural context in which the expression of nationalism is but part of a larger process of creating cultural identities.

Sociological and historical studies of nationalist movements and conflicts often privilege the significance of institutional and state forces over the cultural in the making of national allegiances.[3] Nationalism is usually understood as a state-imposed ideology, reinforced by ethnicized affinity, and mostly examined for its instrumental use for particular political ends. In cases in which nationalism is considered a product of culture, the latter is usually relegated to a mobilized rather than mobilizing status. The fact of nationalism has become such an indispensable pillar for claims of sovereignty in the modern world that inquiries into its making often end up reinforcing rather than challenging its ramifications in cultural life. Military intelligence, political profiles, and occasional cinematic graces of the media, accompanied by crash-course segments on the people, geography, and history of a particular country during times of political crises, signal to us that the knowledge of other people's cultures becomes relevant only on the occasion of political conflicts. We give much less attention to how concepts such as national sovereignty, nationalism, and racial identity and violence grow out of particular cultural contexts layered with historical memories and antagonisms that fuel the emotional resolve of the "nation."

The cultural sensibilities that shape the specific passions of nationalism can benignly form a community in peace or, more likely, incite violent hatred for others. Their centrality in any given culture does not come to the fore only during times of war and violent confrontations, even though those occasions tend most to remind us of their grave importance. "Where does nationalism come from?" is not a question about origins but, rather, one that reflects our incessant puzzlement over why its continually resurfacing presence today should surprise us. Globalization has not diminished but only brought into starker relief the intensity of the claims of "nation" and ethnicity. In an era of promised technological communicability between cultural localities, the desire for separate and, in many cases, incommensurable ways of life and identities has not faded. The insistent and violent will for ethnic and cultural difference as markers of identities persists amid visions of new world order. It would seem that cultural differences are more often reduced and misunderstood than successfully communicated beyond political needs.

Recognizing this, it is timely to rethink our understanding of nationalism and the possibilities for cultural differences when the difficulty of establishing common grounds is the norm rather than the exception. Already an issue in nineteenth-century China, the problem of making legible national intentions in an international framework was central to the efficacy of foreign affairs, increasingly defined by "diplomacy." Reviving the issue in a more modern setting, the diplomatic aftermath of the aircraft collision near Hainan Island in 2001 illustrates the importance of the problem in the context of contemporary Chinese nationalism. Following closely on the heels of the embassy bombing, the collision of a U.S. EP-3 surveillance plane with a Chinese fighter aircraft quickly focused on how to acknowledge culpability in a way that would be acceptable to both the United States and China. The choice of language was carefully scrutinized. This was an awkward negotiation between not only the two governments but also the Chinese government and its populace, some of whom saw the government as taking a conciliatory approach toward the United States. President Bush and Secretary of State Colin Powell were reportedly "very sorry" that the incident occurred and that the American plane entered Chinese airspace and landed without verbal clearance.[4] The Chinese propaganda chiefs agonized over the dozens of different ways one can translate *sorry* into Chinese. In the ensuing months, the wording changed from the initial *yihan*, which can convey a dismissive kind of regret, to *baoqian*, an apology that does not really admit to culpability. China had originally demanded that America agree to the use of *daoqian*, which admits guilt. By the time the letter of apology was published, however, *very sorry* became *shen biao qianyi*, which means a "deep expression of apologetic intents."

The emphasis on apology in addressing international conflicts is in itself interesting. The extent to which an admission of guilt corresponds to righting a wrong is a question that has recently received much attention in discussions of human rights, war responsibility, and political restitution. One scholar argues that the political importance in maintaining a framework of morality with room for adaptation to different cultural contexts demonstrates a new and promising course in building an international community.[5] Apologies show a willingness to engage historical injustices that is crucial for communal healing and overcoming. Even though this is true, the optimism invested in a global morality, the adaptability of which is based on "vagueness and voluntarism," may be overstated.[6] The guilty can initiate a forum inviting victims to come forth; however, the reverse is not often the case. In many ways, discussions of guilt are a luxury allowed by political stability and confidence such that one can afford admitting to a wrong, the egregiousness of which, in all likelihood, can be tangibly compensated for through economic means.

The idea of guilt, however, has a much more complex range of expressions in cultural life and sensibilities than these particular forums for international justice could account for. In the two incidents I have described, for example, guilt lies entirely with the perceived perpetrator. The focus on intent in deriving an apology and locating culpability seems to downplay other, more sensitive questions. Some reports claimed that Americans bombed the embassy intentionally.[7] Although this claim may support China's entitlement to an apology, this does not seem to have been the point. Intentionality was never doubted by the Chinese.

Occupying the premise of the controversy is the insistence that any compensation, short of blood, cannot be the right compensation for this injury. Here we have a preference for the abstract and unquantifiable measure of the act, as opposed to something for which a proper compensation may be desired and negotiated. The externalized outrage, as long as it is not appeased, enables a persuasive expression and assertion of national and racial solidarity. Embracing injury and humiliation stirs a profound passion and coalesces with the love for one's nation. On the wall of the Hainan University dining hall during the detainment of the U.S. spy plane, a large banner read, "Wipe Out Our National Humiliation / Severely Punish the American Military." Is one to assume that national humiliation, an assault to one's national pride, can be redressed only through retaliatory violence? Does the condition of humiliation sustain one's right to call for another's injury in turn? Or can we understand the degree of the humiliation only by the violence we retroactively commit in its name?

The two disputes with the American military have provided the main focus for interpreting Chinese nationalism from the outside in recent years. We cannot fully understand the questions they raise, however, if we were to examine only the rupturing moment of nationalism without a deeper grasp of its cultural impetuses. One of the most overlooked dimensions of claimed national injury is that the claim of victimization reserves, among other things, the right to retaliatory violence. Even if only in theory, the idea that injury demands injury in turn reinforces the position of the disempowered with the passions of vengeance. The claim of injury does not always have as its exclusive preoccupation the original cause of distress. Instead, the position of suffering itself generates something more intimate to the building of collective identity. More tangibly, it comes to acquire particular social and political leverage that makes it attractive to hold on to positions of victimhood. In this sense, in emphasizing guilt and social redress as important tools for building dialogues between cultures and nations, we neglect the possibility that the persistence of the conflict may come hand in hand with its productiveness for maintaining a certain cultural and national identity.

In the absence of such an inquiry, historians have found claims of victimization baffling. That victimization could offer a "peculiar source of pride" or become a "badge of honor" has led to the conclusion that there is an increasing professionalization and commercialization of victimhood.[8] One observer remarks on the trend of competing for historical injustices, such as referring to the Nanjing massacre as the "forgotten Holocaust of World War II" or reducing the Asian American experience to Amy Tan's *Joy Luck Club*. Another historian of China understands this as a reflection of China's self-fashioning into a "professional victim."[9] In a different context, Anthony Appiah sees in the claim of victimhood a strategy for identity building motivated by the fear of the "shallowness" of one's relatively trauma-free identity.[10] In these cases, the position of the victimized is utilized to claim an otherwise undeserved cultural recognition. Instead of being tied to acts that directly engender victims, victimhood becomes a fashioned or strategized identity. Concerned that claims of suffering, lacking authenticity, are just a different way of competing for recognition in identity politics, these observers focus on the derivative aspect of victimization and deplore what they see as diluting the distinctiveness of historical injustices.[11]

Whether historical injustices are distinct, however, poses a question separate from why people claim victimization. Victimization results from different kinds of injustice and abuse and does not in itself argue for the just or unjust recognition of that injury. It does, however, present the state of suffering as being entitled to some kind of compensation. To consider that claim less authentic or derivative misses the reasons for which that position of injury would be socially or culturally desirable. The growing pervasiveness of the phenomenon can perhaps be better understood not as a kind of deplorable opportunism but as an important discursive frame for cultural and national narratives. In ways this book shall examine, victimization does not need to be continually attached to a historically real injury to claim and act on authenticity. Victimization is not only empowering in a framework of international justice that mediates processes of restitution; as seen in the Hainan Island incident, the embrace of victimization can shape cultural passions for national and racial identities. It integrates historical humiliations, such as colonial subjugation, into a resilient narrative of self-invention. Rather than glorified sovereignty, the consecration of humiliation is intrinsic to tales of nation building and national identity, especially for those claiming to recover from fallen status.[12]

It would perhaps be more useful to think of victimization not as something new to historical injustices but rather as a modality of cultural identity. Humiliation can be both a response to injury inflicted by another party and the preserving stake of a cultural claim. In the context of twentieth-century China, how this might work as a cultural experience generating specific passions—benign and violent—and nationalistic and racial ideologies is the subject of this book. The challenge is to provide an account of victimization and suffering not as beleaguered conditions but as terms enabling the articulation of a persistent identity. Rather than take victimization as something that must be sanctified with authenticity, one might consider it in its versatility. In this way, one might avoid the problem of privileging some claims of victimization as real and authentic, thereby dismissing others as more opportunistic or even vulgar. We may not always be morally equipped to judge the intrinsic worth of victimization, but we can consider how it operates within a cultural and historical frame as a way of mobilizing the power of identity.

This task bears intimately on a study of Chinese nationalism, culture, and literature, as well as on issues of multiculturalism, ethnonationalism, and the constitution of individual identities, extending well beyond the specific locus of this inquiry. This study of the formation of modern Chinese identity in its national, racial, and cultural configurations recasts these problems in the frame of "failure." Against our usual conceptions of self-determination, sovereignty, and fulfilled identities, *Failure, Nationalism, and Literature: The Making of Modern Chinese Identity* examines the formation of nationalism, racial identity, and literature during the crucial period of nation building in China from 1895 to 1937.

Out of a real political failure marked by imperial decline, military defeats, foreign occupations, and infelicitous reforms, a different order of failure emerged in the late nineteenth century. The rhetoric of failure incorporated defeat into a narrative of resilience. Inaugurated by the tumultuous history of late imperial and Republican China, failure elaborates on historicity through a rhetorical mode of overcoming and regeneration. This discursive propensity becomes the most productive and pervasive mode of cultural self-perception during the crucial period of nation building. Occasioned by historical crises but worked over by a cultural desire for survival, failure is a modality for overcoming that does not rely on simple triumph as its goal. National narratives are not always committed to a vision of success. The exceptionality of failure in the ideal scheme of sovereignty is what paradoxically holds ultimate sway over the cultural imaginary.

The idea of failure encompasses the range of cultural, political, rhetorical, and literary maneuvers that seek to repair a damaged sense of "nation" and "self" during these formative decades of great turmoil, conflict, and uncertainty. Conceptions of race, nation, and culture developed their own narratives and definitions of a modern Chinese cultural identity. The force of this imperative toward the formation of a modern identity was an imperative unparalleled at this time of westernization, imperialism, and the disintegration of the old social order. Nation was perceived as a much-needed political entity in a new era of globalization. The idea of race (*minzu*)—which means both "nation" and "race" in Chinese—acquired a more precise definition through appeals to evolution and positioning the "yellow race" in relation to "white race." In the cultural imagination, literary modernity was expressed through the construction of new cultural identities, such as the "New Woman" and the "Chinese national character," as well as through the combination of Western narrative forms with the Chinese vernacular tradition of the novel. All three developments, however, coincided in their expressions of unease toward the viability of a declining Chinese civilization. They enabled points of tension and divergence where interpretations of race, nationalism, culture, and imperialism took different courses in the making of a nation's destiny. The unease grew into an insistence on the relentless self-examination of China's weaknesses. It founded multiple narratives of cultural resilience within the experience of an oppression as productive as it was involuntary.

Nation, Race, and Literature in China, 1895–1937

In a volume titled *We Spit on That Kind of Chinese*, contributors from China as well as overseas Chinese are brought together to scrutinize self-representations of Chinese. In their opinions, these images have distorted and disgraced Chinese culture and identity.[13] Among the objects of criticism are the dissident Wei Jingsheng and producer Su Xiaokang of the controversial television series *Heshang* (River elegy) in the late 1980s that, in its open critique of the Chinese government, attracted much national and international attention. The most interesting debate in the volume, however, comes from a series of articles and readers' letters dealing with the controversy surrounding the sign "Chinese and dogs not admitted." This sign is said to have been posted as one of the park rules outside the southern gate of the Huangpu Park in Shanghai until 1928. The first public park in China, Huangpu Park was built in the British concession in 1868. One of the most often-cited reminders of Western imperialism from the so-called one hundred years of national humiliation (*bainian guochi*) starting in the mid-nineteenth century, the equivalence of Chinese with dogs has become synonymous with that colonial history. It epitomizes the humiliation Chinese experienced under Western domination, palpable in everyday life in Shanghai's International Settlement. Thus, when in 1994 someone suggested that the sign was fabricated, an emotional controversy followed.

In a short article published in the Shanghai journal *Shiji* (Century), Xue Liyong briefly recounts the times at which people resuscitated the sign's history in order to promote war patriotism and political goals. Kenneth Scott Latourette mentioned it in *The Development of China* (1917) as part of his denunciation of Western colonialism in China.[14] In 1932, when sentiments against Japanese and Western colonialism ran high, the sign's relation to the humiliating colonial context was brought up again for its perceived political significance. In an article that was reprinted in several journals and newspapers, Xue suggests that the Museum of Shanghai Urban History and Development had fabricated the sign in the 1950s in response to the Korean War and the need to solidify cultural loyalties toward the recent Communist victory. The museum itself never officially opened, but the story of the sign captivated the popular imagination. Witnesses who had lived in Shanghai at the time testified to its existence. Xue, however, dismisses their accounts as confusion with what they actually saw at the museum. Xue states that the existence of this sign cannot be proved. In the 1980s, he explains, there was again discussion about redisplaying this sign in what was formerly the Shanghai Historical Museum. Yet, despite the pressure of popular demand, museum personnel felt it inappropriate to proceed based on inconclusive evidence regarding its origin. In 1989, when the sign and other artifacts were relocated to storage, the movers discarded the sign because the fabrication, Xue emphasizes, was clear even to them. As a gesture of his own protest against the undeserved legendary status of this sign, Xue stomped it to pieces and left them next to a heap of garbage. He claims to have done this for the sake of preempting more unfounded controversies in the future, because "People who would fabricate a humiliating story about China reveal only their rotten Chinese characteristics in doing so."[15]

After the appearance of Xue's article, concerned readers sent in numerous detailed descriptions of the sign and its precise location. Well-researched data based on journals, newspaper clippings, and personal memoirs from the late 1870s through the early decades of the twentieth century flooded the publications department. Xue's skepticism was widely perceived as a disloyal attempt to soften the culpability of Western imperialism. Emotional outcries were voiced both at home and abroad. To remind people of the infamy of imperialism, one author urged them to read the suicide letter left by one of the leading martyrs of early twentieth-century China, Chen Tianhua (1875–1905), who took his own life in the hope of awakening the Chinese to the urgency of saving the nation.

As a result of the extraordinary attention given to this controversy, several historians recently reinvestigated the matter. Whether this sign had in fact existed to the degree that would have satisfied both sides of the controversy is, however, not a question I wish to evaluate.[16] Nor is it, apparently, what was ultimately at stake. The editor's own note best captures the sentiment behind the controversy: "Apart from whether this displayed sign is an original or reproduction, the problem lies in the question: Can we then use it to deny completely the historical fact of western imperialism's brutality and its oppression of the Chinese people?"[17] Thus, the crux of the issue lies not in missing factual evidence but in something much less tangible—a humiliating memory that will never cease to remind the Chinese of their national shame. In fact, the editor's own question already predicates itself on the suspicion that the sign did not exist. It matters not whether the object of anti-imperialist patriotism is real, as long as the relation of the Chinese people to it as a humiliating experience continues to be commemorated. In this way, though Western imperialism engendered the event, its historical memory is divorced from this origin. It is not the nation that he seeks to restore, but the proof of its dejection that he wants to reinstate. In a remarkable moment, nationalism is expressed without nation. The passion of injustice one feels in nationalism lives on without the nation's continual and palpable injury. Failure protects the nation from falling into oblivion.[18] In exchange, however, the nation's humiliating past is remembered without nationalistic glory. Thus, between indignation and commemoration, national allegiance implicates itself in a paradox of objectless and joyless allegiance.

The title of one rebuke to Xue's claim states, "Not forgetting national hatred is by no means a rotten Chinese characteristic."[19] Presumably, insisting on the nation's humiliation reflects a desirable national characteristic. After all, one merely shows one's patriotism by not letting the history of oppression disappear from historical memory. On the other hand, Xue is also motivated by a kind of nationalistic outrage directed at not letting the Chinese be reminded—let alone by a false artifact—of their history of subjugation under Western imperialism. Renan's well-known remark that a nation is founded on collective memories does not seem to take into account memories that do not desire a heroic or honorable past.[20] The possibility of the nation as an identity lies, strangely, in its commemorated injury, its failure to secure a proper recognition, not in forgetting through collective amnesia. The nation, however, is not alone in having failed in some way. The sense of failure also extends to individuals, resonating as a certain failure *in them*, imagined as a fault in the Chinese national character. In fact, *We Spit on That Kind of Chinese* is not the only work published in the 1990s that scrutinizes the question of what is wrong with the Chinese national character.[21] The first complete modern Chinese translation of nineteenth-century American missionary Arthur Smith's *Chinese Characteristics* (1890) appeared around the same time.[22] Another work published in Beijing, *The Quirks of the Chinese*, deals with every facet of the Chinese character from selfishness to superstition. On the cover is a warning to the Chinese people not to become "the ugly Chinese."[23] Our ugliness, it says, comes from the fact that we do not know that we are ugly.

Judging from the number of works that have appeared since then on the flaws of the Chinese, one may speculate that the preoccupation is unlikely to subside. The intensity of national identity remarkably finds its most convincing expressions in negativity. An unrelenting self-scrutiny leaves no flaw uncriticized, no fault unconfessed. The imperative for every Chinese to understand his or her own shortcomings as a prerequisite to self-improvement asserts that behind every pleasing self-image lies a delusion that must be exposed. Despite this open self-chastisement, however, something intimate to the self remains: If only the Chinese knew they were in fact ugly, they might then perhaps not be so ugly anymore. The promise of redemption lies not in the recognition of an object in need of remedy but in the labor of reflection. If only one would turn against oneself in a moment of truthful recognition, one could then dispel the delusion that lies at the root of Chinese characteristics. Here we distinguish a similar move at work in the identification with the nation. By keeping alive China's humiliation as a nation, one can properly keep intact one's passion for its survival. The urgency of national salvation is forever preserved as the most promising possibility for the nation. As long as one has not exhaustively established the source of China's weakness, that weakness has not yet become fatal. The passionate attachment to the nation, furthermore, entails an impassioned commitment to the scrutiny of one's own failure.

The preoccupation with what is wrong with China, though not always expressed in the same way, has never failed to excite nationalistic imagination throughout the twentieth century. Its different articulations originate from diverse premises but rely on a persistent mode of failure. To begin this inquiry into the power of failure in the shaping of nationalistic, racial, and cultural discourses, Chapter 2 deals with this variegated topography by examining the Chinese intellectual discourse on race in the late Qing period. During this time, the transition from late imperialism to modern national and racial consciousness propelled the cultural imagination into unknown territories. The haunting specter of the nation, which later becomes the focus of intense self-scrutiny in the 1920s and 1930s, first found its precipitating images in the two decades before the founding of the Republic (1911).

In the late 1890s, because of a series of military defeats following the Opium War (1839–42), intellectuals could no longer refute the alarming state of affairs of China's declining international status. Reformers such as Kang Youwei, Tang Caichang, and Liang Qichao attempted different strategies to rationalize China's failure. The theory of social Darwinism provided a way of explaining China's tenuous position in the modern world. The yellow race, it was widely said, was in decline, but this decline was not yet systematically theorized. At the time, this mode of rationalization was indistinguishable from the exercise of cultural imagination. The burgeoning of translated Western literature, a feat pioneered by Lin Shu, the leading translator of European and American fiction widely read by Chinese intellectuals, reflects the intense energy in investigating China's possibility of avoiding the fate met by other races, such as the blacks.

Whereas political treatises longed for utopian solutions for the degeneration of the yellow race, fiction reflected as much political allegories as it did the popular appetite for sensationalized adventures. Failure, in another way, inspired rather than devastated. Examining how this works in futuristic fiction, science fantasies, and the larger dialogue on the "yellow peril," Chapter 3 looks at the transformation of the worrisome idea of a race in peril into a celebrated notion of a menacing and triumphant race in popular and fictional imagination. In the last attempts to mediate harsh reality, the cultural sensibilities at the time received the experience of oppression with fantastic ingenuity. With the advantage of historical hindsight, one sees with clarity the trajectory of nationalistic ideology rather than the plethora of those other ideas and fancies that helped to shape it.

Although intellectuals stated the problem with poignancy and eloquence, an array of obscure, unknown cultural opportunists and amateur writers, with their often outlandish views at the fringes of history, allow us a glimpse into the rich milieu to which the intellectual project of national salvation is indebted. Not only intellectuals but also popular writers and commentators played with the specter of China's irreversible deterioration in the scheme of evolution while trying to comprehend its gravity. Reorienting themselves toward a perceived global struggle for survival, observers and writers used the logic behind the laws of evolution to construct China's proper place of superiority. At times inconsistent, the process of forming this racial rationale oscillated between self-doubt and exuberance. In this framework, the yellow race is rationalized, through inventive rhetorical maneuvers, as the only race of all subordinated races—blacks, browns, reds—capable of posing a portentous threat to white superiority. A race in peril turns into a race capable of inciting fear. The weak transforms into the formidable, and failure becomes strength.

The late Qing period experimented with the experience of subjugation as a source of possible entitlement and also initiated a discursive framework for locating the source of China's decline. In the process of attempting to see in themselves the prospect of both ruination and rejuvenation, late Qing intellectuals and writers set a cultural pattern of ambivalent self-scrutiny. The line of inquiry was more persistent than the object it pursued. The racial framework contradictorily sketched out in the late Qing lent itself to a specialized inquiry into racial improvement in the Republican period. Under the influence of a new and much-heralded scientific spirit, eugenics gave expression to both the cultural anxiety about race and a rational faculty eager to dissect the discomfort. The logic of self-scrutiny easily extended from examining the inadequacies of biological constitution to identifying the spiritual defects of racial, national, and sexual "character." Chapter 4 examines these concomitant discourses of race, eugenics, and the national character.

Significantly, "national character" is variously translated as *guominxing* and *minzuxing*. Both *guojia* and *minzu* have been used to translate "nation." However, *minzu* has a distinctly racial connotation, harking back to the notion of clan (*zu*).[24] Racial thinking in modern China draws upon not only Western social Darwinism and racial engineering but also available notions within the Chinese cultural repertoire. This was intended, among other things, to minimize the possible estrangement and resistance to imported Western sources. In the 1920s and 1930s, *eugenics* was variously translated as "study of superior birth" (*youshengxue*), "study of good birth" (*shanzhongxue, shuzhongxue*), "study of marriage and posterity" (*hunyin zhesi xue*), and "study of racial improvement" (*renzhong gailiang xue*). The importance of posterity in Chinese culture is a concept readily absorbed into the advocacy for eugenics. Even though the phrase "superior birth, superior nurture" (*yousheng youyu*) can still be seen posted every few blocks in the central part of Shanghai in the twenty-first century, it has lost much of its nationalistic connotations from the 1930s.[25] During the first three decades of the twentieth century, the period of nation building in China, racial improvement was propagated as the key to national survival. In significant ways, eugenics was not merely an intellectual enterprise. Its indebtedness to the notion of self-improvement, racial or cultural, opened up a narrowly defined social project to a wide variety of unconventional, if not esoteric, ideas, ranging from exercise regimes and breathing techniques to new conceptions of body culture.

In this way, racial decline was not the only category in need of remedy. Critical attention turned to women's undesirable characteristics as another focus of social and literary criticism. Chapter 5 centers on the various proposals and programs outlined for women's new role in the modern society. Beginning with a close examination of the philosophy of a "society based on beauty," advocated by the infamous sexologist and cultural guru Zhang Jingsheng, this chapter traces the issue of femininity through popular sex culture, studies of female perversions and criminality, and literary expressions of the "modern woman." From their physical beauty to their deranged sexual behavior, women were encouraged to reflect on their own ills, liberate themselves from the shackles of traditional China, and assume the responsibilities proper for the "modern woman." Just as the Chinese people were urged to develop a consciousness of being citizens of a nation (*guomin*), women were called on to transform themselves into "new women" (*xin nüxing*).

Available explanations of gender construction and nation in China studies often designate the nation as a coercive institution that exacts definitions of femininity and sexuality.[26] Historians often remind us that women played an indispensable role in revolutions in modern China by resorting to empirical evidence to establish the underrepresented presence of women in modern Chinese history.[27] Literary scholars, on the other hand, scrutinize the making of gender in great detail without providing more rigorous analyses of how that would bear on the cultural context that makes gender prescriptions necessary.[28] In fact, only by taking into account the larger social and cultural context together with particular manifestations does one notice the underlying logic impelling scrutiny of gender, national character, and youth. Everything from the better maintenance of the postal system to the brand of cigarette one should smoke pivots on the question of correcting China's failures. Behind the ostensible optimism of a new and enlightened modern China lies a reluctant, though comforting recognition of a deeply flawed China that only the Chinese themselves could love.

The examination of Chinese "character" as a constitutive element of national strength gave entry to the imperative of national salvation into the individual's interior life. How one behaved in the privacy of one's home, and even in one's psychic life, directly influenced the health of the nation. The individual's private desires and torments bore the imprint of the nation's demise. Just as racial character was a matter of self-surveillance, interiority became the discipline of nationalistic conscience. Whereas questions of the Chinese racial character and the New Woman impinged directly on the nation's ability to survive, the individual's inner conflicts expressed an uneasy relation to the nation. Sexual torments resonated with perceived colonial oppression. Identity was linked intimately, albeit uncomfortably, with the process of identification, just as nation relies on the appeal of nationalism. Whatever has been exacted from one's identity to make possible the nation as a collective identity is accomplished by coalescing the individual's trauma with the nation's trauma.

The abundance of first-person confessional narratives in modern Chinese literature of the May Fourth period beginning in 1919 attests to this commiserated intimacy. The need for self-dissection, as forcefully called for by Lu Xun, was equated with national salvation. Only by scrutinizing what is wrong with them can the Chinese regenerate their atrophied national spirit. Embedded in the short story form, diary writing became widely utilized to convey the interior dramas and torments of individual writers. Chapter 6 examines the making of individuals' interior life in relation to the exigencies of nationalism by focusing on masculinity and masochism in literature and literary culture. The individual's interior life reflected the conflicted relation with the imperatives of nationalism, and that interiority also provided the space for interrogating one's own identity. Reflecting this intense focus on the individual's inner life and desires, Chinese intellectuals' keen interest in psychoanalysis at the time furnished a new perspective from which to articulate their personal and sexual identities. Male writers expressed the apprehensions of masculinity in masochism and melancholia. Self-torment became a gratifying labor offering respite from the impossibility of exoneration. They took pleasure in narratives of masochistic suffering, taunting the audience with their restless, alternating requests for punishment and expiation. This is expressed not only in the short story collections by Yu Dafu and Guo Moruo but also in the private correspondence between Guo, Zong Baihua, and Tian Han in *Trefoil Collection*.

The psychic grievance of individual torment offered a potent source for impassioned attachments. Chapter 7 examines the appeal of suffering both to individuals and to a collective national identity. The experience of suffering encapsulated the political and aesthetic mood for an era of individual torment and social anguish. Wrestling torment from the privacy of individual psyches, the idea of suffering or depression (*kumen*) provided an expression for the modern epoch too powerful to be claimed by any individual. Lu

Xun's translation of Kuriyagawa Hakuson's *Symbol of Angst* bespeaks not only a literary interest but also a profound concern with the experience of modernity in China. *Kumen* facilitated the expression of a modern China as uncertain as it is sublime. It bridged individual restlessness with societal discontent, allowing the projection of, more than anything else, the intellectuals' anxiety over their felt social irrelevance as the legitimate sentiment appropriate to the project of nation building. Artistic creations became synonymous with suffering, reaffirming the centrality of failure to the tasks of national salvation and revolution.

From these very different perspectives—yellow race, racial perils, eugenics, national character, femininity and masculinity, beauty and literary masochism, and confession and suffering—a tale of nation building in twentieth-century China unfolds. It is told many times from multiple locations on the cultural topography, each time differently but consistently in the mode of failure. And it never ceases to be resilient even as it tells a cumulative tale of defeat. The relevance of this complex cultural framework for perceiving oneself in relation to the outside world continues to have its political and social appeal today. In 1991, the novel *Yellow Peril* (Huanghuo) once again revived the specter of the destructive potential of the yellow peril. The trilogy first appeared in a Canadian expatriate newspaper and was subsequently banned in mainland China.[29] It envisions a time of political turmoil following the Tiananmen Square incident (1989) under the threat of nuclear war and environmental catastrophe. Most significant is the third volume, titled *Yellow Peril Re-attacks the World*, in which the fulfillment of the prophecy of the yellow peril is brought to life, as billions of Chinese refugees flood into Russia and the United States, forcing the world economy, resources, and land into decline.

Even more recently, the new epidemic of 2003, severe acute respiratory syndrome, recalls the power of cultural anxieties about biological contamination from an exotic origin. Referred to in certain European presses as "China syndrome" or "Asian flu," the acronym SARS had the unfortunate resonance of "Special Administrative Region," Hong Kong's official name since the 1997 handover. Conspiracy theories of the virus as U.S. biological warfare against the Chinese met with the retaliatory speculation that China's own biochemical labs unleashed the virus on the populace. The exchange of paranoiac accusations hark back to earlier eras of racial and national antagonisms fueled by imagined powers of contamination. Summoning the resolve of patriotic nationalism, Premier Wen Jiabao, on May 4, 2003 — the eighty-fourth anniversary of the monumental nationalistic, anti-imperialistic, and new culture movement in 1919 — called on the nation to carry forward the May Fourth spirit of "democracy" and "science" in the nation's fight against SARS.[30]

The continual cultural power of the invocation of racial and national survival follows a tradition beginning in the late Qing period of imagining the rise of the yellow race as menace and master. The future of the Chinese race is envisioned with a hope driven by the promise of a once-derogatory designation. In journals and newspapers from the 1860s throughout the 1930s, the preoccupation with what is wrong with China only intensifies. The preoccupation with failure will become ingrained as a particular consciousness. The question of China's ills ceases to be posited exclusively as such, for by the 1920s and 1930s, it will have been internalized as the constitutive premise upon which every other question is posited. Failure becomes the embedded consciousness of an identity in search of the "Chinese."[31] Its perpetual lack of fulfillment also enables its intense passion ever to preserve that possibility.

Undoing Idealism

China's nation-building project compels us to think differently, going against our intuitions and desires to deplore abjection and to privilege empowerment. Existing critical approaches toward different national literatures and cultures, however, have not yet adequately met this demand. Before proceeding with the specific analyses of China's culture- and nation-building process, it is necessary to address the conceptual implications it holds for other disciplines. Due to the range of theoretical issues outside the China studies field that the present study engages, this last section will discuss at some length the ways in which certain conceptual approaches designed to deal with cultural alternatives and national literatures have also limited our understanding of the array of possible articulations of different national and cultural narratives.

In the past twenty years, theoretical interest in "third-world literature" has gained focus and intensity, primarily because different national traditions and minor literatures are deemed valuable for a critique of the Western intellectual tradition and literary canon.[32] The project of incorporating the peripheries and minor discourses, however, has recently encountered its own limitations. The practice of literary and critical theory has fallen short of its aspirations for dialogic cultures and global literatures. New barriers to proper recognition have risen to replace and even compound old ones, as the criterion for assessing the value and scope of non-Western or minor literatures remains bound to a question of who wields the power of representation.[33] More problematically, a proclaimed ethical reflexivity, as a more socially responsible approach, has also made the motivations behind well-disguised rationalizations even less transparent.

Amid these battles over ethics and responsibility, there has been little room for reflecting on the different implications of these issues in and from other locales that do not observe the same set of ethics. The genesis of Malaysian-Chinese and Singaporean-Chinese literatures in the early twentieth century serves as an example. Originally a diasporic split from mainland Chinese literature, Sinophone literature in Southeast Asia has been considered minor to and derivative of China's modern literature (New Culture Movement of 1915) well after the declaration of a "South Seas color" (*nanyang secai*) literature by a group of expatriate writers between 1927 and 1932. The fact that literary awards in Taiwan, rather than mainland China, have now become a forum of recognition for Malaysian Chinese writers further complicates the notion of a national center for legitimate "national" literary traditions. The often-invoked notion of "cultural China," a concept used to avoid the pitfalls of a singular geopolitical and cultural identity, was in fact first proposed by these Southeast Asian diasporic writers. Despite the intent behind its original proposal, "cultural China" has largely been limited to Taiwan, Hong Kong, and mainland China, the three most vocal locales in the Chinese heritage world.[34]

The invitation to participate in a more open cultural forum is tempting. It also comes, however, with its own conditions for speaking. The development of modern Chinese literature as a field in the American academy in many ways reflects the intellectual burden created by this kind of framework. On the one hand, subscription to current multicultural discourses (whether postmodern or postcolonial) has undoubtedly provided a more effective way for modern Chinese literature, or any other third-world literature, to create its own academic identity in a cross-cultural nexus. On the other hand, the distinctiveness of different national literatures and traditions are recognizable as long as they participate in the familiar history of oppression and subjugation. Whether it is to expose the secret neuroses of the imperialist legacy or to empower cultural and political exile as productive margins of alterity, attempts at reexamination often stipulate a tale of national suffering and grievance or of indictment and triumph in the face of Western domination.[35] The assumption that empowerment and sovereignty are demonstrated through the degree of extrication from domination, recast as globalization or historically prefigured as imperialism, does not merely underlie analyses of colonial nationalism. The same principle also shapes the way ideas such as individual freedom and self-determination are heralded as universal aspirations, often subsuming cultural differences.[36] It is not always clear, however, whether freedom from bondage, in the way it is conventionally understood, is or should always be the desired solution.

The experience with westernization in China demonstrates the importance of this question. As many historians have pointed out, although westernization held the promise of reinventing a new China equipped with modern science and technology in the late nineteenth and early twentieth centuries, China's optimism was also accompanied by an anxiety over the perceived threat of imperialism.[37] A series of foreign aggressions and territorial occupations beginning with the Opium War quickened the pace of disintegration of the imperial order. By the early twentieth century, China's sense of cultural sovereignty was irreversibly shaken. The ambivalent recognition of both China's weakness and its need to emulate the very source of that subjugation for modernization, widely acknowledged at this time, led reformers and intellectuals to endorse a distinct cultural rationale for national survival. Beginning in the late 1890s, intellectual discussions, political tracts, and popular discourse focused on notions of racial peril and cultural extinction. An intense preoccupation with the failure of an empire, culture, and race led to persuasive articulations of modern Chinese national and racial identity.

On first consideration, admissions to failure, national decay, and racial degeneration may not strike one as a positive discourse in any successful nation-building process.[38] Indeed, in its everyday sense, failure is a lesson learned or a mistake not to be repeated. It hardly elicits a desire for its repetition. A commitment to failure, however, upsets this premise of success. Among other things, it removes the weight of ideals deemed universal from the workings of agency. Thus, Chinese intellectuals may desire democracy without endorsing the condition of freedom, while writers fantasize about self-inflicted pain without conceding to the position of the abject. One might consider, in light of Lydia Liu's recent provocative analysis, the incursive role of "itinerant signs" that continually reproduce asymmetry in the meanings of words and consequently recognition.[39] And the "obsession with China," as so aptly discussed by Chinese intellectual and literary historians for half a century, may in fact display not a mere fixation but a powerful cultural production based on what David Wang insightfully calls a "scar typology."[40] The very unlikely appeal of failure has precluded the critical examination of how national identities, in countries where Western domination is considered a part of their modern and nationalistic history, can survive in a kind of persistence without triumph. Contrary to the grasp of common understanding, nationalism can proliferate around an ever-precarious sense of survival that engenders the continual emotional investment in the idea of the Chinese nation as a collective destiny.

Even though scholars who focus on previously unvoiced narratives of oppression may highlight a certain culpability of imperialism, they also forestall questioning the status of this history.[41] Notions of residual subjectivities that defy and survive subjugation, or subversive and parodic debunking launched from the margins of dominant ideologies, have been inspired by the optimism of revising the notion of hegemony. However, these venues still share the premise that these subversive positions carry the indelible imprint of subjugation, testifying to the authenticity of their suffering as well as confirming the continual role of imperialism in their tales of intervention. Attempts to present different views often resort to the device of claiming an "uncontaminated" tradition and continuity before or following Western presence.[42] The contention often rests on the issue of whether westernization, as in the case of nineteenth- and twentieth-century China, ought to be considered unique and given disproportionate status or contextualized within a longer historical frame that remains centered on China as the primary point of reference.[43]

Whether these concepts—one that seeks to level disciplinary boundaries, and the other that essentializes cultural traditions—can challenge or loosen the historical grip on the definition of subjugation or imperialistic domination is a question that cannot be answered by existing approaches toward critical studies. The prevailing assumption that subjects might through different kinds of empowerment regain the autonomy previously denied them has compelled the line of inquiry itself to return continually to the site of injury.[44] The sanctity of pain remains an absolute condition in which victims as well as vanquishers are bound by suffering and guilt. This drama of social suffering, however, requires reexamination. The appropriate response to victims' commemoration of suffering is not always predicated on the admission of guilt. Yet, continually invested in the notion of authentic selves and cultures, we seem reluctant to forgo the ideal of recovering a kind of individual freedom before the state of bondage. Despite the often-repeated recognition that individuals enter into social existence under a certain conditional sacrifice and that no "individual" stands outside these given parameters, the recovery of individual freedom as a project of restoration remains a driving impetus behind conceptions of what it means to rehabilitate national or individual autonomy.

We have yet to consider articulations of distinct and coherent national identities based not on sovereignty but on the embrace of "failure." A conceptual framework appropriate for such a task has to be created. The practice of embracing failure provides an unexpected solution to prevailing anxieties about national and cultural identities. It relieves nationalism of its ideological prominence by examining its interaction with and reliance on other cultural forms of expressing plenitude and survival. To this end, this study differs from the usual treatment of nationalism, in which "nation" oversees cultural life as its inescapable, dominant referent. Whereas the historical sense of failure is bound with tangible events of deprived sovereignty and national defeats, the concept of failure creates a discursive possibility for considering the value of the struggle for identity outside the commitment to success. Its theoretical implications also challenge the evaluation of the viability of national and cultural survival according to the idea of self-determination. If the recognition of failure, rather than strength, can incite a passionate attachment to the ideas of the Chinese nation or race, then one would have to rethink the extent to which the position of the subjugated actually excludes or compromises the possibility of agency.

One of the ways to approach this problem is to reconsider abjection and victimhood. Abjection and other conditions of psychic pain, such as trauma and melancholy, have contributed to the sanctification of victimhood in current critical discourse. Suffering occupies a narrow scope of interpretation whereby victimization possesses a certain unchallengeable authenticity. More than an analytical category for psychic injuries, abjection has also created an alarming explanatory power for why abject subjects stay as subjects in pain. Often as a project of guilty reflection, the focus on abjection as a state of robbed expression has projected the silent indictment of one's own culpability. Contrary to this theoretical tendency, a historicization of an abject consciousness in defeat, such as one faced with the overwhelming dominance of westernization in China in the late nineteenth century, reveals a great capacity for psychically renegotiating this condition and reinventing the exercise of agency.[45]

That abjection might have a more promising potential for self-assertion than the absence of any kind of subjugation may disturb our usual sense of preferred social existence. The suggestion that people might of their own volition seek out curtailing circumstances for their social or psychological well-being at least goes against what we would like to believe about the pursuit of individual fulfillment. Yet for countries operating under the imperatives of nationalism and imperialism, defined by defeats and hard-won victories, subjugation generates its own condition of persistence beyond ostensible resistance. The embrace of failure belies not a mentality of submission but a strategy of negotiation. Violence, as Frantz Fanon aptly pointed out, remains the brooding fantasy of the oppressed. No experience of subjugation excludes the "secret defiance" that seeks out some way of avenging itself.[46]

Resistance may be most productive, and certainly persevering, when it is not openly expressed but harbored as an unleashed potential of might. Less obvious, however, is that rather than rely on covert subversions, the task of reappropriating agency can be accomplished by openly rushing to one's own subjection. In just this way, the incessant preoccupation with failure in the nation-building period in China enabled Chinese intellectuals to interpret China's cultural decay as something they brought upon themselves. At the risk of muting the effects of Western hegemony, they would insist instead that the damage inflicted by domination remains secondary to what the Chinese themselves did not manage to accomplish. In this way, they continued to invest in an identity of themselves, even if disparagingly. The image of a venerable civilization is grasped with even greater tenacity through adaptive rhetoric, despite the pervasive sense of disorientation regarding the viability of China in the twentieth century.

In significant ways, the challenge posed by an understanding of the productivity of failure in the project of culture and nation building in China stands at the crossroads of contemporary Western critical thought. Theories of power and resistance, from peasants in Malaysian villages to contentions over the Western literary canon, often oscillate between wanting to affirm the potential for inventive agency at the margins of legitimacy and returning to challenge the center for recognition from within.[47] Scholars of nationalism are divided on the intrinsic value of nationalism in view of the power of European Enlightenment discourse it carries. Distinctions between anticolonial, reactionary nationalisms in the non-Western world and Western European nationalisms founder on the issue of origins, as though the focus on different types of nationalisms, such as Eastern and Western, would resolve the ambivalence of nationalism as an ideology as well. Scholars are hesitant to consider the complexity of the motivating passions attached to the nation that are psychologically distinct from patriotism. Psychoanalytical thinking, which seems to offer precisely this much-needed examination of national subjects' interiority, is equally confounded by the resistance of subjects to the fulfillment of their own desires, which turn out to be as much a psychic burden for them to maintain as to disappoint.[48] The complex and often well-disguised ways in which individuals seek the recognition necessary for their desired identities are also at the core of debates on multicultural politics in the United States.[49] How subjects are constituted and why that does not always denote subjugation and domination are questions that these discourses are often ill-equipped to answer.

A consideration of failure puts in question the assumed premise of social interaction that subjects are reliable and liable for the recognition they seek. It asks whether an idealized vision of the autonomous subject and social existence, to which such a liability is attached, offers an effective or meaningful way of assessing cultural survival.

Nationalism, carrying its persistent and intensifying appeal into the twenty-first century, provides an obvious locus for such an inquiry. In its extreme expression, love for the nation assumes an unconditional love, a passion that seems to hold explanatory power for fanaticism, violence, self-sacrifice, and martyrdom. People's voluntary sacrifice in the name of nation has been singled out as the strongest testimony to the extreme and dangerous appeal of nationalism. Beyond the simple explanation of extremism and fanaticism, the curious demand that one die for one's nation has also been continually posited as one of the most puzzling aspects of nationalism. Why, indeed, would individuals who identify themselves with the nation as a source of individual fulfillment be willing to forgo their own well-being? One might well wonder what kind of attachment seeks its own destruction and how that is productive of the sentiment of nationalism or collective allegiance.

Given the multitude of conflicts and disagreements that arise with regard to expressions of nationalism, it is surprising how little has been said about that intuited relation we attribute to nation and nationalism. Seldom examined is how nationalism is practiced as though it were simply about something called the "nation." We assume that the passions of nationalism stem from an allegiance to an entity clearly recognized as the nation. However, nationalistic subjects often endorse the sentiment of nationalism without agreeing on a coherent vision of the nation. Separatist movements and ethnic violence are often sparked by disagreements over a single definition of nationhood.

In this way, nationalism no more takes nation as its exclusive object than identification does any particular identity. Inaugurated in the name of self-determination and national sovereignty, desires for nationalism unleash a process rather than embody a goal. Nationalism is not attached to beliefs or ideologies identifiable as those belonging to the nation as such. Categories usually associated with nationalism, such as self-determination, freedom, and sovereignty, are not in themselves capable of eliciting the emotional attachment proper to nationalism. The process of becoming invested in the destiny of the nation predicates itself on the ability to incite and awaken individual passions. In incitement lies the power of nationalism, its susceptibility to individuals' participation. Subjects' perceptions of themselves as participating in this process reify, in a circular way, the sanctity of the nation. The problem does not reside in the question of what is the proper object of nationalistic allegiance, nor does the blame lie with the irrationalities of nationalism as a sentiment. The inconsistencies that plague conceptions and practices of nationalism alert us that nation, as an object of patriotism, is the product of the ambiguities of identification.

Seldom, however, do we think of nationalism as a process of identification due to the value we place on nationhood as sovereignty. We seem willing to take the authenticity of nation at its word as much as we unquestionably accept the authenticity of suffering. In just this way, most inquiries into nationalism have attempted to naturalize the conjoining of nation and nationalism, primarily because they equate nationalism with the building of state ideology.[50] In this view, nationalism trickles down to the populace, who are instigated or indoctrinated into endorsing ideologies of the state in the name of nationalism. Insofar as cultural experiences of nationalism are distinct from state ideology, the latter possesses the coercive power to reshape and even supersede the former. However, nationalism constructs distinct cultural experiences, because it relies on passions that are intimate to individuals rather than to the nation. The empty abstraction "nation" itself elicits no emotional response. The most powerful tropes evoked in nationalistic rhetoric are often those already familiar and reinforced in cultural life. Nation appeals to kinship, to the naturalness of familial attachment. One's country is, after all, the fatherland or the mother country. The purity of the love for the nation is often declared as a more exalted way of self-fulfillment than romantic love. In times of war, it is one's own mother, wife, and sister who are pillaged, a favored metaphor for driving home the sense of peril threatening each masculinized citizen.[51]

However, all this still explains little, if anything, of the nation itself. Love for the nation is, after all, not the same as love for one's own family or of oneself, both of which are often sacrificed for the nation. In cases of intense nationalism, usually accompanied by a history of colonialism, allegiance to the nation is measured directly against personal sacrifice. In such cases, love for the nation may draw not from the positive feelings one has for the success of a larger entity called the nation but from a complex psychic relation predicated on failure, the willingness and even the desire to fail.

At the core of nationalism lies a perpetually incitable sense of injury. Nationalism does not rely on just any kind of emotion. Rather than pride, feelings of injury provide the most versatile and undying desire for ambition. The reconstitution of national identity is always pursued with the utmost conviction and energy after suffering successful attacks, such as in the two Sino-Japanese Wars (1894–95, 1937–45) and, in the American context, Pearl Harbor and September 11.

The fundamental paradox of nationalism is its testimony not to greatness but to the need for greatness. Oddly, its persuasion and legitimacy derive from the lack of precisely those elements on the basis of which its ideology can be reified. The identity of the nation must be perceived as having failed in some way in order for nationalism to come to its rescue. The endangerment of nation legitimates the pretext for nationalism. A nation for which one cannot enjoy an exalted image is the driving displeasure behind the nationalistic impulse.

Through relentless appeals to one's sense of shame, guilt, and hatred, nationalism becomes palpable to individuals through incitement. Nation is indeed not possible epistemologically without its coalescence with something more intimate to the subject's interior topography. Nowhere is the entity nation palpable without its reliance on expressions that cannot be claimed as its own. One loves the nation through something else, or one feels the perils of the nation through the threat to one's own person, the imagery of one's mother and daughter raped in times of conflict with other nations. In this way, assaults on the nation often translate into discourse on the endangerment of one's own body. To partake in national pride requires knowing intimately one's own sense of shame, for love for the nation is always prompted by an inadequacy of that love. When the occasion arises, one must even be willing to bring that destruction upon oneself as an honorable sacrifice to show just how much one does indeed love the nation.

These feelings of self-berating, conscience, and guilt are the points of fixation around which the psychic life of the individual also unfolds. For this reason, what nation invokes is also infinitely displaceable. The transmutation of nation surfaces everywhere and in all forms during times of national crises. Its persuasiveness, however, does not stem from its obviousness but, rather, relies on its metaphorical promiscuity. Whether it is the brand of toothpaste one uses—as it was in China during the height of the anti-American goods boycott in 1905—or the killing of sparrows under Mao's ordinance, the nation's urgency parallels invasions of one's health and belongings. Metaphors of bodily harm to individuals abound in discussions of the nation's importance to its people's survival. The appeal to the fear of disease and deformity elicits a far greater sense of peril than good health. Likened to the health of the individual, the health of the nation claims immediacy. It is not coincidental that successful evocations of degeneration accompany corrective programs of social reform, nation building, and eugenics. As long as the nation never reaches this state of good health, it can continue to exist as an urgency demanding unconditional devotion. The conviction of failure, rather than sovereignty, makes nationalism possible.

As powerfully evocative as the image of impending ruination is, feelings of inadequacy alone cannot sustain nationalism. Dejection without hope does not elicit the proper nationalistic subject. Compensatory love must be voluntary in its sacrifice. Nationalism does not in itself command this allegiance, for the sentiment of loving the nation means to love it *as though* it were something else. In order for nationalism to appear to enjoy this allegiance, subjects would have to willingly embrace, in a moment of identification, the imperatives of the nation as their own. Perils of the nation are perceived most poignantly when viewed as an extension of the individual's subjective attachments. The required sentiment of national survival easily finds resonance with the survival of one's own desires. Rather than the nation making the demand, subjects exact this voluntarily from themselves. This constitutive moment of complicity, however, is not always readily visible, as passions for the nation become indistinguishable from one's own conviction in the significance of one's death. In this way, the willingness to desire one's own sacrifice not only desires failure but, significantly, fails desire. Indeed, as we will see, the theme of thwarted love predominates in Chinese literature throughout the nation-building period. To escape the imperatives of both one's sense of selfhood and the nation's directives, the protagonist often chooses to renounce love in favor of patriotism.[52] Often voluntarily sacrificed for the nation, sexuality also eroticizes nation as a sexual object.

Strangely, love for the nation constitutes an inward experience that has often been singularly mistaken for an external allegiance. The nation shares an intimacy with individuals, and nationalism appears to promise this indissoluble link. Yet how this intimacy is possible and continually renewed presents a question that reinterrogates the individual's allegiance to the nation. The centrality of sexuality in the individual's passionate attachments to the nation contributes to our understanding of identification. Nationalism makes possible the nation.[53] Critical attempts to provide this link through sexuality have largely been limited to unveiling nation as a constructed category through cultural myths, fables, and the imaginary.[54] How its constructedness relies on the continual psychic participation of individuals in the complicated processes of identification remains unexplored.

The question of how nation and nationalism are severed by the intrusive and disjunctive passion of the subject requires a narrative of interiority. Nationalism's continual sway over the individual's needs to express collective allegiance passionately and even violently prompts us to reexamine the enabling psychological constituents. The naturalized tie between nation and nationalism might thus be better understood as the uneasy relation between identity and identification.

Psychoanalysis, in this way, has contributed much to our understanding of how cultural perceptions interact and shape social realities. It posits a sobering view of the constructed condition of social existence and how individuals survive it. The intertwinement of subject and object, interiority and exteriority, posits the problem of self and other in ways that have exerted a deep influence on the discourse of contemporary cultural and literary studies. Its stature in this way, however, has come up against much criticism, especially regarding the assumption that the language of psychic topography applies across different cultural terrains. Nonetheless, the narrative premise of psychoanalysis has something else to tell us about the theoretical tendency to prefer the position of subjects under siege.

The basic notion that subjects are in search of a foreclosed object, the fulfillment of which constitutes their desires, uncovers a tale of frustrated interior life. In many ways, subjects are, on this psychoanalytic premise, doomed from the start because this relation to the object remains both primal and irreplaceable. Hence the adage of "too little, too late" necessarily plagues whatever attempt the subject makes to retrieve the sense of well-being that she or he once felt with the object as part of the world and self-perception. The state of deferred gratification proves both necessary and interminable, creating an insurmountable distance between desire and its fulfillment.

Such a tragic necessity has been useful for critical thinking. Previously, subjects were explicated in terms of desire. Thwarted, unconsoled, and frustrated, they were driven by a desire that could end only in dissatisfaction, reinforcing the futile search for the ultimate fulfillment. Longing and the unending torture of unfulfilled love were taken, in cultural and literary studies, as solemn testimonies to the human condition in terms of class, gender, and nationality. Because desire is constantly at odds with the demands of political and social reality, the torturous negotiations subjects must conduct to eke out a viable social and psychological existence are channeled into narratives of domination, subjugation, and oppression. Resistance against hegemony, be it class, race, or gender, is also cast in these terms of psychological hardship. The burden of maintaining sanity in the face of deprivation, violence, and trauma, especially in contexts of national histories and colonial violence, is considered an unfortunate but inevitable component of social existence. The operating assumption remains that, given the choice, individuals would not opt for subjugation and would pursue instead a life guided by freedom and self-determination.

However, to live up to this ideal that drives cultural and social critiques, considerations of psychic survival are held up against what amounts to an appealing but impossible state of being. For instance, recent attempts to use melancholia to analyze injured identities, racial and sexual, continue to invest in the idea that there are certain representations that curtail individual freedom from its ideal state of exercise.[55] The one injured is, by definition, a victim of the structures of power and domination. Melancholia, as the condition of grief, deprivation, and trauma, has come to preoccupy reflections on the psychic repercussions from social injury.

Melancholia has become useful for cultural analyses because it provides a topography for tracing shattered identities whose occasion of detriment is brought on by prescribed norms of race, gender, and class. The detriment is inescapable, as it predicates, to varying degrees, the possibility of having an identity at all. However, although credited with founding this insight, psychoanalysis itself does not always unambiguously corroborate this tale of trauma that has come to structure theories of racial and sexual anxieties. For Freud, if we return to one of the foundational studies of melancholia, the melancholic seems enabled rather than incapacitated by suffering in his or her ambivalent need to demonstrate it with insistence and compulsion.[56] On the one hand, the melancholic is characterized by withdrawal and disinterestedness in the surrounding world; on the other hand, the melancholic has a need to address and demonstrate his or her symptoms before an adjudicating audience. The melancholic is characterized by an "insistent communicativeness which finds satisfaction in self-exposure."[57]

The insistence and eagerness with which the melancholic tirelessly acts out the conflicted relation with the loved object casts doubt on the degree to which the melancholic is, as she or he professes, bound to the agent of distress. The compulsion to demonstrate incites, rather than submits to, the pain of loss. If melancholia is likened to a wounding, as it has been in psychoanalytical literature, it is, oddly, a wounding that enjoys the labor of repetition, of rewounding itself. Freud himself overlooks this oddity and believes that the melancholic's rebellion is merely a symptomatic reenactment of the fundamental trauma being suffered, and despite the displayed revolt, the melancholic is ultimately in a "crushed state."[58] It is, however, not clear whether the melancholic subject is incapacitated by the haunting specter of the loved object or in fact exorcising the state of paralysis by turning it into his or her own creation through psychic labor. In other words, it is not certain whether the psychoanalytical premise assumes the inevitability of doom or offers the possibility of relief only by way of detriment.

Significantly, internalized along with the object are the various attachments, love or hatred, that the melancholic subject once had with the object. The relation to the object, rather than the object itself, provides the focus of reenactment. The object cannot be loved or hated, memorialized or murdered, without this relational displacement. We are looking not for an object whose restoration would be ultimately satisfying but a reenactment of the subject's relation to it.[59] For the melancholic, the point of fixation is not the love once known and lost but the love never really known.[60] The significance of the lost object cannot be maintained throughout the melancholic morphology of dejection, withdrawal, disinterestedness, public self-reproach, eagerness for communication, militant self-aggression, and anticipated punishment without itself undergoing a process of transpositions. Suggested through these performances of the melancholic labor is, in fact, another facet of the psychic economy of grief. The penchant for drawing attention to one's suffering takes on a specifically pleasurable dimension.

The economy of melancholia, then, is no longer restricted to mourning but carried over into a kind of triumph in persistent labor. All forms of psychic survival have, after all, a "crushed state" as their originating premise. Yet this price of social existence need not be interpreted solely in terms of that shattering. To survive is to have already begun the disengagement, one should remember, from that moment of psychic trauma. The efforts at reappropriating trauma carry significance in themselves, apart from the "shadow of the object."

In this way, we require some other explanation for the afterlife of an agency that triumphs over loss without exuberance. The insistence of grief points to the proximity of a resilience that is unaccounted for in the focus on melancholia. The vocabulary of psychic grief needs a different language of pain that mediates the excess of pain with the possibility of survival. An unobvious but appropriate choice is the logic of masochism. Distinct from and even antithetical to melancholia's disinterest in pleasure, masochism fetishizes the experience of perverse pleasures in circuitous ways that would seem to be a far cry from the inward grieving over a cherished, loved object. Yet if we consider perversion in its etymological sense of "turning away" from something, be it normalized sexuality or the proper process of mourning, then masochism and melancholia produce two mutually reinforcing orders of psychic survival.

How masochism achieves mastery is helpful in revising the psychoanalytical understanding of how one escapes a psychic allegiance to a loved but overbearing object such as the nation. If we consider nationalism as constituted in injury rather than pride, and if that sense of failure somehow figures as voluntary love, then we can conceive how the painful mode of failure remains productive and consoling for an injured national consciousness. Masochism, in this respect, demonstrates how the psychic labor undertaken in the name of an object becomes reappropriated as self-preserving labor. Identification, articulated in this way under the reign of the object, enables the subject to survive under authority in an inventive way. The masochist escapes authority by adhering most faithfully to its laws and prescriptions to the point of fanatic participation. Pain is pursued with ticklish pleasure. In order not to let any moment of pain go to waste, the masochist meticulously plans the execution of his punishments. The significance of rituals, as once argued by Theodor Reik, belongs to part of the masochist's control over his fanaticism, an intended passionate allegiance that he never completely gives.[61]

If melancholia teaches us anything about preserving an object of love such as the nation, masochism shows how dubious this commitment can be. The embrace of guilt and shame does not admit to the culpability of a crime. It does, however, harbor that culpability as the impetus for atonement. The compensatory remorse, in turn, does not terminate with time or deed. Instead, it proliferates as something that continues to drive one to interminable labor, to life. From this perspective, individual freedom lies in neither the overcoming of defeat nor the restoration of a certain proper identity. Rather, it consists in the intimate knowledge that one has failed and that this failure can and should be compensated through the exercise of one's own labor. Preserving the object in oneself as part of one's identity belongs to a process of identification propelled by unrequited guilt and shame.

A theory of interiority can give us only the contours of the psychic life. Yet placed in the specific context of national and cultural histories, it shows that distinct narratives of survival and failure are not incommensurable as viable, simultaneous narratives of nationalism. From the perspective of nationalism, a consideration of the subjects' interior life offers invaluable insights into how passions informing this attachment are shaped in the cultural imagination. As though anticipating the inevitable challenge to reground considerations of the psychic life in the history of nationalism and cultural modernity, the introduction of Freudian psychoanalysis in China in the 1920s and 1930s, for example, was met with objections on the grounds of cultural specificity. However, leading Chinese proponents found innovative ways of recasting the theory of psychic life in light of China's particular predicament with nationalism and modernity. Self and nation were two irreconcilable categories often contending for the expressions of desire and recognition. China's unique sense of crisis and euphoria during these formative decades led intellectuals and writers to address psychoanalysis, as a theory of the "modern" self, in terms of both failure and rejuvenation. In this sense, psychoanalytical theories were appropriated as a cultural rhetoric in specifying the desires of selfhood and the imperatives of the Chinese nation. The imperative of nationalism in China gave theories of interiority a distinct cultural inflection.

An examination of the particular historical circumstances does not only demonstrate how we can understand psychoanalysis in the Chinese framework. How Chinese writers inflected the theories of interiority through their personalized literary culture of confessions provides an equally compelling narrative of melancholia and masochism unexplored by psychoanalytical and cultural theories. In a way that opens up the question of psychic injury to the broader scope of cultural modalities for experiencing and articulating suffering, failure can offer us invaluable insights into the formation of passionate attachments to nation and identity.

Fundamental to identity, the maintenance of failure is asserted over and above a deeply felt sense of inadequacy. For identity to remain a possible category for desire, failure in this way must be preserved. This is true for nations that find new impetus and energy after humiliating defeats, such as China after the Sino-Japanese War of 1894–95. It is also true for psychic identities that thrive on threats to their own disintegration through either rewounding or self-wounding. The notion of failure articulates the underlying economy of nationalism, racial melancholia, and cultural masochism in diverse terrains of political, social, and literary expressions. It shows how the consecrated object to which one professes allegiance—be it the nation, the loved one, or authority—is offered to the threat of destruction in order for that allegiance to be possible. With an appeal as detrimental as it is persuasive, failure inaugurates a moment of promised reconstitution in which China's tale of nation building unfolds in the late 1890s.

CHAPTER 2

The Yellow Race

THE INTELLECTUAL experience of modern China since the late nineteenth century has been burdened with an intense anxiety about its cultural destiny in the modern world. Identified by various scholars as self-hatred, dissatisfaction, and frustration accompanying the transition from empire to nation, why this tormented self-preoccupation remains central to modern Chinese identity has not prompted further analysis.[1] Beyond the precipitous context of a collapsing dynasty, Western encroachment, and declining cultural glory, the anxiety over China's destiny takes its own exigency as a cultural mode of survival. As early as the late 1890s, it was impossible to miss the pronounced thematization of China's ills. From China's lack of jurisdiction over its own territories to concerns about cultivating personal hygiene and mnemonic habits, the imperative to build a strong nation from the dynastic ruin was unparalleled. Intellectuals, political activists, and writers alike were engaged in strengthening a weakened China. Everywhere, loving the nation (aiguo) was encouraged, instilled, and articulated with growing urgency.

After all, it was not clear whether China would escape the fate of other countries vanquished by Western imperialism. The partition of China was a palpable reality in 1898.[2] Japan occupied present-day Taiwan along with the Ryukyu and Bonin islands under the treaty of Shimonoseki in 1895. Russians controlled Xinjiang, and the French oversaw Indo-China. This alarming state of foreign encroachment was, furthermore, preceded by six decades of steady decline in imperial sovereignty, both at home and abroad, which eroded the confidence of a failing empire. The Sino-Japanese War, as Benjamin Elman recently pointed out, prompted the construction of a narrative of inevitable collapse that interpreted the Self-Strengthening Movement era largely as a categorical failure.[3] This has resulted in the long-standing view that despite the mission to pursue Western technology with the founding of the Anqing Arsenal, Jiangnan Arsenal, and Fuzhou Navy Yard in the 1860s, China's repeated military defeats in confrontations with the West and Japan were unavoidable. Reformers had to reconceive the very idea of sovereignty as the prerogative of modern nation-states, an increasingly important category of self-perception for which China was yet to win recognition.

Apart from the threat of physical partition, the worry also revolved around a cultural menacing threat of "invisible partition." The latter, it was warned, operated in indirect and more nefarious ways. Unlike physical conquest, invisible partition was not limited to the territorial claims of colonialism. Economic exploitation and political intervention, it was pointed out, more damagingly undermined China's sovereignty. Cultural imperialism operated in realms not demarcated by the stipulations of extraterritorial treaties. If China were to survive Western encroachment, it was recognized, it would not suffice to merely ward off territorial transgressions. China must stay vigilant of the greater threat lurking beneath. The imperative for its survival was measured against the impalpability of cultural domination. In this way, the idea of a culpable and pervasive Western imperialism became an indispensable corollary to the impetus for cultural survival.

So pervasive was the expressed sense of China's inadequacy around the turn of the twentieth century that its obviousness seemed to render further analyses superfluous. To the extent that scholars have recognized the anxiety this produced, they often explain it as a passing phenomenon largely due to China's lack of political organization and cultural confidence at the end of its dynastic era. The anxiety, however, over the inability of China to survive as a nation did not abate with China's claim to modern nationhood in the twentieth century. The incomplete project of nation building found no satisfying end.[4] The profound doubt regarding China's survival came to shape modern Chinese sensibilities of the nation in powerful ways. Different fields of discourse converged on the articulation of this uncertainty. Racial discourse, for example, constituted one major domain in which this fundamental doubt operated. Visions of a future China coalesced with narratives of the yellow race. Shifting from "yellow race" to "yellow peril," intellectual conceptions of the yellow race projected, as will be seen, an unexpected trajectory toward imagined triumph.

This chapter traces the development of this shift through an examination of the tensions and complicities between ideas of social utopia, national salvation, inferior races, and the literary imaginary. It examines the making of an incipient modern nationalistic consciousness in a spectrum of discourses, from popularized vernacular newspaper articles and pictorials on national humiliation to intellectual objections to the theory of evolution. It shows how, despite this plethora of expressions, dominant ideas of the day, as articulated by well-known reformers such as Kang Youwei, Liang Qichao, and Tang Caichang, narrowed the scope of national survival largely to racial improvement according to the inevitable logic of evolution. In the process, this racial discourse brought into relief the image of its object, the yellow race, by displacing other races in a perceived racial universe. This intellectual maneuver carried implications well beyond its reformist parameters, as it also legislated a literary moment of racial imagining, as marked by Lin Shu's translation of *Uncle Tom's Cabin*. Recasting the racial hierarchy, the late Qing discourse on race confronted reality with an equally powerful persuasion of fantasy.

Defining "Nation," Knowing Shame

Apart from the physical loss of territorial sovereignty and the possibility of further partition in the late 1890s, the growing anxiety over the decline of Chinese civilization generated a discourse on the specter of cultural and racial ruination. Readapting Spencer's social Darwinism, Chinese intellectuals had a new framework for understanding decline as belonging to the universal logic of natural selection.[5] Dynastic ruin engendered the project of "saving the nation" (*jiuguo*). Much intellectual energy was expended on locating the cause of China's precarious state of affairs. Yan Fu, the first person to introduce social Darwinism into China, advocated the tripartite imperative of cultivating people's "strength, intelligence, and virtue" (*minli minzhi minde*).[6] Of the three, "intelligence," which encompasses technological knowledge as well as moral awareness, holds the key to the search for "wealth and power," the two indispensable pillars in the pursuit of modernization and self-strengthening.

As soon as the goals were identified, however, the question arose as to what kind of modern national subjects would be required to achieve them. The task of social and political transformation relied, of course, on institutional and structural change. As many people quickly recognized, however, it also involved the more fundamental task of reorienting people's consciousness.[7] *Min*, a word designating "the people," had been for most of China's feudal past mired in the subservient relation to *jun*, a word designating "ruler" in political and moral philosophy. Proponents of reform and revolution tirelessly tried to disentangle the two by invoking passages in classical texts to argue that "the people" had, in the earliest times of Chinese history, been thought of as the foundation of society. Using the more recent examples of the French and American revolutions, reformers sought to foreground Western principles of democracy and popular sovereignty in reinterpretations of China's political and philosophical tradition. The phrase "the people" was reinvested with the sanctity of Jean-Jacques Rousseau's social contract, John Stuart Mill's liberalism, and Adam Smith's self-guided individualism.

In order to define what it means to pursue strength, power, and knowledge as part of the enterprise of modernity, one had to first understand the prerequisite consciousness worthy of such aspirations. The proper national subject in this way formed the pivotal issue for many late Qing reformers from Yan Fu to Liang Qichao. Questions such as how to unlock the feudalistic mind indoctrinated by centuries of dynastic rule, awaken the people to their own capacities for thought and action, and reorient the traditional sense of the world to the requirements of the modern era were issues that urgently engaged the attention of intellectuals and political reformers eager to realize China's modern destiny.

The expression of the modern national subject, however, was not limited to the idea of "citizen," most famously advocated by Liang Qichao. Prior to defining citizenry, one needs to envision the civic and national space in which such recognition would have any political or social meaning. Although the notion of citizen has come to dominate our understanding of the political context at the time that called for constitutionalism, republicanism, and democracy, it was only one designation in the wide spectrum of different cultural articulations attempting to define a consciousness, capacity, essence, or spirit that captured the promise of China's rejuvenation.

Whether it is a question of awareness, an innate ability, something quintessentially Chinese, or an abstraction of soul, the making of modern Chinese national and cultural identity needed to legitimate all at once the importance of "self," "nation," and "people." The contemporary vocabulary mobilized for this task included "self-awareness" (*zijuexin*), "the ability for self-governance" (*zizhili*), "national spirit" (*guohun*), "national essence" (*guocui*), "the strength of the people" (*minli*), "the heart of the people" (*minxin*), "elemental essence" (*suzhi*), and "character essence" (*qizhi*). All of these terms emphasize something primordial and unexcavated that, once released, would transform and rejuvenate the Chinese people and culture. Even though the category of self may seem to contradict the demands of the collective nation—a polarity that later crystallizes in debates on literature and politics in the Republican era and continues today—they were at first perceived as complementary. Regardless of how intellectuals politically and ideologically defined these concepts, bringing them to a level of understanding accessible to and embraceable by a largely illiterate populace was quite a different matter.

To this end, popular journals written in vernacular exploit the components of the ideogram for "kingdom" or "nation" (*guo*) in order to invent new meanings readily understood by the popular mentality.[8] Breaking down the ideogram into its components, one author explains that the "outer boundary" shows the importance of territorial enclosure to even the primitive people. As tribes gathered into larger social units, he continues, the Chinese people of former times became fearful of invasion from other races. Within this enclosure, everyone's livelihood and property enjoyed protection. This initial grouping for basic survival further stimulated a desire for community, as people, now united in one mind and body, brought together their families. Bearing the responsibility of preserving the whole, the "people of the nation" are thus constituted. Another commentator, in a more militant fashion, argues that the "spear" (*ge*) within the character for outer boundary reminds us of the need to defend with force and even violence the boundaries of this collective entity. The reason *guojia* appropriately designates every person's relation to the nation lies in its coalescence of "nation" (*guo*) with "family" (*jia*). The author even proposes a new ideogram combining the two characters. The ideogram *jia* can be divided into two components, one resembling the roof of a house and the other, an archaic way of writing "I." This new visualization of the "nation" would affirm the mutual indispensability of self, family, and nation. There is no self without the family, and no family without the nation. Similarly, if one fails to love the nation, one fails ultimately to love and dignify oneself.

The injunction for every person to consider the nation's welfare as synonymous with one's own implies an interesting corollary. The notion of self-worth is immediately measured according to the extent to which it can be renounced in the name of a greater good.[9] This escalating tension pits the "self" (*ji*) against the "nation" but is itself predicated on the mutual dependence of the two. The notion that if one does not love the nation, then one does not love oneself can have two different sets of implications. One is that love for the nation encompasses one's self-love and that national pride would be an incentive for personal pride as well. The other possibility, however, is that the failure to love the nation reflects a prior failure of loving oneself and that the nation's demise is somehow precipitated by this act of personal failure. And indeed, this latter analogy provides the rhetorical foundation for the idea of "national humiliation" (*guochi*), a potent sentiment that fuels the passion of nationalistic rhetoric.

Among the numerous ways that they explain to the average person the meaning of *aiguo*, many commentators also play on a cultural and colloquial sense of personal perils. "The one who knows to love the nation," one writer succinctly formulates, "is not afraid of death (*bupasi*)."[10] Indeed, an age of new heroes is called for. This new mission of nationalistic discourse celebrated Yue Fei (1103–42), a general of the southern Song dynasty, as the first anticolonialist to "reject the foreign" (*paiwai*).[11] Lamenting the scarcity of the likes of George Washington and Napoleon Bonaparte on Chinese soil, advocates invoked exemplary heroes from an array of cultural contexts, from the Japanese samurai to Bismarck and Madame Roland. Most important, however, is the assertion that, absent such aspirations for heroism, one would have no sense of that basic requirement of social life called shame. Thus, alongside calls for loving the nation or avenging national infamy was the equally important task of instilling a sense of national humiliation.[12]

In this vein, "Portraits of National Humiliation" were printed in the effort to incite this sentiment through visualization.[13] Reacting to the aggression of tsarist Russia in northeastern China, one sketch shows the Manchu general Zeng Qi threatened with decapitation by the Russians. Zeng Qi made a secret agreement with the Russians in 1900 that gave them control of Liaoning. He was later found out and removed from office in infamy. Even though Zeng Qi was not executed by the Russians, the picture suggests his betrayal of his own country as well as himself, as is pointed out in the caption: "This is what happens to those officials who succumb to foreigners!"

These visual representations did not merely illustrate current events.[14] Embedded in them was a double message: the culpability of imperialism as well as China's own contribution in allowing the atrocities to happen. The coupling of outrage at foreign encroachment with the shame of one's own passivity was a powerful combination. In a more extraordinary example, another picture used the event of the Boxer Rebellion of 1900 to point out the drawbacks of foot binding.[15] "Bound feet suffer humiliation" refers to the occupation of Beijing by the eight allies (Austria-Hungary, France, Germany, Great Britain, Italy, Japan, Russia, and the United States) in the quelling of the Boxer Rebellion. Because Westerners raped Chinese women of all ages, the caption points out, northerners with unbound feet were able to run away and hide, whereas southerners, with their "three-inch lotuses," could only succumb to such a fate: "This is what happens with those who bind their feet!" The formulaic admonitions at the end of these captions seek to instigate a reflection on the backwardness of Chinese customs as well as reinforce the humiliation China thus brings upon itself. The causal relation is implied in every instance. From mantras to jingoistic songs, to "love the nation" is to know one's own sense of shame.[16] Ignorance is no excuse, for not knowing one's shame is synonymous with shamelessness.[17] In the absence of such a feeling of shame, many argued, one practically invites humiliation at the hands of foreigners.[18]

The mobilization of such a sentiment for nationalistic discourse certainly has a rhetorical dimension. The consequence of not knowing one's humiliation even as one suffers it exaggerates at the same time that it simplifies the role of self-awareness. If all citizens would passionately embrace the nation's infamy as their own, they would perhaps rise up in indignation.

If we were to understand the task of national salvation as something achieved simply by a different frame of mind, it would certainly puzzle us why humiliation still figures so prominently in China's sense of national identity today. The central problematic, in fact, lies in precisely the way we think of the thematization of defeat and humiliation in the late Qing. The then-recent events of the Opium Wars (1839–1942, 1858–60), Sino-French War (1884–85), Sino-Japanese War (1894–95), and Boxer Rebellion (1898–1901) served as immediate catalysts in spurring the sense of urgency in building a modern nation. Historians have therefore traditionally privileged the impact of political and institutional changes on the development of nationalistic discourse. The premise of nationalistic discourse, however, was much more volatile and vague than what can be explained by its original inspiration. Its persuasion lies in its ability to generate visions rather than redeem past defeats. Prompted by concrete events of imperialism and defeat, nationalistic discourse thrived on the memorialization of humiliation. The passion it incited for the nation paradoxically required the perpetuation of the poignancy of injury.

In this sense, allegiance to the nation at the same time involves resentment in regard to its abjection. In this striking fashion, nationalistic discourse justifies its intolerance. To reject what is foreign—be it the refusal of assimilation or outright violence—is legitimated by the logic that one is simply maintaining a minimal threshold of survival. The dividing line was drawn in different ways. Discussions on effective and ineffective methods of anti-foreignism distinguish between "civilized" (*wenming*) and "barbaric" (*yeman*) measures. Reminiscent of "using the barbarians to control the barbarians" (*yiyi zhiyi*), a tactic used by early proponents of westernization in the 1860s, the notion of "rejecting the foreign," however, is legitimated as something intrinsic to the maintenance of all national identities. The category of barbarism no longer applies to foreigners but refers to the Chinese themselves. In one case, to reject what is other is loosely defined as the common disposition of all human beings.[19] Regardless of the level of civilization, it is said, xenophobia exists as the fundamental basis for people's discernment between their own community and others. However, the "civilized" way of xenophobia does not require brute force. In this vein, many intellectuals and writers disapproved the Boxer Rebellion at the time as a disorganized uprising that reflected the worst of the Chinese collective mentality.

In contradistinction to visible forms of antagonism, some advocated a formless, spiritual kind of rejection based on self-transformation. The problem of the "outside" (*wai*) is inverted to that of the "inside" (*nei*), redrawing the line of resistance from a rejection of the foreign to a focus on self-governance (*zizhi*) and self-cultivation (*zixiu*). This inner cultivation ensures a kind of civilized compliance on the outside while maintaining inner autonomy. Self-accused barbarity enables a rhetorical strategy that appropriates rather than debunks the capacity for cultural legitimacy. The objection to rejecting what is foreign lies not in the principle but the execution. In 1904, the radical revolutionary student journal *Tides of Zhejiang* formulated one of the earliest definitions of nationalism as "uniting the same race and othering the other races" (*he tongzhong yi yizhong*).[20]

Although recollection of past humiliations and projections of future perils are at the forefront of nationalistic discourse, other ways of building national consciousness also aim at a similar incitement. Conservative or radical, nationalistic discourse is not impassive to its own self-deprecations. The intensity of self-criticism engenders an equally strong resolve to turn it all around. In this way, the affirmative image of a glorious racial and cultural heritage also worked alongside the image of abjection. In accordance with the desire for an exalted origin, the mythical figure of the Yellow Emperor, first invoked in the Han dynasty (202 BCE–220 CE), was revived. Leading journals of the day, conservative or revolutionary, featured portraits of the founder of the Chinese Han race, who reputedly reigned from 2697 to 2597 BCE. The use of the Yellow Emperor's dates for calendrical notation—as opposed to the Western calendar—was not only advocated in intellectual discussions but also debated in fiction. Liu Shipei, one of the conservative cultural essentialists advocating the preservation of national essence, expounded this idea at length in 1903. Liang Qichao, representative of the opposing view, justifies the use of Western notation as a matter of convenience and efficacy.[21] Often, both the Yellow Emperor and Western calendars appeared side by side in print, laying competing claims to the temporal propriety of the modern era.

Reified along with the Yellow Emperor were both time and origin. Theories of the origin of the yellow race and civilization, influenced by contemporary Western anthropological and racial thinking, were varied and mutually contradictory. Some said Babylon was the birthplace of the yellow race, whereas others proposed South Asia. There were those who claimed that the Chinese civilization broke off from Western roots, a claim vehemently opposed by those who asserted a Sinic origin distinct from that of all other civilizations.[22] Regardless of the place of origin, these discussions converge in the larger preoccupation with finding a source that best exemplifies a former era of lost glory. People used the notion of a pure Han race founded by the Yellow Emperor to corroborate as well as reframe the recent knowledge of Western racial hierarchy. The "yellow race" found its place within this scheme of racial evolution. But it was also able to contest this order based on its own mythologized racial authority.

In this vein, many objected to the universality of evolution as pertaining to the Chinese case.[23] The theory of evolution, some objected, disguises the superstition of fatalism with scientific language. Invented by Western imperialists to justify their subordination of other peoples, evolution was a descriptive rather than prescriptive process.[24] Only those who are content with subjugation endorse the theory of the survival of the fittest so as to escape the harder task of self-strengthening.

Such observers argue that the idea that some cultures, due to long-term stagnation, become less viable than others is fundamentally false when applied to China, because its problem lies in not the resistance of but susceptibility to eternal change. As a result of the extraordinary sensibilities nature has bestowed upon the Chinese and the cultivated wisdom reflected in their extreme responsiveness to the world, one author argues, their ever-changing perceptions precluded unity and consistency in their political actions. Other commentators claim that, if anything, China has advanced too far along the path of evolution, having reached its apex while the Europeans and Americans still dwelled in the age of barbarism. In any case, the hierarchical distinction between the yellow and white races does not reflect the inevitability of evolution, a limit imposed by nature (*tianxian*). It is, rather, a restraint imposed by the Chinese themselves (*jixian*). Losing sight of their own superiority, unparalleled over centuries of glorious cultural prosperity, they wrongly suspect the imminence of a racial demise following the examples of the black and red races.

Whereas discussions of China's national and racial survival tend toward the simple dichotomy between the yellow and white races, the yellow race as a discursive category was only recently homogenized. The evolutionary creed of struggling for survival, widely acknowledged as the rule governing China's fate in the modern world of competition for hegemony, did not at first have the white race as its sole opponent. Although China's struggle for national sovereignty quickly became discussed as a struggle against Western domination, racial antagonism was not initially perceived as merely a problem brought on by the white race. Radical revolutionaries of the day, such as Zhang Binglin and Zou Rong, blamed China's weakened status on Manchu rule, which by usurping Han sovereignty led the Chinese civilization into dire straits.[25]

Not atypically, anti-Manchu sentiments were part of the revolutionary fervor that would later be directed solely at Western imperialism. At the time, the distinction between ethnic rivalries and racial antagonisms was only secondary to the nationalistic rhetoric of incitement. In the vein of Russian Nihilism, outright proposals for assassinating Manchu officials were put forth.[26] "The rise of the Han is the death of the Manchus" (*Hanren qiang, manren wang*) was a belief not only espoused by the conservatives in the Qing court who opposed reform but also, for the opposite reason, embraced by the anti-Manchu radical revolutionaries.[27] For those who saw the more urgent task as the eradication of the Manchu elite from Han society, the former was seen as an inferior fringe race that illegitimately ruled the Han race. Reminders that the Manchus were merely another variant of the barbaric tribes culturally subservient to the Han Chinese equated the Manchus with other lesser tribes designated with animal radicals, such as sheep, dog, or deer, in the Chinese script.

However, there were also those who saw in this internal racial division the dangerous potential of further fragmenting China's fragile social unity. For them, the Manchus had already both racially and culturally assimilated into the Han, and the real object of deserved animosity should be Western imperialism and the white race.[28] Internal racial oppositions, in this view, would only further expose China's weakness to the aggressive designs of the imperialists. Eventually, the latter view dominated the early revolutionary agenda. Racial survival became a contest between a subjugated China and Western imperialism. The ethnic diversity within the yellow race was subsumed under a largely self-proclaimed role of China struggling against the formidable opponent, the white race. "Ousting the Manchus" (*paiman*) more generally meant "ousting outsiders." Equated with one's loyalty to the nation, xenophobia was an essential testimony to loving the nation. Driving out the foreigners was seen as a matter of survival rather than aggression.

Reemphasizing this distinction, Zhang Binglin once sought to legitimate anti-Manchuism by privileging the Chinese race's prior physical presence.[29] Responding to objections concerning whether Manchu's usurpation of Han sovereignty deserves any more legitimation than the Han's subjugation of the indigenous Miao people in southwestern China, Zhang states that whereas the Han race cannot exactly be considered an outsider to China, the Manchus are of a clearly other origin. Thus, their expulsion belongs to a matter of restoration rather than subversion. In this regard, Zhang even makes the unusual distinction between the Manchu population in general and the Manchu government, for whom he reserves exclusive antagonism.

Other staunch anti-Manchu proponents, however, are less discerning. Zou Rong's 1903 inflammatory anti-Manchu nationalistic tract *Revolutionary Army* (Gemingjun), for example, called for the massacre and rape of the

Manchus in order to wash away the humiliation endured by the Han race.[30] Citing Manchu atrocities against the Hans at the fall of the Ming dynasty, as narrated in *Ten Days in Yangzhou* (Yangzhou shiri ji) and *The Massacre in Jiading* (Jiading tucheng ji lue), Zou poignantly enumerated the series of defeats and humiliations endured by the Chinese that had been long forgotten. Chen Tianhua's no less impassioned writings, political and fictional, such as *Bell Alarming the World* and *The Lion's Roar*, express in equal intensity a resentment toward the Manchus doubled with a reproach toward the Chinese themselves.[31] The martyrdom of both men epitomized the intertwining of personal shame and national injury: one died from illness during imprisonment in 1905 and the other committed suicide in the same year in hope of awakening the Chinese to the shame of not avenging China's humiliation.

These three figures represent the radical contingent of revolution and nationalism; however, views on the fate of the yellow race were not always expressed in extreme, militant language. The context for racial discourse in the late Qing was marked by not only the intensity of nationalistic passion but also the energy of a vibrant cultural imagination that creatively argued for the survival of the yellow race. The concern with how a subscription to the idea of racial hierarchy could work to justify one's own racial advantage never trails far behind the conception of race in modern China. The elimination of all other races—brown, red, and black—as possible contenders in all Chinese discussions of the survival of the fittest race attests to this underlying concern. Standing prominently at the fore is the dichotomy between the white and yellow races, the only two races considered superior enough to have the capacity to survive in the modern world.[32]

From the outset, race was embraced not only for its implied system of differentiation but also, more significantly, for its promise of an innate capacity to rule over others. In this significant way, China's preoccupation at this time is not so much a question of what is wrong with China but, rather, why its people cannot enjoy its rightful superiority. Justifications of why China deserves to survive and be distinguished from other vanquished races and nations appear alongside discussions of its imminent doom. Some authors distinguish between "vanquished nations" (*mieguo*) and "perished nations" (*wangguo*).[33] Whereas vanquished nations such as China are subjugated but not broken in spirit, the argument goes, perished nations such as India, Poland, and Egypt do not even dare hope for regeneration. The more insistent is the thought of doom, the more exalted the aspiration of reclaiming China's past supremacy.

Reflecting this paradox, intellectuals and reformers often expressed their anxiety with a certain utopian exhilaration. One of the best examples of such utopian sentiments, Kang Youwei's 1901–2 *Datongshu* (The book of the great union) embodies this curious exhilaration that bolsters his notions of racial superiority and hierarchy.[34] The book itself sketches out a utopian vision of a world in which China plays a central role. Yet it soon becomes clear that a world of equality and the assurance of China's prominence are two different desires often at odds with one another. Its attempt to resolve this conundrum deserves to be examined in some detail.

The Utopia of Racial Harmony

The influence of Kang Youwei on revolutionary and reformist thought in the political and intellectual climate of the late 1890s is well known. His views on race exemplify the vision for national greatness, both in its grandeur and oversight. Kang's ideal that social, class, and political divisions should tend toward greater unity entails the simplification of the races. To ensure equality in a world of great union, Kang believes, one must do away with privileging distinctions. He envisions a world with no boundaries, national or racial. For Kang, however, the absence of distinctions does not mean equal consideration. Kang proposes that the colored races be gradually brought to extinction by intermarrying with the white and yellow races, a eugenic project that would take thousands of years to materialize. Although this implies the eventual disappearance of certain races, the yellow race, however, does not quite follow this greater scheme toward simplification. In regard to whether the yellow race would also gradually be lightened and integrated with the white race, Kang puts forth a more complicated rationale:

> In the world, people of the silver race traverse the earth, and the people of the gold race are in the majority. It is a world belonging to the yellow and white races. Even though the white race commands strength and occupies a position of superiority, the yellow race is large in number and possesses wisdom. Thus, it is only logical that the two should join and integrate. And by no means ought the yellow race be destroyed. I see our people traveling to England and Australia. Those who meticulously select their diet and cultivate their health with good western methods have a ruddy facial color like the Europeans. Those who ingest half-cooked beef still bloody look as though they were wearing rouge after being away for a few months. If they were to spend more time in the sun, inhale fresh air in well-ventilated spaces, and undergo two or three generations of racial integration, whereby the southerners relocate to the north and mountain dwellers to the seaside, the people of the yellow race would all gradually become white in no more than one hundred years. With the additional help of racial communion (*tongzhong*), they would naturally meld. One would not have to wait

for the completion of the Great Union for all the yellow people to turn into white people. These two races will have blended into one color with no distinction between them. Only the brown and black races, who are qualitatively far distant from the white people, will indeed be difficult to integrate.[35]

Intermarrying the inferior races to the yellow or white race, according to Kang, would be the only possibility for the less fortunate to survive. This survival, however, paradoxically entails their extinction. To Kang's mind, these less desirable races would somehow require little persuasion to sacrifice their own continued existence in the name of a "universal good" to which all humans aspire.[36]

To achieve equality and great union, one must begin by leveling physical differences. Kang concedes, however, to the difficulty in convincing a white woman with her beauty to interbreed with a black man, an unappetizing mismatch Kang likens to that of a goddess and demon. No "magical medicine" or "saint healer" could make the African race attractive for such an interracial union.[37] Thus, Kang offers a few incentives. He calls for monetary compensation and distribution of medals inscribed with the distinction of "improved race" (*gailiang renzhong*). Courageous women who are willing to content themselves with less satisfactory mates for the sake of the entire human race will be rewarded with public acknowledgment.

Although Kang explains why the interbreeding between the yellow and white races would be favorable for racial harmony, he is remarkably silent on why the white race would desire such a union. After all, for a beautiful white woman to interbreed with an inferior yellow man would presumably also go against the logic of promoting the great union. Kang's attempt to posit yellows and whites as complementary races in fact betrays his expressed hope that, with proper physical cultivation, the yellow man might one day shed that "pickled yellow" tinge.[38] With all its wisdom and numerical advantage, the yellow race appears equally inferior in its physical attributes to the white race in the scheme of racial amalgamation.

If it is considered an improvement for the black or brown race to upgrade to the yellow race, then to move from being yellow to white must be better still. Yet Kang has difficulty reconciling himself to this inevitable realization of the scheme. Slipping from the exclusively "white" outcome to the ambiguous "white and yellow" union throughout his treatise, Kang is ill-prepared to conclude that eventually even the yellow race will have to be completely assimilated into the white to achieve the world of great union. On the one hand, he emphasizes that the particular adaptability of the yellow race may even warrant the optimistic prediction of achieving whiteness well before the completion of the great union. On the other hand, his vision stops short at the point where the whites and yellows—races into which the brown and black races will have disappeared—jointly populate the world.

Even though the scheme of racial union aims at doing away with hierarchical distinctions, Kang merely takes homogeneity as a measure of equality. To achieve the state of ideal racial harmony, even if it means that only the yellows and whites survive, is synonymous with bringing about racial equality. Races tend toward simplification, defined in terms of whiteness. Kang accepts that although equality is a "just principle" (*gongli*), the fact that things are not equal belongs to their intrinsic disposition.[39] Kang, commenting on the condition of the blacks in the American South, despite Abraham Lincoln's abolition of slavery in 1863, explains that this is the reason why white Americans still refuse to consort with black slaves. What makes the yellows more amenable to becoming white lies in their relatively small physical difference. Though they may be well educated, blacks' obvious physical markers—such as "unbearable bodily stench," "chest full of long hair," "pitch black limbs," and "bestial" facial features—doom any prospect of leveling racial distinctions.[40] Carrying his eugenic premise to its logical conclusion, Kang argues that those members of the brown and black races whose dispositions and physical appearance are simply too repugnant or who have incurable diseases should be sterilized.[41]

According to the Chinese intellectual historian Zhu Weizheng, *The Book of the Great Union* was in all likelihood composed in the ten years prior to the Revolution of 1911.[42] The sources for Kang's inspiration have been traced to foreign works such as Edward Bellamy's utopian socialist novel *Looking Backward 2000–1887*, which was serialized in *Globe Magazine* (Wanguo gongbao) from December 1891 to April 1892 and in which *utopia* was translated as "a world of great union" (*datong zhi shi*); as well as to *Imagined Excursion to the Planets*, by the Japanese philosopher Inoue Enryō (1858–1919). Kang also had in his possession one-fourth of the foreign works translated by the Jiangnan Arsenal's Translations Division, which was one of the earliest Chinese institutions to systematically translate Western scientific knowledge.[43]

The influence of Darwinism and natural selection is apparent in Kang's *Book of the Great Union*. The topic of racial survival in intellectual discussions was so pervasive at this time, however, that its full significance cannot be simply attributed to any one source.[44] Contrary to the prevailing view, by the 1870s, both Darwin and the interpretive context for the theory of evolution had been introduced into China, forming a sophisticated, albeit not entirely understood, framework for thinking about racial evolution.[45] The content of Darwin's *Origin of Species* had been introduced to the Chinese audience as early as August 1873 in the newspaper *Shenbao*, twenty-five years before Yan Fu's 1898 translation of T. H. Huxley's *Evolution and Ethics*, generally considered the first Chinese source on Darwinism. In fact, in Kang's disciple Liang Qichao's letter to Yan Fu commending his translation of *Evolution and Ethics*, he remarks that what he and others read in Yan's translation was everything he had heard from his teacher Kang Youwei but had never fully understood.[46] Although Kang never provided any systematic analysis of Darwinian ideas, he had incorporated them into his own political thinking on race.

Premised on the feasibility of racial communion, Kang's desired racial superiority amounts to diluting inferior races through interbreeding with the superior ones. This interpretive use of racial improvement differs significantly from the context of Western eugenics. Rather than reject the fundamental premise of Western eugenics, the hierarchization of the races with the whites at the top, Kang accepts the premise but simply readjusts the hierarchy by placing the yellow race alongside the white. In Western eugenics, the fear of contaminating the racial superiority of the noble stock prompted measures of sterilization and euthanasia. Whether the feared contamination was from the lower classes in one's own society (as in England), from a group defined as racially inferior to the Aryan stock (as in Germany), or from undesirable emigrants from southern and Eastern Europe (the concern for American eugenicists), the main objective was to protect racial purity through a reinforcement of racial hierarchy.[47]

Kang, on the other hand, wants universal racial impurity in order to obfuscate the distinction of inferiority. Anticipating the objection that racial communion would endanger the superior races by mixing pure with inferior blood, Kang gives a grimly optimistic response:

> There is no harm. I predict that after thousands of years, there will not be many of the brown and black races left. People of the yellow and white races will be everywhere. To cross-breed billions of yellows and whites from the fine race (*meizhong*) with one or two brown and black members of the rotten race (*e zhong*) is to save and ameliorate a small number of the rotten race with billions of the fine race. By the time of the Great Union, the quality of life will be greatly enhanced with few worries. The state of medicine and hygiene will be far beyond what today's Europe and America can match. The speed of transformation will be so fast that we need not worry about the decline of the human race.[48]

The equality envisioned in the realm of great union disguises the reinstatement of domination. Kang maintains an unambiguous racial order in which the yellows and whites appear to be the logical rulers of humankind. A weakened China is once again elevated to the status of master. Two distinct contradictions, however, are sutured in this vision. To idealize the supremacy of the yellow race is to place it in the position of the recognized conqueror, the white race. Yet the yellow race must be reinstated without betraying its reliance on an identification with the white race. The idea of racial communion asserts a kind of sovereignty and power China does not possess. The felt sense of China's inadequacy both drives and plagues the vision of the great union.

Racializing China both distances the yellow race from the inferior races and aligns it with the superior breed. Racial hierarchy does not merely subordinate the yellow race to the inevitability of its logic. It also offers the yellow race the possibility of domination. The reconceptualization of the yellow race in the configuration of races occupies center stage in the Chinese intellectuals' sense of world order in the late 1890s. In 1897, the late Qing reformer Tang Caichang, who was the editor of influential reformist newspapers such as *Sichuan News* (Xiangbao) and *Sichuan Studies Newspaper* (Xiangxuebao) and perhaps most well known for the failed uprising of the Independent Army in Hankou in 1900, compiled a detailed description of the various races of the different nations in the world.[49]

At the beginning of his *Geguo zhonglei kao* (An investigation into the races of various nations), Tang recalls reading Yan Fu's 1895 essay "On Strength." It brought about such a profound epiphany in him that immediately upon finishing, he rolled up the scrolls and cried, "What is the most pressing concern of today? Indeed, it is race! Race!"[50] Despite this initial tribute to Yan Fu, Tang actually draws largely from Chinese translations of a wide variety of foreign sources, such as the journal *Gezhi huibian* (Compendium of science), edited by the English translator and entrepreneur John Fryer; *Wanguo shiji* (A history of myriad nations), which was based on the Japanese translation, *Bankoku tsūten* (Historic encyclopedia of all nations), by Okamoto Kansuke (1839–1904); as well as an 1874 translation of *Blair's Chronological and Historical Tables*, by John Blair (d. 1782), titled *Siyi biannianbiao*, published by the Jiangnan Arsenal's Translations Division.[51] *Investigation* is a survey of the four races—white, yellow, black, and red—of the five continents. After each section consisting of quoted references, Tang provides his own commentary.

From the onset, Tang was impressed by the Darwinian idea that, as summarized by Yan Fu, all species began as one. Because of the passage of time and the shifts in environmental factors, this unity evolved into multiplicity over millions of years. To regain that original unity would be nearly impossible. What struck Tang in particular in this evolutionary scheme were the tasks of "rushing to struggle for one's survival" (*ji zicun*) and "leaving behind fine seed" (*yi yizhong*).[52]

Every species looks after its own survival through favorable reproduction. It is the way of nature, Tang observes, for races to evolve from "inferior" (*jian*) to "superior" (*liang*) breeds. To permit races to decline to the point of extinction would be to go against the natural order of things. Not only are the races hierarchized, as in Yan Fu's translation, but there is also a clear dividing line between the white/yellow and red/black races: "The yellows and whites are intelligent, while the reds and blacks are stupid; the yellows and whites are masters, while the reds and blacks are slaves; the yellows and whites are noble, while the reds and blacks are disorganized."[53] After completing his survey, which, unsurprisingly, only ends up confirming his predisposed view of the racial order, Tang advances the notion of racial amalgamation.[54]

"On Racial Communion," the first of the two postscript essays attached to *Investigation*, proposes interracial breeding as a way of upgrading the yellow race. Tang begins by quoting the travel diary of the nineteenth-century Chinese ambassador Xue Fucheng. In the essay, written during his travels to Hawaii in 1891—eight years before Liang Qichao's better-known *Notes from Traveling to Hawaii*—Xue remarks on the decline in the native Hawaiian population to one-tenth its original figure during the hundred years since the settlement by the Americans, Europeans, and Chinese. Since ancient times, Xue observes, this has been the tendency of the survival of social groups on earth. Just as the Native Americans and the indigenous Ainu of Japan were vanquished and forced into decline, other tribes and races failed to survive. The Chinese, who are the descendants of the divine, are the "noble race" (*guizhong*). Europeans, even though they are only slightly behind the Chinese, Xue remarks, are also wise and prosperous. Other than the Europeans, whose origin, Tang hastens to add, can be traced to Asia and who demonstrate a capacity similar to that of the Chinese, no other comparable people exist. Even in the Americas, Europeans reign supreme. In cases in which members of the indigenous group somehow rose through the ranks, the enabling condition was invariably that they married into a European bloodline and thereby altered their racial composition.

From this passage in Xue's diary, Tang arrives at the idea that in order to build a heavenly nation, unite all religions, and enter into a time of peace, racial communion holds the key. This vision, much like what Kang proposes in his *Book of the Great Union* three years later, is ominously supported by changes Tang perceives as already in motion in the world. Among the ten pieces of evidence he presents is the fact that the Japanese, for instance, do not forbid interracial marriage between their people and the Europeans. In the Pacific islands, including Singapore and Hong Kong, the descendants of mixed parents have already proved to be of superior intelligence. Moreover, Tang continues, even though England, Russia, France, and Germany are separate countries, they are in fact interrelated through kinship and marriage, a blood cohesion that accounts for their shared political outlook. The fact that mixed couples are not an unusual sight in China's treaty ports and that prominent Chinese do take Western wives shows that Westerners themselves do not consider it demeaning to marry the Chinese. A more mystical support for his argument is Tang's observation that because all humans exist in the same ether and thus have similar bodily compositions, there should not be any differentiation among them.

Beneath this grand project of uniting humankind, however, lies a much more localized desire to strengthen the weakened yellow race. Despite Tang's attempt to advance the idea that interbreeding the white with yellow race has proved successful and superior in every case, he reveals his inner anxiety when he breathes a sigh of relief at the fact that white people do not express their disgust at the idea. Clearly, Tang asserts, "the westerners do not take the weakness of China and the stupidity of the Chinese people as reasons for considering intermarriage an act of defilement."[55] This last point concludes his ten justifications for racial communion as a general good for all races. He then proceeds to discuss the importance of racial communion for the yellow race:

> To achieve equality among the myriad nations and their sovereignties, nations open to one another so that politics can be shared. Once politics is shared, then knowledge can be exchanged. Religion follows the sharing of knowledge, and the melding of dispositions follows that of religion. Why should one, then, be skeptical of racial communion? Should one allow one's own short-sightedness to inhibit its natural course? I say that if the yellow and white races embark on this process quickly, the rise of the yellow people's strength is within sight. If the process were to take place slowly, then their strength would not be regained until after thousands of years. If our people are decidedly against racial communion, then they voluntarily become the likes of the African and American savages. Westerners, who observe the creed of the evolutionists, will then treat us like savages and be repulsed by the idea of racial sharing. In that case, the survival of the yellow race would not at all be certain. Most likely is their continuing debilitation and the absence of rejuvenation.[56]

Tang's notion of racial communion, like Kang's vision of the great union, does not actually dispense with racial distinctions. More important for him is the danger of the yellow race becoming like the red and black races. By becoming more white, the yellows may hope to survive. The desire to identify Chineseness with whiteness, however, is more duplicitous than a desire for sameness. Tang attempts, as Kang also does, to align the yellows and whites as the reigning masters of the races. He is as much repelled by the undesirability of the darker races as he is attracted to the idea of the yellow race's superiority over them. Whiteness holds an appeal not because of its proven authority but because of its example as an attainable position. The obvious contradiction between racial equality and hegemony does not escape Tang. After describing the myriad races and nations in *Investigation*, he offers the following concluding argument:

> After surveying all the races of various nations, one sees that, following the deluge, all human races originated and developed from Asia. It is absolutely confirmed that all races originated from one source. Formerly, races proceeded from unity to multiplicity. For multiplicity to later return to unity is but the usual course of events between heaven and people who follow logical principles. How can there be objections under the pretext that this goes against the meaning of things and confuses the ways of the world? Those who are small and cowardly and who fail to recognize the deeper significance of things must deem my words inappropriate. Those who blaspheme and criticize me will not understand the truth in my words without themselves having to undergo the catastrophe of heaven's destruction. Alas![57]

If the yellow race verges on extinction—as has already happened with the red and black races—it can survive only through racial communion with the white races. Yet, reversing the logic, Tang insists that this is in perfect keeping with the way of evolution, for all races originated as one. Furthermore, because the originating race was in Asia, interbreeding with the white race merely restores the status of the yellow race as the origin of all races. The idea of the original unity was stated in Yan Fu's translation of Darwin. The "deluge" Tang refers to, however, comes from the biblical tale of Noah's ark, which he then combines with the notion that Asia is the birthplace of the human race. The last point is indebted to early theories in Western anthropology cited by Okamoto Kansuke in his *Historic Encyclopedia of All Nations* and reiterated in Xue Fucheng's diary.

The sources of Tang's inspiration, however, remain less interesting than what he did with them. His fail-safe logic runs as follows: The yellow race faces imminent extinction; if it is to survive and avoid the fates of the "truly" inferior races, it must align itself racially with the whites; however, this need for racial communion does not really mark the weakness of the yellow race, because all races started with the yellow race anyway. Racial communion secures in essence a recovery of our proper selves. There is no reason not to undertake it, because it merely restores something that the yellow race in any case already owns.

Indeed, in the order of racial hierarchy as perceived by Chinese writers and intellectuals around the turn of the century, not enough distance separated the yellow from the "inferior" races, such as the red and black.[58] No sooner is an identification with the oppressed made than it is immediately denied. The yellow race is often seen as coming dangerously close to following the footsteps of once-great nations and races that fell into ruin. The sentiment expressed at such moments of epiphany, on the surface, often voices regret and sympathy. Great nations with venerable traditions such as India, Persia, and Egypt, for instance, were once as great as China. Yet because they failed to strengthen themselves in ways appropriate to the demands of the modern world, they fell into enslavement under the domination of the superior white race. If, such negative examples notwithstanding, China fails to regenerate itself, such ill fate would also befall its people, henceforth reduced to the state of ruined civilizations. Thus, the less the yellow race has in common with the undesirable races, the closer it approximates a position of superiority. Against this prevailing sentiment of impending ruination, Liang Qichao attempts to mobilize this same sense of peril for building a national consciousness.

Although Liang remains one of the most important and influential late Qing reformers, his arguments for building China as a modern nation and race are not without ambiguity.[59] In an 1897 essay, "On China's Imminent Rise" (Lun Zhongguo zhi jiang qiang), Liang remarks, quite optimistically, that China has no reason for decline but every chance of strengthening itself. Arguing for the natural propensities of different races, Liang explains,

> The reason for India's decline is due to its race. People of the black, red, and brown races cannot compare to the white people because of the kind of microorganisms that exist in their blood and the angle of their crania. Only the yellows and whites are not so far apart. Thus whatever the white people can do can also be accomplished by the yellow people. Japan's imitation of western ways is a case in point. Since the Japanese race originated in our country, it would be illogical to say that we cannot accomplish what they can.[60]

Liang demonstrates a perception that breaks down racial composition into biological components. Racial identity defines what is intrinsic to oneself as a natural physical trait, a biological disadvantage resulting in defect. In Western eugenics, the naturalization of rational constructs as having a biological basis is a familiar tactic of legitimation.[61] However, the way in which the rationale of biologism applies only to the "inferior" races is striking. Liang implies that the yellow race remains safe from such fallibility. The certainty about the status of the yellow race thus obtained, however, is almost immediately thrown back into doubt by the uneasy elision between not only the white and yellow races but also the Japanese and the Chinese.[62]

Despite his propagation of such an idea in persuasive terms, Liang's attempt to justify modern China on the appeal of race is neither original nor conclusive. He reflects, in many ways, the different debates going on at the time on reform, revolution, and political legitimacy. The move to legitimate the Chinese as the ultimate source of Japan's rise to power since the Meiji period closely resembles the Sinification rhetoric already deployed in discussions about westernization in the 1860s. However, Liang reinvests the racial order with the imperatives of nationalism in an unusual way. Liang does not speak of a utopian world in which all humankind is united in harmony. He does not couch the strong desire for China to rise as the superior nation and race in the conciliatory terms of racial amalgamation with the white race. Instead, he puts forth with great conviction the defense that China's racial identity represents something not only worthy of but also crucial to the modern world.

He accomplishes this by embracing the threat of peril as, first and foremost, a sign of strength. Whether a nation survives, Liang argues, depends solely on its citizens and not the aggressive intentions of other nations.[63] Recasting the sense of imminent extinction as self-willed survival, Liang builds a positive foundation for national consciousness by reappropriating the external threat as self-inflicted destruction. Once that reappropriation is accomplished, the task of saving the nation remains only a matter of indoctrinating a proper sense of national citizenship. This initial move remains essential to his nationalistic thinking. In this essay Liang reiterates his claim that the superior quality of the Chinese race cannot be likened to that of the Turks, Indians, or Africans. Therefore, if the Europeans try to treat China in the same way they treated these vanquished nations, domination would not be easily achieved. In fact, Liang asserts with exuberance, the Chinese will become the most powerful race of the twentieth century.[64]

The ways in which Liang argues this claim are both astonishing and counter to the usual understanding of his critique of the negative traits of the Chinese. One of the reasons for the yellow race's inevitable success lies in the fact that, Liang points out, the Chinese have a very strong sense of "self-governance." "Civilized nations" (*wenming zhi guo*) of the West place such a value even above political sovereignty. It is true, Liang concedes, that China lacks internal political unity. Local governance acts, in effect, independent of central authorities, and this has contributed to the historic lack of patriotism among the Chinese. Liang also acknowledges the obstinate ways in which the Chinese refused to assimilate with others, the one base habit foreigners most complained about. He argues, however, that this actually shows the true mark of the Chinese people's unrelenting independence and inner strength.[65] Precisely because of this indifference to authority, the Chinese have developed a great sense of self-reliance. Such are the ways of "blessings in disguise."[66] Exploiting the negative signification, Liang redeems China's institutional and bureaucratic inefficiency and corruption by accentuating their inadvertently positive effects, further arguing for the Chinese people's remarkable capacity to overcome adversity.

Thus, when it comes to the contentious issue of the mistreatment of Chinese laborers abroad, a continual source of nationalistic outrage that culminated in the Anti-American Goods Boycott in 1905, Liang advances a similarly unconventional interpretation. Drawing from the general criticism that the Chinese are cowardly and lack a sense of curiosity and "appetite for adventure" (*maoxianxing*), he points out that Chinese have managed to settle in foreign lands, braving the most perilous conditions. Unlike their European counterparts, whose governments supported and financed such ventures, the Chinese sojourners enjoy no such protection. The Chinese government not only discourages but also forbids its people to settle in foreign countries. In cases in which the disloyal members return to China, their prior sojourn would be considered an offense punishable by death.[67] Other nations, like parental figures, protect and nurture their citizens abroad. China, however, forsakes her citizens as orphans are abandoned. If it were not for these harsh legal prohibitions, Liang remarks, the Chinese would not have had the chance to prove themselves to be unstoppable and proceed anyway to populate other parts of the world on their own initiative.[68]

Here, Liang's argument intersects the contemporary criticism of the Qing government's gross negligence of its people's welfare abroad as politically "uncivilized," compared to the recognition of citizenship of Western nations. However, instead of engaging the debate, Liang redeploys this point to argue something different: The fact that the Chinese have been nonetheless undeterred in their desire to settle abroad and "self-populate at a time when the struggle to survive of the races is at its most vehement" proves that the Chinese race will once again rise in strength.[69] The Westerners used to compare China to India and Turkey, yet, Liang asks passionately, do the Indians or the Turks display strength of this scale by which a people can be so self-reliant without their nation's support? Because the Europeans do not have the physical capacity to endure the hardship of settling in remote places in the world, the Chinese are the only people capable of performing the great task of "opening up the world." The whites are arrogant and cannot endure physical hardship, whereas the blacks and browns are "lazy and stupid." Besides the yellow people, Liang asks, who can take on such a task? In a remarkable moment, Liang candidly states the ambition afforded by these rhetorical questions: "Today, North America and Australia are colonies of the white race. One day, South America and Africa will be the colonies of the yellow race."

In this essay, Liang essentially tries to change contemporary perceptions of the shortcomings of the Chinese race. The lack of independence and political allegiance are, after all, common complaints about the so-called feudalistic and slavish mentality of the Chinese.[70] The absence of identification with the collective good, as has often been criticized, lies at the root of China's lack of national consciousness. The metaphor likening the Chinese to a tray of loose sand, something for which Sun Yat-sen and Lu Xun are often given credit, had already circulated widely in the late 1890s. Often employed to describe the lack of political consciousness in the Chinese people, the metaphor carries a disparaging tone. Yet Liang, acknowledging this, turns it around to show how the Chinese actually benefited from this lack of political unity.

The exploitation of Chinese laborers abroad, increasing in great numbers in the second half of the nineteenth century, became a sensitive and contentious political issue by the early twentieth century. Often kidnapped and shipped out from the southern provinces, such as Fujian and Guangdong, "piglets"—as they were sometimes referred to because they were dispatched like livestock—were mostly sent to the South Pacific. Sympathy for uneducated peasants, the group most susceptible to such victimization, both led to an intense disillusionment with domestic social conditions and directed nationalistic sentiment against the Americans' treatment of Chinese laborers in California. At the renewal of America's Chinese Exclusion Act in 1894, Chinese were outraged by the unequal treatment. The Qing government's inability to secure rights for its citizens abroad exemplified China's incompetent diplomacy. China's lack of established diplomacy, perceived as a necessary skill in coexisting with other nations in the modern world, added yet another item to its long list of racial weaknesses.

Against this sentiment, which quickly grew into nationalistic fervor, Liang's assertion regarding the Chinese laborers' adventurousness expresses national pride in an unexpected way. He puts aside a defense against China's state of debilitating international authority and emphasizes, instead, its gravity in order to accentuate the racial survivability of the Chinese. Failure is celebrated as power and strength. The Chinese laborers' suffering testifies all the more to their capacity to endure hardship. Rather than a source of outrage, their suffering demonstrates a commendable characteristic that entitles them to the prospect of establishing their own colonies in South America and Africa. Taking it a step farther than Kang Youwei ever could in a vision of future harmony, Liang's idea of the yellow race does not complement but usurps the dominant status enjoyed by the white race.

The national consciousness Liang instills relies on a sense of racial heritage inherent to the Chinese of which foreigners cannot deprive them. Liang appeals to people's national consciousness not through the image of the nation but through the eternity of race. Yet this communal sense of race draws from the recognition of national failure. His reappropriation of the Chinese laborers' maltreatment as testimony to their laudable perseverance provides a pivotal turn in nationalistic rhetoric, by which failure is recognized as resilience and humiliation turned to pride.

Like Kang Youwei and Tang Caichang, Liang envisions an imminent future world in which the yellow race reigns supreme. Kang and Tang sought to fulfill such a vision by overinvesting in the supremacy of the yellow race as a universal, utopian ideal. Their professed humanitarian appeal to racial communion disguised their anxieties regarding the viability of the yellow race. Liang, however, exploits the anxiety by bringing it to the fore. He by no means desires the abolition of racial boundaries. Instead, he utilizes this anxiety of failure to spur the sense of urgency for the Chinese race to survive and claim its own hegemony. Kang and Tang recognized but still hoped to remedy the failure of the yellow race in their writings. With Liang Qichao, however, the embrace of failure became something desirable in itself.

Nationalist rhetoric incorporates the recognition of failure as the very productive method of building the Chinese race. Inherently antagonistic toward ideas of "great union" and "equality," the nation-building project thrives on the assertion of difference. What intellectuals wanted at this time was not a state of equality or the abolition of the logic of hegemony, which they unhappily witnessed from the receiving end under Western imperialism; rather, they wanted to know what was required for China to be able to exercise a similar kind of domination over others.[71] The project did not repudiate aggression; it just did not want China to be the victim. Most extraordinary in this pursuit of national sovereignty is how effectively a discourse on, paradoxically, failure and humiliation, drives the nationalistic claim.

The late Qing intellectual discourse on nation, anti-Manchuism, racial harmony, cultural legitimacy, evolution, and ruination constructed a complex matrix for thinking about racial demise along with national rejuvenation. This was not an easily accomplished task, for the persuasion needed the participation of the cultural imagination as well. It required metaphors and sympathy, common experiences of oppression as well as differentiated views endorsing the possibility of one's own recovered superiority. In this way, the idea of the yellow race, its survival and its justification for continual existence, rallied to its cause the tales of other oppressed races.

Specters of Racial Ruination

The cultural logic of failure shares, at the same time that it rejects, an identification with the subjugated races. If it were intolerable to be treated like the inferior races, it would be even more shameful to be mistreated by them. Abuse at the hands of those who are themselves low in the racial order would be offensive indeed. To consider oneself even worse off than perished races such as the blacks or reds strikes at the heart of nationalism. Intellectual discussions as well as fictional fantasies proliferated around the haunting specter of partition. In the five chapters that appeared in the influential revolutionary journal *Jiangsu*, Xu Zhuodai's "Our People After the Partition" (Fengehou zhi wuren) paints the horrific vision of a partitioned China.[72] The scholar protagonist, Huang Shibiao, is led by an old man in his futuristic dream to visit the "perished nation" that is now China, where the official language is English. The most humiliating sight, however, was Indian soldiers deployed on every block by the British as the local security force in Shanghai's International Settlement. Despairing at the fact that even "people of perished nations" (*wangguo zhi min*) can wield a club of authority on Chinese soil, Huang Shibiao laments that the Chinese cannot even hope for such slavery. Another short story, "Tomorrow's Partition" (Mingri zhi guafen), relates the humiliating details of white dominance over the Hans, replacing the no less shameful Manchu rule.[73]

In significant ways, the underlying desire for supremacy in intellectual and political discussions cannot be fully understood without the larger cultural context from which intellectual articulations are lifted. The experiences of other subjugated races, which had only occupied the periphery of intellectual discussions on the yellow race, abound in literary expressions of racial ruination. Black slavery in America, the extermination of the Native Americans, and the colonization of the Pacific islands and South Asia were warnings of what would befall the Chinese. Among the black, red, and brown races, the experience of black slavery carried a particular poignancy. The word for slave and bond servant (*nu*) was also used to describe despicable and shameful behavior or conditions, exemplified in the concept of, for example, a traitor (*maiguonu* or *wangguonu*) or in the slavish character a traitor displayed (*nuxing*). However, *nu* can also have a connotation of pity, as *wangguonu* can refer to either one who causes the ruination of one's country—that is, a traitor—or an unfortunate member of a perished nation.

This inflection from shame to pity is seldom registered in political discourse on nationalism. Not until the translation of Harriet Beecher Stowe's *Uncle Tom's Cabin* by Lin Shu (1852–1924) does it find its most expressive content. Lin's voluminous translations of Western novels into classical Chinese exerted an indisputable influence on the later May Fourth generation. Well noted as a predecessor of Butterfly and Mandarin Duck fiction, Lin Shu is less known for his purported mission to save the yellow race, a purpose specifically stated in a number of his prefaces to the early translations. His famous 1901 collaborative translation of Stowe's *Uncle Tom's Cabin* uses the black slaves' experience of oppression to forewarn the yellow race of a similar fate.[74] In his preface, the blacks' experience is both to be sympathized with and avoided:

> Examining the history of America, one learns that the black slaves of Virginia were transported on a Dutch military vessel in 1619 to be sold in Amsterdam. This was the beginning of the whites' treatment of the blacks as slaves. At the time, America had not yet established itself as a nation. With a sense of public equality, Washington governed his country and did not treat it as private property. Yet he was still unable to abolish slavery. It was not until the time of Lincoln that slaves began to win their freedom. Recently, what had been the way to treat the black slaves is gradually becoming the way to treat the yellow people. A scorpion that cannot fully release its poison must gnaw on shrubs and plants to vent its venom. People who later come to touch the withered stalks will be paralyzed even if they do not die from it. Must we the yellow people touch those dead stalks? Our nation, though rich in natural resources, is not being developed. With their poor and meager livelihood, people cannot sustain themselves. Thus they start to work and live on the American continent, even envying its way of life. American statisticians, worried about the drainage of capital, cruelly mistreat the Chinese migrant workers and ban their entry. The gross abuse suffered by the yellow people is in some instances even greater than what the black people endured. Yet, because the strength of our nation is weak, our emissaries abroad are too timid to protest. There is, moreover, no one in the know who can document such incidents. With no way of finding out, the only written precedent at our disposal is *A Record of Black Slaves Lamenting, "Heaven!"* Originally entitled "A tale of black slaves under oppression" (Heinu shoubi ji), it is also known as "Uncle Tom's Cabin" (Tangmu jiashi).[75] It was written by the American woman writer Situhuo [Harriet Beecher Stowe]. Out of a disdain for the title's lack of classical appeal, I changed it to the present name. The poignancy of the detailed narratives of the tragic circumstances of the slaves is not affected by the cleverness in eliciting pathos. Rather, because what was recorded in the original text touches on the imminent death of the yellow race, the sorrow grows all the more overwhelming. Nowadays, those who clamor about are already too obstinate to listen to cautionary words. Those who are fond of the other race, furthermore, mistakenly believe that the westerners treat their subjects with generosity. They therefore wait eagerly to head over there to join them. We cannot afford to have less of those who might be awakened by my humble translation.[76]

Lin Shu was known for the emotional appeal of his translations. Perhaps it is against this reputation, first established in 1899 with his widely popular translation of Dumas' *La Dame aux camélias*, that he contrasts his more serious intent behind translating *Uncle Tom's Cabin*.[77] Stressing the absence of sensationalizing artifice in his translation of *Uncle Tom's Cabin*, Lin reassures

his readers that the horrific events he relates require no stylistic embellishments to convey their gravity. The tragedy teeming from the events themselves suffices to draw forth tears of sorrow from the readers. The yellow
people will, upon reading the experience of the black slaves, naturally see it
mirrored in their own condition. Having said this, however, Lin quickly
adds that a change in title was necessary for the translation, for he disliked
the original title for its lack of "classical flavor."

Lin's sensibilities as a translator are evident throughout his voluminous
corpus. However, this particular note about the title seems to contradict his
insistence on the absence of artificial assistance in heightening the novel's
emotional appeal. Lin claims that the original title was *A Tale of Black Oppression* and also *Affairs in Tom's Cabin*, neither of which carries as strong a
resonance as *A Record of the Black Slaves Lamenting, "Heaven!"*—his chosen
translated title. Lin purposefully inserts a point of sympathy and identification, through which the oppressed experience of the black slaves can be
readily felt as that of the yellow people. The preference of *lu*, the word for
"record," and *ji*, the word for "tale," also suggests a desire to present the
translation as historical testimony. A note after the preface explains that
the title *Heinu yu tian lu* does not signify an observer's sigh of sympathy at
the knowledge of the black slaves' suffering. Rather, "*yu tian*" is a quoted lament coming from the slaves themselves when, forced to toil in the fields,
they raise their heads toward the sky and cry out, "Heaven!"[78] Striving to
convey a sense of immediacy, he intends the translation as a citation of suffering, as a way of seeing what it is *really* like. This somehow substitutes for
the kind of historical testimony, Lin claims, lacking in the case of the maltreatment suffered by the yellow people in the United States.

There were, however, a number of contemporary accounts of Chinese laborers' experience in the United States, especially in Honolulu and San
Francisco. Liang Qichao, for example, published a series of articles regarding the conditions of the Chinese laborers in America in the newspaper
Zhixinbao in 1897.[79] Articles on their treatment were also available in various journals.[80] If Lin was not aware of these publications, that did not deter
him from asserting that the laborers' suffering was far worse than that of
black slavery. The relevance of the black slaves' experience, according to
Lin's preface, lies in its convenient substitution for the documentation lacking on the treatment of the yellow people abroad. Yet the point of identification and sympathy is made to enable the vision of a reality much worse,
much more repugnant to the dignity of the yellow people. In this way, the
act of sympathy also enables differentiation. That experience of suffering belongs, after all, to the black slaves, not to the Chinese. The yellow people

may very well follow in the steps of the black slaves' ruin, but only if they fail to be awakened from their ignorant slumber.

In a biographical postscript, Lin briefly introduces the life of Stowe, as well as more precise details regarding the Chinese laborers:

> Mr. Wei and I translated this book in collaboration not for the sake of winning unsolicited tears from our readers by relying on our cleverness in narrating sorrow. Because the fate of enslavement is impending on us, we cannot but let out a cry for the common people. In recent years, America has strictly prohibited Chinese laborers. They installed wooden shacks in the wet marshes. Gathering up hundreds of Chinese who have come from afar, they lock them up inside. After a week, they let one or two go. There are those who after two weeks were still not released from incarceration. This is what I mean by "slave pen" in the novel. It has always been the case that civilized nations do not examine personal correspondence. Today, when it comes to the personal letters of the Chinese, none can escape careful scrutiny. If the word "America" were at all mentioned, it is as though some federal crime had been committed. Arrests, expulsions, persecutions, and ostracizations follow, leaving no energy unexpended. Does China have any claim to being a nation? From observing wisdom for governance and befriending books, I came to understand that, as for people without a nation, even those who are civilized can treat us with barbarism. If one day we the Chinese open up another page for slavery, would it not be a direct result of this? Japan, like us, is also of the same yellow race. When the Americans insulted a noble Japanese woman under the pretext of checking for vaccination, the Japanese were outraged and protested. They even set up associations of resistance against the American government. Brave are the Japanese indeed! If there were any officials in China, how can they not know that their citizens, guiltless of crime, are dying in incarceration and humiliation? The concerns of the upper and lower echelons are as different as the Kingdoms of Chu and Yue. What further need is there to speak of the decline of national might? Now, as political reforms are just beginning to take motion, my book could not have been completed at a better time. Everyone is eager to abandon the old knowledge in diligent pursuit of the new. Though my book is shallow, it nonetheless suffices to strengthen our will and come to the aid of loving the nation, preserving the race. To the discerning gentlemen, who among you deem these words indiscreet?[81]

There are a number of issues Lin touches upon in his preface and postscript that are already familiar from the discussions of reformers and revolutionaries. First, the treatment of the Chinese laborers abroad was, at the time of Lin's translation, a pressing issue reflecting the incompetence of the Qing government in protecting its citizens abroad. Incarcerated in the infamous shacks (*muwu* or *muzha*), Chinese laborers were, by many accounts written in Chinese, subjected to strict physical examinations and vaccination upon arrival in the United States. Because the "strength of the nation is weak," China lacked the international authority to contest the issue effectively.

Second, using the blacks as a negative example of what awaits the yellow race falls directly in line with the preoccupation with racial extinction. That the yellows might end up repeating the fates of the "inferior" races was a feared possibility that weighed heavily on the literary as well as the intellectual imagination. The comparison with Japan as a member of "the same yellow race," furthermore, underscores the racial characteristics of bravery and prowess that the Chinese lacked in their own national character. Whereas the Japanese were quick to resist the Americans, the comparison suggests, the Chinese merely gave in.

Finally, Lin Shu sees his translation project as part of the larger task of "loving the nation, preserving the race." This desire is strongly expressed in a number of the prefaces to his translations.[82] After translating *Uncle Tom's Cabin*, Lin went on to translate *Aesop's Fables*, a number of which were chosen out of an expressed concern with the treatment of Chinese laborers.[83] It is imperative, Lin asserts in one of the prefatory remarks to *Aesop's Fables*, that the yellow people quickly rid themselves of the "slave mentality," the detriment of which can already be witnessed in the treatment of the black slaves.[84] The sheer number of the population, apparently a source of pride for some, Lin laments, is more the result of indiscriminate reproduction than discreet cultivation.[85] Of those remaining from the destruction of disease and war, few take learning seriously and most squander their lives away.

Interestingly, Lin's complaint about the Chinese taking pride in their reproductive capacity rejects the kind of self-comforting rhetoric previously expressed by Kang Youwei regarding the numerical indestructibility of the yellow people. His translation collaborator, Wei Yi, also sees "Chinese slave characteristics" (*zhinaren nuli xingzhi*) as the problem *A Record* helps to identify. In the translator's preface to H. Rider Haggard's *People of the Mist*, Lin warns of the "robbery of those who destroy other races" and remarks, "If the white race can swallow Africa, they can similarly take over Asia."[86] He further reiterates the view that "the red people have no intelligence, and so they were pillaged by the white people. The intelligence of the yellow race is no less than that of the white race. How can the yellow race, therefore, willingly become even less than the Native Americans?"[87]

According to Sun Jilin, the influence exerted by Lin's *Record of the Black Slaves Lamenting, "Heaven!"* was no less than his widely popular translation of *La Dame aux camélias*.[88] It was also pivotal in Lin's decision to direct his translation efforts at alerting the world to the perils facing the Chinese. *A Record* was his first collaboration with Wei Yi, and it took an unusually long sixty-six days to complete. In a letter to Xie Meiru shortly after its completion, Lin remarks that he had for three years regretted not having the opportunity to show his loyalty to his country.[89] Now, however, with the completion of this novel, he could devote himself to the task of translating books that will awaken the people and thereby help strengthen the nation's will.

If Lin Shu was looking for an ideal reader that could be stirred into loving the nation and preserving the race, he needed to look no farther than a 1904 review article published in the journal *Juemin* (Awakened citizen).[90] The author, "Enlightened Stone" (Ling Shi), claims that he had difficulty locating a copy of the popular work *A Record*. Once he did manage to wrest it from a friend's hands, he could not help but "read and weep, weep and read," echoing Lin Shu's own patriotic labor at translation whereby he "cried and translated, translated and cried."[91]

For Enlightened Stone, Lin's collaborative translation with Wei not merely gives lament to the blacks' bitter conditions but presages the fact that 400 million yellow people will soon play out the sequel to black slavery. The perils of the Chinese need not wait for the future, adds Enlightened Stone. They are already visible in the treatment of the Chinese in America and other nations, a treatment much worse than what was allotted to the blacks. The white race arrogantly purports to be the ruler over all other races but practices barbarism under the fake banner of "civilization." Even so, says Ling Shi, changing his tone, a nation must already be weakened within in order to be conquered from without. If one does not stand on one's own, how can others be faulted?

Upon reading *A Record*, Ling Shi states, "I take joy in the fact that my fellow people have not reached the state of the black people. . . . Yet I fear the danger that, because our national consciousness is so weak, they may not be able to avoid reaching that state."[92] The fact that the "yellows" could be but have not yet been treated quite like the blacks is both a consolation as well as a reason for seeing themselves as somewhat different from the other oppressed races. Ling Shi extrapolates from *A Record* the representative scenario of all those threatened by white domination. The novel represents the experience of the black race as well as incorporates the experience of oppression of all those who are subjected to another race. However, in his view, the yellow people are somehow still in a position to avoid that fate if they would strengthen their national consciousness. No law of inevitability governs the subjugation of the yellow race as it does the other colonized races. For the yellow race, the possibility of prevention and self-assertion remains open.

Seen from this perspective, the issue of the Chinese laborers is also placed at a certain distance from the nation-building project. The reportage of the yellow people's oppression abroad drives home the need for building a nation-loving consciousness. The sense of outrage that fuels the passion for the nation, however, is prompted by an experience of substitution with the black slaves. It is as if without seeing someone else standing in for the experience one dreads for oneself, the mere knowledge of one's potential suffering lacks ultimate persuasion. Oppression and injury are most poignantly felt in the moment of identification, in which the reflective distance afforded the spectator produces the most convincing testimony to affliction. As remarked by Ling Shi at the end of his essay,

> Reading *A Record of the Black Slaves Lamenting, "Heaven!"*, I take the tears I shed for the black to weep for the yellow people. Seeing the black people's past, I weep for the yellow people's present. I wish to place a copy of the book in the homes of every yellow person. May all who read this let out sobs of filial emotions and tears shed for heroes. I bid every story-teller in tea houses and bookstores to relate this story. They may awaken the citizens of our nation with their skills in narrating extreme sorrow and cruelty. I wish to ask the famous painters of Shanghai to paint an illustration for each of the forty-two chapters. Using my crude skills at making verse, I shall write a few lines so as to compete with the reputation of *Strange Tales from a Chinese Studio* (Liaozhai zhiyi). Children and women enjoy a good show and surrender themselves readily to common tastes. I hope that all good men and women will give copies of this book to others. Those who encourage others to practice goodness may buy this book as a way of repaying the grace of heaven.[93]

Fiction, after all, was able to solicit the kind of tearful nation-loving consciousness Lin Shu had hoped. Ling Shi's response to *A Record* would have pleased the translator. Even more appropriate is the fact that at least one of Ling Shi's wishes materialized. Lin's translation was soon adapted into a play and performed in Japan and China by two different Chinese societies of Western-style "civilized drama" (*wenming xi*).[94] Spring Willow Society (*Chunliushe*), the first modern Chinese drama society, was founded by a Chinese student organization in Tokyo in 1906.[95] With a mission to "open up knowledge and invigorate the spirit," the main founders of Spring Willow Society, Li Xishuang and Zeng Xiaogu, inaugurated the society with a performance of Dumas' *La Dame aux camélias*, also based on Lin Shu's translation.[96] Because of the overwhelming reception of *La Dame*, they decided to perform Lin's *Uncle's Tom Cabin* in five acts later that year (see Figure 2.1).[97]

The reputation and success of the performance reverberated throughout the Chinese student community both at home and abroad. In response, Wang Zhongsheng organized Spring Sun Society (*Chunyangshe*) in Shanghai and premiered *Uncle Tom's Cabin* in the city in 1907. Even though Wang had not seen the Tokyo performance, he experimented with his own mix of traditional and Western elements of drama, using classical Chinese instruments and forms of dialogue but with modern lighting, stage set, and Western costumes. The attempted realism of *Uncle Tom's Cabin* was apparently limited by the fact that, despite the portrayal of black slaves in the American

FIGURE 2.1   Photograph of the cast of the Spring Sun Society's production of *Uncle Tom's Cabin*. Shanghai, 1907.
Source: Shanghai Academy of Social Sciences (Shanghai shehui kexue yuan)–Center for Shanghai Studies (Shanghai yanjiu zhongxin), Shanghai.

South, the actors' faces were painted white in traditional stage makeup (see Figure 2.2).[98]

The appeal of Lin Shu's translation reached far and wide, from the birth of modern drama to revolutionary tracts. Zou Rong's influential work *The Revolutionary Army*, for instance, eulogized Harriet Beecher Stowe for shedding light on the oppression of other races. A 1909 novel, *Tokyo Dreams* (Dongjing meng), even narrated a performance of the play in its last chapter. A group of Chinese students in Tokyo performed, as in real life, *A Record of the Black Slaves Lamenting, "Heaven!"* and featured an Indian student, attesting to the communal experience of oppression of all colored races.[99] In 1957, a former member of Spring Willow Society reconstructed the script, changing the title to *The Hatred of the Black Slaves* (Heinu hen) to reflect the increasing anti-imperialist resentment after the Korean War (1950–53). It was performed on the fiftieth anniversary of the birth of modern Chinese drama. According to Tian Han, the father of modern Chinese drama in the May Fourth period, performances in the 1930s impressed upon the Chinese populace the atrocities of racial discrimination as part of American imperialism.[100]

The appeal of oppression, vicariously experienced and witnessed through *Uncle Tom's Cabin*, reveals the complex relation between the perceptions of the yellow race and the acknowledgment of those who belonged to the inferior races. Nationalistic imagination proliferates around a confirmation of

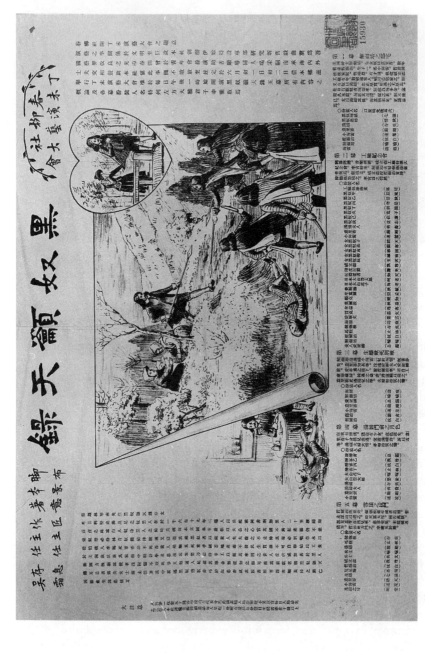

FIGURE 2.2 Poster for the premiere of *Uncle Tom's Cabin* by the Chinese drama society Spring Willow Society. Screenplay adapted from Lin Shu's translation. Tokyo, 1906.

Source: Tsubouchi Memorial Theatre Museum, Waseda University, Japan.

its own feared inferiority. It also gathers around what it reassuringly distances itself from in sympathy or contempt. Racial hierarchy is heralded because it spurns the weak (the black and brown races) and crowns the victorious (the yellow and white). To escape the fate of the weak, one must survive at the expense of others. Yet to sense that possible extinction as urgent, one clearly has already identified with the weak. Such is the ambivalence of nationalism, driven not by love of the nation but by the recognition of its inadequacy.

Although Lin Shu's translation is the first and by far most influential literary articulation of this ambiguity, it neither exhausts nor concludes the racial imagination unleashed by late nineteenth-century cultural conceptions of racial survival. The literary fascination with the specter of racial demise extended well beyond the experience of the black slaves (*heinu*) and built on others' tales of oppression. The circuit of cultural imagination did not cover just the topography of oppressed races. It was also in dialogue with Europeans' fears of their own racial decline. The fascination with racial failure, as expressed in different nations' conceptions of themselves, diffracted through the lens of race the horror of one's own destruction. How this figures in the popular imagination and why this vision of peril appears prominently in empowering a sense of racial identity is the subject of the next chapter.

CHAPTER 3

The Menace of Race

But on May 1, 1976, had the reader been in the imperial city of Peking, with its then population of eleven millions, he would have witnessed a curious sight. He would have seen the streets filled with the chattering yellow populace, every queued head tilted back, every slant eye turned skyward. And high up in the blue he would have beheld a tiny dot of black, which, because of its orderly evolutions, he would have identified as an airship. From this airship, as it curved its flight back and forth over the city, fell missiles—strange, harmless missiles, tubes of fragile glass that shattered into thousands of fragments on the streets and house-tops. But there was nothing deadly about these tubes of glass. Nothing happened. . . . Had the reader again been in Peking, six weeks later, he would have looked in vain for the eleven million inhabitants. Some few of them he would have found, a few hundred thousand, perhaps, their carcasses festering in the houses and in the deserted streets, and piled high on the abandoned death wagons. . . . Had there been one plague, China might have coped with it. But from a score of plagues no creature was immune. The man who escaped small-pox went down before the scarlet fever. The man who was immune to yellow fever was carried away by cholera; and if he were immune to that, too, the Black Death, which was the bubonic plague, swept him away. For it was these bacteria, and germs, and microbes, and bacilli, cultured in the laboratories of the West, that had come down upon China in the rain of glass.[1]

In 1906, Jack London published "The Unparalleled Invasion," which described the coming of the "yellow peril." His futuristic vision vividly captures the American and European imagination of the inscrutable and menacing East at the turn of the twentieth century. In "The Unparalleled Invasion," the jubilant clamor over Japan's victory in the Russo-Japanese War awakened China to test her own powers. Under the friendly tutelage of Japan, China engaged in fantastic technological advancements already enjoyed by America and Europe. The technological prosperity of "machine civilization" rendered the Malthusian principle inapplicable, as China's population growth exploded. Peasants and workers, compelled by the increasing scarcity of resources, poured into neighboring Asian and Southeast Asian countries. Terrified by the prospect of an invasion of Europe, Western nations called for a Great Truce, suspending their disagreements in order to consolidate their efforts toward containing the "over-spilling monstrous flood of life."[2] After a number of ineffectual military campaigns, the Europeans and Americans resorted to an unprecedented bacteriological warfare against China in 1976 that they had to sanction especially for the occasion. After completely obliterating the Chinese race, they repopulated China with their own settlers and began a prosperous era of cultural "cross-fertilization."

London's fantastic tale was not based merely on the conceits of the literary imagination. As a war correspondent for the Hearst syndicate during the Russo-Japanese War, London, in his reportage on the then-widespread concern with the yellow peril, reflects the perceived objective reality. The threat from the East inspired awesome fear and anxious admiration in its Western onlookers. The image of a faceless yellow horde invading the borders of Western civilization invoked, in a powerful moment of externalization, the sublime vision of Western cultural apocalypse. In retaliation against this phantom image, Western nations struck down the yellow peril with a method of warfare considered too inhumane to be used on each other. The yellow slant-eyed face represented the external enemy whose destruction would reaffirm the faith in the democratic ideals of "humanity" and "peace."

A colonial fantasy recoiling on itself, the yellow peril loomed ominously in the Western cultural imagination as the embodiment of at once its own strength and demise. American and European minds were filled with a great sense of power from unparalleled hegemony but were simultaneously haunted by the fear of it coming to an end. From the perspective of the imperialist imagination, the revival of the yellow peril in the early twentieth century offered a pretext for further reasserting this might. The menace from the East provided the pivotal point on which the imperialist fantasy turned from awe to fear, self to other.

On the other side of things, however, a different historical interpretation and cultural fantasy were in the making. Whereas the specter of the yellow peril gave the American and European imaginations a glimpse into their worst fears, it offered the Chinese audience a reflection of their coveted prowess. The ominous racial specter raised by the West circulated widely in China through literary and journalistic translations and provided the screen on which cultural anxieties and desires were projected and exchanged. The continual construction of the identity of the yellow race no longer restricted itself to the pages of utopian treatises or to the social ideals of racial communion. Absorbing and reinventing the voices of other threatened races, the Chinese, in their perceptions of their own racial survival, no longer relied solely on black slavery as a metaphor. They took in the haunting tales of others, such as the Native Americans, Filipinos, and Jews. Consolidating the racial front of the colored races against the white race in the cultural imagination, the yellow race claimed the authority to speak on behalf of the former in expressing grievances and justifying retribution. Playing on Western and Japanese discussions of the yellow peril, Chinese commentators and popular fiction writers accessed a reservoir of global racial anxieties of which China loomed as the formidable object.

To understand the ways in which racial anxieties legitimated a sense of peril and grievance, this chapter examines how this discourse evolved and how the identification with perished races transformed itself into a revitalized embodiment of the menacing yellow peril. Lin Shu's little-known translation of Western ethnography, for instance, demonstrates a different facet of racial discourse that displaced the experience of China's inferiorization onto that of other races. *Minzhongxue* (Ethnology), adding a critical dimension to the understanding of Lin Shu's stature as a literary translator, reveals how an inquiry into China's own racial rejuvenation accompanied an ethnographic curiosity that classified an order of racial superiority and inferiority. This chapter explores this hierarchy through an examination of serialized and novel-length popular fiction rife with images of vanquished peoples—such as blacks, reds, browns, and Jews—with whom China keeps a discreet distance couched in ostensible sympathy. It also broadens the historical perspective on the European and American notion of "yellow peril" by examining the origin of that discourse as it was revived in nineteenth-century Europe and, oddly, embraced by the Chinese as a way of empowerment. Finally, focusing on science fantasies such as "Electrical World" and *New Century*, this discussion extends the previously examined parameters of late Qing intellectual discourse on race to incorporate less canonical views of racial power from largely unknown popular writers.

The Fate of Perished Races

Although reformers such as Yan Fu, Kang Youwei, and Tang Caichang propounded the logic of evolution with a sense of certainty, the idea that races are doomed due to physical inferiorities was not an inevitability for popular writers. A rudimentary understanding of ethnicities and races, it was believed, revealed reasonable explanations based on classifications of primitivism and civilization. The literary fascination with vanquished races, or "inferior races" (*liezhong*), was in significant ways an imagined ethnography in the making. Closely related to this ethnographic inquiry, Lin Shu's *Uncle Tom's Cabin* presents one of the earliest literary cases in which an oppressed other race is cited with sympathy and fear. The intent behind introducing its content to the Chinese was to forestall the same scenario from befalling the yellow race. Yet, in an even more explicit way, Lin Shu was actively engaged in this kind of ethnographic investigation.

Shortly after their first collaborative effort in translating *Uncle Tom's Cabin*, Lin Shu and Wei Yi were both hired by Imperial (present-day Beijing) University's Translations Bureau, overseen by Yan Fu.[3] Although Lin Shu is known primarily for his role as a translator of fiction, he translated three nonfictional works as well, all of which are little known today.[4] Two of the three are historical works: *The Second Punic War* (1886) by Thomas Arnold (1795–1842), which Lin translated in 1903; and *The History of Napoleon* (1829) by John Gibson Lockhart (1794–1854), which was translated in 1904. Although the two historical works were written well before their Chinese translations appeared, the third was translated within an astonishingly short time. An early anthropological study, *Ethnology* was translated into English in 1900 by J. E. Loewe from the German original, *Völkerkunde*, by Austrian ethnologist Michael Haberlandt (1860–1940).[5] Haberlandt was the first professor of ethnology at the University of Vienna and cofounder of the Society for Austrian Ethnic Studies. The English translation of *Ethnology* was published in The Temple Primers series, designed for a lay audience. Three years after the work appeared in English, Lin Shu completed the Chinese translation, *Minzhongxue*, or "a study of ethnic races."[6] The choice of "ethnic races" (*minzhong*) rather than "race" (*renzhong*) emphasizes its study of races as cultural and racial collectives. As pointed out in the English preface, ethnology is a comparatively modern science: "Although knowledge of foreign countries and peoples has been a natural consequence of trade and travel, it has never been given a systematic survey as would be provided by ethnological study."[7]

In Lin Shu's own preface, he gives the importance of ethnology a different emphasis. Upon reviewing Western ethnology, he takes great pains to justify the existence of ethnological thinking in the Chinese tradition. Westerners claim that the Chinese have no practice of documenting the customs and habits of different peoples. However, the fact that Sima Qian's (145–86 BCE) *Historian's Record* already provided accounts of outside peoples such as the Huns and the Koreans demonstrates that the Grand Historian possessed "civilized" thinking and did not discriminate against foreign peoples. The claim to ethnology was important for Lin to make, because he believed that Westerners' curiosity about other peoples and cultures cultivated their ambition for expansion. Without it, the Phoenicians would not have sailed outside the Mediterranean, nor would Columbus have reached the Americas. The reason Westerners' intelligence may be higher than that of the yellow people lies in the fact that their minds are not closed to the outside. With the knowledge of other cultures at their disposal, they are used to viewing the customs of others as primitive and thereby holding them in contempt. For that reason, the ones who roam the earth wielding might today are Westerners. By translating and reading their recorded observations, Lin remarks, the Chinese could learn with efficiency their acquired knowledge. The Chinese must carefully scrutinize the reasons for the Westerners' contempt and subjugation of others and take that as a warning to themselves. In this vein, Lin Shu's notion of ethnological inquiry implied the conviction that China can somehow spare itself the fate of the inferior races by identifying the signs of their decline.

Much like his stated mission in translating *Uncle Tom's Cabin*, Lin Shu's interest in *Ethnology* stems from the hope that there is a key to understanding why certain races are destined to extinction and others not. The perils of the yellow race, while motivating such a quest, are subsumed under a larger map of varying degrees of civilization and barbarity. Seeking to confirm rather than challenge the inequality between the races, Lin Shu strives for an order of knowledge that would give the Chinese the power to classify the inferior races according to their deserved status. Thereby turning the inferior races into the object of inquiry, Lin Shu's investigation is curiously neutral about the sources of the yellow race's decline. This is particularly striking in the objective stated in *Ethnology*, whereby studying the "mental, moral, and physical characteristics" of the Americans, Pacific islanders, Malays, Asians, Africans, and Mediterranean race is rendered into the tripartite "moral, mental, and physical cultivation" (*deyu zhiyu tiyu*). These are, after all, just a slight variation of the familiar three areas of decline identified by Yan Fu as requiring urgent corrective measures for China's national salvation and racial survival.[8]

Lin Shu's translation dispenses with the fifty-six illustrations scattered throughout the original—pictures of natives in their indigenous ornaments, dress, and domiciles and with their weapons. He also refrains from additional comments in the section on the Chinese and Japanese. Yet he is eager to translate ideas of community and nation into terms familiar and relevant to China's own preoccupation. Where Haberlandt remarks on how the states of most nations have evolved not from the "consciousness of national affinity" but from the growing domination of the individual, Lin renders this feeling of national affinity into *aiguo aizhong zhi xin* (the sentiment of loving the nation and loving the race), a phrase that closely recalls *aiguo baozhong* (loving the nation and preserving the race), which he had previously used in his preface to *Uncle Tom's Cabin*.[9] He also translates "primitive people" according to a clear hierarchy of racial value as *liezhong zhi ren* (people of inferior race) rather than *yeren* (savage).[10]

At times, Lin Shu disagrees with what was in the original. Where Haberlandt talks about the upheaval experienced by the indigenous people of Brazil upon the arrival of the white settlers, for instance, Lin Shu does not hesitate to insert his own comment: "The white race inundated the whole continent . . . the natives all perished . . . and the continent became the colony of the white people (*bairen zhimin zhi di*)."[11] Haberlandt, on the other hand, had only gestured toward the upheaval, without any reference to "the white race" or "colony," by writing, "In no continent of the world have such fundamental revolutions and changes in the fates and development of such tremendous areas taken place in so few centuries as in America."[12]

Lin himself probably did not make the decision to translate *Ethnology*. It was most likely assigned to him, as were the two other nonliterary translations he completed during his tenure at the Translations Bureau. Yet it is curious that this particular book was chosen. After all, it was written only three years earlier as part of a series. Little time had passed for it to acquire the kind of fame most of Lin Shu's chosen texts for translation had enjoyed. From Lin's preface, more perfunctory and noticeably less impassioned than his preface to *A Record*, we know that the objective was, as in *A Record*, to teach the Chinese a lesson through example. This time, however, the lesson lies less in the solicitation of sympathy than in the experience of an oppressed race. The goal is to inquire, in an increasingly systematic and deductive fashion, into how the inferior races came to be the way they are and where they stand on a world map of anthropological imagination.

As critical distance substitutes for sympathy, an objectification of the oppressed races replaces the yellow race's own emotional accounts of suffering. The anthropological imagination about the oppressed peoples finds its way into the "indigenous" Chinese literary imagination as well. Here the woes of the yellow race are recast in the voices of the "truly" inferior races. Instead of the Chinese themselves telling the tale of oppression, other races, irreversibly vanquished and abject, take on the narrative in multiple voices. "Xieleihen" (Traces of bloody tears), serialized in one of the most outspokenly nationalistic student journals founded in Tokyo, *Hubei Students World*, provides one such example.[13]

A young Irish girl, Josephine, travels with her father to Hong Kong. On the way, they stop in Barcelona, where in a bookstore they come across a book called *Revenge of the Red and Black Peoples*. The author, Li Sha, is a Filipino who studies at the University of Spain. Intrigued by the fact that the author is not white, Josephine skips the preface and eagerly reads on. The story takes place in 2201 and opens with the escape of a man and a woman of the red race from a zoo in North America. On the way to the mountains where the pair hope to find remaining clans, they accost a black couple who have similarly escaped from their masters. The four agree to travel together and find a remote place in a harsh climate unpopulated by white settlers too tender for such hardship. Exchanging their stories of oppression, the Native Americans recall the time when the people of the western hemisphere did not know about the American continent. The Native Americans remember with pride:

> Our ancestors were kings and emperors. When Columbus discovered America, he also had to call himself subject and pay tribute and revere our ancestor as the Grand Emperor of the Heavenly Kingdom. He didn't use his own language but learned ours and practiced our customs. Our ancestors were deceived by him and went along with what he suggested. At first, he brought more people under the pretext of observing our ways. Who could have known that, having mastered our geography and customs, he and his people would kill our ancestors and murder our women and children? From then on, they proclaimed themselves the favored sons of heaven (*tian zhi aozi*) and enjoyed the utmost authority. Though we are unenlightened primitives who should for generations serve as slaves, today we cannot even be allowed such luxury. They lock us up in the zoo like beasts. Each day we are fed, clothed, and served—a fate truly better than the one allotted to our fellow men. But yesterday I heard one of the tourists saying that there are only thirty families of the red race left in this world. In another year, the red people will become extinct. Upon hearing this, my woman and I were determined to escape in order to gather our lost clans and seek out survival in the mountains.[14]

Commiserating with their red companions, the black slaves relate an even bleaker tale. Oppression in Africa, they note, shares a similar history with that of the Americas. Although the population on the African continent once was at least ten times greater than that of the Native Americans, the slave remarks, now there are not even three families left. Adding to the tragedy, however, is the fact that the foreigners were not the ones forcing the blacks into slavery. Rather, their fellow countrymen sold them as one of Africa's exportable indigenous goods. After the American Civil War, the blacks were emancipated, but they continued to seek after that word *slave*. The rich flaunt their wealth by the number of black slaves they keep. So people treat blacks like livestock. Because of the social and economic prestige slave ownership signified, the white people did not want the blacks to go extinct; on the contrary, they wanted them to reproduce. Whereas the Native Americans may bemoan the fact that they cannot even enjoy being slaves, the blacks, with their irreversible slave mentality, can only wish for their own racial extinction.

Having compared their experiences, the couples then parted to pursue the task of saving their own races from extinction. Eventually, neither couple was successful. They reunited at a later date and decided to follow the example of Adam and Eve to create their own offspring. Through an unforeseen encounter with wild animals, however, the two men died, taking with them the hope of preserving the race. At this point, the precocious reader, Josephine, realizes that she has bought only the first of the two volumes of the novel. Apparently, the first volume deals only with the suffering of these people, whereas the second provides a tale of revenge. But the second volume is conveniently missing. Returning to read the author's preface, then, Josephine finds the following words:

> I am a member of the brown race. My fellow men have been enslaved by the foreigners for over four hundred years. After slumbering all this time and wasting away our given talents, we have developed no thinking on freedom and sovereignty. I inquire in haste the ways of independence and racial strengthening, while lamenting the extinction of my fellow men. . . . Alas! The reds and blacks have not completely lost their lines of descent. There are still a paltry number of remaining clans. Thus they cannot be said to be extinct. My fellow men! Do not tread on their final paths but keep their ambition alive! The world belongs equally to all. How can we allow the white people to monopolize it? [15]

Although only the first installment of *Traces of Bloody Tears* appeared— short-lived, as most serialized fiction from the late Qing was—it serves as a significant literary artifact. Despite the array of vanquished races displayed in the narrative, these various experiences of oppression from different racial perspectives ultimately converge into one. The Chinese, and not the Native Americans, after all, were the ones who had a long history of tributary relations with vassal states. The idea of acculturating barbarians with the language customs of the Middle Kingdom is awkwardly applied to the way the Native Americans received Columbus's arrival.

Apart from the displaced historical details, the story also incorporates contemporary discussions on the Chinese migrant workers. Some observers pointed out that if not for the Chinese, who were willing to endure and work under the most perilous conditions, be it the tropical heat of Southeast Asia or malaria in Peru, European imperialism would not have succeeded. Westerners, with their fair skin and delicate constitution, were not considered sufficiently robust to withstand physical hardship. In *Traces of Bloody Tears*, this exploitation is also seen as the last refuge for the oppressed red and black races, who may perhaps find a haven outside the reaches of Western civilization. The least credible testimony from the oppressed themselves rests on the notion that the Native Americans would consider themselves "unenlightened primitives who should for generations serve as slaves" or that the black slaves would fault themselves for their own "slave mentality." Such self-disparagement is unlikely to be corroborated by the oppressed themselves.

However, this is precisely the kind of self-disparaging rhetoric the Chinese were so fond of using at the time. The complaint about Chinese "slave mentality" can be found in innumerable journal articles dealing with the problems of China. Uniting the brown, black, and red races in the telling of China's own tale of suffering at the hands of the white race, *Traces* demonstrates the complex location of the yellow race in this fantasy of others' suffering. The ones who really want to tell their tale of suffering recede from the picture. Instead, the presence of every other "inferior" race is solicited in its place. Their experiences of oppression articulate the grievances of the one who is absent. One chapter title from *Traces* is quite revealing: "Reading the novel, one's heart becomes tied to the heroes; mourning perished nations, one deeply feels for the races." Suggesting that reading performs an act of compassion by which one becomes emotionally invested in the fate of the heroes, the couplet likens it to mourning, whereby sympathizing with an object appropriates its suffering as one's own. In this way, unless the object suffers, that process of identification is not possible. Race is most deeply felt when it becomes the object of sympathy and sacrifice. Imagining that other inferior races suffer somehow enables the certainty of one's racial demise. To make someone else suffer and to be witness to the suffering, therefore, become indispensable to this sympathy and love for oneself.

The interest and admiration expressed for what is perceived as perishing nations' last gasps abound in much of the literature from the early 1900s through the 1910s. One sees its continuation well into the May Fourth period, when the oppressed become the Eastern Europeans. Among the ones most often sympathized with are the Native Americans, blacks, Filipinos, and Jews. The constructed author of *Revenge of the Red and Black People* is a Filipino student trying to save his nation from extinction. In addition to this work, a number of historical literary works concerning the colonized experience in the Philippines under Spanish and then American rule were serialized in Chinese journals in the first few years of the 1900s.[16] In the self-preface to "An Unofficial History of the Philippines" (Feiliebing waishi), published in the first volume of the renowned journal *New Fiction*, the author expresses his admiration for the last remaining "healthy one among perished nations."[17] The unrelenting resistance of the Filipinos, he remarks, has enabled the name to illuminate the whole world.

The people of perished nations are mourned for being deprived of their homeland. In this conjunction, apart from the black slaves, seen as having been taken away from their native lands and abused in a foreign country, Jews were considered to exemplify the despair of statelessness. Many of the literary narratives about the oppressed are often given as historical accounts, as testimonies from the oppressed themselves. Yet none tried more painstakingly to create this air of authenticity than the 1903 novel, *Ziyou jiehun* (Freedom of marriage).[18]

In her preface, the translator states that the novel was originally authored by an American Jewish gentleman by the name of Vancouver. The Chinese translator, Liberty Flower (Ziyou hua), a young woman twenty-eight years old, made his acquaintance after moving to Switzerland with her father, a watchmaker. A self-proclaimed "abandoned citizen of a perished state" (wangguo yimin) Vancouver wishes to deliver to other oppressed peoples the message that even among perished states, there are still those who harbor the hope of saving the world. Moved by this sentiment, Liberty Flower translated *Freedom of Marriage* into Chinese as *Ziyou jiehun*. Divided into three parts, the novel is supplemented throughout by a traditional style of commentaries by the translator. Liberty Flower also explains three kinds of notation, designed to alert the reader to either particularly moving parts or references that have a specific Jewish context. Cueing the reader to instances of cultural substitutability, Liberty Flower emphasizes the adaptability of the Jewish experience to Chinese circumstances. The English original, Liberty Flower claims, has no preface and hence the first chapter serves as the author's own preface. If the reader should find the writing style in that chapter slightly perplexing, she explains, she hopes to make it up in honesty, because she had done little to disguise it literarily and the oddity belongs to the strangeness of Western writing. Because the translator herself is not adept at verse making, she notes in modesty, any suggestions or submissions from the readers would be most appreciated. Creating a sense of extratextual authenticity, Liberty Flower even provides a mailing address for sending such comments: Miss Liberty Flower, 367 Gaumonne Street, Geneva, NE, Switzerland.

According to its original conception, the novel was to be written in three parts. The first part, according to Liberty Flower, discloses corruption in society as seen through the eyes of its young protagonists. Employing a classic late Qing narrative technique using the eyes of a traveling or wandering narrator, the first volume resonates to the style of its more well-known contemporary novels of social criticism, such as Wu Jianren's *Ershi nian mudu zhi guaixianzhuang* (Twenty years of witnessed strange phenomena, 1903) and Liu E's *Lao Can youji* (Travels of Lao Can, 1903). The second part, featuring the protagonists later as students, deals with their efforts to reinvigorate the spirit of learning in the academic world. Again, this harks back to other contemporary novels, such as *Huang Xiuqiu* (1905) or *Ku xuesheng* (The suffering student, 1905), featuring student protagonists who, as cultural novices, embody, for better or worse, the signs of new knowledge. The last part focuses

on the deeds of heroes who embark on the great task of nation building. However, of the three parts mentioned, only the first two appeared. Like *Revenge
of the Red and Black Peoples*, the perfected future of gratification and recuper-
ated sovereignty remains an unwritten, and perhaps impossible, account.

However, a different reason for this omission stands behind the case of
Freedom of Marriage. The alleged translation is actually not a translation but
a Chinese original. The author, Zhang Zhaotong, was a Chinese student of
political science at Waseda University in Japan and contributor to the radical student journal *Jiangsu*. The third volume never appeared in print because it was never written, even though in the preface Liberty Flower alludes
to it as part of her translation.[19]

This fictitiousness of the novel was not simply a contrivance of authentic
authorship. Like so many novels since the seventeenth-century classic *Dream
of the Red Chamber* (Hongloumeng), the play on mirage and reality heightened all the more the consistent purpose of moral pedagogy. The blatancy
of irony did not detract from the focus of moral reflection. The prefatory
chapter telling Vancouver's story of how he met Liberty Flower demonstrates this point. The Jewish gentleman had for some time lamented his
statelessness and contemplated the possibility of reviving the will of his nation's people. One day, he learns from the newspaper *Freedom News* that a
Jew founded Freedom School on an island in the Pacific called Freeland. He
visits the campus, located on Independence Road on Freeland, and gives a
lecture explaining freedom, a concept he demonstrates with the example of
freedom of choosing one's own mate for marriage. Vancouver then discusses
his novel and meets its soon-to-be translator Liberty Flower for the first time
at her residence, which she named the Apartment of Freedom. The content
of chapter 1, therefore, makes no pretense at sketching out an allegorical
world, in which words such as *freedom* and *independence* tirelessly resurface in
personal names and locations. At a time when these concepts were still
newly translated Western liberal values, they were cited with not only a
sense of novelty but also suspicion. The novel was described as a "political
novel" with a focus on reforms and social critique. Throughout the twenty
chapters, however, the events narrated are no more credible than what was
introduced in the preface and chapter 1.

The significance of this novel, however, lies not in its impersonating
imagination but in the attribution of its source to a "forgotten citizen of a
perished state." The moral story drawn from the Jew's suffering is that China
must improve upon its own ills to avoid the same outcome. The spectacle of
another state in ruination mobilizes one's will to recover one's own national
destiny. The story itself is retold with Chinese formulae, replacing the Jewish context. The experience of oppression is easily transposed onto another's

national humiliation. As aptly expressed by a Chinese reader in a verse dedicated to the novel and published in 1904 in the journal *Women's World*: "Before the barbarians are destroyed, one sighs at homelessness. The people of perished nations weep with tears streaming down their faces like strewn hemp. Showing my sympathy, my heart aches ever more. Holding the silk cloth, I stitch Liberty Flower."[20]

The pain of racial destruction is felt as though one were subjected to it as well. The communion of national consciousness lies in its ready identification with tales of suffering. Be it the black slaves, red natives, colonized brown race, or the stateless Jews, the specter of perished peoples and races poses a displeasing scenario for the Chinese themselves. The possibility of a parallel course toward extinction and the end of sovereignty speaks all too well to what are by now deep-seated fears. At the same time, however, this image is kept at bay. The assurance that these lessons, if properly learned, could save China from a similar fate often concludes the comparisons with the other colored races. In a way that offers not only hope but also a new venue for extending nationalistic ambitions, oppression is not yet a fatal condition for the Chinese as it is for all the others.

Whereas the narratives of the less viable races absorb China's sense of victimization, they also furnish the justification for its revenge. The projected fantasy of other races' ruination serves to shield the yellow race from the fates of the less fortunate races. Though China may not actually share in the suffering, the nationalistic fantasy takes up the cause of the oppressed. Of the events and protagonists in the novel, one detail stands out in particular in relation to this framework of ambivalent identification. The young male protagonist, who together with his female counterpart, Guanguan, manages to change political trends and enact social reforms, is named Huang Huo, which means the "Yellow Peril." On the day his father was executed for not assisting Western missionaries in the killings of antimissionary Chinese, Huang Huo's mother gave him this name as a way of memorializing his father as well as the national infamy that accompanied his birth. The significance of naming in this novel, however, was not alone in its implication of racial vengeance. The name Huang Huo would not be so remarkable in itself if it did not pinpoint a widespread practice in literary naming at the time.

Surnames such as Huang, Hua, and Xia, in fact, appear frequently in novels from the early decades of the twentieth century before the founding of the Republic.[21] Just as huang (yellow) carries a particular resonance for the Chinese racial identity, hua (blossom) and xia are also designations for China and Chinese culture. However, huanghuo, in this case, is not merely a neutral self-designation. Even though in some novels characters with the name Yellow Peril embody all the negative characteristics of a backward and self-enclosed feudalistic mind-set, in other novels—such as *Freedom of Marriage*—protagonists with such a name are reformist and revolutionary figures who hold the promise of aiding China's entry into the modern era. This discrepancy points to something larger than merely an inconsistency in literary preferences.

By the time *Freedom of Marriage* appeared, in fact, discussions of the yellow peril in a broader cultural and political context were well under way. While the fate of China remains precarious and its territorial sovereignty vulnerable under the threat of partition, a resilient political rhetoric takes pride in pointing out the difficulty for any one power to entirely engulf it because of its size. Discussions of the yellow peril become a venue for psychological comfort and discursive maneuvering. A number of commentators find encouragement in the fact that if China is being oppressed, at least it is not passively subdued. The prophecy of the yellow peril, created by the Europeans themselves, now finds its true embodiment in China. The self-distinction we have seen made by the Chinese with respect to other oppressed peoples now deepens with confidence in the idea that the yellow peril is somehow the thorn in Western imperialism's side, a formidable threat no other vanquished race has the power to pose.

From "Race" to "Peril": China and Japan

The notion of the "yellow peril" was first used in Europe in response to the sixth-century invasion of Attila the Hun. It became part of the European memory of Asia and its barbarian hordes from the time of Genghis Khan and the Mongol invasions. This term was brought to the fore again in European discourse in the late nineteenth century. Spurred by the Malthusian prospect of uncontrollable population growth and its inverse relation to available resources, yellow peril was originally the economic and demographic disaster that China and Japan together potentially posed. Depending on the political exigency, four different versions of who is meant by the designation existed. At times, Japan's fulfillment of this role appeared as the most fearsome prospect. The enormity of China's population, at other times, seemed more plausible to the literary imagination, such as that expressed in the works of the American writers Jack London, Ambrose Bierce, and Bret Harte.[22] The heated controversies over Chinese immigration in California in the nineteenth century, in particular, stoked this fear with poignancy. A third view is a composite of the two—Japan with its political might, and China supplying the numbers—which argued that, under Japan's military tutelage, China's unbridled population of 400 million would unify to subvert Western imperialism and thereby bring an end to Europe's era of supremacy. The

fourth view, often used defensively by Chinese who thought the title unflattering, proposed that Russia, being geographically situated in Asia itself,
should be considered the real yellow peril, especially given its designs on
northeastern China. This last view gained the least currency and quickly
dropped out of discussions, as yellow peril was soon equated with the revival
of China's racial hegemony.

The reappearance of discussions on the yellow peril in the late nineteenth
into the early twentieth century was situated in the complicated power matrix between Russia, France, England, America, Germany, and a quickly
emerging Japan.[23] The Sino-Japanese conflict in the mid-1890s left Asia vulnerable to further territorial acquisitions by the Europeans. Eager to secure
Germany's share but cautious to maintain his alliance with other European
powers, Kaiser Wilhelm II of Germany issued warnings of the imminent
threat from the East.[24]

In 1895, he propagated the idea of the yellow peril through a drawing (see
Figure 3.1). In the sketch, Archangel Michael, a symbol for Germany, stands
on a cliff before a group of seven women with shields and armor. Facing

FIGURE 3.1 Kaiser Wilhelm II's vision of the "Yellow Peril": "Völker Europas,
wahret Eure heiligsten Güter!" (People of Europe, guard your holy heritage!). Artist: Hermann Knackfuss. 1895.
Source: Huis Doorn, The Netherlands.

them, Michael points his left hand east to a cliff on the opposite side, where Buddha, in a halo of ominous rather than peaceful light, sits facing them. The caption reads, "People of Europe! Protect your most holy grace!" According to one commentator, the Buddha figure looked upon destruction with "unmoved and cold eyes." At the order of Wilhelm II, Hermann Knackfuss, a professor of art history at the Kasseler Art Academy in Kasseler, fleshed out the vision in a final sketch.[25] Wilhelm II then sent copies of the drawing to various heads of state, including Tsar Nicholas II, as well as his top associates, such as Bismarck, who was admittedly puzzled over the meaning of the painting but nonetheless placed it under his Christmas tree.[26] It reached Russia and, as it was printed in *The New York Times* in 1898, America as well. The drawing was also disseminated among the populace and readily accessible on the steamboats of the German East Asian Cruise Line as decorative art.[27]

Though often credited with reviving the idea of the yellow peril in late nineteenth-century Europe, Wilhelm II was not the only source responsible. Claims of origin are often contradictory or unreliable. Even an American dentist who once served the kaiser claims to have coined the phrase. As early as 1870, Ernest Renan spoke of a danger posed by the East, although at the time he meant Russia. In an atmosphere of a surfeit of imperialistic ideology that tended to perceive threat rising from all peripheries of Europe, Wilhelm II merely instrumentalized a discourse that had been gaining momentum since the 1870s.

Though warnings of the yellow peril circulated widely, their interpretations were seldom uniform. Significantly, much disagreement resided in the discussion of yellow peril itself. Sympathizers with Asia, such as Anatole France, jeered at the Europeans themselves and maintained that "yellow peril" was a phenomenon created solely by the "white peril." Even as European critics were attributing the rise of the yellow peril to European imperialism, they were also launching a moral crusade against their own political cultures. Another American commentator wrote an essay titled "Bogey of Yellow Peril" in which he sought to demystify the object of the hysteria exaggerated in European and American discourses.[28] Indeed, in many ways, yellow peril bespeaks the phantasm created in the European and American minds. Japan's quick rise to power and the scale of the popular uprising directed against Westerners during the Boxer Rebellion in 1900 gave substance to the worrisome prospect. Interestingly, both sympathizers with and opponents of the yellow peril share a common apprehension about the end of European supremacy, economic and moral. If yellow peril was the fear that needed expression in the European cultural and political imagination, its potential for proliferating cultural anxieties did not end there. What was originally set up as a specter of doom for the European finds its embodiment fully gratified in Chinese political and cultural reinterpretation.

Although there are variations and different emphases, the Chinese reception of the idea of yellow peril has two general aspects, both of which aimed at mastering China's difficult position in the international hierarchy of power. One mode of reception, first precipitated by the realization of Japan's might, sought to credit the Chinese for Japan's rise to political and cultural power. This justification, often demonstrating painstaking powers of rationalization, put China on the map as a participant, even if peripherally, in the war game between East and West. Hopeful speculations about China's ability to pose itself as a formidable foe to the West were at first put forth cautiously. The discussions focused more on the future of Sino-Japanese than on Sino-Western relations. Through a series of discursive strategies, however, the parameters of discussions expanded to incorporate Western perceptions of Japan. This second mode of reception often expressed confidant jubilation in China's prowess, measured against its ability to rise as a threat to the West. Providing a point of reflection and diffraction, European discussions of the yellow peril were selectively scrutinized for any hint of crediting China's role in the perception of the yellow peril.

The continual rise of Japan reached a new level of recognition after its victory over Russia in the Russo-Japanese War. As events unfolded during the war, they were not only carefully monitored by the European powers but also avidly reported in the Chinese print media. Even the ailing Ottoman Empire, the "Sick Man of Europe," whose example inspired the designation "Sick Man of East Asia" (*dongya bingfu*), felt rejuvenated by the prospects in Asia and aspired to be the "Japan of the Near East."[29] Journals such as *Alarming Bell News* were founded for the sole purpose of reporting the events.[30] Other journals, such as *Eastern Miscellany*, one of the most widely read journals at the time, republished many articles from more specialized journals and circulated them among a wider audience.

China's reception of Japan's victory was fraught with ambivalence. On the one hand, Japan's rise to international prominence was a reflection of China's dwindling status. Not only was China ill-equipped to compete with Western nations led by the white race but it also appeared incapable of keeping up with a fellow member of the yellow race. The simple dichotomy between the white and yellow races hitherto maintained in late Qing intellectual discourse was ruptured by this change of hierarchy within the yellow race. Appeals and pleas for the consolidation of the yellow race quickly rose in response. Japan, it was argued, should not forget its symbiotic relationship and racial affinity with China. Their alliance was crucial to both nations' continued survival, like the mutual dependence between "teeth and lips" (*chunchi xiangyi*).[31] Ultimately, the yellow race must unite in an alliance against the invasion of the white race.

On the other hand, Japan's victory provided an important piece of evidence for the Chinese. The law of evolution, by which the strong (white) subordinates the weak (colored), was irreversibly challenged. Even though opponents of evolution had already charged the theory with Western imperialist connotations, this was the first time that a real military conflict between the yellow and white races proved the fallacy of the logic of white supremacy.[32] As reported in various articles rejoicing in the prospects of the yellow race, Japan's rise led to the important insight that the white race was neither the legitimate nor the necessary ruler of the world. The law of natural selection had not proved invincible. China, too, could rise to prominence and a position of international domination. The whites were, after all, not superior to the yellows. After Kang Youwei's imagined realm of the great union, the Russo-Japanese War was perhaps the first historical event to furnish this coveted desire for hegemony with tangible evidence.

The ambivalent reception of Japan's victory as both threat and promise resulted in a difficult topography for China to negotiate in claiming its own racial and national superiority. Racial solidarity with the Japanese was important for this justification vis-à-vis the white race. However, it was equally vital that China maintain its presumed role, even if only psychologically, as the leader of the yellow race. Out of this ambivalence, two primary views were reiterated. One way of coming to terms with Japan's prominence was to rationalize its indebtedness to the Chinese culture. Representative of this view is an article published in *Diplomacy News* in 1904, "On Japan's Lineage from Tang Culture."[33] Appearing at a time when Japan's superior capabilities were increasingly evident, the article was reprinted in other journals, such as *Eastern Miscellany*. The author chastises those who blindly subscribe to the primacy of the law of evolution in predetermining the roles of the strong and the weak. There are intellectuals, the author remarks, who readily surrender to this fatalism, opening themselves up to the exploitation of foreigners who happily use evolution as a pretext. Now, with the clear victor in view, the discourse on the natural racial boundaries collapses. From this point on, all who try to hide themselves behind the idea that the whites are superior, and yellows inferior, demonstrate only their own cowardice.[34]

The author disapproves of those "self-disparagers" who seem ready to submit to the creed of evolution and white racial superiority; however, he mobilizes a similar kind of sentiment in his reassertions. On one level, he recovers the premise on which China can claim to be the source of Japan's glory. On another level, however, his argument reflects a kind of rhetoric regarding China's failure that is steadily taking shape at this time.

He willingly concedes the fact that China today is not as great as it used to be. And rightfully so, he emphasizes that China's weakness does not lie in the foreigners who encroach upon its land and humiliate its people by calling them unkempt and unsanitary. It lies, rather, in the willful abandonment by the Chinese of the ancient ways that had made China a great empire. Because the Chinese somehow failed to preserve the ways of their forebears, this tradition has now crowned someone else's glory. The source of China's ills is to be sought not in foreign invasion but in one's own failure to claim what is properly one's own. Reminiscent of Liang Qichao's assertion that China's racial extinction lies in the hands of its own people and not those of foreign powers, this argument relies on the rhetorical force of self-blame as a way of projecting China's otherwise unhindered destiny of greatness.

In this way, the embrace of failure gives an unexpected leeway for discursive maneuverings. The inquiry itself into failure itself, rather than its content, becomes a persistent form of self-illumination. The confidence of remedying the problem once it is properly identified underlies each described item of China's ills. Paradoxically expressed through self-disparagement, this new optimism surfaces in all forms of discourse around this time in which the need to reconcile one's superiority and the opposing reality required rhetorical and psychological reassurances. It demonstrates the readiness with which self-attributed failure can become a powerful tool for self-accreditation.

Apologizing for the burden pushed onto the Europeans and Americans to maintain international order and peace, an anonymous writer, "Man of Leisure," argues that the West has been forced into a state of competition and rivalry by events in the East. [35] The struggle for dominance within Europe and between Europe and America drove these nations to extend their spheres of influence in the Pacific and South Pacific. However, if China had not shown signs of vulnerability to the designs of imperialism, Western nations would have been kept at bay and thereby compelled to live in peace with one another. According to the author, if only the people would endeavor to revise their political institutions, renew their learning, and rejuvenate their national strength, there is no reason why China could not, in alliance with other Asian nations such as Japan and Korea, keep in check the rivalry between the Western nations. Quarrels among the Europeans would then be confined to the negotiations of coexistence without escalating to violence and hostility over territorial acquisitions.

Of course, it is shameful that the Chinese, possessing such great powers of initiation (*zhudongli*), do not use them to increase their own strength but, instead, allow them to go to waste. In view of the fact that Japan's prowess and success have removed evolutionary obstacles to the fulfillment of the yellow race, it is only appropriate that China fulfill its "god-given duty (*tianzhi*) as a member of the same continent, the same race" and "repay the generous will of her good friend [Japan]" and together reign as masters of the East.[36] The author finally resigns himself to the fact that the safety of the East is tied to China: "The gains and losses of the world also depend on her. Heavy indeed is our responsibility!"[37]

If it is difficult to sell China's importance to world peace, a claim of responsibility in the name of good conscience seems to do a better job of solicitation. In this view, China's demise becomes capable of affecting the state of world politics. The necessity of China overcoming the demise itself turns into an obligation to contribute to international stability. The shame to its own people notwithstanding, China's weakness is reasoned to have wide-reaching effects on global harmony.[38] If China were to take the initiative and play the active role as Asia's master, Western nations would not be tempted to expand their territories abroad. More important, they would not be tempted to risk the destabilization of their amiable relations with one another. Imagined in all its recognized failure, China turns out to hold the key to a peaceful world order. How self-disparagement can suddenly become a hyperinvested self-image is perhaps no less puzzling than how Japan, the hated vanquisher of 1895, turns into a "good friend."

A prime example of the unreliability of alliances is the fact that, even though advertising a close bond with Japan may have its discursive advantages for Chinese commentators, Japanese writers were more interested in dissociating themselves from Sino-Japanese affinity. The warm embrace of Sino-Japanese cultural relations sat awkwardly with Japan's political agenda. Eager to establish an Anglo-Japanese alliance at this time, Japan found no advantage in the idea that China and Japan shared a common culture. An article published in the Japanese newspaper *Jiji shinpō* and then translated into Chinese as "Fei tongzhong tongwen" (Not of the same race and culture) flatly refutes the idea of a Chinese-Japanese racial and cultural affinity.[39] Citing anthropologists' use of craniometry as a way of determining racial origin, the author points out that the racial affinity shared by the Chinese and Japanese is not any more specific than what is shared by all Asian races. This distinction, he continues, hardly holds greater precision than saying that all Europeans are of the same racial family. In fact, there are different standards for cranium size and, by extension, for racial classifications within the larger category of race.

The fact that racial affinity in any case means little more than mere taxonomy, the author argues, can be corroborated by examples such as America and Britain, and Japan and Britain. Although America and Britain are of the same race and language, those affinities are inconsequential when it comes to a conflict of political interests. Britain and Japan, on the other hand, having no racial relation, can nonetheless become allies. Therefore, the Japanese should not carelessly appeal to the feeling of "same race, same culture *tongzhong tongwen*" with regard to China and mislead foreign observers into thinking that Japan has a certain special relationship with China. This might give rise to a concern over the yellow peril. There are already those among the English who would not hesitate to mobilize racial and religious differences to undermine the formation of an Anglo-Japanese alliance. It is fine to have occasional commercial dealings with China, the author warns, but to attribute this to the affinity of "same race, same culture" will hardly win Japan the kind of allies it wants.

This article, soon translated into Chinese and published in *Diplomacy News* and *Eastern Miscellany*, is interesting for two reasons. First, it points out that appeals to racial identities are subsumed under larger political motivations. This move, in many ways, also indirectly refutes another piece of Japanese propaganda at the time, one that attempted to present China and Japan as racial allies in order to facilitate Japan's expansion of its sphere of influence in Asia. In this sense, this essay is remarkably candid about the political interests that animated discussions on the yellow racial alliance. Second, this discussion itself is motivated by precisely such an interest. Japan must not resort to racial affinity as a viable political premise, because in order to present itself as a desirable ally to the British, it must distance itself from China. To be accepted by the white race, in other words, one must pass as somehow racially impartial. Yet only the recognition that race in fact does matter can give expression to such a disclaimer. In the shifting game of the yellows versus whites, racial alignment carries an ineluctable persuasion.

The Chinese translator of this article attaches a postscript expressing his own opinion. With regard to Europeans' concern with the yellow race, the idea of "same race" as a form of solidarity has much appeal to various nations in Asia. However, as far as international relations are concerned, the translator continues, nationalism is the basic premise on which international dealings operate. Beginning in the late 1800s, the Japanese became increasingly unhappy with the intervention of Russia, England, and France in the Far East, and they promoted the idea of "same race, same culture" to secure their influence in China. Now that the Anglo-Japanese alliance is secure, they fear the jealousy of other nations and seek to deny them access to the same claim. Neither of these ideas—"same race, same culture" or its refutation—contains any substance. They are no more than the tactics of foreign policy makers. In short, the author concludes, if it were not the case that our nation is so weak, things would not be this way.

The Chinese translator's remarks acknowledge that impassioned calls for racial alliance were no more than political games. Nations were engaged in rivalry, and racializing nations is merely a way of differentiating the order of hegemony. The sober recognition of the constructedness of racialized discourses, however, by no means dilutes their emotional appeals. As a source of power and self-annihilation, the claim of race enables the conviction in one's perseverance as well as formidability. Race not only is a claim about one's cultural or ethnic legitimacy but also promises the investment of power in the conception of who one is in relation to others. As a structurally hierarchical category, its discursive invention is premised on the question of domination and hegemony. Pivoting on the question of might and subordination, the notion of the yellow race inevitably evolves into a preoccupation with its destructive capacities. Posited through a series of discursive distortions, a race under subordination reemerges as a race of threat. Rather than put on the defense as menace, yellow peril becomes a title of legitimate prowess.

Embodying Menace

Avidly consuming the contents of debates on the yellow peril in newspapers, journals, and treatises published in Europe, America, and Japan, the Chinese audience was especially interested in the Europeans' and Americans' concerns with Japan as the yellow peril. Against, but often inspired by, these racial views, the Chinese audience re-created the image in accordance with their own desired vision.[40] The primary journalistic forum for these reappropriated views, *Waijiaobao* (Diplomacy news) and *Jingzhong ribao* (Alarming bell news), in particular, provided lengthy coverage between 1904 and 1905, when discussions on the yellow peril reached a new height because of the Russo-Japanese War.[41] Attempting to rally support for their cause, the Russians warned the European powers of the imminent rise and domination of the yellow race if Japan were not subdued. The French subscribed to this view to some extent, but the British and Americans were more skeptical of Russia's own ulterior motives.[42] The fact that Russia, as part of Asia geographically and the real aggressor, would be more appropriately called the yellow peril was a detail not lost on the British commentator.[43] Of the foreign articles translated into Chinese, British and Japanese sources were in the majority. The Japanese were largely preoccupied with refuting the notion of the yellow peril, whereas the British voiced the strongest skepticism. Keeping a cool distance from all the excitement, one journalist pointed out that the threat of the "yellow peril" was no different from what was clamored about as the "American peril" a few years before.[44] In the same vein, "white peril" and "German peril" were equally unreliable coinages thrown into discussions on the configuration of power in Europe. Rather than reject Japan on the basis of a racial myth, British and American supporters praised Japan for taking the lead among Asian countries by behaving like a "civilized nation."

While the British and Americans attempted to dispel the threatening myth of the yellow peril, the Japanese were also trying to dissuade Europeans from endorsing such a view.[45] Dissociating themselves from the category of the yellow race by denying the "same race, same culture" affinity with China, the Japanese feared that the notoriety of being the yellow peril would further disfavor their future alliance with Western powers. Although Japan sidestepped any association with the name, the Chinese seemed eager to assume it. One Chinese translator's short commentary attached to one of these articles states that the yellow peril, rather than infamy, promises the national strength coveted by China: "When the white people first created the theory about the yellow peril, it was meant to denote the Mongol invasion. The so-called Mongol race includes China. Now, because Japan is winning over Russia in strength, the emphasis has shifted to the Japanese. If China were to emulate Japan's efforts and seek its own strengthening, the peril would be even greater."[46] At stake is the question of who embodies the true yellow peril capable of arousing fear in Western nations. The ambivalent relation China has with Japan's prominence can be no better demonstrated than by its preoccupation with claiming this title. The pejorative connotations of yellow peril became a confirmation of one's formidable strength. In another postscript to a different article, one translator comments on how the yellow people should not despair that they will not be able to bear out the prophecy of the yellow peril.[47] The yellow people should put every endeavor into materializing this feared prophecy rather than allowing the white people to jeer at their lack of potential. Carrying out the impassioned plea for the yellow race to rise up to the occasion, late Qing reformer Huang Zunxian calls out, "In great harmony the five continents unite in one—the time for that has not come. The black ghost and red barbarians fell under the whites. Now the whites fret of the 'yellow peril.' What is the yellow peril? It is we Asians! We! We! We!"[48]

As a way of resolving the ambivalence toward Japan's glory and China's weakness, Chinese observers enthusiastically anticipate their eventual role as the true yellow peril. While Japan tries to keep the name at arm's length, China offers an eager embrace. Significantly, even after the Russo-Japanese War, the privileged status of being the yellow peril remained vividly in the minds of the Chinese. A 1908 article from an American newspaper discussed the various problems with the presence of Chinese laborers in California and other parts of the world.[49] Worried by the inevitable course of evolution, the author fears that because of overpopulation yellow people will start pushing into Europe. He foresees racial conflicts between Asians and Europeans, as can be already extrapolated from the racial conflict in the Unites States between the whites and blacks. Unlike the blacks, who have no civilization, however, the yellows will be much more troublesome. Taking the recent influx of Chinese immigrants into Australia as an example, the author states that the yellow peril is embodied by the Chinese and not the Japanese. In response, the Chinese translator's postscript is as brief as it is revealing, as the only conclusion he arrives at is the tantalizing suggestion that "according to this article, the yellow peril is not the Japanese but the Chinese. It speaks of East Asian people's characteristics in comparable terms. Should we Chinese not rise up in excitement upon hearing this?"[50]

Inspired to put forth their own views on the yellow peril, Chinese commentators were excited about the prospect even after the discussions had subsided in the West.[51] Reinterpreting the discursive phenomenon of the yellow peril itself, a Chinese observer remarks that Japan's unwillingness to assume the role unveils the true identity of the yellow peril. Japan's intense lobbying for the abolition of the phrase has not contributed to the diminishing interest in the subject. Although Japan has stepped onto Russian soil and showed its might, that in itself would not have sufficed to shock all of Europe. Japan's subjugation of an already decrepit and corrupt empire was not enough to start the rumor of the formidable yellow peril. The only explanation, the author states, must be that China was what was truly meant by the yellow peril.

The notion of yellow peril has enabled nations to envision their own destruction as well as triumph. For China, in particular, it provides a discursive position of substitution. Its uneasy relation to its presumed leading role in the yellow race finds reconciliation in the simplified dichotomy between whites and yellows. The tension between China and Japan is subsumed under the larger imperative of racial conflict. Yet in desiring to be the yellow peril, China has internalized both its promise and failure. A racially pejorative term is desired not because China was unable to reflect on its more imperialistic connotations but because the yellow peril carried an unintended profit. The status and confirmation offered in being the yellow peril outweigh the insult.

The Jubilation of the "Yellow Peril"

China's fascination with the yellow peril lies in its potential to substantiate China's own promise of fulfillment. Through complex rhetorical maneuvers, an originally derogatory term directed at the Japanese transforms into self-affirmation for the Chinese. The idea that China could rise up one day and fulfill this prophecy, to the detriment of the Western colonial powers, offered an attractive vision. Whereas political discourse gives only sparing occasions for articulating such a heavily invested self-image, popular fiction writers express it with exuberance and sensationalism for their urban audience. Supplementing the intellectual social utopia constructed up by Kang Youwei and Tang Caichang, futuristic fiction spells out the narrative of the yellow race's domination in no uncertain terms.

The newly emerged genre of science fantasies in the late Qing provided the medium through which Western technology and Chinese hegemony could become one.[52] Concomitant with the proliferation of classified genres ranging from detective and nihilist fiction to the more esoteric "fiction of fishing industry" and "fiction of advertisement," science fantasy grafted onto the materiality of Western military power the imagination for a future of Chinese supremacy. Rewritings of classical novels provided an easy forum for projecting the modern onto the old. More original conceptions attempted to construct an entirely new world to showcase China's desired image. Exemplary in this regard is a little-known yet highly revealing novella published in *Xiaoshuo shibao* (Fiction times) in 1909, "Dian shijie" (Electrical world).[53]

As one of the earliest works of science fiction in China, "Electrical World" brings into focus the various tensions between Western technology, scientific optimism, a growing nationalistic passion, and the desire to avenge a humiliating history of colonialism. Beginning in year 2010, the novel narrates the following two hundred years. We first learn that by the twenty-first century, China has reclaimed full jurisdiction over all foreign settlements and treaty ports. It has at its command enormous naval fleets and ground troops, confirming its status as one of the most formidable nations on earth. Mining projects of China's rich natural resources were fully operational and, more important, domestically owned. Under China's own supervision, its railway system reached a state of sophistication far exceeding that of even colonial times. If these achievements still do not convey China's unparalleled prowess and confidence, the male protagonist's name, Huang Zhenqiu, which literally means "the yellow that shocks the earth," drives the message home. As the hero of future China, he is also known as Electric King (Dianwang). Planning for China's continual prosperity, Huang proposes the ambitious plan of creating a new world supplied by enhanced electricity, rendering traditional energy sources obsolete. With new transport vehicles such as flying electric ships and electric cars, costly railways are as redundant as they are cumbersome to build. With a bit of time and capital, Huang promises, "in not more than fifty years, China will easily become the master of the entire world" (*quan shijie zhuren weng*).[54]

The next day, Electric King opens an exhibition of New Electric Studies at his private factory. The range of offerings is disorienting, as visitors are entertained with electronic music, transported in mobile chairs powered by electricity, and served delicacies on electric conveyer belts. Huang unveils a new element he has created from a piece of fallen asteroid that carries an electromagnetic energy five thousand times greater than the most powerful magnets. From this he has extracted a kind of metal that can serve as the basic raw material for unthinkable technological innovations. With one look at this unassuming, small object, visitors feel as though "the electricity in their pupils was almost sucked away" by its mesmerizing power.[55]

Apart from objects that exert an almost supernatural power over the human mind, included in this array of technological novelties are also state-of-the-art weaponry, entertainment, and communication devices. There are more than one thousand electric guns, hundreds of different varieties of electric fans, electric films, electronic music, and wireless telegrams, all of which were unknown before. After meandering through more than one thousand exhibition rooms, the visitors come to three preservation rooms. In contrast to the awe-inspiring Chinese exhibition, these rooms store twentieth-century technological relics, mostly of Western origin and now valuable only for their historical reference.

Apart from arranging this spectacular display, Electric King himself is also an awesome spectacle, using a pair of electric wings for his own personal transport. The technological realization of the fantastic, it is explained in the novel, follows the logic of adaptation of species to their environment in the progressive scheme of evolution. Thus, by means of these wings, Huang is able to maximize any given evening by dining in San Francisco and still making it back to Shanghai in time to go to the race track before any of the courtesans have begun their nightly carriage excursions on the streets.[56]

Amid this picture of China's prosperity, news of an invasion spreads. The nation Xiwei (Western Might) has dispatched an air fleet to destroy the yellow race. It is quickly approaching Dongyinguo (Nation of Eastern Shadow) and will reach China in a matter of days. Located somewhere undisclosed in Europe, Western Might had trained a special flying fleet in 1999. Over five years, it had used the fleet to destroy other powerful nations on the continent. Since then, Western Might has been scouting out Asia as its next target. Eastern Shadow has tried to appease them, but Western Might, believing in the prophecy of the "yellow peril," plans on invading the small nation regardless. Led by Napoleon X—harking back to one of the many Western heroes admired by late Qing writers—Western Might's flying fleet carries as its best weapon a shrapnel bomb. At the news of the imminent invasion, the Chinese try to locate Huang Zhenqiu, but to no avail. Just as the Chinese people begin to panic, they learn that Electric King, armed with only his pair of wings and a newly invented electric gun, has single-handedly dealt a major blow to the forces of Western Might.

Having no spare time to relate the news himself, he sends a quick message to the world's news agencies and sets off to subdue the remaining enemy forces, in fear of their retaliation if not quelled once and for all. As it turns out, Electric King has already known about Western Might's plan to destroy the yellow peril for some time. Always a step ahead of any threat to his people, his research on developing a new electric energy to strengthen China's defense has already been in progress for two years.

In retaliation for Electric King's dispatch of troops into Siberia, Napoleon X orders the execution of all Chinese traveling in Europe. All diplomatic channels having failed, Electric King is left with only one choice— to destroy the enemy. He shows great reluctance to inflict violence of such a scale, but holding back his benevolent tears, he arms himself with a powerful electric gun. With one sweep, he unleashes thousands of streams of fire at the enemy troops, annihilating them in a giant explosion, the magnitude of which is said to be so great that all of Asia could hear it.[57] After three days of fire bombing, Western Might and its people are finally destroyed.

After this demonstration of China's might, other nations come with their peace offerings. Meanwhile, the Chinese emperor bestows an official title on Huang as a token of gratitude. The outcome of racial apocalypse finds restored harmony only in the sealed mandate of the emperor in a postnationalist empire. Huang continues with his exploits, such as mining gold in Antarctica, building a storage place for gold in Iran, and refining an element capable of climatic warming originally discovered by a German scientist. Because any peaceful society rests on education, he invents electric microphones and projecting screens to facilitate multimedia pedagogy. As a corollary, he also promotes traditional moral education, in the spirit of which he creates a "desire-quelling drug" (*jueyuji*) that suppresses people's sexual desires until they are fifty, the said age of emotional maturity.[58]

Flying cable cars improve the efficacy of public transportation by loading and unloading passengers on vertical belts. Huang's counterfeit-proof bills, printed with a distinct signature using electric pressure, rout out fraud and distrust in society. To expand the possibility of inhabitable space in the world, Huang also creates electric machines capable of controlling weather patterns, facilitating the ease of setting up colonies underwater. As for the surviving European laborers who are recruited to develop these projects, Huang shows kindness by also improving their living conditions and allowing them leisure time to pursue hobbies. The narrator consciously contrasts his benevolence with the cruel treatment suffered by the Chinese laborers in the nineteenth century. Significantly improving the quality of life for all,

Huang achieves a "world of great union" (*datong shijie*) that, in short, would be the envy of Kang Youwei.

Occasionally, members of White Resistance conspire to assassinate Huang. They are, however, always apprehended beforehand and reeducated accordingly. One group, for instance, hoarded gold from the mines in Antarctica in preparation for a war of independence. Upon their arrest, they are banned from the enjoyment of the public park, a punishment the lightness of which the novel distinguishes from the humiliating ban on the Chinese from entering Huangpu Park in Shanghai in the nineteenth century. In the end, pleased with his task but disillusioned with the ease of success, Huang Zhenqiu sets off alone to travel throughout the galaxy in his electric balloon to survey other planets. Ever thinking ahead, he aims to set up space colonies in the future once the finite resources of the earth have been exhausted.

"Electrical World" underscores the importance of fantasy in the conviction of China's greatness. The tale posits a morally superior scenario of the yellow peril. China not only thwarts the design to exterminate the imminent yellow peril but also takes that rationale to the extreme. The yellow race takes technology to a level that its Western inventors could not. Many of the scientific gadgets invented are Chinese improvements upon existing Western technology, much as the tale itself is a series of original embellishments on the other's primordial fantasy of the yellow horde. Inspired by the lure of menace, the notion of the yellow peril is taken, improved, and recast as the benevolent supremacy of the yellow race.

"The yellow that shocks the world" succinctly captures the idea of celebrating the yellow peril. Together with an imagined gesture of mercy toward white laborers, references to the treatment of Chinese coolies abroad and the infamous park sign, "Chinese and dogs not admitted," work to rehabilitate the sense of lost sovereignty under Western domination.[59] Banishing that history to a superseded past, the three rooms full of Western technological relics from the twentieth century reduce the military might of imperialism to a state of inert enshrinement.

But the satisfaction does not come only from reversing the memory of former subjugation. "Electrical World" consciously sets its claimed power apart from the practice of Western hegemony by installing its own values of spiritual superiority. Mobilizing every appeal of legitimacy, the character Huang Zhenqiu is at times described as a world savior with Buddhist connotations. Although the white race is portrayed as ruthless and oppressive in its rule, the yellow race, once in the position of power, shows merciful governance over its white subjects. When pushed to violence, a decision for which Huang always shows initial reluctance, he does it unwillingly and with regret. The world of great union, achieved under Huang's efforts, posits a political ideal only the yellow race is fit to materialize. Thus armed with moral rectitude, the yellow race in its continual territorial expansion underwater and into outer space, the single most developed theme in the book, fulfills the most feared prophecy of an overpopulated yellow race as foreseen by the Europeans. The thought of not only the earth but also an entire galaxy being overrun with people of the yellow peril incites as much horror in the Western imagination as it does pleasure in the Chinese vision.

Yellow peril not only embodies the colonial fantasy to which the yellow race is subjected but also locates the source of China's possible triumph. Revealingly, fictional visions often posit a futuristic utopia with the threatened sovereignty of the yellow race as its starting premise. Seldom does the yellow race actually initiate the aggression. With great moral reluctance, the yellow race is provoked into demonstrating its perilous formidability, always accomplished with awesome efficiency in the end. When moral recognition alone does not suffice, sophisticated weaponry ensures that China's spiritual supremacy can be backed with force. The separation of the winners from the losers may also require the inscription of enforceable statutes, as are incorporated into a more aggressive scenario in a different novel published in 1908, *Xin Jiyuan* (New century).[60] Written by someone under the pen name "Master of the sapphire lotus house," the novel opens with a strong and vital China in the year 1999. As in "Electrical World," coastal treaty ports are back under Chinese jurisdiction and the institution of foreign settlements has long been abolished. The new China, distinct from the old, enjoys wealth, power, stability, and a successful constitutionalism, all of which are safely guarded by a defense budget one-third of total state expenses. Fearing China's status and acting on a prediction of an imminent catastrophe as a result of the yellow peril, the white nations plan their preemptive attack. An opportunity presents itself when China proposes to systematize the use of the Yellow Emperor's calendrical notation in all nations populated by the yellow race. Among them are two republics formed by the descendants of Chinese laborers in Australia and America. Exploiting this occasion as a pretext, the white nations call for an alliance against the yellow race.

The event unfolds, through the rest of the twenty chapters, with detailed accounts of the technological warfare employed in a struggle that, as stated at the beginning of chapter 3, will "determine once and for all the superiority of the yellow and white races."[61] The weapons employed are often of purported Western origin with improvements made by the Chinese, an enhancement that always pays off in the latter's favor. Despite the author's initial disclaimer that "since [he] is no science expert, the novel does not serve as explication," detailed introduction to each new weapon is set off in a separate paragraph in the text with the date of its invention, the inventor's name, and a short description of its powers.[62]

Heroes with names such as Huang Zhisheng (yellow's prosperity), Huang Zhiqiang (yellow's strength), Yang Guowei (flaunting the nation's prowess), or Hua Rixing (the day of China's rise to prominence) are but a few examples of the patriotic pride expressed throughout the novel. Women heroes also demonstrate great scientific expertise and often work alongside, and even come to the rescue of, their male counterparts against the demonized white enemy. The white race, portrayed in all its ruthlessness, lifts the ban stipulated in a war convention prohibiting the use of chlorine gas in order to combat the yellow peril, resonating to Jack London's story from just two years before. To no Chinese reader's disappointment, however, the yellow race quickly creates an antidote. After their plan backfires, eventually the white race is subdued, as a result of which they are forced to sign the following treaty drafted by the Chinese:

1. Beginning the first month of the Yellow Emperor's year 4707 (March 2000 in the Western calendar), all nations will recognize Xiongyelü as China's protectorate.
2. All naval fleets and ground troops sent by all nations to Xiongyelü will leave its soil within one month. In addition, they will pay an indemnity of 50 trillion taels of silver.
3. Henceforth, all nations of the same race as China will use the calendar system of the Yellow Emperor. Those who are not members of the yellow race but who wish to use this calendar system may do so without interference from other nations.
4. All nations will pay an indemnity of 1,000 trillion taels of silver for the military campaign incurred, and of this amount 500 trillion will be distributed among the various nations of the yellow race over a period of ten years.
5. Places in Africa, Australia, and the Americas where Chinese immigrants have resided will become the extra-territories of China for purposes of commerce. China will enjoy full legal jurisdiction in these settlements.
6. China's naval fleets may dock in the ports of Singapore, New Zealand, Suez Canal, and the Adriatic Sea. They will also enjoy the right to navigate in the waters of the Suez Canal and the Mediterranean Sea.
7. Those Chinese who wish to spread the teachings of Confucius may do so in any country on the European and American continents and enjoy full protection from their respective governments.
8. Chinese immigrants residing in America and Europe who suffered financial or commercial loss will be compensated with the sum of 50 trillion taels of silver. In addition, they will be given the right to conduct commerce along the Panama Canal.

9. On this said day on which the treaty is agreed to by all signatories, China will call back one-third of its fleets in the Adriatic Sea. All nations who have lent similar support will follow suit.

10. On this said day on which the treaty is agreed to by all signatories, China will return all prisoners of war to their respective countries. The expenses will be borne by their home countries.

11. Upon the completion of this treaty, all nations may still send their ambassadors to Beijing, and vice versa. Amicable relations will resume just as before.

12. This treaty is written in both Chinese and English. Should disputes arise regarding the definition of any of the above clauses, the Chinese version will serve as the text of reference.[63]

Almost all twelve clauses bear some relation to the series of humiliating treaties to which China had been subjected since the Opium War. The recognition of China's territorial sovereignty now extends to her new protectorate, Xiongyelü. The then-astronomical 1901 Boxers' indemnity of 450 million taels of silver now translates with a vengeance into hundreds of trillion taels per white nation in the envisioned 2000. The historical injustices suffered by the Chinese workers in Africa and the Americas are redressed through territorial concessions. Even if spreading the teachings of Confucius was not considered a national priority, the resentful memory against Western missionaries warranted the retaliatory clause 7. Most revealing is the final clause, which takes the Chinese version of the treaty as the text of reference for all future disputes. Since the 1870s, the Chinese had become increasingly aggravated by America's changes to the terms of the Exclusion Acts. Linguistic barriers often offered an additional venue for manipulation. Adding clauses rather than having to seek agreement on a new treaty each time, Americans were notorious for exploiting the interpretive slippage between "clause" (*tiao*) and "treaty" (*yue*).

Despite the satisfaction of retaliation, however, *New Century* seems unable to bask in the victor's glory in good conscience. As though the appropriation of the colonizer's triumph could not be enjoyed without also sharing its culpability, the novel ends abruptly with the white race's protest against this unilateral treaty. England and Russia refuse to sign the treaty on the grounds that it in effect authorizes the enslavement of the white race, a humiliation with which any Chinese reader of the novel could easily sympathize. In any case, the promised sequel was never written, even though the popularity of the first volume lasted at least through its eighth reprinting in 1936.

Imagined racial wars between the ultimate contenders, the whites and the yellows, provide a frequent setting for science fantasies. Often reiterated is the familiar view that because the red, brown, and black races have declined to the point of extinction, the yellow race remains the only viable contender against the whites in the racial hierarchy.[64] Even though science fantasy provides the most receptive outlet for the imagining of a political and social utopia, the idea of strengthening a failed race remains fundamental to other genres of fiction as well. *Ku xuesheng* (The suffering student), for instance, deals with the experience of racial discrimination as seen through the eyes of a Chinese student studying in America. It begins with an allegorical war between two groups of ants, one yellow and the other white, fighting over the remnants of a piece of melon the narrator dropped on the ground.[65] Huang Xiuqiu, the name of the female protagonist of the novel with the same name, meaning "yellow embroidered earth," provides a similar allegorical tale of building a house, reminiscent of the boat analogy for immediate destruction in *Lao Can youji* (Travels of Lao Can). Be it political (*zhengzhi xiaoshuo*), such as Liang Qichao's *Xin Zhongguo weilaiji* (The future of New China), social critique (*shehui xiaoshuo*), utopian (*lixiang xiaoshuo*), or scientific (*kexue xiaoshuo*), much of late Qing fiction resorts to a logic of the fantastic as the way to foretell the regeneration of a failed yellow race.

The Perils of Nation

The struggle between the white and yellow races remains the driving impetus of the modern Chinese national identity well into the 1920s and 1930s. For the most part, the survival of the Chinese race is presented as a precarious possibility threatened by imminent extinction. However, this insistent apocalyptic vision cannot be fully understood without also considering its attempted reconciliation. Failure is neither an absolute condition nor fixed identity. Yet by taking it as a narrative structure most intimate to themselves, intellectuals and writers were able to use it productively for self-regeneration. Their expressed belief—political or fantastic—in the inevitability of racial extinction underscores not a resignation to prescribed racial order but an intense desire to make it into a problem only they themselves can resolve. This does not simply reflect an anxiety from which the Chinese attempt to extricate themselves. Nor does this vision demonstrate an unshakable belief in the inevitability of evolution, of racial conflicts as a natural part of the struggle for survival. There are, after all, many discussions from the period that argue against the necessity of evolution.[66] Apart from what Japan's superiority in the Russo-Japanese War demonstrated, Chinese commentators have pointed out that the law of evolution only justifies exploitation by the strong. Having convinced the rest of the world of the law of evolution, it is said, the white race erected a racial order in which the white race alone was destined to subordinate the yellow, red, and black races.[67] The Chinese must realize, one author repeatedly urges, that their flaws, rather than being irreversibly inscribed in the law of evolution, can be remedied by the Chinese themselves.[68]

In this way, what was originally a source of unquantified anxiety for China becomes a productive episteme, offering the alluring prospect of regeneration and resilience. Whereas the perceived superiority of the white other had once prompted utopian dreams of racial amalgamation, the concept of recovering superiority finds new anchorage in the construction of China's own agency. Instead of faulting the white race for tricking the Chinese into the scheme of evolution, the yellow race will now assert its own place in an evolutionary order determined by the Chinese themselves. Subjugation is rationalized as self-empowerment. An insistent self-inquiry will triumph over the foreigners' jeers and insults, as no one will be as harsh on the Chinese as the Chinese themselves. The task of self-improvement lies, first and foremost, in the proper identification of China's ills.[69]

In an ostensible mode of self-blame, failure generates an opposite effect. China's greatness, it is ultimately reasserted, is not in doubt; nor is the prospect of its restoration uncertain. However, in order to make good on this promise of recovery, one must scrutinize one's flaws ever so carefully. The impediment to greatness can be broken down into manageable aspects of individuals' daily lives; it is located in their undesirable characteristics, bad habits, and lack of a properly Chinese national consciousness. Failure as a mode of self-inquiry creates a parallel obsession with what is wrong with China, a question posed not in search of an ultimate satisfying solution but in the service of a continuing tale of nation building.

In this way, race engenders a sense of urgency and peril, which in turn concretizes the abstract existence of "nation." However, its most productive imprint on the formation of national consciousness lies in the sense of failure, against which love for the nation finds its most compelling reason to endure. The presence of nation is continually fueled not by the positivistic identity of the yellow race but by the unabated failure that threatens to take over. This rhetoric taking shape in the discussions on the imminent extinction of the yellow race will serve as the foundation for the Chinese eugenics discourse on nationalism and the "national character" in the 1920s and 1930s.

CHAPTER 4

Loving the Nation, Preserving the Race

BY THE 1920S, the development of nationalism in modern China was well underway. Joining the discourse on race, national survival readily assimilated the imperatives of racial survival. Racial extinction became an object of serious and systematic contemplation, carrying over into debates on demographics, population control, and disease. In the ferment of the May Fourth period, an incredible variety of speculation and ideas about national and racial survival were expressed with passionate conviction. Quickly absorbed into the general milieu of celebrating the power of scientific knowledge, the problem of race did not seem out of reach to the modern mind of rationality. The intellectual landscape of the 1920s and 1930s, however, was still unable to free itself from a felt sense of personal and national crisis, as a new series of unsuccessful political attempts to secure international recognition and domestic stability led intellectuals and students not only to vehemently protest the hegemony of Western imperialism but also to delve deeper into the structural inadequacies of Chinese society.[1]

The appeal of scientific rationality as a way of analyzing China's problems gradually replaced the fantastic and utopian hopes for a future China as expressed in late Qing political and literary discussions. The fervor of anxious nationalism sought answers in different aspects of intellectual and cultural life with energy and focus. The task of saving the nation hastened the search for new methodologies and ways of thought. Among the most intensely examined issues, sexuality and race sparked heated debates on family, love, marriage, and reproduction. Amid the excitement of new and controversial ideas, something more fundamental and of lasting impact was also steadily taking shape with "scientific" precision. Some began to consider the feasibility of Western eugenics as a response to the need to overhaul the Chinese national character. Explaining biological and psychological defects, these discussions

mutually reinforced a cultural obsession with finding faults. Each specific inquiry into China's decline made an attempt at another self-reorientation. Indeed, constructions of racial engineering and sexual modernity carried the
indelible imprint of a consciousness plagued by failure.[2]

Although Western eugenics originated from the concern with the feeble
and the weak within their own societies and was then later extended to the
idea of racial hierarchies in an era of imperialism, Chinese eugenics at its inception was propelled by the perceived threat of racial extinction under the
pressure of Western domination.[3] The ambivalence accompanying such a
project of appropriating a discourse in which one is unfavorably placed still
presents a pressing issue in current discussions on nationalism or claims of
sovereignty in defiance of colonial powers.[4] The dilemma of seeking self-
assertion from the very racial ideology that bolstered European imperialism
and colonial empire presented a peculiar choice for Chinese intellectuals
tempted by the potential of racial engineering. In complex ways, however,
this was a secondary if not false dilemma produced by an underlying cultural
logic of survival during China's nation-building period. We have already
seen the workings of this rationale in the late Qing, but it now manifests itself in specific areas of inquiry in the early Republican period.

The following discussion navigates through this difficult topography by
tracing its contradictions through some of its central and emblematic figures. It first gives a brief overview of the general framework of discussion as
a way of understanding the context against which the intellectual project of
eugenics offsets itself. The idea of failure turns into an underpinning discursive current driving contentious issues from racial engineering to Lu Xun's
literary treatment of the Chinese national character. While eugenicists attempt to recast the problem of national salvation in racial terms, the continuing cultural preoccupation with "Chineseness" reveals the importance of
racial or character faults in the conceptions of Chinese identity.

Eugenics and Nation

In the mid-1920s, earlier ideas of racial union seem undesirable, if not impossible. The sober recognition of the extraordinary magnitude of China's
social problems tempers former fantasies of the yellow race's easy triumph.
Unlike earlier responses to the "yellow peril," concerns about the viability
of the "yellow race" acquire an intensified focus, sharpened by the enthusiasm for scientific approaches. At the same time that science highlights the
natural law of evolution, it also promises corrective measures for the consequences of its inevitability. By this point, Kang Youwei's vision of a world
united in great harmony is widely recognized as an impossible illusion. Even

within the white race, it was pointed out, racial tensions are insurmountable, as evident in the conflict between the Anglo-Saxons and the Teutons in World War I. To the Chinese observers, this conflict revealed the vulnerability of even the whites to the problem inherent to race—racial degeneration. Whereas earlier identifications with the yellow peril in the late Qing period still looked to the Europeans and Americans for confirmation, now each race is recognized as plagued with its own problems. Directed toward a scientific solution and social engineering, the Chinese eugenics project solidifies the idea that China's failure lies in the racial body.

The notion of racial improvement had already been introduced in journals by the 1910s as a new way of perceiving and explaining nations' rise and fall.[5] Translations of Western introductory texts to eugenics proliferated, seeking to familiarize the Chinese audience with the severity of the possibility of racial decline.[6] Scientific reasoning of how the problem might be remedied extended into discussions on population control, migratory patterns, and geography.[7] Even the question of why China did not produce its own geniuses like Einstein or Shakespeare, for example, was explained in terms of the distribution of China's geographic resources.

Establishing correspondence between collective survival and individual health, analogies between race and the body multiplied. Races age, much as human bodies do.[8] Just as bodies are susceptible to the buildup of toxins and useless cells, races can fall into decline if not purged of the bad habits and customs that have accumulated over time. Reversing the prior defense that China's early advancement along the scheme of evolution accounts for its present state of decrepitude, cultural conservatives reluctantly recognized the exhaustion of an antiquated civilization. China, being one of the oldest civilizations on earth, verged on becoming dangerously frail. Although it is every creature's instinct to struggle for survival, it was said, survival itself would not mean anything without a proportionate rise in quality. It was not enough merely to hold on to the thread of life. China needed to be restored to good health.

Those asking whether China was indeed too old to be resuscitated eagerly found symptoms to confirm the anxiety. Some identified syphilis as the cause of racial degeneration. Other kinds of "illnesses of civilization" (*wenming bing*), such as tuberculosis, neurosis, and insomnia, were also popular contenders.[9] There were still others who loosely attributed the lethargy and lack of creativity of the Chinese to their "phlegmatic" nature according to the Aristotelian view of the four humors. Suggestions of venereal disease and ancient Greek physiology offered plausible diagnoses, while medical journals increasingly reported on the measures and results of racial improvement, primarily as practiced in Britain, America, and Germany.[10] In this cli-

mate where intellectuals were more open than ever before to the idea of societal transformations, from within and without, eugenics caught their eye
as a viable solution for racial reconstruction.

The enthusiasm for scientism alone, however, did not guide their aspiration. Veiled under the perceived threat of racial decline was the more fundamental preoccupation with how Chinese civilization, in particular, might
survive this universal danger. With this central question in mind, Chinese
eugenicists, writers, and other authorities considered more dubious viewed
eugenics with a very keen interest in producing the exact cause of China's
racial decline. Although they often did not agree on the guidelines for eradicating China's ills, their visions—scientific and utopian—bespoke the anxious hope for a society reborn. Cultural debates about the national character, modern identities such as the "New Woman," and ideologies of the May
Fourth period proliferated around these different visions. Even though current Western theories of modern nationalism seldom deal with the issue of
national character, the idea of a "character" or "essence" proper to the Chinese race and nation was crucial for distinguishing the Chinese national consciousness in the process of nation building. Racializing views, as has been
pointed out, were not lacking in traditional Chinese cultural and political
consciousness.[11] But the new frame of reference, drawn from Western racial
theory, played an interesting role in the competition for authority among
the different ideologies in Chinese cultural and intellectual life. Its assigned
capital in the Chinese discursive frame dissolved the claim of origins in the
exercise of appropriation. Conflicting persuasions and cultural ideologies
converged on racial decline as their shared anxiety.

In a 1928 article, "Why Should We Study Eugenics?" (Women wei shenmo yao yanjiu youshengxue?), published in *Student Magazine* (Xuesheng zazhi), one of the most influential journals at the time targeting young adults,
the author Wu Zhenzi outlines four reasons: for the human species, the race,
the nation, and the individual. Taking his cue from Arthur de Gobineau's
The Inequality of Human Races (1915) and Madison Grant's *The Passing of a
Great Race* (1916), Wu suggests a parallel between the threatened continuation of the Teutons and the extinction facing the Chinese. Reiterating the
views of Western eugenicists and hereditary specialists on controlling the reproduction of undesirable constituents, Wu, however, raises a very specific
concern for the Chinese context:

> If we do not hurry to some measure of improvement, and allow the situation to
> continue evolving in this way, people like them (the insane, the criminal, etc.)
> would increase everyday. Moreover, the other races in the meantime will be dili-
> gently improving themselves. Not only will we be extinguished by other races,
> but—even if they do not come to put us out of existence—we cannot possibly

continue to exist on this earth, as we witness our own decline and inevitably lose our own status and worth.[12]

At first glimpse, the feared prospect for Wu appears to be the uncontrolled reproduction of the eugenically unfit within the society. However, the measuring stick against which he senses the urgency of such a problem is the imminent destruction of the Chinese race at the hands of other races. Wu predicates the possibility of national survival on the implementation of eugenics alone. He posits racial extinction as an inevitable outcome if the Chinese were to proceed as they are, gradually lagging behind the advances made by other races. Strong and weak nations alike, such as America and Japan, and Brazil and India, or old and new countries, such as England and France, Russia and Czechoslovakia, all have some kind of organization promoting the practice of eugenics. The reason is, Wu explains, that eugenics is inseparable from the expression of nationalism in a world in which racial engineering extends beyond national boundaries and refigures the order of international colonialism. To prove its own nationalism, China must improve the physical and psychological health of its citizens.[13] The imperative is all the greater, Wu underscores, because China already enjoys the unflattering reputation of being the "Sick Man Nation." It is only half the nation that it can be. Thus, failing to implement a eugenics program would be failing to fully express the claim to one's own nationalism.

Wu's point is a simple one. The nation is, among other things, an ideality the fulfillment of which is held out as a promise to its constituents who are thus enticed into embodying in themselves a vision of proper citizenship and "national character." To be a nation among nations, China needs to reverse its state of ailment and, in every way, it is within the power of its citizens to avoid catastrophe. Wu's solicitation of individuals' racial responsibility, however, actually assumes the impossibility of such a promise, because, as he also warns, the process of decline would take over even without the pressure for survival from competing with other nations. It is as though the "Sick Man Nation" would inevitably bring about its own ruination, thus becoming a self-ascriptive rather than descriptive prophecy. Any promise of regeneration also recalls the fear of the unstoppable process of self-degeneration. Founded on the inevitability of racial extinction as a premise, the desire of eugenics becomes productive of, instead of dissociated from, further anxieties. Interestingly, all this does not dampen Wu's optimistic belief in China's exceptionality. The specter of ruination is what each individual citizen must believe as real, but the collective destiny as embodied in the nation leans toward an opposing utopian vision. The fear of failure is meant to disguise in proportion the fated greatness of the Chinese race, as the lesson he draws from the apocalyptic scenario is an even grander vision of a world united under Chinese leadership:

> When we have become a strong nation, after improving the citizens of this Nation of Sick Man day by day according to the principles of eugenics, not only can we forever stand in the arena of the competition among the powerful, but we can also use our peace-loving national character—a characteristic which the people of our nation have possessed for thousands of years—to promote world peace and walk together, hand in hand, into the Realm of Great Union.[14]

Resonating late Qing utopian views about the hegemony of the yellow race, eugenics discourse in China, despite its scientific pretensions, also relays the desire of cultural fantasies. For one of the early eugenicists, Zhou Jianren, Lu Xun's youngest brother, this was paramount to instilling a way of thought. In one of his earlier introductory treatises on eugenics, he stresses that the practice of eugenics relies not on legal coercion but on the indoctrination of a certain belief, which may then hopefully be naturalized as a habit.[15] Once educated about the principles of heredity, people would understand the dangers of "bad character" (*liexing*) for racial improvements. Using "peaceful means," eugenics preempts the violent advent of natural selection by taking necessary measures to ensure racial fitness. The most important of these measures is to teach people their share of responsibility (*zeren*) in promoting racial well-being.

As though volunteering for this task, someone under the pseudonym "The Responsible Rustic" (Youze pifu), wrote a treatise titled *The Present Remedy for China* (Zhongguo xianzai de bujiufa).[16] The author begins with the statement that "China is that which belongs to us the Chinese."[17] Whatever may befall China is the sole doing of the Chinese people. He chides the Chinese for faulting foreign imperialism rather than themselves, because blaming someone else for one's decline is also to forgo the possible agency in one's rejuvenation. The reemphasis on China as the exclusive problem of the Chinese also means that the Chinese, not the foreigners, are the sole determiners of its fate. To this end, his prescribed remedies include various corrections for the racial character as well as a set of nineteen physical exercises aimed at promoting strength and endurance. In this way, racial health translates itself into individual physicality. Each national subject pledges his or her allegiance to the nation through a physical incorporation of its ills and health. Taken from a variety of esoteric and historical sources such as Taoist treatises, *History of the Later Han*, and *Huainanzi*, the set of nineteen exercises—with the aid of dumbbells—also draws from the understanding of bodily composition in Western anatomy and, in particular, the training program devised by a contemporary Japanese physical educator. Among other things, this physical regime promises to make one immune to extreme temperatures and ensures the vivaciousness of one's offspring, as would be evident in their increased physical stature.

On the surface, these prescribed exercises appear to focus exclusively on physical strengthening. However, the author warns against focusing on purely mechanical movements. In a semimeditative state, the practitioner should also actively engage his or her mental energy (*jingshen de yundong*). The salvation of China lies in not only physical strength but also a corresponding spiritual discipline. In the end, every average man and woman needs to know that saving China lies in his or her own hands. If that power were not exercised, then China's continual ruin would be his or her doing as well.

Discussions such as this abound in the Republican era. "The Responsible Rustic" provides an unusual instance of prescribing a specific physical training program as a way of improving racial quality. In a way that treads the boundary of martial arts manuals from this period, *The Present Remedy for China* sees the fortification of mind and body in unison as solidifying national strengthening as well.[18] Others analyzing China's national character see it as a less tangible withering of the racial spirit (*minzu jingshen*), largely blamed on centuries of cultural inertia. The Chinese are said to lack a progressive spirit and dawdle their time away in lethargy and imprecision.[19] Among the more nostalgic critics, one author reaffirms that the Han is an unquestionably superb race but has regrettably been in decline since the Qin and Han dynasties, taken as the pinnacle of civility and social order.[20] In this view, one should not assume that China's current "ailing condition" (*bingtai*) is its usual state of affairs (*changtai*). The stress on China's present situation as a temporary departure from an otherwise superior norm reinforces a rationale that resurfaces repeatedly in identifying areas of its weakness.

The interest in eugenics in China in the 1920s and 1930s, of which Zhou Jianren is one of the more representative authors, lies in restructuring and reeducating the spirit and "character" of the Chinese. As Zhou espoused in the late 1910s and throughout the 1920s, eugenics offers a way of preventively improving and recovering the superiority of the Chinese race. However, by the time of the Communist takeover in 1949, he had drastically altered this view. Having witnessed the detriment of racial politics as carried out in international and class conflicts in both world wars and China's own civil strife, Zhou tempers his previous optimism regarding not only eugenics but also, more generally, Western science. In *On Eugenics and Racial Discrimination* (Lun youshengxue yu zhongzu qishi, 1948), published in the same year he joined the Chinese Communist Party, Zhou soberly recognizes that the "peaceful means" he previously described has in no way settled the question of racial struggle.[21]

For Zhou, the presumed distinction of a superior racial stock within a given society has only justified the imperialistic logic of colonizing the inferior races abroad. Science, like politics, follows the strategic interests of domination. Eugenics, in this way, has been used as the ruler's weapon, replacing the fatalistic superstition of the past with the modern superstition of science.[22] Pointing out that Darwin's fieldwork was possible only because he was working as a naturalist aboard a British navy ship, Zhou notes that the enterprise of British imperialism was foundational to the propagation of race as science.[23] As far as eugenics in China is concerned, it only gave rise to the revival of feudalistic concepts under the new rubric of science. More damagingly, it cultivated an inferiority complex in relation to Western imperialism, whereby the Chinese acquiesced to their own subjugation. Because most of China's knowledge of eugenics was imported from the United States, the admiration for Americans' racial views reinforced the vicious cycle of self-loathing in awe of a superior other.

Zhou Jianren's revised views on eugenics reflect his intensifying concern with class struggle in the late 1940s and throughout the Communist period. His demystifying analysis of eugenics as an instrument of Western imperialism corroborates a redefined Chinese nationalism, directed exclusively toward anti-imperialism and class warfare. However, even though eugenics comes to be subsumed under the historical narrative of imperialism, its cultural place and context have much more to disclose. Eugenics brought together a number of concerns that are deeply revealing of the particular cultural sensibilities in the 1920s and 1930s. What Zhou Jianren can now disparage as the sole effect of imperialism was a phenomenon far more complex. Self-disparagement worked in unexpected ways in securing the kind of confidence required of a nation attempting to rejuvenate not only its political might but also its "spirit." To fully appreciate this cultural topography, one must trace out the different dialogues with which eugenics sought to engage. China's first eugenicist, Pan Guangdan, figures prominently in this cultural matrix.

Eugenics and Conservatism: Pan Guangdan

During the Republican era, at least twenty-five books were published dealing exclusively with eugenics and racial improvement.[24] Some were introductory primers, whereas others were translations of various American and British eugenicist tracts, such as C. B. Davenport's *Heredity in Relation to Eugenics*, Havelock Ellis's *The Task of Social Hygiene*, William Robinson's *Eugenics and Marriage*, and Leonard Darwin's *What Is Eugenics?*[25] In addition to these direct translations, two others were based on Japanese translations. Five

books, however, were by the same author, Pan Guangdan, the first eugenicist in China. Having studied at Qinghua University in Beijing and then in
the United States at Dartmouth College and Columbia University, Pan began editing and publishing in journals in China on the subject of eugenics
and racial hygiene in 1924.[26] He first put forth his ideas to a Western public
in a virtually unknown early article written in English, "Eugenics in China:
A Preliminary Survey of the Background," published in 1923 in the American journal *The Eugenical News*.[27]

Pan points out that the death rate in China has decreased with the influx
of Western culture. Although he concedes that the real problem with over-
population is quality, not quantity, he also states that the problem in China
is not as serious as it is in the West. Therefore, the measures appropriate to
China aim "more at prevention rather than at correction."[28] Pan later revises
this view that postpones racial degeneration as an eventuality. For the purpose of this article, Pan underscores the fact that a eugenics program appropriate to China is not possible without accommodations to its cultural and
racial background. Among these are the propensity of the Chinese to "breed
out" and a traditional family system that enjoys the same institutional sanctity as that of the church in the West. Pan's recommended eugenics education, to be disseminated among the population at large, includes "supplying
and popularizing new and correct ideas" and a reinstitution of the family
structure, which, "like the church in the West in the last century or two, is
just now receiving heavy blows from all sides."[29] Consistent with his more
conservative stance against the general anti-iconoclasm of the New Culture
Movement, Pan attempts to redeem the value inherent in the traditional social institutions that, in his mind, have been the foundation of Chinese culture. The popularization of ideas on eugenics in China, Pan adds, can take
as its model the Eugenics Record Office and the Eugenics Education Society in London, which could be transplanted after some modification.

Although Pan had initially presented his eugenics program to his Western audience as more preventive than corrective, his later treatment of the
subject acquired a more poignant tone due to the Japanese invasion in 1931
and the internecine fighting between the Chinese Communist Party (CCP)
and the Nationalist Party (GMD) in the 1920s, cataclysmic events that
brought to the fore the urgency of increasing national strength and solidarity. In a 1931 article, "Minzu yuanqi pian" (On the primary essence of race),
published in a short-lived journal Pan himself founded, *Yousheng yuekan* (Eugenics monthly), he bluntly describes the state of affairs:

> Like a patient, the Chinese race has reached the stage at which the doctors say
> that a very big needle is required. For the past thirty or forty years, innumerable

stimulants have been injected, but no sign of improvement has been seen. At the most, there have only been short-lived enthusiasms. Now it remains to be seen how effective this big needle is. If not, then one can say—all politeness aside—that China is doomed.[30]

Unlike social scientists who like applying terminology discovered in the biological sciences to social pathology, Pan states that when "[he] says that the race is ill, [he] means a real illness and not a metaphor."[31] The biologized discourse on racial survival privileges itself as the point of reference. It is not, in other words, a metaphor for the consequence of imperialism or loss of cultural splendor. The Sick Man of the East does not suffer from some amorphous cultural malaise. His spiritual ailment can be explained by a physical inadequacy, a biological condition that, once identified, can be corrected by means of racial hygiene. Racial degeneration becomes the sort of fault that one can rectify. No attachment proves more vulnerable to one's sense of well-being than an undesirable bodily feature. A biological defect can be more easily corrected than the more amorphous and abstract problem of the national character. Once the problem of nation building is transposed onto physical improvement, it is amenable to calculation, measurement, diagnosis, and, most significantly, remedy. The suggestion that one's own inferiority is really the result of one's negligence in properly cultivating racial hygiene offers much comfort to those in fear of irremediable racial degeneration. The diseased nation resides in one's very own body. The inadequacy of this bodily foundation, furthermore, accounts for the weakening of the people's essence (*minqi*) and the deterioration of the national character.

Unlike the Indians or the Jews, who faced the threat of extinction from the outside, Pan explains, the death of the Chinese race is due to the inner depletion of its essence.[32] Whereas other races and civilizations lack the capacity to resist Western imperialism, China has a reservoir of racial superiority it has not yet tapped. The parallel usually drawn in the late Qing between China, India, and other ancient civilizations marked a point of differentiation for Pan. The old fear that China risked suffering the same fate as other old civilizations unable to cope with the demands of modernity finds a new rationale in his thinking. China is ill, but, unlike the case of India, its endurance is far from exhausted. For Pan, "Chinese culture cannot be deemed as ancient, for we are still in the midst of evolving, hence have much more hope and space for unfolding than races which have been either hurled along too recklessly towards change or who have cowered too easily before it."[33]

The haunting anxiety of an old, festering civilization on the brink of collapse is now celebrated as a youthful potential yet to be exhausted. The two incongruous elements of this paradoxical claim are reconciled in an opposition within an analogy. By distinguishing cultural tradition from racial maturity, Pan divorces culture from race. In doing so, he gives up neither China's claim to cultural superiority nor its need to prove its given racial viability. The superior tradition of a culture need not be incommensurable with the threat to its survival, for the latter occurs on a racial, biological level. In other words, the need for racial improvement is less a realization occasioned by external threat or foreign domination than a biological upgrade long overdue the Chinese. Hence, "China has not reached its maturity."[34] Had that been the case, its present situation would not be possible. Therefore, the determination of what fruits this "young" race will bear depends solely on the actions of its own members. The task of recognizing and rectifying this lack is transferred back to the Chinese themselves as responsibility and agency.

The biologization of racial illness conveniently allows Pan to locate the cause of China's decline. As remarked by his contemporary, Li Jinghan, a sociologist who wrote the preface to Pan's *National Characteristics and Racial Hygiene* (Minzu texing yu minzu weisheng), eugenics allows for the precise, scientific diagnosis of China's weakness. Contrary to all other attempts to evaluate China's national crisis, Li writes, eugenics refreshingly identifies its source scientifically as physical inferiority.[35] However, Pan's emphasis on the biological foundation of China's racial decline is not without inconsistency. In the following key passage from "On the Primary Essence of Race," Pan clearly explains not the literal but the metaphorical meaning of a biologized race. Having just insisted on the strictly "biological" and nonmetaphorical nature of racial illness, Pan continues, "Strangely enough, the grave illness we are speaking of today is not the illness itself, the depletion of the primary essence, but, rather, the fact that the ill do not know that they are ill. Not recognizing that little is left of their primary essence, they are still indulging in its dissipation."[36]

Oddly, the literal returns once more to the metaphorical, as we learn that the illness is the lack of awareness of defect, rather than the defect itself. The provocative force of the literal image gives way to its figurative evocation. Pan's rhetoric remarkably resembles that of Lu Xun, who, lamenting the multitude trapped in a state of slumber in the iron house, comments on several occasions that the defect of the Chinese people is precisely that they have no consciousness of it.[37] On the one hand, a proper consciousness of one's own defects ensures that a remedy is within reach. On the other hand, the insistent questioning of whether the Chinese are capable of acquiring this kind of awareness precludes the possibility of an affirmative answer. The preoccupation continues to posit the Chinese people's lack of awareness as a condition that cannot be overcome. If Lu Xun's self-dissection also perpetuates the need to dissect, Pan, in a similar way, takes negativity as the positive foundation for racial strengthening. The same insistence on excavating what is most undesirable in the Chinese people drives both metaphors of self-dissection and recognition of bodily defect.

The significance of this critical self-reflection for the "national citizen" is not merely a concoction of the literary or cultural imagination. The susceptibility of cultural anxieties to ideological use can be no better exemplified than in the idea behind the New Life Movement. Taking over the cultural rhetoric of failure, the movement relies on the power of invoking shame. Advanced by Jiang Jieshi (Chiang Kai-shek) in 1934 in an effort to promote national salvation through the inculcation of proper national consciousness and personal hygiene, the movement was an attempt to individualize the urgency of national revival. The aim was to "awaken" (*juexing*) in all citizens the appropriate awareness of their individual responsibility to national salvation in the conduct of their everyday life. Focusing on personal hygiene, the movement's mission was to revive the moral purpose of a corrupted and degenerate people. Due to its short duration and lack of success, the movement is seen today as one of the Nationalists' many failed attempts to mobilize and sustain mass support outside their urban centers of operation, a failure that has come to serve as an explanation for their ultimate defeat by the Communists.[38]

Ironically, the movement was designed to rally support on a scale similar to that of the Cultural Revolution. It has been pointed out that the catalyst for the movement was provided by the Nationalists' recent struggle with the Communists in Jiangxi Province. The Communists' deftness at inciting the masses into supporting their cause was an advantage the Nationalists had recognized. However, the vision of the New Life Movement, apart from its failed execution, reflects the larger preoccupation with reforming the Chinese mind and character that had been intensifying since the turn of the century.

The idea of a proper Chinese essence to be recovered was propounded by the Society for the Protection of National Learning (Guoxue baocun hui), whose journal, *Guocui xuebao*, was founded in 1905. Its founder, Zhang Binglin, was one of the most vociferous anti-Manchu advocates, and his ideas made a profound impression on an entire generation of young reformers and intellectuals who would later take on the task of nation building in the 1920s and 1930s.[39] National essence, in the sense meant by Zhang, was a racial and ethnic essence proper to the Han, as distinct from that of the Manchu. The legitimate identity of the Han was said to manifest itself in the classics. Hence, a return to the classical tradition would offer the kind of cultural authenticity vainly sought in Western learning and modernization.

Among the journal's well-known editors and contributors are Liu Shipei, Deng Shi, and Huang Jie. However, Huang's serialized essay, "Huang Shi" (Yellow history), has come to represent the journal's mission to claim a Chinese cultural identity. Even though the National Essence project did not survive the onslaught of the New Culture Movement, the idea of a national essence stayed and was given another voice of support in 1922 by the *Critical Review* group led by Mei Guangdi and Wu Mi. Although the point of reference for "national essence" shifted from fervent anti-Manchuism to an embrace of Western humanism, the central focus on distilling a national essence proper to the Chinese remained undiverted.

In this way, the New Life Movement had immediate cultural precedents, and not merely political events, for its inspiration. This point of commonality also makes visible the intimate resonance shared by political visions and general cultural sentiments, of which political agenda is but one institutionalized, albeit powerful, expression. In this light, it would be difficult indeed to dismiss, as most historians do, the significance of the New Life Movement. Its short duration and failure cannot be perceived solely on the level of the Nationalists' struggle for power with the Communists. One clear demonstration of the larger historical context to which the New Life Movement responds is the way in which the hygienic habits of the Chinese are taken as a source of national shame under the guidelines of the movement, as put forth in Chiang's programmatic *Outline of the New Life Movement* and *Necessary Knowledge of New Life*.[40]

Among these habits that "ill-befit the times and the environment" are spitting and urinating in public; disregard for public decorum, such as not standing in line and waiting one's turn; and keeping a sanitary domicile. Largely grouped under the four rubrics of "clothing, food, residence, and behavior" (*yi shi zhu xing*), one's personal conduct within the privacy of one's home as well as in the public domain is, ideally, equally subjected to the scrutiny of national consciousness. The grounding four principles of conduct—propriety, righteousness, integrity, and shame (*li yi lian chi*)—are the more abstract notions of the attributes of citizenship extracted from the discipline of the four basic cares.

However, although the four guidelines are given equal weight in definition, it is "shame" (*chi*) that begins the series. The four are continuous and mutually reinforcing, yet all stem from or are "released by" (*fa*) the sense of shame.[41] In this way, "shame" occupies a particular place in the ordering of the four principles. Without shame, one would have nothing to illuminate, execute in action, or express in form. The prerequisite sense of shame sets into motion the desire for improvement and discipline, despite its last position in the idiomatic *li yi lian chi*.

The four basic cares in personal hygiene, in fact, were already familiar in the long repertoire of cultural shame prior to the New Life Movement. The image of Chinese spitting randomly on the streets and their association with filthy and disease-ridden residences had been a constitutive part of the Chinese discourse on the lives of Chinese laborers in California and Chinatowns since the late 1800s.[42] As anti-imperialist as these reports were—many of them by leading reformers—they also expressed dismay at the ways in which these Chinese laborers confirmed the grounds for foreigners' contemptuous treatment. For example, the travel diaries of influential reformers such as Liang Qichao and Huang Zunxian, while voicing outrage at widespread racial discrimination, also expressed shock and shame at the conditions under which the laborers maintained themselves. The complex ambivalence of being outraged and at the same time unable to defend their pride often gave rise to intense patriotism and national consciousness in their subsequent writings. The idea that these sources of shame must be rectified drives the premise behind Pan's eugenics project. Eugenics provides the ideological and psychological transition between the vulnerability of shame and the desire to turn it into something one can overcome. In the background, the pressing imperative is how to make the degeneration of the Chinese race a problem every citizen can embrace as his or her only hope for salvation.

Thus, the inconsistency in Pan's emphasis on the biological and metaphorical descriptions of racial decline pivots on the greater issue at stake. Pan's oscillation between the "universal" appeal of a biological decline and the racial particularity of Chinese degeneration parallels the tension between his desire to alleviate the anxiety over national failure by broadening its scope as a universal, biological problem and his equally strong impulse to recast China's ills as something still within the possibility of remedy, still as "Chinese." The significance of the primacy Pan gives to the biological foundation of race lies in its relegation of national boundaries to secondary importance. Pan Guangdan envisions the potential for international, global participation for Chinese eugenics discourse. For him, China's racial predicament differs little from an ailment to which all humans, Chinese or European, are susceptible in the process of natural selection. In the same way that in the late Qing a "yellow race" defined against the "white race" served as a rhetorical rubric subsuming inner racial tensions, participating in a kind of racial decline suffered by humankind as a whole removes the focus from China's impoverished status in international politics. This makes it possible to rationalize China's weak position as a product of inner racial fault rather than external subjugation.

The envisioned effect grounds the threat of China's national and racial extinction in a global struggle for survival of the fittest. The way in which this discourse appropriates the autonomy to speak and, even more significantly, to confess its own weaknesses, departs from the realm of subversive discourse. Eugenics discourse in China, as Pan constructs it, provides an all-encompassing, universal framework in which the urgency of China's national survival also happens to be addressed. China's predicament partakes in the manifestation of a universal principle, which is in turn locally utilized to justify China's own right to national survival.[43]

In this light, the slippage between the literal and the metaphorical in Pan's conception of race reflects less a theoretical inconsistency than an attempt to reconcile two simultaneous imperatives. On the one hand, faulting Western imperialism for China's decline leaves little room for articulating a genuine possibility of survival for the Chinese race. By arguing that the reason of detriment is in fact a universal, biological decline rather than the superiority of one nation over another, Pan appears to resolve this dilemma of agency. If the decline is one's own doing, then Western dominance can make less claim on the power of detriment. On the other hand, this biological explanation remains in the service of a desire to awaken a specific national consciousness fueled by a sense of inadequacy. The particularity of national consciousness undermines the very universal appeal of eugenics. Thus, the literal—the biological—cannot help giving way to the metaphorical, for the biologization of racial decline is itself a metaphorized attempt to displace the cause of national humiliation.

As a result, this new awareness affirms oneself as the precipitating force rather than as the victim of a process of racial decline beyond one's control. The self-consciousness produced doubles back as a reflexive awareness of one's own failure of self-recognition. Whatever suffering or humiliation may be inflicted by Westerners on the Chinese can never match the candor with which the Chinese relentlessly expose their own weaknesses. If the Westerners are harsh in their critique of the Chinese, the Chinese are harder still on themselves. If anything, Westerners' unsympathetic and condescending views toward the Chinese would only better promote the purpose of self-examination.

The stakes, then, for eugenics in China are clearly mapped. Pan recasts the international vying for domination as a war against racial degeneration. The national- or racial-specific quality of "Chinese" is curiously subsumed under the necessity of a biological ailment. The biological supersedes national boundaries in urgency and necessity. Once Pan rationalizes the particular fate suffered by China as a metonym for a biological and evolutionary fact encompassing all national destinies, then the discourse on racial improvement becomes a strangely self-empowering act of failure. The anxiety of China's national failure is now mollified by the consolation of universal, biological science. Yet this should not be understood only as a consequence of the May Fourth fascination with scientific objectivity. This relentless inquiry into the source of China's racial failure underscores the transfer of knowledge back to the Chinese.

Eight years after "On the Primary Essence of the Race" and into the War of Resistance (1937–45), Pan sought to reconcile the idea of racial decline with war patriotism. This piece, "The Racial Significance of the War of Resistance" (Kangzhan de minzu yiyi, 1939), bespeaks the imperative facing both war rhetoric and, later, the Communist revolution.[44] The self-deprecating aspect of China's illness had to be artificially replaced by the euphoric vision of its cure, even though the idea of failure remains alive in the background. National morale and pride superseded all disbelief and hesitation. The cultural rhetoric of failure was exorcised of its rhetoricity in favor of a united front. The idea of racial degeneration, in the same vein, can no longer appeal to a sense of crisis comforted by reassurance. By the time Pan wrote "The Racial Significance of the War of Resistance," the biological significance of race was subsumed under the imperative of the abstract notion of the "Chinese race" and its "primary essence."[45] The problem of race no longer concerns the survival of the entire race in general but, rather, points to the "primary essence" making possible its survival, an essence that Pan suggests is the "life strength" (*huoli*) or the "strength of competing for survival" (*jingcunli*).

In the attempt to promote this positive outlook on the devastation of war, Pan states that the War of Resistance actually gives the Chinese an opportunity to test their primary essence. Against critics who denounce the war for depleting the race of its most viable male constituents, Pan argues for its positivity from the vantage point of the "strength of competing for survival." He draws a more mundane but popular analogy in arguing that the test of war is like that put before the young monks trained in the Shaolin Temple where, upon the completion of their training, they would have to fight their way out of the temple as an act of confirmation. It is the "rite of passage" for every youth. Here, Pan harks back to his notion of a youthful and inexperienced rather than an old and decrepit China.

In this vein, Pan modifies his prior position of 1931 as expressed in "On the Primary Essence of the Race." He acknowledges that he was indeed too negative and pessimistic in his outlook on the state of Chinese primary essence. Recalling his earlier view that the inner dissipation of China's racial essence was the cause of foreigners' encroachment, Pan now takes a more optimistic stance. Whereas earlier the Chinese could not have even accepted this test of racial strength, now—in the midst of the War of Resistance—China has proved itself more than capable of taking on this challenge. The experience of fighting in the War of Resistance has shown the Chinese in a more poignant fashion than ever before the nakedness of their weaknesses. The Chinese may have known these faults in the abstract before, but they only now truly recognize their severity. Hence, the War of Resistance has been beneficial for the Chinese race, for it has brought about the recognition that the Chinese need to rectify themselves.

Although Pan still advances the notion of undesirable Chinese characteristics, he now mobilizes their positive aspects for the sake of war patriotism. War hastens China onto the path toward self-fulfillment. The internal scrutiny of racial inadequacy, in his modified stance, should not lead to despair in times of war. Rather, one should rejoice in the prospect that war brings one closer to the self-awareness necessary for victory. The disclosure of one's weakness not only awakens the sense of shame but also propels one toward the goal of greater self-realization.

Thus, something has fundamentally changed in the 1930s. It is no longer the case that seeking China's salvation in Western science would produce the dilemma experienced since the late nineteenth century: how, under the dominance of Western cultural articulations, to express a distinctly Chinese identity. A Chinese identity is no longer premised on positivity but recast as a defect. This insistence on defect, furthermore, protects the primacy of the Chinese consciousness in the search for a remedy. The obsession with one's own failure overrides all other concerns such that external threats can only pale in comparison. Anything that can be employed in the service of this recognition becomes inflected with this consciousness. The use of eugenics as a possible remedy propagates, first and foremost, the preservation of this self-knowledge. And the object of this self-inquiry turns into the problem of the national character.

National Characteristics and Racial Hygiene

In his 1936 preface to *National Characteristics and Racial Hygiene*, a collection of his writings from the previous eight years, Pan explains how each essay found its place in the development of his thinking. The earliest work that made an impact on him—and to which he will refer again and again in his writings—is a book published in 1924, *The Character of Races*, written by Ellsworth Huntington, a research associate in geography at Yale University. Four chapters in the book, Pan is pleased to note, are devoted to the subject of the Chinese race. Pan had already introduced them in *Chinese Students Abroad in America* (Liumei xuesheng yuebao), a monthly journal to which he regularly contributed while a student in the United States.

Huntington's detailed analysis of Chinese racial characteristics, using the principles of natural selection and migration, impressed Pan. Huntington himself had been attempting to expound the importance of environmental determinism in natural selection since his first publication nine years earlier, *Civilization and Climate*. He had come to inquire into natural selection as "arising most frequently under the stress of over-population and migration."[46] A study of famines in China, Huntington believed, disclosed the importance of this principle. Hence, he solicited information from various missionaries, such as Arthur Henderson Smith, who was a missionary for the American Board of Commissioners for Foreign Missions in Zhili and Shandong from 1872 to 1926.

Smith had firsthand experience with famines and relief work in China and remained influential in American perceptions of China. His correspondence with government officials shows that some of his views managed to have figured into U.S. policy toward China.[47] Known for his animated demeanor and Shandong accent, Arthur Smith was a cultural informant of sorts for both the Chinese and Americans.[48] He was also the author of *Chinese Characteristics*, which Pan had translated and published in *Golden Era* (Huanian), a journal he founded with an intended popular appeal to succeed the short-lived, more specialized *Eugenics Monthly*.[49] Although he had read Smith's work before, Pan first saw its relevance to his own race project while translating Huntington's *The Character of Races*. He later included fifteen (out of the twenty-seven) chapters from Smith's book in his collected volume, *National Characteristics and Racial Hygiene*. Although Pan had known of *Chinese Characteristics* at least prior to 1928, he did not yet have an intellectual framework in which it could provide a conceptual leverage.

Pan notes that, in recent years, Chinese scholars in the field of psychology had taken an interest in the question of national characteristics. Because the field was still in its infancy, however, no systematic hypothesis could be extrapolated. Hence, "with no other choice, we will have to make do with a Westerner's work and take his authority as a substitute. Even though we well know that it is the impression of a single individual without scientific basis, it will still make us feel better than if we omit it altogether."[50] Smith's portrayal, Pan continues, has its own value, for it is the result of years of observing Chinese peasant life. Even in light of the theory of natural selection, Smith's depiction contains some truth, for under the particular circumstances of China's natural and cultural environment, natural selection produces a certain trait or specificity of behavior that then becomes a racial characteristic.[51] Having said this, however, Pan makes the following criticism: "Smith has only presented the mere result and not explained the cause. I am afraid that in truth he does not really understand either where the explanation lies. Yet for those of us who discuss natural selection, it is clear."[52]

Chinese Characteristics fulfills the function, then, of portraying the consequences of what Pan had already identified as the cause, the racial degeneration of the Chinese. Smith's *Chinese Characteristics* is not valuable for Pan as the unchallengeable Western missionary authority expressed as "native" expertise—it neither conveys an indisputable truth about the Chinese people nor confirms for Pan the ineluctability of colonial power. It is valuable as an outsider's view that reconfirms the racial failure Pan has already recognized in his own people, an externalizable narrative that corroborates what Pan can claim as an insiders' problem. As a Westerner's "objective" impressions recast as a self-perception of failure, *Chinese Characteristics* provides that very pristine, unscientific—if not naive—account of the Chinese that Pan can then reshape as a confirmation of their own undesirable racial characteristics. The power of prescribing truth about the other is neither conceded to the missionary nor reenacted in complicity. Rather, the power of truth is lent to him in order to sustain his own discourse.

The deployment of the "Western observer" is made clear in Li Jinghan's preface. Prior to Western imperialism, Li claims, the Chinese had no measuring stick for their weaknesses. Only after successive defeats did they realize that, as a race, they were ill. Hence, the quest for an appropriate remedy began in order to find a path to self-renewal. Pan, Li continues, is the first one to cast this problem in the concrete terms of science and biology, a task others failed by posing only abstract questions regarding the essential spirit (*yuanqi*) and diseased characteristics (*bu jianquande minzuxing*) of the Chinese people. However, Li continues, one might ask, What kind of inquirer is really capable of recognizing the Chinese racial characteristics? Who is the most appropriate person to explain it? To these questions, Li provides a detailed answer:

> Some people seem to think that only the people of this nation can understand themselves. For a foreigner to understand a race utterly different from himself, especially one as different as Chinese, is simply not possible, because as he observes the Chinese, he inevitably sees them through a colored lens. On the other hand, it is not a simple task in any case for an individual or a race to recognize himself so clearly, especially in a recognition that is just, healthy, and sober. . . . Furthermore, *it takes courage* to recognize one's own flaws. There are often various taboos or embarrassments in doing so. Of course, as a foreigner observes us, he inevitably measures us against his own standards. Yet it is precisely because he has such a different set of standards that he can so clearly see our characteristics . . . unlike the way we are with ourselves, the foreigner is much more unreserved in giving his opinion. Therefore, in order to really recognize and understand ourselves clearly, we need to, of course, on the one hand, rely on our self-analysis; but on the other hand, we should not neglect but value the opinions of foreigners about us and use them as a reflection, especially when these opinions result from meticulous observation.[53] (emphasis added)

Like Pan, Li is not unaware of the prejudice inherent in Western representations of the Chinese. However, the point of this exercise of self-recognition lies not in who provides it but rather in how it is employed in serving one's own end. The Westerner is not obeyed for his authoritative discourse in which a Chinese is orientalized but rather solicited as an "objective" viewer who can all the better analyze what is plaguing the Chinese race. Interestingly, in *Chinese Characteristics*, Smith remarks that the Chinese accept criticism with remarkable readiness, a fact he considers to be a great virtue. For Li as well as for Pan, however, the ability to accept criticism underscores the capacity for relentless self-analysis. The Western authorities he cites as evidence are not chosen by him as indisputable discursive authority. It matters not whether the Western missionary is "right" about the Chinese. One's insistence on the inadequacies of the Chinese national identity is what makes the Westerner's view useful as an alibi.

In this way, Pan's perception of westernization is more complex than the mere imitation of ideas and cultural practices. In fact, he directs one of his most consistent criticisms at China's indiscriminate importation of westernization during the May Fourth period. In *The Problem of Eugenics in China* (Zhongguo de yousheng wenti), he divides the reception of westernization into three stages: the period of "isolation," from the Ming to the mid-Qing dynasties; the period of "adaptation," from mid-Qing to his present; and a future period of "selection," which he envisions and emphasizes as the crucial stage in which the adaptation can be evaluated in terms of its feasibility for Chinese racial survival.[54] He translates "adaption" [*sic*] as *weiyu* in the manifesto in the opening issue of *Golden Era*, a journal he founded after *Eugenics Monthly* ceased publication. Indiscriminate adaptation without selection, Pan warns, would result only in China's replication of the mistakes made in the West.[55]

Applying the principles of eugenics to his own cultural source of origin, Pan cleverly uses the "westernization" he criticizes on the one hand and affirms the specific locality of the Chinese context on the other. Commenting on the discussion at a recent symposium on the project of China's cultural construction, Pan supports a new "Sino-centrism," shedding the usual negative connotations associated with the arrogance of the Middle Kingdom and adopting, instead, a more self-reflective attitude. This new self-centering approach, Pan states, has three dimensions: the environmental, the cultural, and the racially specific. The absorption of Western culture, Pan concedes, presents an absolute imperative for modern China. However, he hastens to add, to have the capability and conditions for fulfilling this imperative is quite a different matter. China should absorb what is appropriate to its racial character.[56] The primary task fundamental to Chinese racial survival, it seems, lies in the proper awareness of the ways in which the Chinese racial character is defective, rather than in placing one's hope solely on the importation of Western culture. The instillation of a certain self-consciousness both leads the task and ensures that China remains centered in itself, despite the facile solution of westernization.

In the biologization of the problem of nation and race, national differences are actually suspended rather than accentuated, for this discourse in itself—complete with the power of objective analysis—is an act of legitimation, giving oneself admission to a racializing framework where one, rather than being spoken for, speaks for oneself. Exercising this prerogative, Pan Guangdan did not just talk about the racial characteristics of the Chinese. He also analyzed the Japanese and Germans for their inclination to pessimism and suicide, as well as Indians and Poles for their inherent propensity to be dominated and exploited.[57]

Pan reproduces, in fact, the exact framework in which Chinese characteristics were placed in the Western context. In review articles of books published between 1850 and 1900 in American journals, for instance, national characteristics were discussed in terms of every nationality, not just American. The idea of national characteristics, moreover, was not always accepted uncritically. Amid the general positive reception of Smith's *Chinese Characteristics* in leading American journals such as *The Nation* and *The Athenaeum*, it was pointed out that the book nonetheless "impressed one always with the idea that the author is applying European weights and measures to gauge characters which have no counterpart in Europe at all."[58] This sobering contemporary view, significantly, speaks to current analyses of colonial authority in missionary discourse. The attribution of "national characteristics" to the power of imperialistic discourse has as its precondition the accepted primacy of these European "weights and measures." Because the possibility that the idea of racial characteristics could have no European counterpart at all is not examined, it is continually limited to its colonial indebtedness.

Once we understand the context of racial discourse in which Pan situates the idea of Chinese characteristics, however, we recognize that contemporary explanations of self-objectification, self-colonialization, or self-orientalization only give a very partial picture of what was in fact a complex act of self-empowerment. By joining an international debate on race, Pan places China on an equal discursive footing with Western nations for whom racial hierarchy constituted both discursive and cultural capital. His design is clear, as can be seen in a chart he produced, in which each country and its own eugenics movement, including its founder, were listed, complete with dates and purpose. On this global map of racial advancements, Pan's name appears prominently as the founder of the Chinese Eugenics Society established in 1924.[59]

The Search for Defect: Ah Q

Although Pan's vision for a eugenics discourse in China constructs different sets of external imperatives such as national survival, traditional conservatism, the institution of the family, and the universalizing framework of biologized race, the discourse of race and national character carried a resonance in the depths of the formation of cultural identity. The idea of failure not only reveals the intellectual underpinnings of eugenics discourse on racial character but also underscores a foundational moment in the conception of a national character in the literary imagination. Lu Xun's *The Official Chronicles of Ah Q* (A Q zhengzhuan) marks such a moment in the genesis of modern Chinese literature. Translated into various languages and adapted into plays and films throughout the twentieth century since its appearance in 1921, *Ah Q* holds an iconic status in literary historiography and popular culture alike. Often compared to Don Quixote, Hamlet, and Faust, Ah Q embodies a certain cultural image of the Chinese. Intended by Lu Xun as a portrayal of the "Chinese national soul," the image of Ah Q has undergone diverse interpretations, depending on the ideological orientation.[60] For twentieth-century China, not lacking in vehement political upheavals, the reception of *Ah Q* follows an equally politicized course in literary history. Shen Yanbing, who under the pen name Mao Dun became one of the most important voices in twentieth-century literary criticism, identified it as the "crystallization of Chinese characteristics." His enthusiasm for the deeply subjective resonance of *Ah Q* prompted him to make an impassioned address to the young audience of China, mired in angst and irresolution:

> If you read this more than twice, you will ultimately have to acknowledge that in there casts your own shadow. Don't you have your own "device for psychological victory?" Have you not, like Ah Q, been content to quickly forget unpleasant hardships? In the midnight hours of your dark broodings when you're down on your luck, have you not comforted yourself with the thought, "my son will be much better off?" It's fine, I don't need to ask further. In sum, Ah Q is the crystallization of the Chinese people's "lack." He may not know how to order fancy dishes or speak western tongues, and he may not know "Europe" or "America" . . . yet those "new sons and daughters of old China" who know how to enjoy fancy food and speak western languages but still suffer from "lack" can only lay claim to being half an Ah Q at the best.[61]

Mao Dun's excitement over the representation of the Chinese character encapsulates the impact of *Ah Q* even at its inception. However, the question of whether Ah Q's power of representation is limited to that of the Chinese soon formed the crux of subsequent contentions. Xu Guangping, Lu Xun's common-law wife, said that Ah Q did not just represent the weakness of the Chinese. His character expressed a globalizing racial weakness, especially that belonging to the oppressed. Ah Q, throughout the 1940s and 1950s, came to embody anything from the peasant, to the slave, to the proletariat. His tale has been alternately narrated as that of personal distress and class defeat. A debate between two critics that lasted almost ten years centered on the global character and historical particularity of this literary figure of humiliation and triumph.[62]

Without exception, *The Official Chronicles of Ah Q* has always been taken as a critique of the Chinese national character. The often despicable behavior of Ah Q in the face of defeat and humiliation is assumed to provide a negative example of the Chinese themselves. In the 1980s, however, critical attempts tried to retheorize Ah Q as a phenomenon of world literature. Ah Q's undesirable characteristics were taken as a reflection of culture in general. Although some still insisted on interpreting Ah Q's spirit as the consequence of class, economic inequality, and imperialism in China, others saw his global potential as an expression of the universality of human nature.[63] One emphasizes the specifically national (Chinese) character of Ah Q; and the other, his universal appeal as a thwarted individual. The continual legacy of Ah Q aside, the obsession with national character and, more important, its ills, remains one of the fundamental concerns of modern China.

Discussions of Ah Q remain at the core consistent in the continual dichotomy between his embodiment of the "Chinese" and his representation of the oppressed in general, but Lu Xun's own interest in national character has been illuminated in a different way. One mainland Chinese scholar believes that Lu Xun's interest in the Chinese national character was brought about by his knowledge of American missionary Arthur Smith's *Chinese Characteristics*, a book he came across while studying in Japan.[64] Taking this a step further, another scholar puts forth the provocative notion that it was only after reading Smith's book in its 1896 Japanese translation that Lu Xun became engrossed in the concept and that the notion of "Chinese characteristics" was "imported" to Asia from the West.[65] Lu Xun's criticism of Chinese national characteristics, as is argued in both instances, uncannily resembles that of Arthur Smith.

This insight draws attention again to the important epistemological role played by missionaries in the Chinese perception of themselves via the West. This critical emphasis exposes the ethnocentrism in Western conceptions of Chinese characteristics and points at a specific historical encounter whereby cultural difference is established.[66] The story of Lu Xun and national char-

acter, however, has much more to tell us. Under the guise of borrowing
Arthur Smith's authority, Lu Xun refracts the image of the undesirable Chinese character through a series of outside specular positions whereby sameness becomes a fascination with an external perception of oneself. What
made the appeal of "national character" possible was not the interpellatory
power in Smith's words but the complexity of Lu Xun's participation in intentionally propagating someone else's corroboration of China's faults. We
would do well to reexamine Lu Xun's own account:

> I didn't have much money, so I only bought Yasuoka Hideo's *Chinese Character-*
> *istics as Seen in Their Fictional Works* and then left. It's a thin book with bright red
> and dark yellow colors. The price was a dollar and two cents. The author is quite
> polite, for he states in the preface that "this applies to not only the Chinese. Even
> in Japan, I am afraid, few people can escape the same criticism." Still, "once we
> consider both the degree and scope, even if we praise them as Chinese charac-
> teristics, we need not feel reserved about expressing our opinions." At this point,
> being the "zhinaren" that I am, I could hardly help breaking out into a nervous
> sweat.[67] One glance at the table of contents and it's clear: 1. Introduction, 2. Ex-
> cessive attention given to external appearance and demeanor, 3. Fatalistic and
> give up easily, 4. Capacity to bear and endure, 5. Lack of sympathy and abun-
> dance of cruelty, 6. Selfish individualism, 7. Excessive frugality and abnormal
> greed . . . 9. Deep superstition, 10. Indulgence in pleasure-seeking and lustful
> pursuits. . . . He apparently fully endorses Smith's *Chinese Characteristics*, which
> he cites often. Twenty years ago, there was already a Japanese translation called
> *The Demeanor of the Zhinaren.* Yet we the "zhinaren" hardly took notice of this
> book. In the first chapter, Smith talks about how the "zhinaren" are quite the-
> atrical. At the slightest excitement, they become actors, exaggerating and culti-
> vating each gesture of the hands and feet. Rather than having been spontaneously
> spurred into such actions, they're actually just trying to put on an impressive
> show. This is because they put too much emphasis on "face," always trying
> to build themselves up. That's why they have the nerve to talk and act that way.
> All this is to say that the key to the important national characteristic of the
> "zhinaren" lies in "face." . . . If we use this to analyze and reflect on ourselves,
> then we would realize that this conclusion is not overly malicious. . . . Of the for-
> eigners I've met, quite a few diligently study the so-called "face" of the Chinese.
> I'm not sure whether this is from the influence of Smith or their own experi-
> ences. Yet I feel that they've not only already arrived at some conclusion, but also
> applied it. Once they become even more skilled at it, I'm certain that they will
> win over not only diplomatic relations but also the friendship of the upper ech-
> elon "zhinaren." At that point, they would not even use the word "zhinaren"
> anymore but, rather, "Chinese," for that in itself concerns the very face of the
> "Chinese."[68]

As demonstrated in the four instances in which Arthur Smith's *Chinese*
Characteristics is mentioned in the Lu Xun corpus, Lu Xun's interest in
Smith's book lies in how it has colored the Japanese representation of the

Chinese "essence." In Lu Xun's preface to Uchiyama Kanzō's *The Ways of a Living China* (Ikeru Shina no sugata), he remarks with interest that the Japanese are said to be a race fond of drawing conclusions.[69] Whether in discussions or readings, they are not satisfied until they reach some kind of conclusion from the experience. This preference for self-contentment, Lu Xun notes, is evident in Japanese Sinology from the Meiji period, a study that, Lu Xun believes, has been largely influenced by the work of "some British author" on Chinese characteristics.[70] Now, however, Lu Xun remarks with sarcasm, new developments in the discipline have emerged. One traveler by chance walks into a grand Chinese official's house and sees an impressive collective of ink slabs. Immediately, he concludes from this empirical evidence that China is a great civilization that values the art of learning. Similarly, if a tourist in Shanghai buys a couple of pornographic pamphlets and picture books, he can just as well decide that Chinese culture prides itself in lechery. By the same logic, the fact that people like eating asparagus in the Jiangsu and Zhejiang provinces must indicate the embedded libidinous psychology of all Chinese people.[71] If they see something that they cannot understand, then they can always resort to the inscrutability of the Oriental as an explanation.

Lu Xun complains about cultural reductionism, a fact he takes to be unfortunate but hardly avoidable. If even among people of the same country an understanding cannot be taken for granted, he remarks, one can hardly be surprised by the kind of misunderstanding that arises in encounters between different cultures. As an example, Lu Xun refers to the opportunistic self-representation of Chinese students abroad as specialists in the literature of their cultural tradition, with which they no longer share any affinity upon returning from years of study abroad. What concerns him is not the ineluctability of "Chinese characteristics" as a category of truth; rather, he is more interested in how different cultural mediums of prejudice relay and essentialize the Chinese as a set of characteristics.

Arthur Smith, whose name Lu Xun hardly recalls and whose nationality he confuses in this 1935 preface, provides one such example. For Lu Xun, *Chinese Characteristics* provided the "blueprint" for misrepresentation by the so-called China specialists (*zhinatong*) in Japan.[72] Although he considers Smith's book to be better than what Japanese scholars have produced on the same topic, Lu Xun also notes its many mistakes. He neither naively accepts the authority of Smith's ethnocentric description nor would have thought it interesting had it not served as an apt example for his criticism of racial stereotypes. Lu Xun was not simply looking for evidence of Japanese prejudice against the Chinese in order to discredit and dismiss the Japanese. Despite the fact that he recognized the uninformed sources for the Japanese views of the Chinese, it was no less instructive for him to use these "outsiders" to dissect China's weakness. Using them to reinforce the need for harsh self-scrutiny, Lu Xun returns once more to his preoccupation with the primacy of self-reflexivity in identifying China's failure.[73]

Probably for these reasons, Lu Xun never spoke of Smith's work in isolation but only in terms of his larger concern with how the book gave legitimacy to derogatory constructions of the Chinese character by the Japanese. In his recollections, Lu Xun's close friend Xu Shoushang tells us of the conversations he had with Lu Xun about national character while studying in Japan between 1902 and 1909. Current speculations about the linkage between Lu Xun and Arthur Smith's book are based only on the approximate temporal coincidence between this period and the appearance of Smith's book in Japanese translation.[74] Thus, it is still uncertain whether Lu Xun himself even read the book during the formative period of his thinking on national characteristics. It is important to point out that the "national" specification of the notion of Chinese characteristics is a slippage that Lu Xun himself makes.[75] *Guominxing*, the word for "national character," is neither in the title of Arthur Smith's book—in English or its Japanese translation— nor in any of the Japanese studies Lu Xun mentions on the Chinese racial character or essence. He could have with equal plausibility learned of Smith's book and its Japanese translation through Yasuoka Hideo's constant references in *Chinese Characteristics as Seen in Their Fictional Writings*, a book Lu Xun bought much later in the summer of 1926. In "Uchiyama Kanzō zuo *Huo Zhongguo de zitai* xu" (Preface to Uchiyama Kanzō's *Ikeru Shina no sugata*), Lu Xun mistakes the American missionary as British and does not seem to even recall his name.[76]

Question of origins aside, the more intriguing fact remains that Lu Xun embraced the concept of Chinese national characteristics for its participatory complicity in his lifelong project of cultural self-critique.[77] He was not lured by a missionary's representation into identifying it as his own. He was himself engaged in a more radical commitment to a Chinese character preserved in failure. The text that has come to claim its literary genesis exemplifies the complexity and centrality of this act of self-dissection. The economy of self-critique operates much more ambiguously on the literary register than what has been claimed in the cultural legacy it engendered.

Lu Xun's 1921 *The Official Chronicles of Ah Q* narrates the life of an unremarkable and at times pitiable man whose infelicitous circumstances coincide with historical and political calamities. From Ah Q's humble birth to his final execution, his behavior has been said to reflect the worst of the feudalistic mind-set of the Chinese. Most well known of these undesirable traits is Ah Q's penchant for demonstrating his "spiritual triumph" (*jingshen shengli*), accomplished through a psychological reversal of his suffering. In his mind, specific instances of defeat are only insignificant details of others' petty jealousy. He turns himself from being the object of jeers and contempt into the empowered subject confirmed in his superiority. Despite the fact that he has claim to neither distinction nor pedigree, he fabricates blood relation to a local elite family in order to enjoy some benefit of fame or, once his deception is discovered, infamy. By maintaining the logic of this consciousness, he manages to remain undisturbed in the face of most adversity. Normally, slighting the other as his own offspring—paternal attributions are insulting for the implication that the person making the claim slept with one's mother—suffices in retrieving some illusion of confidence. Yet Ah Q also transposes the sense of victory onto his own humiliation:

> The pile of white shiny silver that is his—it's now all gone! Even if he rationalized it as having been stolen by his own bastard, he still feels unhappy. If he called himself a bastard, he would still feel the same. Now he finally begins to feel the pain of defeat. Yet he immediately turns defeat into victory. Raising his right hand, he then slaps his own face twice in a row. It stings somewhat from the burning pain. Afterwards, however, he feels much calmer, as though he himself had done the slapping, and the one slapped is another self. Soon it is as though one had slapped someone else. Though it still stings, he happily takes a rest in victory.[78]

Psychological victory, in fact, is not a completely self-aggrandizing act. In this series of complicated attributions of insult, Ah Q's triumphant recovery is inseparable from an act of self-infliction. Degrading his foes as his bastard sons, in this case, does not quite alleviate the humiliation of having all his prize money stolen. The next move, then, is to call himself the rogue who allowed this to happen. Thus deserving the ill luck, Ah Q resigns himself to the recognition of his own inadequacy. Yet this secondary maneuver at regaining comfort fails as well. Finally, as the feeling of defeat settles in, the psychological self-humiliation turns into physical degradation, as he expels the image of the abject self as an other in need of punishment. This is the process by which Ah Q "turns defeat into victory."

The splitting of the self in the process of appropriating the shame of defeat somehow maintains psychic survival. The logic of self-expulsion works as violence against oneself, but in a way that does not reproduce but rather repossesses the moment of transgression. Significantly, Ah Q has to rationalize the agency of the act, for even though it is clear to us that he had just slapped himself, it is only confirmed in his fantasy—"*as though* he himself had done the slapping." The sense of victory for Ah Q, as both the subject and object of this act, lies in enjoying as well as suffering the infliction of pain. The significance of the act lies in the relief from one's own humiliation—"the one slapped is another self"—through the demonstration of one's capacity to suffer at one's own hands.

Ah Q's self-slapping spiritual triumph does not merely serve as a spectacle to be seen from a disapproving distance. Self-triumph captures for Lu Xun a painful rejuvenation, experienced as self-inflicted humiliation and punishment, which is fundamental to the survival of the national character. It is striking that as one of his favorite psychological reversals Ah Q pretends that he is being beaten by his son. The implication here is less that his opponent is thereby diminished in a patriarchal hierarchy than that the idea of being defeated by oneself offers a much more tolerable and even comforting kind of suffering.

In this way, Ah Q's recognition of self-failure connects much more intimately to Lu Xun's preoccupation with the Chinese national character than has been conventionally understood. Lu Xun's use of other people's criticisms inevitably returns to the central problem of one's own inadequacy, as can be witnessed in his justifications for translating the works of foreign scholars and writers such as Kuriyagawa Hakuson.[79] In this conjunction, one might also recall Lu Xun's famous, though little-appreciated remark that whenever he relentlessly dissects other people, he is even more harshly dissecting himself.[80] Self-attributed failure ultimately confirms the subject who is capable and willing to inflict the pain of this truth on himself, thereby, if nothing else, reasserting the persistence of his own consciousness.

Although most commentators agree that Ah Q embodies the undesirable national characteristics of the Chinese—for example, avarice, cowardice, opportunism, and megalomania—few would entertain the possibility that Ah Q, as a literary and cultural phenomenon, actually helps produce a viable self-image of the Chinese. The need to perpetuate the interpretation that Lu Xun produced a humiliating figure to encapsulate the Chinese national essence, accompanied by decades of scholarly and cultural fascination with studying this undesirable character, leaves a legacy as revealing as it is enduring. Excavating the character flaws of the Chinese has become an importantly productive and impassioned industry of building modern Chinese national and cultural identity.

Since Lu Xun's literary invention, Ah Q has become the everyman, the negative icon of the Chinese national character. He also carries the humiliating symbol of the Manchu rule, as the name "Q" itself is said to capture the image of the queue that Chinese men were forced to wear during the Qing period. In Ah Q, "national character" (*guominxing*) is synonymous with "rotten character" (*liegenxing*). Since its inauguration during the May Fourth period, the preoccupation with Ah Q and the meaning of the Chinese national character have found audiences in fields as diverse as social psychology, literature, cultural criticism, and even popular reading. A renewed interest in the 1980s spurred new treatises on the topic. *The Ugly Chinese* by Taiwanese writer Bo Yang was only one of several works prodding at the old wounds of a diseased national character. Some seek to further the critique using more precise measures of social science, whereas others try to mitigate the harsh self-critique with emphasis on the positive aspects of the Chinese national character. Often reflecting currently politicized incidents, such as the controversy over the television series *River Elegy* that launched an undisguised attack on the Communist regime in 1989 or the dispute over the existence of the colonial Shanghai park sign "Chinese and dogs not admitted," ruminations over the Chinese national character often express much self-resentment.[81] Apart from the newly fueled sentiment against the despicable behavior of the Chinese, retranslations of Arthur Smith's *Chinese Characteristics* appeared as recently as 2004. One writer points out that the "sick pride" (*bingtai zizun*) of Ah Q is not what we need now.[82] Racial pride should be built on a clear, objective understanding of the different facets of one's national character. Another social psychologist justifies his study as providing an occasion for "self-reflection" (*fanxing*).[83] Both authors are somewhat dismayed at the function of self-debasement in the expression of a Chinese national character.

Extending beyond the realm of specialized discourse, national character also finds popularity among the average population. A series titled Chatting About the Chinese produced single volumes dealing with particular aspects of the Chinese character, such as superstition, life view, and leisure. Another series, The Psychology of the Chinese, focuses on studies of the Chinese approach toward happiness and contentment. The fact that one might pick up a book on Chinese national character for pleasure reading or sociopsychological critique is deeply revealing of its embeddedness in cultural life.[84] In addition to print, there was also a television lecture series, *Conversing About Racial Character and Modernity*, broadcast by Central People's Broadcast Network between April and July 1991 on the show *Learning*. The lectures were subsequently published as *Talking About the Chinese*. Whether it is to further dismantle or rehabilitate the image of Ah Q, the unabated interest in just how one survives in a state of debasement continues to express the preoccupation with the quintessential "Chineseness."[85] Conditioned by disease and ugliness, the Chinese national and racial character is what one loathes to love, but would hate even more not to loathe.

In 1934, thirteen years after the appearance of *The Official Chronicles of Ah Q*, some people began to voice the concern that the Chinese might have lost their confidence as a race.[86] In response, Lu Xun points out that the problem is not the lack of confidence (*zixin*) but the susceptibility to self-deception (*ziqi*). Resonating his 1908 remark on China's national megalo-mania, Lu Xun's greater worry—which he consistently articulates—is that the Chinese are impervious to real self-critique. They have always been re-luctant to analyze themselves.[87] He once enumerated the five ways in which this racial arrogance has been expressed: (1) "China, with her expansive ter-ritory and wealth of natural resources, became civilized the earliest; her mo-rality is unparalleled in the world"; (2) "While foreign nations have a higher level of materialistic civilization, China has an even higher spiritual civiliza-tion"; (3) "Whatever the foreigners have, China has already had them; what-ever type of western science is just as someone in China had once ex-pounded"; (4) "Foreigners also have poverty, thatched huts, prostitution, and stink bugs"; (5) "China is best when barbaric. You may say that Chinese thought is without order, but that is precisely the fruits of our enterprise as a race. Beginning with our ancestors and down to our posterity, we were disorderly in the past, and we will continue to be disorderly in the future. There are four hundred million of us. What are you going to do? Extermi-nate us?"[88]

Most concerned about the last phenomenon, which he considers the most recent, Lu Xun fears that this celebration of nationalistic barbarism draws its legitimating pretext from the laws of heredity. Racial arrogance, easily turned into fervent nationalism, is only a step away from the appalling suggestion of extermination. Although this represents a more radical end of the spectrum of cultural nationalism Lu Xun warns against, the close danger of falling into a maniacal self-deception is precisely what motivates his proj-ect of relentless self-dissection. The assumption is that no matter how harsh the Chinese may criticize themselves, there is always the tendency to dilute the self-recognition with an underlying, ineradicable arrogance. Inciden-tally, those five enumerated items are not the products of the lack of reflec-tion on China's condition. They encapsulate and reiterate an intellectual and cultural logic focused on self-scrutiny, as expressed in popular writings and social treatises since the late nineteenth century. Lu Xun could hardly have expected that the obsession with dismantling precisely the delusion of na-tional pride could itself become a sustaining mode of cultural identity. Even less could he have foreseen that this insistence on exposing the failures of the Chinese national character would acquire a much more complicated and, most important, productive cultural stance than he had despairingly thought. From eugenics to the literary construction of the Chinese racial and national character, the sense of incompleteness is not a flaw but the driv-ing force behind loving the nation and preserving the race (*aiguo baozhong*).

CHAPTER 5

The Quest for Beauty
and Notions of Femininity

THE INDISPENSABILITY of defect in the narrative of nation building enabled nationalism to tap into the anxieties of everyday life. Yet the notion of faulty character did not belong to nationalistic discourse alone. It carried a greater versatility than the proliferation of racial anxieties. Instead of defining the discourse of failure, nationalism shared in its appeal. In this web of diversity, notions of racial ruination existed alongside those of beauty and ideal femininity. The question of the national character extended into a quest for the "New Woman" as well.

In the search for the ideal modern woman, critics reevaluated her role in the family and society. This polarized the supporters of women's liberation into those who retrenched to ideological conservatism, on the one hand, and those who embraced the opportunity to revamp gender roles, on the other. As the proprietors of scientific racial discourse, eugenicists shied away from the inevitable conclusion of granting women's freedom, while the unabashed outspokenness of the infamous Zhang Jingsheng, known as "Dr. Sex," threw them into disarray. Zhang managed to propagate the concept of racial improvement among the average populace, a feat the eugenicists were unable to accomplish with equal success.

The tussle over the ownership of racial discourse played out in discussions of femininity, as the preoccupation with eradicating undesirable traits combined the project of racial improvement with the enterprise of redefining the feminine. This chapter examines how the idea of defect inspired visions of beauty in society, as proposed by Zhang Jingsheng. It looks at the ways in which defect, in race or national character, legitimated the founding of the "New Woman" project and made claim to the psychic topography of the feminine.

Working against these assumptions, women writers often opted for a kind of femininity that would rather operate under the imperative of self-discipline. Contrary to Zhang Jingsheng's ideals of beauty and Pan Guang-dan's diagnosis of psychosexual perversity, the works of leading women writers delineated a complex set of imperatives for what it meant to embody femininity in literature. Examining the various articulations from eugenicists, sexologists, and female writers such as Ding Ling and Xiao Hong, the following analysis juxtaposes a variety of notions about the feminine. From vehicles of racial propagation, vanguards of an ideal society of grace and beauty, to objects of psychosexual inquiries and ascetic literary heroines, perceptions of the modern woman moved between her outside appearance and her enigmatic psychic life.

A Society of Beauty: Zhang Jingsheng

Eugenics discourse provided a scientific framework for reconceptualizing the task of racial survival. Motivated by the same preoccupation, Lu Xun's literary portrait of Ah Q inquired into the individual's psychology in hope of awakening the Chinese to their degenerate selves. Independent of one another, both Pan and Lu Xun corroborated a view of "characteristics" that somehow defined the Chinese racially, culturally, and psychologically. The search for the root of China's illness marked a tendency contradicting the very project of modernity. Although many heralded modernity as the new and cosmopolitan, the cultural focus in which it was received incessantly dwelled on excavating more of China's ills, ever deferring the possibility of completely eradicating deep-rooted characteristics stubbornly defined against change.[1] The May Fourth Movement may have ushered in an era of largely antitraditional positivism, but it also precipitated the closer scrutiny of the underside of progress, continually fueling the project of modernity with a driving sense of incompleteness and discontent. The recognition of a flawed race and society gave rise to aspirations of corrective measures. The higher and more exalted these aspirations were, the more extreme the measures it entailed. As eugenics proposed pseudoscientific solutions, it unwittingly lent itself to parody in the popular realm. Yet this unintended caricature also expressed its own serious intent in restructuring the society. The appeal of sexual and racial perfection reached outside the narrow scope of scholarly and scientific discourse. How to run a society in which fault can be corrected by beauty is a question that brings us to a peculiar figure standing at the fringe of mainstream eugenics.

The notorious Chinese popular sexologist Zhang Jingsheng (1888–1933) represents an odd voice in an intellectual milieu driven by scientism and new epistemologies. His name, Jingsheng, is taken from the Chinese translation of the creed of evolution, "struggle for existence among the species, survival of the fittest" (wu*jing* tianze, shizhe *sheng*cun). Zhang studied in France from 1912 to 1919 at both the University of Paris and the University of Lyon. He decided on the subject of philosophy after an attempt to pursue the art of gardening was thwarted because of stipulations attached to his fellowship.[2] Like many intellectuals and observers of the event around the world, Zhang was disillusioned by the outbreak of World War I. Immersed in the thinking of revolutionaries, novelists, philosophers, and sociologists such as Jean-Jacques Rousseau, Auguste Comte, Emile Durkheim, and Henri de Saint Simon, Zhang received his Ph.D. in philosophy from the University of Lyon in 1919. Upon his return, he became involved in education reforms in Guangdong Province and was known for a pedagogical style unorthodox for his time.

He taught English by physically acting out the meaning during enunciation and wrestled with his students on the athletic field.[3] Joining the ranks of China's foremost revolutionary and anarchist thinkers, such as Lu Xun, Chen Duxiu, Li Dazhao, Zhou Zuoren, Liang Shuming, and Wu Zhihui, Zhang began teaching at Beijing University in 1920. The first volume of his *Xingshi* (Sexual histories) appeared in 1926, and it was immediately labeled as pornographic. Posters were put up on university campuses forbidding its circulation, an action that elicited exactly the opposite response.

Sexual Histories belonged to the first of many categories of research conducted by the Committee of Folk Customs Investigation at Beijing University. The committee members agreed that the category of sex warranted an independent inquiry. Zhang placed an advertisement in the supplement to *Crystal Newspaper* calling for submissions from the general population. He asked the readers to share their conventional or unconventional sexual experiences with the public for the sake of "knowledge"—a catchword for scientific spirit during the May Fourth period—and the cultivation of proper sexual habits. At the same time that Zhang asked for honest confessions, he also reminded the readers that they should aspire to make their sexual histories as brilliant as poetry and as intriguing as fiction.[4] The call for submissions asked for detailed accounts and encouraged the audience—in familiar second-person address—not to be bashful but to tell all, confessing their sins and sharing their glories.

Sexual Histories consists of seven such submissions from readers, most of whom were young adults. At the end of each submission Zhang attached a short commentary on the questions their personal accounts raised, though his comments dealt more generally with the issues of sexual health and relationships. Reacting to Zhang's unconventional methods, the Chinese eugenicists, despite their differences, united in a common cause against what they considered the vulgarization of eugenics and the lofty idea of racial improvement. Pan Guangdan remarked with dismay in 1925 on the multiplication of sensationalist journals such as *Sex Magazine* (Xing zazhi), *Sex Drive Weekly* (Xingyu zhoukan), *Sex Newspaper* (Xingbao), and Zhang's *New Culture* (Xin wenhua). He disapproved of their pandering to vulgar tastes under the guise of promoting general sexual health.[5] Yet these publications attracted a wide audience. For example, the heated exchanges between the eugenicists and the sexologist over the mysterious "third kind of fluid," or female ejaculate, became the focus of much controversy as well as layman curiosity.[6] This not only made Zhang more popular but also gave other journals free publicity to exploit. In a 1927 issue of *Sex Magazine*, for example, Pan's very attack on Zhang Jingsheng was reprinted without authorization and unwittingly lent legitimacy to the magazine's purported "inquiry" into the scientific basis of "the third kind of fluid."[7]

The hostility between the sexologists and the eugenicists was significant. Zhang's unabashed confessional style intertwined with his pedagogical views on sex education left his more conservative counterparts exasperated. The title "Dr. Sex" (*xing boshi*) was equated with lechery and pornography. Even Wen Yiduo, a close friend of Pan Guangdan whose specialization in classics and poetry exempted him from the sex fray, cannot help letting the reference of "Dr. Sex" slip into his discussion of the *Book of Odes* (1122–256 BCE).[8] Taking his cue from the revered Romantic thinker Rousseau, who was the subject of his Ph.D. thesis in Lyon and whose *Confessions* he subsequently translated in 1929, Zhang wrote about his life freely, sparing few details.[9] Pan, in particular, maintained his disdain for the sexologist, even well after the latter's disappearance from Shanghai's public life in the late 1920s. Persistent in his diligence to expose the charlatan doctor, Pan reported on Zhang's continual legal mishaps with a vengeance. In 1933, the people of Zhang's home district, Raoping, allegedly filed a public complaint against Zhang. In pursuit of his original academic quest, he was detained by the authorities in Shantou on August 22, 1933, for farming on unauthorized land and licentious practice.[10] Pan was less interested in the fact that the "licentious practice" was a gross exaggeration of a personal relationship Zhang carried on with a young woman whom he hired as the principal at his elementary school.[11] Deemed indiscreet by the townspeople, the relationship raised a few eyebrows. As he was concerned only with yet another exposé on Dr. Sex, Pan was happy to note the good prospects for outlawing books of perversion. With some satisfaction, he concluded that such "specialists" of sex need to consult specialists of their own.

Despite the pretext of scientific objectivity, however, the opposition between the eugenicists and the sexologists is less scientific than ideological. Like Pan, Zhang also envisions a certain eugenic ideal in a society based on principles of perfection and beauty. What he has to offer, he explains at one point, is neither strict science nor pure philosophy. If anything, it proposes a kind of art combining the two. Here Zhang does not differ greatly from Pan's ideas for a better China. Unfortunately, Zhang's notoriety as Dr. Sex has largely obscured the similarity his society of beauty shares with other, more accepted visions of racial and national rejuvenation, such as Jiang Jieshi's New Life Movement and Pan Guangdan's eugenics project. Taiwanese scholar Peng Xiaoyan rightly points out that Zhang distilled his vision of a society of beauty from his knowledge of Eastern and Western discourses on social utopias.[12] In fact, before he acquired the infamous reputation as Dr. Sex with the publication of *Sexual Histories* in 1926, Zhang had been pursuing a serious teaching career for five years at Beijing University as professor of philosophy. In 1924 and 1925, respectively, he published *A Way of Life Based on Beauty* (Meide renshengguan) and *Organizational Principles of a Society Based on Beauty* (Meide shehui zuzhifa). No analytical treatment has yet been provided of how ideas as diverse as "third kind of fluid" and regular beauty pageants jointly operate in Zhang's philosophical framework.

For Zhang, any historical progress, social organization, or individual creation has as its goal the fulfillment of beauty. He defines "a way of life" as the pursuit of marvelous and amusing effects transcending the drudgery of material life. Neither scientific in the narrow sense nor Confucian in its nature, Zhang's thinking employs both scientific and philosophical methods. He states that inherent in life is "energy." This is divided into "accumulative energy" (*chuli*) and "expansive energy" (*kuozhangli*). The principle of beauty encourages one to direct this cumulative force into an expansive, external expression in the most optimal and efficient manner possible. The eight areas in which to pursue the principles of beauty are "clothing food residence" (*yi shi zhu*), "physical cultivation" (*tiyu*), "profession" (*zhiye*), "science" (*kexue*), "art" (*meishu*), "sex education" (*xingyu*), "entertainment" (*yule*), and "a way of life based on beauty" (*meide renshengguan*) itself.

From the outset, Zhang rejects the idea that scientific rationality with its bureaucratic reasoning and administrative logic alone could achieve a perfect society. "Organization" (*zuzhi*) itself serves merely as a transparent medium through which spiritual exaltation can materialize. For Zhang, organization progresses from nonexistent to existent, small to large, bad to good, chaos to order. It is incumbent upon individuals themselves to practice beauty for a society to embody fully its principles. Here, Zhang advances notions of personal behavior remarkably similar to those later promoted in the tenets of the New Life Movement. The first of the eight categories, "clothing food residence," for example, is only one item short of Nationalists' "clothing food residence behavior." Even the missing category of "behavior" is implied in the practice of the principles of beauty underlying each area. Clothing, apart from cleanliness and practicality, is specifically designed to counter some of the less desirable aspects of the Chinese.

Zhang locates the most obvious sign of the "old sick Chinese man" (*Zhongguo lao bingfu*) in his external appearance. With the founding of the Republic, Zhang jeers, one has only managed to cut off the queue and change the flag, but the sickly (*bingtai*) and ugly (*chou e*) accoutrement remains. If the Chinese were to change this, which is one of the major failures of the Republic, their spiritual improvement would surely follow. Men's traditional long gowns, round-tip shoes, and pointy caps only accentuate the sloppy and awkward look of corrupt decadence. Those who are accustomed to shoes made of cloth inevitably drag their feet when taking strides because of weakened ankles. As a consequence, they slouch from the lack of support in their soles. Men's shoes should be made of leather rather than cloth to correct this problem. Their hats should be modeled on the Turkish fez to help conceal their short stature. Thus, the look of the "sick man" will be transformed into that of the "majestic great man" (*xiong jiujiu de wei zhangfu*).[13]

As for women, Zhang assesses, their clothing requires greater reform. Because of women's greater subjection to rites and traditions, their clothing has always been designed to cover fully the arms and cruelly flatten the breasts. Hence, when they walk, they inevitably show a disproportion between their fronts and backs, as their bound breasts and sagging behinds disrupt the grace of movement. Women should use, instead, primarily silk and chiffon for their clothing and avoid wearing the big hats fashionable among European women so as to keep their petite proportions.

From design to production costs, Zhang goes to great lengths to promote these new vestments for the society of beauty, especially while lecturing to his young students.[14] The sketches he includes suggest an inspiration taken from European women's clothing at the time, no doubt impressed upon him during his stay in France. In general, Zhang's theories make no pretense at depersonalized objectivity, as at moments of excitement he would interject personal revelations from either his own sexual experiences with French women or his conviction concerning a free-body culture. Short of founding his own utopian colony, Zhang professes his enthusiasm for playing the self-appointed vanguard of the new society of beauty. For these very reasons, whenever his authority is not altogether discredited, his theories are received with skepticism. His concerns, however, are often the same as those propounded by leaders of the New Culture Movement. The idea that China is on the brink of decrepitude and will remain so without proper measures of rejuvenation propels the project of building a new nation. His consistent invocation of "big old sick man" (*laoda bingfu*), "old sick Chinese man," and "the people of a rotting old country" (*fubai de laoda guo ren*) resonates well with contemporary concerns about China's survival as a race and nation.

The minute details of everyday life on which Zhang places so much emphasis are strongly reminiscent of "undesirable Chinese characteristics." As with his contemporaries who find Chinese habits of hygiene appalling, Zhang focuses on the manner of ingestion. He stipulates, for instance, that one keep one's mouth closed right after delivering the food so as to avoid inflicting on others the unpleasant sight of progressing stages of mastication.[15] Rather than throw leftover bones onto the floor, the proper guest would, instead, leave them in the rice bowl for the servants to take away. Spitting, as with the public relief of flatulence, should be discreetly avoided. Further eliminating the unsightly mix of biological functions, Zhang stipulates that spittoons be removed from the dining area and kept strictly in the bathroom.

For Zhang, physical needs should be supplemented by spiritual enjoyment. Distinguishing need from pleasure, he promotes elevating the gratification of physical needs to the level of aesthetic enjoyment. In regard to eating, he recommends the "internal ingestion method" (*neishifa*). This exercise entails an inhalation that "tastes" the aroma of the food without necessarily physically swallowing it. It emphasizes enjoyment rather than nourishment.[16] Each instance of ingestion need not be solely for the sake of need. Instead, one can heighten the experience of eating such that it can be simply for enjoyment. In the same vein, Zhang advocates the "spiritual communion method" (*shenjiaofa*) as a way of taking sexual pleasure. Because sex requires less frequency of satisfaction than food, Zhang proposes, its sublimation into a spiritual experience should be simple enough to do.

On the subject of sex, Zhang, expectedly, has well-articulated views. The purpose of sexual cultivation, he carefully distinguishes, is not embodied in the act of ejaculation. It should not be treated as a purely hedonistic indulgence or meaningless cultural dictate to continue the family line. The point of intercourse is to maximize the spiritual pleasure for both men and women. If it so happens that they wish to procreate, then impregnation should be treated as one of the marvelous effects of conjoining two bodies and souls.[17] In this way, there are two facets to sexual education based on beauty. One is to minimize the frequency of intercourse and, instead, turn the fulfillment of physical drive into the gratification of desire. The other is to use the energy of sexual desire (*xingyu de jingli*) thus kept in reserve to expand one's capacity for thought, artistic creations, and actions. All great deeds, Zhang affirms, are created by a transmuted sexual force (*bianxiang de xingli*), which he coins as *jingbian* (essence change), in contradistinction to *bianjing* (change essence, i.e., externalizing sperm), which he derides as the bestial reflex of ejaculation. The average person, Zhang states, wastes his essence by engaging in routine intercourse as bland as eating a bitter melon. In any case, from the perspective of beauty, the importance of spiritual connection outweighs the need for frequency. Sexual intercourse primarily facilitates spiritual elevation, which has the power to enhance the accompanying physical pleasure.

If Zhang's proposals seem mystifying to the modern reader, they also elicited a mix of curious voluntarism and involuntary amusement from readers at the time. One reader, for example, was rightly puzzled by the spirit's capacity to fulfill a biological need, but cited with enthusiasm references from religious tracts to decipher Zhang's proposal.[18] Despite his usual sympathy for Zhang's unorthodox views, even Zhou Zuoren felt that both the "internal ingestion method" and "spiritual communion method" were too much like Taoist tenets on withholding semen during intercourse.[19] Even though he applauded Zhang's refreshingly honest promotion of pleasure and entertainment in contrast to the sick moral pretense of Chinese society, he found it "unscientific" (*fei kexue*). Nonetheless, he recommended Zhang's book for its "poetic" quality. Here, Zhou's inadvertent comment points to the peculiar style of Zhang's book. In the preface to *Organizational Principles of a Society Based on Beauty*, Zhang remarks that it matters not whether readers consider his book a practical social treatise or outlandish fiction.[20] At another point, he denies that the book is designed to be any kind of utopian bulletin or heavenly oracle.[21] He is content with merely putting into words what he senses in the world around him.

Beautiful Eugenics and Its Regulations

Zhang's fundamental message is that a life principled on beauty is always a matter of elevating the spiritual and breaking out of the confines of materiality. He does not deny the conflict between need and desire, because antagonism carries with it the true experience of beauty. In this way, his idea of sex education involves teaching youths about both the materiality and spirituality of sex. Whereas the materiality of sex amounts to physical climax, emotional transcendence constitutes the spiritual aspect. Youths will learn that physical impulses have a greater capacity for realization than can be momentarily satisfied in the mere act of ejaculation. Whereas excessive ejaculation drains one's mental energy, a preservation and transmutation of one's essence will have a more spiritual impact.[22] This way of understanding neither represses nor denies the physicality of sex. It discourages youths from

foolishly dissipating their energy on what they can only perceive as the se-
ductive object of guilt and taboo.

Zhang's paternalistic pedagogy, however, is accompanied by a more pragmatic view of its realization. Rather than a matter of free and unrestrained
expression, sex is also subjected to a strict regime of perfection, discipline,
and emotional elevation. In Zhang's ideal society, men below the age of
twenty and above fifty-five, and women below the age of eighteen and
above forty-six, are not allowed to engage in sexual intercourse. He equally
discouraged masturbation, not out of moral objection but on the grounds of
wasting one's essence without proper emotional elevation. For men and
women who are sexually active, the prescribed frequency is no more than
once every few days.

In this vein, Zhang advances the notion of a "new eugenics" (*xinde
youzhongxue*) or "new fetal education" (*xinde taijiao*) based on the practice of
transcendent sexual gratification.[23] Disciplined measures, combined with
modernized fetal education, will foster the ideal mind and body befitting the
principle of beauty. The more diligently the expecting mother conforms to
the principles of beauty—by wearing comfortable clothing, maintaining
good hygiene, and holding a content spirit—the more eugenic her child
will be. This formula, Zhang adds, differs from traditional fetal education,
in which it is believed that the child inherits the mother's disposition. By
new eugenics he means that the level of the mother's physical well-being is
directly proportional to the quality of the environment her child needs in
order to live in fulfillment of the principles of beauty. New eugenics promotes the aspiration for and practice of beauty rather than the breeding of
good genes. The eugenicists' hope of creating intelligent and well-bred children, Zhang states, is truly an overestimation, for intelligence and personal-
ity are the effects of nurture, not nature.[24]

Zhang's more respectable contemporaries brand him an opportunistic
charlatan, but that stigmatization reflects more the authority-making process
of the New Culture Movement than the intrinsic value of Zhang's views.
His utopian framework is not all frivolity and play. In his own way, he attempts to reconcile the demands of individual freedom with communal
good, subjective passions with structured expressions. Beneath the surface of
social perfection, and coextensive with the expressions of individual creativity, are stringent, uncompromising rules regarding how individuals' behavior must be governed. This instrumental rationality puts the idea of a society based on the principles of beauty in a more somber light.

In *Organizational Principles*, Zhang outlines a eugenics program for fos-
tering private behavior in accordance with the principle of beauty that takes
ideas from Western eugenics, anthropology, and aesthetics. The proposal is

intended to be revolutionary and emancipating for women. He promotes a "system of lovers" (*qingrenzhi*) as opposed to the institution of marriage. Under this system that allows the exercise of free love between men and women, women enjoy more freedom of choice, for without the institution of marriage men would always have to compete for their affections. As a result, love is neither a gift nor possession but, rather, a way of "appreciation" (*xinshang*). No one takes courtship for granted. Every union is earned and can be terminated at will if it fails such standards. Relationships remain fluid, compelling each participant to always strive to become a better and more attractive candidate. Thus, men and women always conduct themselves in the most beautiful and desirable manner possible. In this way, women's status in society will improve, for they will no longer be burdened by marriage and its primary task of reproduction. To ensure that the best possible unions are between the most qualified and competent in the "evolution of love" (*aide jinhua*), Zhang calls for free and regular state dispensation of birth-control pills.[25] Without the pressure of reproduction, only the best possible offspring will be produced, for their parents will be making that choice under the most free and thus optimal conditions.

Zhang's vision of perfection does not limit itself to one culture or nation. Complementing the "system of lovers" is also the "system of exogenous marriage" (*waihunzhi*). Unlike the system of lovers, which underlies the inner principles guiding a society's evolution, Zhang's system of exogenous marriage aims to bring about a kind of utopian world in harmony. Like Kang Youwei's vision of the realm of the great union, Zhang's world greatly benefits from interracial marriage. However, he takes it a step further by making it the central institution in materializing the ultimate principle of beauty—love. The system of exogenous marriage is defined as men and women of one locality marrying those from another. Zhang cites Australian aborigines as proof of the benefits of such a practice. Not only does exogenous marriage provide for Zhang the best way of promoting and expanding the system of lovers but he sees it as the "best method for achieving mutual understanding between different races and the great union of the world (shijie datong)."[26]

Following eugenic principles, however, Zhang encourages interracial marriage only with those races that possess strength where the Chinese race is weak. He does not take the world of great union for granted. Russians, for example, with their "adventurous, mysterious, and imposing character," would be a perfect complement to the "tender and benevolent" disposition of the Chinese.[27] Zhang predicts that the future "Asia for Asians" (*yazhouren de yazhou*) will be dominated by the mixed race (*hunhe renzhong*) of the Chinese and Russians. In the same way, he advises, the Chinese should intermarry with Europeans and Americans as well. Zhang recalls that when there were many Chinese laborers in France during World War I, Chinese men were quite popular among the French women. Thus, the Chinese should not be intimidated by the snobbish manners of the Europeans into thinking that, like toads dreaming of tasting the swan, they are not good enough. True, Zhang concedes sympathetically from personal experience, there are those French women who look down on Chinese men. However, one need not seek one's mate in that echelon of the society. Instead, he continues, one could turn to the class of the common masses (*pingmin jieji*). Rather than travel abroad for a few months or pore over foreign books for years to acquire worldly sophistication, one would expedite the process by bringing home a foreign wife.

The issue of Japan, however, requires a slightly modified rationale. Despite the fact that the Japanese have none of the talents of the white race but show twice the contempt for the Chinese, Zhang notes, they should not be excluded. Even though the politicized call for "Sino-Japanese affinity" (*zhongri qinshan*) has become a platitude, there is no reason not to apply it in good faith where interracial marriage is concerned. When the Chinese men are in "dire straits," they can also marry women from India, the black race, and the South Pacific. The goal lies in leading the "weak and barbaric peoples" (*shuairuo yeman de minzu*) onto brighter paths. In this way, not only should the Chinese reach up for (*pangao*) interracial marriage with the whites but they should also connect (*lianluo*) with these "lower" races. This scenario works, however, only with the right timing. Before a matrilineal society can be materialized and as long as Chinese women are bound to go where their husbands go, they should not marry the men from these races, for they will be inevitably downgraded (*daixia*). Chinese men, on the other hand, could marry these natives to "elevate" (*tigao*) the latter's racial status.

One of the duties of governance based on beauty (*meizhi*) is "racial improvement" (*renzhong gailiang*).[28] Zhang argues that the state should regulate marriage and matchmaking. No man under the age of twenty-five or woman under the age of eighteen should have access to marriage. They have to be free of venereal diseases and the like. In accordance with contemporary ideas on eugenics, the mentally retarded and the insane will be sterilized to eliminate further "damage" to society. Apart from disincentives, the state can also take positive measures such as setting up "official matchmaking bureaus" (*guanmeiju*) that keep the records of qualified young men and women on file. To protect this privileged information, only the same pool of selected candidates will have access. The state reserves the right to use "scientific methods" to investigate people's backgrounds to ensure truthfulness. These "scientific methods" do not exclude subjecting individuals to physical and intelligence tests so as to ascertain their true competence.

The foundation of Zhang's perfect society of beauty rests on individuals' consciousness and, failing that, the state's power to awaken that self-reflection. In this capacity, Zhang calls for annual state-sponsored beauty pageants for men and women. The five beauty queen pageants are designed to recognize those who have perfected principles of philanthropy, beauty, arts, talent, and community service. The three days during which the pageants are held are celebrated as national holidays finishing off with an extravagant parade. Held on May 5, these pageants are complemented by the eight king pageants on August 8. In addition to having the five categories of their female counterparts, the males in the pageants also compete for titles of adventurousness, technical skills, and strength. Upon their coronation, these thirteen kings and queens will join in a tour around the country. Under the official pretext of preaching to the masses the standards of beauty for a society, the real purpose of the tour is to encourage romance between the participants in hope of producing "superior seeds" (*youliangde zhongzi*).

Although the principles of beauty are positively reinforced in individual consciousness through communal festivals such as beauty pageants, they are also carefully controlled. In Zhang's society of beauty, policing has the peculiar duty of both exemplifying and disciplining the conscience necessary for beauty. The investigation unit (*jiuchadui*) provides encouragement as well as surveillance. Sent to the streets, theaters, dance halls, restaurants, and even private banquets, the police may cite people for spitting, public indecency, and unkempt appearance.

Less expected, however, is their power of intervention in matters such as playing bad music or being an uncoordinated dancer at a ball. The idea is that having two left feet, apart from the motor distress it may cause the wrongdoer, could prove noxious to a society's sense of beauty as well. This exactitude in the pursuit of beauty may seem less draconian once one learns that the police themselves undergo intensive training at special schools set up by the Office of Rites (*liyisi*). Each police officer is well versed in the classics of rites, song, dance, and music. The notion of policing in the sense of invoking individuals' self-policing is best exemplified in the remarkable choice of "weapon": a hand mirror in preference to guns or clubs. Those who transgress upon the rites or show poor taste in music shall have the mirror held up before them. Facing his own reflection, the perpetrator will come to recognize his "ugliness and the wrongfulness of his acts."[29]

The idea of beauty instills a consciousness that shames one into adhering to the utmost demands of perfection. Coupling vanity with humiliation, each citizen works as a self-correcting machine. Reproduction becomes a competition among well-groomed contestants. At every moment, one is subjected to the lofty standards of self-image that, if overlooked even for a moment, would be quickly called to mind by an external device of reflection. Zhang's society of beauty, however, does not rely exclusively on a properly vain conscience. Supplementing the inspiring calls for making oneself as beautiful as possible is a more coercive approach toward those for whom grace and elegance may not be incentive enough. This dimension goes beyond the moral psychology of shame and adopts a medical model of antisocial behavior.[30]

There are three types of wrongdoers in Zhang's society.[31] The lack of proper education in the arts and rites produces the first kind. Fortunately, this kind of offender could be easily rehabilitated in Zhang's society through proper training at either the Office of Rites and Rituals or the Office of Music and Dance. The second type of wrongdoer commits crimes prompted by physical or psychological impairment. If the problem is physical, the state would provide the wrongdoer with a living stipend until the problem is rectified. However, if the problem is psychological, such as indolence, Zhang suggests that the offender be injected with an "anti-indolence serum" (*buduojiang*), which would excite the wrongdoer into seeking a livelihood. In this capacity, Zhang imagines a society motivated by shame but regulated by medical measures. He proposes what he considers a parallel scenario: a woman commits a lecherous act and a doctor is appointed to locate the cause; if the doctor finds that the problem is due to her abnormally large labia majora, they will then be removed to restore her to her sane self. Reflecting an interest similar to Pan's in the cause of female hysteria, Zhang proposes a medical solution for every criminal act. In cases where the criminal's psychosis is too great, Zhang recommends electrocution during slumber. As would be argued four decades later by British and American criminologists and behavioral scientists, in Zhang's society of beauty, there are "no prisons but hospitals, no bullets but pills."[32] For him, the purpose of the beauty corrective in a society parallels a doctor's desire to cure patients.

At the center of Zhang's envisioned society, however, is the woman whose cultivation will be able to transform institutions and behaviors. His definitions of beauty are most precise when applied to women's dress, demeanor, and social etiquette. Not only their liberation but also their consent to conform to the kind of role Zhang envisions is essential to the system of lovers and the system of endogenous marriage. Zhang also expects women to conduct international relations. Women diplomats carry the task of using their beauty and charm to defuse potential conflicts between nations. Mingling with powerful heads of state and top officials at galas, women are expected to behave in a way somewhere between that of a hostess of French salons—to which Zhang was probably denied entry—and that of a nature-loving nudist.

Although Zhang claims to be an advocate for women's liberation, he shares Pan Guangdan's unhappiness at the situation with China's modern New Woman. Young, educated women clad in Western clothing clamoring for independence and liberation from the shackles of domestic life are unlikely to return voluntarily to the domestic duties or reproductive tasks Pan prescribes. Nor do they demonstrate the proper grace appropriate to the society of beauty Zhang imagines. The discrepancy between New Woman and the women embodying the image opens up the issue outside the immediate parameters of the debate on women's role in modern China. Its full implications involve not only the reevaluation of the family structure but also the scrutiny of New Woman as a question of character.

The "New Woman" Project

The progressive pursuit of the New Woman project in the 1920s was quickly tempered by a new set of criteria for her modern reinvention. Her sexuality became a question of character. The idea of women's liberation sat uncomfortably with the reality of China's uneasy cultural transition into the modern era. While some scrutinized the "modern woman" according to a principle of faulty character, others, such as the eugenicists, expressed increasing reservations regarding westernization and its meaning for women's movements.[33] In 1923, Pan was already advocating the reinstitution of the Chinese family structure that came under attack during the May Fourth period. He disagreed with the abolition of traditional institutions, such as the civil exams system, which had for centuries sustained the stability of China's social system. This, Pan argued, had at least ensured the distinction of those who proved more outstanding than others; it provided a process of selection that standardized means of identifying superior stock. The quick embrace of individualism and sexual equality in the May Fourth period destroyed these old institutions without providing viable alternatives.

In a 1931 preface to the Chinese translation of the British sociologist Meyrick Booth's work on women's new liberation, Pan expressed his enthusiasm for Booth's conclusion that women's greatest task, in the end, was to propagate the race.[34] He thought, however, that Booth's argument did not go far enough to discard the term "equality" in preference to "justice" in the demand for women's liberation. "Equality," Pan explains, is misleading, because it overlooks the biological and inherent differences between the sexes and misrepresents the issue as a matter of securing the same social rights. "Justice," on the other hand, governs people's social interactions according to their roles and capabilities. The interaction between men and women falls under this rubric.

Whereas the previous women's movement had as its goal individual liberation, the new eugenically defined goal should be racial and societal evolution. Pan points out that Booth's negligence of racial tasks, as with other writers, had helped inhibit the process of evolution. Future society, in fact, depends solely on the propagation of race.[35] The misplaced emphasis on individual liberation for women, Pan believes, predisposes women to blame the family as an institution of oppression. As a result, they fail to recognize that the family is a place where they can exercise their exclusive prerogative of reproduction. Education for women, for Pan, is all for the good, to the extent that it enables women to make more intelligent and eugenic mating choices. As long as women realize that their greatest task and contribution to society lie in selective reproduction, an early experience in a career can even help prepare women for managing domestic tasks.

Distressed at the burgeoning articles in women's journals dealing with the issue of free choice in love and marriage, Pan is ultimately less optimistic about the place of individualism in the future.[36] Even though love may initiate a relationship leading to marriage, Pan warns, it cannot be relied upon as the sole guiding principle for marriage. If that were the case, there would only be endless courtships and no institutionalized consummation. Pan notes that only 32 percent of the women polled by *The Ladies Journal* in its special issue on love and marriage were prepared to have families. He takes this as the ill consequence of the often-distorted view that women who are not economically independent are "parasitic" or "dependent." Little do they understand, he laments, that the sanctity of motherhood in racial propagation far exceeds the importance of economic independence.[37] Citing what Liang Qichao once said about the concept of rights in the West, Pan stresses that to apply the concept of rights to intimate relationships in China such as that between father and son, or husband and wife, is utterly incomprehensible to the Chinese. To transfer the concept of rights to the Chinese context would be a gross misapplication of one cultural context to another.[38]

In response to Pan's article, Zhou Jianren—the youngest brother of Lu Xun and a generally recognized eugenicist—disputes Pan's subordination of individualism to racial propagation.[39] Zhou believes in the euthenic, or environmental, over the eugenic, or genetic, determination for the quality of racial improvement. Because the instinct to reproduce underlies all biological organisms, the reason they do not reproduce must be due to adverse environmental conditions. Moreover, even if these conditions were optimal, that would only encourage indiscriminate rather than selective reproduction. If, according to Pan, feudalistic institutions in China, such as the family, civil examination system, and even feminine chastity, already embodied the principles of eugenics, then, Zhou asks, why are the Chinese not already the strongest race in the world after centuries of practice?[40]

While rebuffing Pan's suggestion to resuscitate old feudalistic institutions for their eugenic function, Zhou's position has its own reservations. Built upon recently sanctified May Fourth ideals such as individualism and women's liberation, his overt support for the sanctity of individual choice against Pan's downplaying of individualism is nonetheless restrained by his sober recognition of women's actual conditions. In "Women and Society" (Funü yu shehui, 1921), Zhou claims that the call for women's liberation stems from men's own grievances from having to take on a disproportionate number of social tasks.[41] When they realized that keeping women out of the workforce actually worked to their disadvantage, men started clamoring for women's liberation. Zhou reminds us that, after all, matriarchal societies once existed, as is well documented in anthropological literature, yet there must have been good reasons for their replacement by patriarchal rule. After enumerating various biological differences, Zhou concludes that women's dispositions better suit nurturing and reproductive tasks. Elsewhere, he stresses that the perceived need to transform the family structure remains more conceptual than pragmatic. In reality, women's roles and conditions are much more restricted. Thus, to speak of the amorality of marriages not based on love—a creed of the Western reformers—is still, Zhou concedes, too distant from the Chinese reality.[42]

In Zhou's own view on women and the family, much like Pan's, women are still bound to the task of reproduction, albeit with a stronger emphasis on the transformation of societal rather than hereditary forces. The similarities Zhou shares with Pan are hidden in the overt difference pivoting on the issue of individualism. Although Zhou espouses individualism, it is—in much the same way as his perception of the demand for change in the family structure—much more a conceptual ideal than a realistic depiction. The idea of individual freedom during the May Fourth period was clearly connected with the impetus for women's liberation, but applying the principles of individual sovereignty to women proved much more difficult. This conflict, deeply embedded in the New Woman project, reveals more the contradictory vision harbored by its supporters than the innate imperviousness of women to change. To understand a different layer of this ideological and historiographical problem, one needs to see it in dialogue with the literary context as well.

Scholarship on women, literature, and nationalism in the past fifteen years has steered the course of feminist studies toward the field of cultural and ide-

ological critique.[43] Gender, which until recently has largely meant femininity, is often pitted against nation, identified as an ideology of coercion.[44]
Whether this is accomplished through prescription, co-optation, or canon-
ization has been a question less attended to than the politics of subversion.
Even though race is recognized to share a similar need and critical vantage
point against the nation, the attempted alliance between gender and race is
not always successful or transparent in itself.

It has been argued that the literary image of the May Fourth New
Woman was largely constructed out of male fantasies and that the female
body, in particular, was appropriated as the focal point of that imagination.[45]
Even in cases such as that of Mao Dun, who out of genuine interest advocated for women's liberation and literary production, the project of the
"New Woman" is overtaxed with the eager, if not anxious, expectations of
the male intellectual whose desire for the new Chinese nation included novelties such as the modern woman herself.[46] However, the discourse of this
new nation itself is already founded on a sense of inadequate citizenry and
undesirable character. Nation itself has first of all laid claim to failure. Significantly, the tension does not reside merely as a male intellectual problem
in face of an enigmatic, feminine other. The articulation of this fraught relation with an object requiring one's remolding and reform draws from the
discourse on the "national character."

Already in 1920, eight years before the appearance of "Creation," Mao
Dun's most famous short story on the construction of the New Woman, an
article on "Some Negative Characteristics That the 'New Woman' Should
Get Rid Of" (Xin funü suo yinggai chanchude jizhong liegenxing) had appeared in the widely respected *The Ladies Journal*.[47] The author notes the
rampant use of "New Woman," a fashionable image propagated by the May
Fourth Movement and in which women love to see themselves. By New
Woman, however, the author adds, he means a distinction made not on the
basis of seniority, as though younger women are by definition more progressive than the old, but something fundamental to women themselves.
Whether in belief, taste, habit, attitude, responsibility, or social status, the
New Woman differs completely from women of prior times. As long as she
can demonstrate change in what women had not been able to accomplish
for thousands of years, she can truly call herself a New Woman. What we
have to remember, the author says and repeats a familiar May Fourth slogan,
is that without destroying the old, we cannot build the new. What the author means, however, is an uprooting of a very particular sort:

> The reason why most women of the old tradition remain impervious to change
> is no other than the fact that a number of negative characteristics have been

firmly planted in them. Not only do these traits linger, they are also passed on, one by one, to their offspring. In order to become a New Woman, one must first get rid of these negative characteristics, then infuse oneself with the elements of the New Woman. These negative characteristics are like a poisonous sore. The poison has seeped so deep that the skin is completely rotten. Now, in order to grow new muscles, one has no alternative than to amputate it. If not, even if one were to cover it over with some sort of medication, I fear that the wound would not only react against the medicine but also, worse still, trigger some adverse effect. Wouldn't that stunt the little new growth that the patient has so eagerly hoped for? [48]

The reconstruction of women as New Women, is in fact a measure of racial improvement. Although these negative traits—dependency, vanity, resistance to change, and superstition—inhibit the emergence of the modern woman, the author expresses more alarm at their hereditary effect on future generations. The solution, however, is as difficult as it is contradictory, because, as the author admits, these negative traits are also distinctive social behaviors shaped by cultural forces disallowing women's access to independence and education. The author juxtaposes the idea of negative characteristics throughout the essay with an ideal woman type to be fulfilled in accordance with her natural duty (*tianzhi*). He suggests that these stubborn, negative characteristics are still correctable according to some inner capacity, despite the fact that they are no more intrinsic to women than the amorphous "natural duty" women are said to possess for their correction. Because the "resistance to change" itself is among the four undesirable traits, the call for change seems to be a failed project from the start. This, however, does not deter him from exploiting the compelling idea of "heredity" and the rhetorical force of a faulty character.

The reconstruction of the New Woman is not possible without positing an internal decay.[49] The idea of negative characteristics as something infectious to the individual as well as her children mobilizes the same fear in racial discourse. If only women themselves would recognize their inner decay, they would have no trouble embarking on a process of self-liberation. After all, the author explains, the call for liberation, though voiced passionately by both men and women these days, is a task left ultimately to women themselves. The first step toward that goal, it seems, lies in the recognition of the negative characteristics they inherently possess. The proper recognition of this inner inadequacy, oddly, becomes central to the rehabilitation of their autonomous agency. As with the Chinese national character, New Woman faces the simultaneous imperatives of both positing an irredeemable image of herself and laboring to retrieve that impossibility.

Mao Dun's 1928 short story, "Creation" (Chuangzao), bears an interesting testimony to the problems reflected in this discussion on women's characteristics eight years earlier. He writes in the preface that the short story collection *Wild Roses* (Yeqiangwei), to which "Creation" belongs, marked a turning point in his life. He had just renewed his revolutionary beliefs after a period of political disillusionment. As the resulting literary gesture, "Creation" tells the story of a woman, Xianxian, who outgrows her husband who had carefully molded her to fulfill the image of the New Woman. Taken as a Chinese Nora, Xianxian's final act of leaving her husband behind to brood over his failed project of reforming her demonstrates her newfound self. Under the rubric of love, Mao acknowledges, all five stories featuring women protagonists express ideological consciousness of class.[50] It is not difficult to see that Mao Dun invests in the New Woman an ideological significance no less distorting than the one he professes to repudiate.[51] This ambivalence, however, not only belies the strategy of using gender to advance the then-new ideology of class but also predicates itself on the conjunction between gender and the patriarchal survival of the nation. Anxieties about the New Woman as well as the Chinese national character coalesce in rhetoric as well as fantasy.

One of the little-noted scenes in "Creation" is the male protagonist Junshi's reverie on how he came to embark on the project of creating an ideal woman. His father, who died when Junshi was twenty, sternly disciplined him into harboring and realizing righteous ideals. He passed on the doctrine of "saving the nation and strengthening the race."[52] Having planned his son's future, Junshi's father, however, left incomplete his project of creating his son as an ideal type.

Replicating this "desire to create," Junshi searches for the ideal woman, a search thwarted by a series of disappointments. At the suggestion of an old schoolmate that he look for a European woman—who would much better fit Junshi's vision of a modern woman—Junshi refuses, because "a foreign woman, without the background of Chinese racial characteristics, and without the heredity of five thousand years of Chinese culture, is also not [his] ideal of a wife."[53] His ideal woman, Junshi realizes, must be created in his own image. Thus, he finds Xianxian, who is quick at learning new things and "easily influenced by her environment."[54]

Xianxian, however, also "inherited" certain habits from her father, such as a disinclination to read newspapers and an optimistic character. Concerned that her sexual modesty might be passed on to their offspring as cowardice, Junshi even sought to coach her in that respect, only to be quickly outdone by the talented novice. Once Xianxian's progress as a modern woman continues, with more success without Junshi's guidance, Junshi's last attempt to bring her once more under his influence articulates a problem of the New Woman we witnessed earlier in eugenics. Drawing an analogy from politics, Junshi explains to Xianxian: "It's like in politics: everyone talks about democracy, but that does not mean that they really want to democratize politics. It is only because everyone knows that such a concept exists. If someone who hears about it decides to take it seriously, then there is nothing but chaos."[55]

Echoing Zhou Jianren's recognition of the conceptual rather than practical appeal of women's liberation, Mao Dun's text upsets this observation by framing this very view as the enlightened male intellectual's last desperate attempt at securing a patriarchal rationale. In his solitary brooding, Junshi soon reasons that his so-called creation was no more than destruction. He had successfully uprooted Xianxian's naive optimism, but materialism took its place. He corrected the aversion she had for politics, an aversion also "inherited" from her literatus father. Instead, she has become politically extreme in her outspoken views. He destroyed her modest demeanor only to be confronted with the threatening sexual appetite that has arisen in its place.

On one level, Junshi's recognition recasts the argument put forth in "Some Negative Characteristics That the 'New Woman' Should Get Rid Of." Once the New Woman rids herself of these so-called negative characteristics, the creation of this new figure would acquire an autonomy beyond what was originally intended by her male creator. On another level, this lesson in turn makes obvious the shortcomings of the male creators Junshi and Mao Dun and their attempts to fix the problem of modernity by replacing its focus with the problem of the New Woman. This displacement is as insistent as it is convincing. As Junshi admits that Xianxian was right in telling him, "Your ideals were destroyed by your own hands," he is still confronted with an ideal he envisioned, without which Xianxian's transformation would not have been imaginable.[56] Ultimately, the reference for understanding the New Woman is unreliable but indispensable, for the Chinese Nora has to endorse the myth of her own liberation in order to seize that possibility as her own.

Apart from the complexity of deflected recognitions of new femininity, there is, however, a third level on which the question of New Woman intersects the larger issue of China's national character. Junshi's original intent in creating an ideal woman, one recalls, included the desire to create. His entire aim to create was guided by his father's unfulfilled hope in shaping Junshi for the task of national survival and racial strengthening. Yet Xianxian's surprising development not only resulted in her newfound sense of autonomy but also destroyed any expectations of her committing herself to the task of child rearing.

The fear that the New Woman could endanger racial propagation thus resurfaces once more on the topography of May Fourth discourse on women. The eugenicists' fear of modern women disinterested in motherhood returns in "Creation" as a failure of ideological persuasion. In the name of racial viability, conceptions of the ideal woman had to be adjusted accordingly. Under the careful scrutiny of male intellectuals who ostensibly seek her liberation, the discovery of her flaws stakes out a new territory for investigating and diagnosing femininity. Taking on the task of understanding and outlining her new role in a modern society, male observers are puzzled by the unpredictability that accompanies her uninhibited desires and autonomous actions.

That the forces of modernization unleashed and created behaviors that could not be explained by existing theories required intellectuals and social reformers to look elsewhere. The psychic constitution of the feminine became an appealing point of reflection for old and new social ills, especially when associated with criminality and sexual violence. In 1932, Pan Guangdan took great interest in a contemporary case of lesbian homicide.[57] The two young women involved were students at West Lake Art College in Hangzhou. The torrid love affair between Liu Wenru and Tao Sijin ended in tragedy when Tao, thrown into a jealous rage by Liu's affections for a new lover, killed her. According to friends, the two had a dramatic relationship punctuated by violent disagreements. Tao would strangle Liu with a handkerchief only to collapse later into her arms seeking reassurance.[58] Tao often tried to sabotage Liu's various involvements. Liu, on the other hand, would seduce anyone to whom Tao was attracted.

The incident caused a great sensation, especially because it was a case of "same-sex love" (*tongxinglian*). However, Pan himself does not refer to it as same-sex love but, rather, as "same-sex adultery" (*tongxingjian*).[59] During the duration of Tao's trial, members of her clan held a public meeting attended by lawyers, medical experts, politicians, and academics. After lengthy discussions, they concurred that her actions did not reflect the quality of her lineage or even her generally kind disposition. Interest in the jealous lesbian murderess reached a new height when Tao was sentenced to death by the High Court in Zhejiang. The *Evening News* opened up a special column just to publish readers' views on the incident. College students attempted to organize a "Forum on the Tao / Liu Crime of Passion" on campus. Discussions on whether "crimes of passion" (*qingsha*) were more excusable than "crimes of hate" (*chousha*) filled the "Blue Light" column of *Shishi xinbao*.

Unswayed by public sympathy, Pan himself is suspicious of the exonerability of jealous passion, perceived by some as an innocent emotion coming from love. Against the argument that same-sex love is more pure than opposite-sex love, Pan maintains the primacy of moralism, for, unlike animals, "humans practice distinctions of gender."⁶⁰ Pan thus calls for a deeper investigation into Tao's background, where he believes the blame lies. The first sign of social dysfunction (*bujianquande biaoshi*), he points out, is Tao's predisposition to "same-sex adultery." The consequent homicide only adds further perversion (*biantai*) to dysfunction.

This sensationalized affair reflects a growing fascination with female sexuality that, in its same-sex configuration, challenged the power of May Fourth rationality. The figure of the woman and the femininity she embodies are areas of undisciplined knowledge. For Pan, the perversion found in same-sex love has greater implications for understanding the angst of modern life.⁶¹ Femininity offered a reserve of psychic disorders that could explain and satisfy the question of "character," gender or racial, female or national. Of course, his conservatism sits awkwardly with the implications of female psychic disorders: while attempting to restore women to their proper traditional place, albeit enhanced by modern education, Pan is at once the social scientist eager to dispel myths and the traditional male intellectual still invested in capturing a certain "ideal" woman, even if she is expressed through dysfunction.⁶²

Both of these roles come together in Pan's interest in the life of a well-known seventeenth-century literary figure, Feng Xiaoqing (1595–1612). The life of Feng Xiaoqing as a poetess and concubine inspired Pan to write a psychoanalytical inquiry on narcissism, unlike his studies of Jews in sixth-century China and of the pedigrees of famous actors.⁶³ This was his attempt to examine the complexity of sexuality from a theoretical perspective (see Figure 5.1).⁶⁴

Xiaoqing, as Feng Xiaoqing is more generally known without a surname, was a reputedly extraordinarily talented female poet whose gift is brought all the more into striking relief in light of her unduly tragic life as a concubine in early seventeenth-century China. Since the mid-seventeenth century, it has been debated whether Xiaoqing really existed.⁶⁵ According to one of her three biographers, she was the concubine of Feng of Hangzhou. At the age of ten, Xiaoqing was able to memorize the entire *Heart Sutra*, taught to her in one sitting by an old nun. Awed by her extraordinary gift but aware of the ill fortune that may befall a woman with intelligence in such a world, the nun warned that if she wished to survive to the age of thirty, she must not educate herself in reading.

Married to Feng at the age of sixteen, Xiaoqing led an expectedly miserable life as a concubine, in no small measure due to the hostility of the principal wife. Sequestered in a family residence on Lonely Mountain, Xiaoqing led a solitary life in despair. As her only companion during this period,

FIGURE 5.1 Original illustration by Wen Yiduo for Pan Guangdan's study *Feng Xiaoqing: A Study of Narcissism*. Shanghai: Xinyue shudian, 1927.
Source: International Culture Publishing Company (Guoji wenhua chuban gongsi), Beijing.

Madame Yang once tried to persuade her to extricate herself by remarrying. Yet Xiaoqing refused on the grounds that this was her fate, as envisioned in her own inauspicious dream in which she "broke off a branch of flowers and the blossoms dropped one by one into the water."[66] Soon after Madame Yang moved away, Xiaoqing fell ill, which Pan interprets as a sign of her lesbian attachment to Yang as part of an eroticized maternal relationship.[67] Not wanting to contaminate her body, Xiaoqing refused to take medication. However, even though she was so weak that she could only sip pear juice, she attended to her makeup and clothing with great care. She even commissioned a painting of herself. Dissatisfied with the first attempt, Xiaoqing asked the painter to capture her spirit with his brush. She wanted to be captured in a state of animation, so she would get up and carry on daily activities, such as fanning the stove for making tea and looking at books and paintings. When the portrait was finally done, she offered a libation to the woman in the portrait, uttering, "Xiaoqing, Xiaoqing, I consecrate my spirit to you," and wept over her fate. At the height of her despondency, Xiaoqing died at the age of eighteen.

When Feng found her body, she was impeccably dressed in all her radiance. He then discovered a draft of a letter she had written Madame Yang. Learning all about her sufferings, he was overcome with regret, vomiting blood in his despair. Her poetry, left behind along with her first portrait, were burned by the principal wife. However, ten verses did fortuitously survive and were discovered in a barely legible state on two sheets of paper. The reason they escaped destruction was that, attesting to her self-effacing modesty, Xiaoqing had used her own written poetry as wrapping paper for someone's gift just the day before she died.

The story of Xiaoqing has been propagated in various dramas and classical prose narratives since 1624.[68] Her delicate frailty, coupled with expressive sensibilities, appealed to centuries of male literati and prompted them to both admire and sympathize with her plight. Scholars have explained this fascination as the literati's sense of frustration with their own lack of recognition and official advancement. Through the image of the tragic poetess destroyed by a cruel social environment, male literati refracted their own discontent, elevating them to a new level of unjust female suffering.

Other female personas such as He Shuangqing (b. 1715) and Liu Rushi (1617–64), who have had similar legends built around their lives of great misfortune and talent, continue to exert a powerful force over the cultural imagination of suffering women. The legibility of the feminine is problematized on both the metaphorical and literal levels. The testimony to Xiaoqing's tragic existence is conveniently captured in the perilous survival of her poetry. He Shuangqing, whose legend resembles that of Xiaoqing, is reputed to have written her verses with powder on cassia leaves.[69] The precarious verses they composed, preserved in fragments and ruination, testified equally to the ephemeral existence these tragic poetesses led. The solitude in which they quietly expressed their talents and their tenuous evidence, salvaged under the most accidental and miraculous circumstances, underscores both the impenetrability and the importance of recovering their lost legibility.

Pan's particular interest in Xiaoqing, however, reveals a different aspect of this enterprise. At the same time that women are seen in a new light, empowered by access to education and new autonomy, the consequences of centuries of tradition find new expression in the vocabulary of modern psychoses, especially in the realm of sexuality. Ten years before the lesbian homicide case, Pan was already deeply invested in inquiring into female psychological abnormalities that lead to destructive behavior. In 1922, he published his psychoanalytical study of Xiaoqing. Revealingly, he does not question the falsity of her existence but disputes the details of her biography, using a scientific logic drawn from the psychoanalysis of Freud and his contemporary Trigant Burrow (1875–1950). For example, he classifies Xiaoqing's various habits as those of a narcissist, citing parallels from Greek mythology. Xiaoqing's penchant for talking to her own shadow when alone and excessive attention to cleanliness even in a state of grave illness suggest to Pan that she takes herself as the loved object. Strangely, Pan uses details from the myth of Xiaoqing to refute the myth itself, as he earnestly argues that it is not possible for her to have had the coterie of male literati around her, as was recorded in certain versions of her biography. Her narcissism clearly excludes normal social interactions with men. Had she been able to maintain such interactions, Pan repeatedly emphasizes, she would not have suffered a psychosexual disorder.

Taking as his point of departure the familiar association of women with narcissism and dementia, Pan, however, is more interested in how a theory of narcissism explains the workings of same-sex love, the same issue preoccupying him in the lesbian homicide case. The precise nature of Xiaoqing's psychosexual disorder, Pan ultimately concludes, traces a thwarted trajectory toward healthy heterosexuality. Pan takes Xiaoqing's refusal to remarry, as stated in her letter to Madame Yang, as an acknowledgment of her own inability to successfully cope with a heterosexual (*yixinglian*) environment.[70] The trauma that precipitated her departure from the expected trajectory, Pan believes, stems from both her sexual prematurity in relation to Feng and her long-term isolation from any kind of sexual gratification thereafter. Ultimately, Pan returns to the problem of sex education in China as the key to improving the quality of the Chinese race. Society's lack of interest in investigating sexual perversions has left uncorrected female disorders such as lesbianism and, consequently, the deterioration of traditional social institutions such as marriage, family, and reproduction, all of which bear on a nation's survival.

Rather than build a eugenic society on the ideals of beauty and open sexuality, Pan's idea of social restructuring is to investigate and rectify physical and mental deformities. Whereas Zhang Jingsheng idealizes women as ambassadors of grace and beauty in promoting peace and well-being, Pan sees them as psychosexually complex subjects in need of not so much liberation as reform. Women who "do not have the understanding of society and who do not know how to adjust themselves or find ways of moderating themselves are truly regrettable."[71] The same concern leads Pan to emphasize the need to investigate Tao's psychological background. For Pan, a healthy sexual development would have discouraged complete narcissism and same-sex attraction or a regression of object-libido. Proper education for women (*nüzu jiaoyu*) would lead to the decline in same-sex love and promote, instead, a healthy heterosexual development. A possible perversion can be preempted by the indoctrination of normalcy.

In many ways, "Creation" provides the literary counterpart to Pan's concern with women's reform and education. Mao Dun's Xianxian represents the ideal modern woman who does not conform to the original inspiration of the male mentorship. The scenario of the perfectly educated woman may be too perfect for its male visionaries, ultimately exposing their own inadequacies. Although Pan or Mao Dun may attribute the problem of femininity to either male or social expectations, the interior topography of femininity reveals its own restraints and dilemmas in the writings of women writers. If "Creation" exemplifies the thwarted male project of creating the ideal woman, an inspiration shared by sexologists and eugenicists alike, one might seek recourse and dialogue in the works of women writers such as Ding Ling and Xiao Hong. However, instead of a defiant counternarrative, articulations of femininity often speak in a double voice, distant from subversive intentions.

Femininity Without Nation

Critical attempts to reclaim a female tradition in May Fourth literature have focused on revising the literary historiography established by male feminist intellectuals such as Mao Dun or Ye Shengtao.[72] As two scholars have recently pointed out, however, the initial male proprietorship of feminist discourse is not uncommon in other national literatures.[73] The challenge to understanding women's literature in the modern period is perhaps not an exercise in intervention but a reflection on complicity. Whether they are writing tales of oppression or of self-liberation, prominent women writers in China in the 1920s and 1930s claim suffering as a condition. Although variously assigned to political, revolutionary, and social consequences, bitter suffering remains the fate most intimate to women's lives. Its invocation somehow retrieves a sense of authenticity from which no woman escapes.[74] The culpability of masculinity or nationalism has been set up as an indispensable negative to feminine "authenticity."

Recent studies of women writers patronized by May Fourth male nationalist historiography have made great contributions in shifting the focal point away from the requirements of nationalism.[75] Writers such as Ding Ling, Bai Wei, Xie Bingying, Lu Yin, Shi Pingmei, and Xiao Hong are examined in their personal rather than revolutionary voices, as the feminine experience is regrounded in the maternal body rather than war, private memory instead of patriotic allegiance. Few scholars have, however, ventured to understand femininity as something that may desire to appropriate, rather than to cast off, the structure of suffering. Indeed, the interpellation of nationalistic ideology is also imbued with a feminine voice that speaks back without speaking in expected symmetry. As a profound testimony to female writers' sense of self, the desire for self-vigilance at the price of psychological pain complicates our understanding of their feminist discourse in several ways. The ostensible limitation placed on the female voice can no longer be simply attributed to, nor subversively disengaged from, masculinity, paternalism, or nationalism.

How a discourse can be inhabited by the same desire but for different ends is a difficult question to disentangle. We are asked to understand a female identity in suffering without having to concede to masculinity or nation as its oppressor or liberator. Yet, without having to foreclose any possibilities, this difficulty also allows us to interrogate masculinity and nation as categories vulnerable in themselves to the formulation of femininity. In the same way, the female body is neither exclusively subjugated nor required to give up its relation to the nation in order to be reclaimed. A consideration of how suffering can be a desired condition can give rise to a parallel examination of how domination is inhabited by its own vulnerability. To this end, the following analysis demonstrates how the torments of femininity, as expressed in Ding Ling's and Xiao Hong's works, reinforce the necessity of a self-imposed sacrifice that underlies the literary figuration of national allegiance. Their literary articulations show how, unlike Zhang Jingsheng's or Pan Guangdan's understanding of what would grant women their liberty, the restriction of feminine agency in many ways enables the real possibility for its own voice. Female suffering can inhabit subjugation in such a way as to preserve rather than sacrifice agency.[76]

Market Street (Shanshi jie) was published only eight months after Xiao Hong's most well-known novel, *Field of Life and Death,* written during her stay in Qingdao in 1934.[77] A collection of forty-one semiautobiographical essays, *Market Street* documents the life of poverty that Xiao Hong shared with her lover, the writer Xiao Jun, in Harbin between 1932 and 1934, just before their escape from the Japanese occupation in northeastern China.[78] *Market Street* focuses on a private narrative of female suffering without the presence of nation. Unlike *Field of Life and Death, Market Street* does not insert the female body into the national topography of war. It does, however, demonstrate in an important way how the physicality of suffering is inseparable from a psychological reflection on femininity. In this way, *Market Street* already sets out the crucial terms of suffering that later make possible the application of the nationalistic metaphor in critics' reception of *Field of Life and Death.* On one level, hunger, loss, and poverty are expressed as a physical deprivation to which both lovers are subjected. On another level, however, this physical hardship is internalized as a recognition particular to the female narrator. The psychic pain she extrapolates from bodily suffering is coextensive with her sober recognition of femininity.

Howard Goldblatt, Xiao Hong's biographer and translator, observes that the "self-demeaning" female narrator repeatedly forgives the male character Langhua, despite his excesses and male-centered selfishness.[79] Indeed, the text itself gives ample evidence of a repeating drama of selfish acts, ensuing guilt, and passive forgiveness. Tolerance for transgression, very much at the center of their relationship, becomes a token of love. The more the female narrator endures, the more absolving proves her love. Moreover, her sacrifice is always taken for granted. For example, we watch, as she does passively, Langhua devouring the few scraps of food they manage to buy on a meager and irregular income. He remarks on his own selfishness in eating her share of the food, while avariciously putting it in his mouth. She imagines his mouth to be an abyss into which objects—including herself—disappear, a theme that continues to resurface throughout the narrative.[80] Victimization figures as a crucial element in the relationship between the masculine subject and the female body in Xiao Hong's works. However, also embedded in the scene of victimization is a hidden logic of feminine agency:

> The cold air he had brought in with him gave off a rank odor. Drops of water dripped off his nose every once in a while as he ate the bread. "Come and have some!" "I'll be right there." I took the toothbrush mug downstairs to get some water. When I got back, about the only thing left of the bread was the hard outer crust. He quickly said, "I really ate fast. How could I have eaten so fast? Boy, am I selfish. Men sure are selfish." I handed him the mug filled with water. He wasn't going to eat any more. I told him to go ahead, but he refused. "I've

had enough," he said. "I'm full. I've already eaten your half; isn't that enough? Men are no good; they're only interested in themselves. Since you've just gotten well you should get enough to eat." He chatted on about wanting to open a "school" where he could teach martial arts and also teach a little of this and that. As he told me all this he was reaching for the crust. Then his other hand moved into action and, before he knew it, he had twisted off another piece, put it into his mouth, and swallowed it. He reached out again, but this time he said, "I shouldn't eat any more. I've had enough already." His cap was still on his head, so I reached over and took it off for him, putting another piece of bread crust into his mouth at the same time. When he drank the water, it was the same thing all over—he didn't hand any to me until I asked him. . . . On the following day, the bread-filled basket was waiting for me out in the corridor. But this time I didn't open the door. Other people were out there buying bread from him. Even with the door closed I thought I could still smell the fragrance of wheat. I began to be frightened by the bread. It wasn't that I wanted to eat any. I was afraid that the bread would swallow me up.[81]

Langhua carries out his acts of transgression with remorseful confessions. The female narrator, however, neither condemns nor despises his acts. She does not respond with an acceptance of his guilt. Instead, she acquiesces to the acts by voluntarily surrendering the remaining scrap of bread crust that would have been hers. She offers him water without being the least surprised that the same selfish scenario would happen "all over again." The cycle of transgression completed, her sacrifices return to persecute her. The nourishment she was deprived of now frightens her into further renunciation. The bread, now embodying the masculine imperative of her self-sacrifice, threatens to "swallow" her if she does not renounce it voluntarily.

However, missing from this scene is the specificity of oppression. The female narrator observes Langhua's actions, as though they were expected to happen in just that way, repeatedly and without a surprise outcome. She anticipates his moves by filling the mug with water before he asks for it, taking off his cap without his order, and giving him that last piece of bread before he could make another apologetic gesture. The more he acknowledges his selfishness in taking, the more she gives. She responds to demands with disciplined renunciation and gives her renunciation before he even voices the demand. Langhua, a constant source of distress to her existence, compounds rather than creates this willingness for renunciation. Just as her renunciation requires no outside authority, the loss that structures her psychic identity takes no comfort in fulfillment. She likes putting herself in Langhua's clothes, which hang loosely on her, a vacuity accentuated by her ill and frail body. He jeers at her resemblance to a "pocket," and she agrees. Moments of her imaginative reveries inevitably return to the themes of disembodiment, unfulfillment, and emptiness. Yet she is also most at home in the state of deprivation, as not its victim but possessor. She seeks not an escape from but an extension of this condition as the primal metaphor of her sense of being a woman.

As much as hunger signifies a deprivation suffered by both Langhua and the female narrator, it carries an additional meaning for her. The experience of hunger diverges from its physicality when the female narrator displaces it as a psychological event. In one scene in which she chases after Langhua to find out when he will return home, disappointment and loneliness envelop her as she remarks, "Although I'm eating the sesame cakes, it is as though I would collapse from hunger."[82] Hunger, apart from its persistent thematization throughout the narrative as lack of means for livelihood, figures as an intangible deprivation for the female narrator.

Within the event of suffering and deprivation, the female experience thus occurs on two different registers. Her reflection on her pain enables a space for self-consciousness not available in the physicality of pain. For her, pain embodies not an externally inflicted loss but a sustaining condition of female consciousness. In her moments of utmost destitution and solitude, we witness also the sobriety of her self-awareness. Hence she often describes her moments of physical pain as though she were detached from her body. The severance of pain from corporeality occasions less a sublimation of her suffering than a return to her own reflection. The ostensible figure of oppression, Langhua, is not its source but an exteriorized refiguration of her intimate sense of impossible fulfillment:

> After we returned home, I used what rice was left to make a pot of gruel. With no salt, no oil, no vegetables, all we could do was warm our stomachs a little. But even that didn't help. We heated some water and poured it into a cookie tin, but it leaked. Langhua tried to fill a glass bottle with the hot water, so that I could drink it and warm up a bit, but as soon as he poured it in, the bottom of the bottle fell off, spilling the contents all over the floor. He picked up the bottomless bottle and blew into it like a horn. With the tooting sound from the bottle ringing in my ears, I lay down on the ice-cold bed.[83]

The abdominal pain that had plagued the female narrator at the beginning returns. This time, however, hunger is reinforced as a condition irremediable by external means. The male subject, Langhua, again fails in his task of offering her fulfillment. Whereas previously he could only apologetically take her share of the food, this time he completely misses the significance of fulfillment to her. He blows into the bottomless bottle like a horn, as though that substitution—the most that he can offer—could somehow give her relief. His attempt at filling it with water proves futile. More important, this failure shows how his role as her masculine protector inadequately addresses her suffering.

Interestingly, the female narrator invests in Langhua precisely this inflated image of the male subject. Despite his repeated failure, she continues to rely on him, as though he had all the answers she needed. This is particularly striking in how she quietly listens to his criticism of her unscientific or irrational thinking, or how he laughs at her childish remarks and patronizes her. She seeks from him something he can neither accomplish nor know, for he represents merely an expression and not the center of her consciousness of loss. She ostensibly relies on the male subject for making that loss good. However, his parodic effort in the end bespeaks a masculinity that fails to understand that a woman's loss is not arrogated to his doing. Her sacrifice is not for him, just as his compensation proves inadequate for her. Feminine agency lies in the fact that it does not need to be a response or reaction to the requirements of masculinity. Subjugation itself is neither fatal nor complete. In female suffering, as articulated by Xiao Hong, the exercise of agency remains a real and practiced possibility. The assumption that this suffering can only be the evidence of subjugation, however, seems in every way crucial to the imagining of a hyperinvested authority such as the nation. Against this inflated image, not only feminine but also masculine subjects are measured. Under such demands, as we will see, the possibility of self-preservation lies in the desire for masochism and renunciation, the desire for failure.

Disciplining Femininity

Xiao Hong's embodiment of the female in suffering has been commemorated both in literary and nationalistic discourse.[84] Unlike her, Ding Ling has been received with a different sort of enthusiasm. Consistently outspoken against the conflation of politics with women, Ding Ling's work has been canonized, in many ways, as the vanguard of women's literature in modern China. Her defiant female literary heroines subvert male-centered desires and reappropriate the female body from objectification.

This assessment of Ding Ling's heroines, however, has not been able to extricate itself from reinforcing the primacy of oppression as a limiting experience. Precluded from view is an articulation of femininity against internal, not external, opposition. This is particularly important because masculinity and nation are, after all, not the only imperatives femininity tries to defy. The price of femininity must be understood as a consequence both of the domination of power and of a kind of self-discipline contributing to an assertion of autonomy. Reclaimed in a moment not of liberation but inward discipline, the emphasis of agency can fall on overcoming oneself rather than defying outside opposition. In this way, literary expressions of femininity, with their focus on the inner conflicts of female protagonists, reveal the complexity of fighting against the self. These articulations demonstrate how extrication from external demands entails the more difficult task of forcing discipline upon oneself as a kind of recuperative agency.

Missing from contemporary accounts of women's emancipation, through racial improvement or cultivation of principles of "beauty," is the acknowledgment that this reflexive exercise of self-renunciation defines femininity somewhere between liberation and imprisonment. The character of femininity creates not a corrective task incumbent upon social reformers and sexual liberators but an inner space of continual self-struggle. Even if working against itself, female identity does not necessarily find its desired articulation under the guidelines for its emancipation. In this regard, in Pan's disapproval of the same-sex choice that he takes as the source of the case of lesbian homicide, he fails to understand the spectrum of female behavior independent of heterosexual desire. Ding Ling's canonical work, "Miss Sophie's Diary" (Shafei nüshi de riji), on the other hand, demonstrates how the triumph of female agency resides in the sustaining struggle of self-renunciation, for which no triumph can be ultimately claimed.

"Miss Sophie's Diary" has been heralded, more than any other literary text by women writers of the May Fourth era, as an exemplary text for a feminist critique of male ideology.[85] Despite frequent revisitations, however, its double articulation that critiques feminist reading itself has remained largely outside the scope of analysis. At times, the text is mobilized to demonstrate the difficult feat in constructing an unprecedented image of the New Woman. Sophie answers, however ambivalently, the call for a Chinese Nora such as Mao Dun's Xianxian, who, upon leaving the confines of domestic space, must still find a way to resolve the problem of her identity in a society little accustomed to the idea of female autonomy.[86] The inner torments suffered by Sophie testify to her insistence on actively participating in the making of her own desires.

This torment is central to her assertion of selfhood. In many ways, the agony of femininity in "Miss Sophie's Diary" commemorates the oppressive burden of patriarchy borne by female subjects. Torment embodies the condition from which the modern woman seeks liberation. At the same time, her will to survive is also measured against her suffering, even though suffering itself is the condition to be undone. The torment of the female subject becomes, then, a condition she can claim as neither completely subjugating nor self-willed. Her agency is intimately bound up with bondage. In this way, the absence of domination, even if that were possible, would not guarantee her autonomy. One could argue that this paradox itself is a further production of the power of ideological subordination. I suggest, however, that the predicament is also interpretive. It confronts us with a different articulation of agency, one that does not claim a glorified sense of sovereignty. In a way that compels us to rethink the significance of meaning-making subjects, "Miss Sophie's Diary" grapples with just such an unrecognized notion of self.

The first entry in "Miss Sophie's Diary" already demonstrates the ambivalence and torment that have come to define Ding Ling's narrator. Every day gives new occasions for Miss Sophie to get upset. She tires of reading newspapers, because every reported incident fills her with disgust. She resents that there are no fresh "complaints and dissatisfactions" to infuriate her.[87] She adamantly refuses to be responsible for Weidi's devotion to her, for she thinks that a woman should have the prerogative to act heartlessly toward her suitors, even be bored and repelled by them: "I act as a woman is supposed to act."[88] She wonders, out of no small measure of self-pity, why her friends and relatives would be devoted to her, even though there is nothing to love except her arrogance, difficult disposition, and tubercular condition. Repelled by their words of comfort, she laments, "Those are the times that I wish I had someone who really understood. Even if he reviled me, I'd be proud and happy."[89] When no one comes to see her, however, she feels abandoned and angry.

In one way, Sophie's frustration stems from her need for both adoration and the independence defined by the absence of that need. In a different way, however, her desire is structured precisely by such a simultaneous repulsion from the sources of comfort, including herself. She reviles herself for desiring. As a result, desiring becomes reviling, giving gratification through rejection. She idealizes the person who truly understands her as the one who would know when to reproach her and thus make her "proud and happy." She is not looking for someone who would fulfill what she ostensibly desires but one who would make her feel inadequate for his desire.

The same ambivalent self-relation plays out in her relation to Weidi, her loyal suitor, whom she pities and feels unworthy of at the same time: "Don't love a woman so undeserving of your attention as I am."[90] Unworthy as she professes to be, however, she continues to show her contempt for his inexhaustible patience and affection as a way of asserting her worth as a woman. The success of her desire depends on how much she can keep it within bounds. This discipline against herself becomes the game by which she rejects and embraces the man she falls for, Ling Jishi:

> I haven't invited Ling Jishi over, either; and although he's asked several times how things are going now that I've moved, I've pretended not to get the hint and just smile back. It's like planning a battle. Now I'm concentrating all my energy on strategy. *I want something, but I'm not willing to go and take it. I must find a tactic that gets it offered to me voluntarily.* I understand myself completely. *I am a thoroughly fe-*

male woman, and women concentrate everything on the man they've got in their sights. I want to possess him. I want unconditional surrender of his heart. I want him kneeling down in front of me, begging me to kiss him. I'm delirious. I go over and over the steps I must take to implement my scheme. I've lost my mind.[91] (emphasis added)

Ling Jishi, who turns out to be a rather unremarkable and shallow man, is the source of Sophie's torment. Although she attributes the impediment to the fulfillment of her desire to the conventions of society, the greater obstacle lies in herself. Societal expectations and her stringent self-demands form two different levels of discipline. By exacting from herself the demand for renunciation, she acquires a position of defiance in regard to social norms. However, even this act of defiance relies on an internalized enforcement of sacrifice for the sake of social norms. The external forces of a perceived male-dominated society do not inhabit her entirely. Reclaiming that power over herself, she internalizes the relation of domination and subjugation within her.

Strikingly, for a literary heroine whose defiance has been equated with her unabashed expressions of desire, Sophie is remarkably inefficient at obtaining the desired object. Instead of taking what she wants, which is within her capacity to do, she opts for a more circuitous, "tactical" way of strategizing and planning. Even when there are no obvious obstacles standing in her way, she erects a different order of rationed gratification, the end result of which is always her own frustration. As we learn from one of her friends, Yufang, Ling Jishi is not at all the unscrupulous masculine beast Sophie tries to tame or should be tormented by. Yet obsessed with implementing a laborious scheme in which the man would be ultimately won then recast as a dangerous, prodigal womanizer, she imagines the masculine threat by which she would be victimized. Interestingly, creating this scheme is the only way for her to feel that she is in complete control. Mirroring this projection, her confidence in understanding herself so well is actually a tautological prescription of what it means to act like a woman. The "self" she thinks she understands contradictorily emerges as the self that is "a thoroughly womanly woman" (*nüxing shizu de nüren*). Her true interest lies not in the pursuit of a man who can fulfill her but in the desire to painstakingly figure out what it means to embody real femininity.

In fact, Sophie's obsession with what it means to be a "womanly woman" introduces a duplicity within femininity itself. Her torment over her own female identity, in this light, points less to the external restraints of society than to an inner uncertainty. If being a woman does not guarantee femaleness, then implied in Sophie's melancholic suffering is the alternative of being an unwomanly woman. Interestingly, when she first meets Ling Jishi, she filters her impression through the eyes of another man, Yunlin, Yufang's boyfriend whom Sophie treats as a brother: "Yunlin looked so insignificant and clumsy by comparison. . . . Pity overwhelmed me. How painful Yunlin would find his own coarse appearance and rude behavior, if he could see himself. I wonder what Yufang feels when she compares the two, one tall, the other not." [92]

Processed from different perspectives, Sophie's reflection traverses several layers of identification. She imagines Yunlin and Ling Jishi as two male contenders trying to win over female desire. She identifies, however, more readily with Yunlin's sense of inadequate masculinity than with Yufang's female viewpoint, as she assumes Yunlin's comparative unattractiveness as her own in a shared feeling of shame and insignificance. Against Ling Jishi's embodiment of masculine plenitude, Sophie judges her own inadequacy as both a masculine and female subject. The wish that if only "[Yunlin] could see himself" diverts that desire to see *herself*, for her desire is always doomed to a sense of disappointment and renunciation. To imagine Yunlin's felt detriment at the sight of the handsome Ling Jishi, for Sophie, implies seeing herself in his place as the one tormented by an impossible ideal of sexual identity. Finally, Sophie "wonders" what this comparison might mean for another female spectator, Yufang, in whose eyes the perceived incongruity between the two men indicates the perspective of female desire, a field of vision oddly inaccessible to Sophie herself. Further demonstrating her uncomfortable placement, she is the one inserted into the triangle as the object of female desire, as she empathizes with the sense of inadequacy the male subject must suffer at the recognition of his disappointing masculinity. In the final analysis, Sophie's secret torment seems to be whether she embodies the femininity desirable for a woman.

Sophie's habit of stopping herself short of obtaining the male object she wants suggests that she desires a different object. In her obsession with how to act like a woman capable of fulfilling and manipulating men, Sophie makes little effort to act like one at all. She chastises herself for behaving in a way that no "decent woman" would. The criteria by which she reviles herself conveniently distract her from becoming precisely the woman she clearly does not want to be. The fact that she never successfully behaves quite like a proper woman in relation to men ensures that she will never have to become one in relation to male desire. Sophie's struggle with what it means to be a "womanly woman" seems to be a task of evasion rather than embodiment.

The figure of Yunjie, Sophie's former schoolmate, becomes pivotal in this consideration. Yunjie is mentioned in two of Sophie's journal entries. Through Sophie's record of Yunjie's letters to her, we learn of her increasing destitution after marrying someone with whom she shares little emotional intimacy:

> Today I received a letter from Yunjie in Shanghai that has plunged me into a deep depression. How will I ever find the right words to comfort her? In her letter, she said, "My life, my love are meaningless now." Meaning, I suppose, that she has less need than ever for my condolences or tears shed for her. I can imagine from her letter that married life has been like even though she doesn't spell it out in detail. Why does God play tricks on people in love like her? Yunjie is a very emotional and passionate person, so it's not surprising that she finds her husband's growing indifference, his badly concealed pretense at affection unbearable.[93]

Yunjie's unhappy fate confirms for Sophie the kind of suspicious and cynical view she herself has of marriage. Ostensibly, to escape from this fate that constitutes the suffering of women, Sophie refuses to give in to her desires. Men and their affections are certain to disappoint, and Sophie sets them up in her own mind to fulfill just such a function. Presumably, she never wrote Yunjie back. Our next news of Yunjie is her death, which Sophie records in her diary twenty days later. This temporal lapse also coincides with Sophie's own brush with death. As though echoing Yunjie's passing, she was herself hospitalized for a tubercular attack.

The presence of Yunjie in "Miss Sophie's Diary" barely occupies the margins of a plot driven by a "modern" woman's daring trysts with men. Yunjie's silent role, however, structures Sophie's response to men in important ways. We are never given a description of what their relationship was like. Her two appearances in the diary indicate that she was, at least at one point, an important person in Sophie's life. If this was Ding Ling's attempt to complicate the different aspects of female desire in order to offer a subversive challenge to legitimate, heterosexual, male-centered love, it nonetheless carries a specific purpose in the story. For Sophie, the mournful loss of a close female companion fundamentally metaphorizes her relation to heterosexual love. The disciplined renunciation she so intently exercises on herself attests to both the loss of female bondage and the inadequacy of masculine love. This double relation most obviously plays out in her treatment of the young, sentimental Weidi.

As her most devoted admirer, Weidi brims with tenderness and sentimentality. Whereas Sophie forces herself to smile whenever she feels hurt or sad, Weidi feels little restraint in expressing his feelings. Sophie sees in him her polar opposite in disposition and strength. Expressing the emotions Sophie denies herself, Weidi often cries liberally in front of her to express his pain at her continual rejection of his affections. As though keeping his company just to prove the consistency of his shortcomings, Sophie shares her private writings with Weidi at two pivotal junctures in the narrative. Upon reading Yunjie's letter, Weidi could only sob uncontrollably, something Sophie then contemptuously attributes to "the only thing instinct gives him leave to do."[94] These are the tears, however, Sophie herself finds difficult to shed for her loss. Interestingly, Sophie's disappointment with love is displaced onto Weidi, as he is shown in all his helplessness. Sophie "watch[es] him impassively as his eyes turned red" and "taunt[s] him with a cruel running commentary on his little crying jag."[95] The cruelty, however, seems more intended for herself for not being able to register the death of Yunjie.

The male subject becomes the passive point of deflection for both Sophie's desire and her femaleness. In a later entry, Sophie reveals that the reason she had begun writing a diary at all was because of Yunjie. Sophie wants to continue writing as an act of commemoration. This diary, Sophie remarks, holds something intimate to her, and she wishes it to be read by no one besides Yunjie and herself. Against this professed privacy, however, she decides on one occasion to show it to Weidi under the pretext of giving him one more chance at understanding her. If he were to pass the test, Sophie thought to herself, then she would embrace and kiss him, and "become the most beloved, beautiful woman in the world, *the woman of his desires*."[96] Of course, Weidi expectedly fails yet again:

> Weidi read through the pages once. Then once again. All the while he remained self-composed despite tears. I had not anticipated this.
> "Do you understand me," I said.
> He nodded.
> "Do you believe me?"
> "Concerning what?"
> Finally, his nod made sense. . . . Weidi was afraid that I'd thought he's not fully understood me, so he burst out, "You love him. You love him! I'm not good enough for you." I nearly tore the dairy to pieces out of spite. I'd debased it by letting Weidi see it—how could I claim otherwise?[97]

As though she wants him to fail, Sophie shares her most private writing with the person least likely to understand her. Weidi, after all, has consistently misread her at every turn. Yet Sophie makes a solemn occasion out of a moment that she knows full well will be desecrated. She relies on failed masculinity in order to defer indefinitely the image of the perfect woman of male desire. Masculinity thus inadvertently facilitates Sophie's escape from having to desire heterosexuality at all. She thereby preserves the intimacy she shares with Yunjie by offering it most nakedly to the male eye. It is not surprising that Weidi fails to read her, but where he fails, the narrative possibility of femininity recommits itself. For Weidi, the letters could only convey a male object for Sophie's desire, as he cries, "You love *him*!" He could not see the possibility of a female love choice for Sophie, for whom his jealousy bespeaks the blindsight of masculinity. Finally, she nearly tears up the diary, destroying the legibility that cannot be read by him in any case.

Sophie's attempted escape from femaleness underlies her stringent self-discipline. The renunciation she repeatedly imposes on herself accesses a venue for escaping the demands of femaleness. In the same way, her continual torment of unfulfillment offers the only way out of the prescribed commitment to an idealized, self-assured image of the "modern" woman who has to fulfill all the expectations of an ideological novelty. The more she fails to normalize to this vision, the more normalization becomes a vision of failure. Indeed, in "Miss Sophie's Diary," the ambivalence so well recognized in Ding Ling's female character does not merely reflect the conflict between the old and the new, oppression and self-awakening. It also maintains a critical distance from the promise of modernity to restore femininity's authentic voice.

In this light, an examination of femininity can move beyond the usual conceptions of subjugation. Neither masculinity nor femininity enjoys the possession of plenitude; masculinity is a demand from which male subjects also seek relief. How does one, then, distinguish femininity at work in absence of any easy source of oppression—such as patriarchy—against which it can rise in subversion? There are clearly narratives, literary or social, that assert other kinds of femininity—or what it means to be a "womanly woman"—and invest just as much in the identities of women. Lesbianism or female same-sex love offers only one of these expressions.[98] Even within same-sex love, there are different possibilities of attachment and allegiance. Subjects' discipline against their own desires presents a complicated scenario of identification, for which the assignation of sex can provide only a partial answer.

"Miss Sophie's Diary" provides an apt example of the easily missed tension within subjugation of femininity. The ostensible source of domination lies in neither invulnerable masculinity nor external oppression. Apart from the burden of male desire, there remains the more haunting question of knowing one's own desire. Sophie shows how the latter demand is constituted and negotiated in self-discipline and self-renunciation, whereas Xiao Hong's female protagonist provides a narrative of strength above and beyond the tale of female suffering.

The ideological battles over the figure of the New Woman not only renewed the examination into her social role but also laid claim to her psychic constitution. Zhang Jingsheng's society of beauty relied on the external poise of the feminine figure and focused almost exclusively on her physical attractiveness. Suggestions for her autonomous existence in society entailed mainly her greater accessibility to make herself more desirable. Pan Guang-dan, on the other hand, sought to rehabilitate her through an explanation of her inner life, measured against her lack of socialization with men. In this view, her withdrawal from normalized life can be explained only by her deranged choice of same-sex love. Instead of mapping her psychic life according to the exactions of masculinity or social expectations, Xiao Hong and Ding Ling, however, rewrote the interiority of female identity as, first and foremost, the place of alternative agency.

Beneath her docile surface amenable to inscription, the modern woman is as illegible to the male writer as she is tormented by her own will to transparent meaning. Femininity remains elusive of diagnosis, just as masculinity is uncertain of itself. Nonetheless, the ideological contestations, utopian fantasies, and literary narratives surrounding the modern woman reveal her ineluctable hold on the imagination of the modern. Furthermore, she seems indispensable to the definition of masculinity, as she will be once again brought into the constitution of male identity in its own search for expression in masochism and nationalism.

6

Community of Expiation:
Confessions, Masochism, and Masculinity

YU DAFU, MORE THAN any other writer of the May Fourth generation, enjoys the notoriety of indulging in graphic sexuality, sexual perversions, and
excessive sentimentality in his writings. His contemporary, the celebrated
poet Xu Zhimo (1896–1931), once compared his literary works to the unsightly sores on a leper who wails incessantly about them in order to draw
attention to himself. Often singled out as a promoter of moral debauchery,
Yu, however, belongs to a generation of influential male writers and, later,
revolutionaries whose early writings disclose a kind of masculinity not readily acknowledged in literary or political historiography. The ostensible de-
pravities that the male protagonists of these short stories often engage in give
an unsettling expression of masculinity and nationalism articulated in seeking pleasure in physical punishment. This often-dismissed exhibitionist behavior, however, underlies an important way of exploring national identity
when it is thought to be defunct. It suggests that one's allegiance to the nation entails a sense of personal inadequacy and that such a correspondence is
somehow brought about in the psychic register.

Intellectuals of the May Fourth generation did not just use literary language to articulate this fraught relationship between masculinity and nationalism. Many laid claim to the knowledge of psychoanalysis, which at the
time provided a new venue for delving into the private psyche of the modern individual. While Pan Guangdan was translating and studying Havelock
Ellis's works on social pathologies and perversions, Zhang Jingsheng was reputedly the first to translate Freud's *The Interpretation of Dreams*. Unlike the
social scientists and utopian philosophers, however, Chinese fiction writers
encountered the perversions theorized in psychoanalysis in a more intimate

way. Their involvement was less analytical than inventive, for they sought to incorporate a theoretical model into literary creations bearing their personal imprints. Psychoanalysis was not merely a Western theory popular for its novelty. Writers risked and confronted their own sense of moralism and perversions in their engagement with theories of sexual repression. Their literary use of psychoanalytical categories such as dream analysis, free association, paternal authority, fantasy, fetishism, repression, maternal fixation, or desire veils only a deeper preoccupation with expressing a culture of confronting objects of repulsion in oneself as well in others.

Reflecting this troubled sense of the modern self, Lu Xun's attempt to use psychoanalytical concepts to revamp the classical Chinese tale of original creation in "Mending the Sky" (Butian) ended in a frustration he himself has difficulty explaining. Guo Moruo, who ventured deeper into dream analysis and persevered through an entire short story, "Late Spring" (Canchun), was still dissatisfied with his literary excavation of the unconscious. He also regretted having too facilely appropriated the clinical concept of "pathological associations" in his psychoanalytical reinterpretation of Qu Yuan in the play *Xianglei* (Woes on River Xiang).[1] Even though they read about wish-fulfillment and the unconscious, Oedipal complex and sexual repression, male writers explored a different psychic topography in their works. The perversion they chose to exemplify was masochism.

The perception of the nation's failure as an object of allegiance is confirmed and reenacted on a literary level as a masculinity plagued with the inner torments of masochism. The excision of cancerous sores, a favorite metaphor for curing national and even feminine characters, gives way to images of self-laceration in the works of Yu Dafu and Guo Moruo. The nationalistic metaphor of cutting away poisonous sores from the racialized body turns into a literary masochism of cutting into oneself. In this way, masochistic suffering deepens the problem of interior life with the uncertain articulation of masculine identity, as national failure becomes indistinguishable from a sense of personal and sexual failure. Whereas eugenics locates national degeneration in the diseased racial body, male masochism in literature expresses the difficulty in loving the nation in individuals' tormented inner lives. "Dissecting" the national soul carries both a physical and psychological imperative, as male protagonists pursue physical ruination as the only psychically real way to experience the nation's demise.

Even though the portrayal of sexual perversions by Yu Dafu was at the time reprimanded by staunch defenders of May Fourth's new morality, the significance of the literary phenomenon of male masochism has remained largely outside critical scrutiny. It is striking, for example, that sexual perversions invite strong criticism of Yu's stories, yet they are silently tolerated in Guo Moruo's works. Guo's later political stature in Communist China has erased this earlier literary anomaly, even though these works were composed in the same period as "Goddess," Guo's most celebrated and pioneering contribution to modern poetry. The heroism built around Yu's death in the underground resistance to the Japanese in Sumatra during World War II also disconnects his earlier literary preoccupation from the valor of political martyrdom. Retrospectively, the early 1920s, when most of these young male writers made their debut, is seen as a period of emotional confusion and personal exploration. The preoccupation with themes of sexuality and homoeroticism, when acknowledged, is often explained away as experimentation.[2]

This chapter argues, instead, that this excess of sentimentality, configured as guilt and masochism, constitutes an important part of the experience of a national identity and literary community. My discussion departs from the familiar terrain of Chinese literary historiography on male writers. It does not trace their experimentation with Western psychoanalytical theories as a kind of one-way importation, nor does it limit itself to either an acceptance or denial of the premise of Freudian psychoanalysis. Instead, the following looks at how this encounter transforms theory into context through the discrepancy between knowledge and preferred reception. To this end, it provides both a historicization of Freudian psychoanalysis in China and an account of how it is punctuated by a literary culture of confessions and masochism. An analysis of the literary phenomenon of male masochism reveals its wider relevance to the idea of a despised Chinese national identity, often encapsulated in the derogatory designation *zhinaren*.

Far from being an isolated literary phenomenon, masochism also figures in the private correspondence of male writers who share a penchant for using a confessional vocabulary of guilt and expiation in relating to one another. In this way, the interest in the interior life of subjects cannot be fully appreciated without understanding that self-recrimination formed a powerful aspect of the aesthetic appreciation of the modern self. This chapter looks at the articulation of masculinity in these writers' fictional works as well as personal writings to one another, as epitomized in the collection *Sanyeji* (Trefoil). Drawing in other closely associated figures such as Wen Yiduo, Zheng Boqi, Zong Baihua, and Tian Han, this chapter examines the intricate relationship between national allegiance and male masochism, a literary community of guilt and its constituents.

From Psychology to Psychoanalysis, Dreams to Masochism

The introduction of Freudian psychoanalysis in China was preceded by more than thirty years of Chinese intellectuals' interest in the development of modern psychology in the West.[3] The learning of scientific psychology began as early as 1889. Yan Yongjing (1839–98), a scholar who became a pastor in 1871, translated American theologian and philosopher Joseph Haven's *Mental Philosophy: Including the Intellect, Sensibilities, and Will* (1858) into Chinese in 1889. Educated in America from age fifteen to twenty-three, Yan later collaborated with the Episcopal Church of America and founded St. John's University in Shanghai in 1879, where he also served as director for eight years. He began his translation of Haven's work while teaching psychology as part of the curriculum.[4]

At the time, "psychology" was gradually emerging from the field of philosophy in the West as a separate discipline. After around 1820, American philosophy was falling into two different camps: "mental science," or "mental philosophy"; and "moral science," or the study of "active powers." Around the time of Yan's translation, China itself was also undergoing new divisions and changes with regard to traditional and modern classifications of knowledge. One scholar suggests that Yan's chosen title, *A Study of Mental Spirit* (Xinlingxue), influenced by contemporary interests in the question of soul and universal spiritual essence by thinkers such as Tan Sitong, reflects a lineage of knowledge brought by Western missionaries and their translations.[5] The term we know today for psychology (*xinlixue*) did not gain currency in China until after 1897, when Kang Youwei mentioned a Japanese translation of *Mental Philosophy* in his catalog of Japanese books.[6]

It is well known that much of modern Chinese technical and scientific terminology is indebted to the initial coinages made by the Japanese through their shared use of classical Chinese script. Less often, however, do we get a case of direct competition between both a Japanese-coined Chinese loanword and a Chinese-coined term. Nishi Amane's (1829–97) translation of Haven's *Mental Philosophy* offers one such example. Published in 1875–76, Nishi's translation appeared fourteen years earlier than Yan's under the title *Shinrigaku*. Known for his enrichment of the Japanese language through the making of new vocabulary for Western concepts, Nishi reputedly coined 787 new terms, 42 percent of which remain in the general Japanese vocabulary. Of this percentage, almost three-fourths can be traced to a prior source in classical Chinese literature.[7] Ultimately, it is his rendition that survived the language reforms of the Republican era.[8]

Different branches of Western psychology trickled into China in the form of direct translation from German, from English, or via Japanese. Appearing piecemeal in journals, treatises of psychology appeared alongside commentaries and studies of psychology as articles, introductory notes, or book reviews in Chinese journals. Leading academics and education reformers such as Cai Yuanpei, Zhu Guangqian, and Wang Guowei contributed to interpretations and translations of psychology. In this susceptible climate, the introduction of Freud's psychoanalysis came relatively late.[9] In 1920, *Eastern Miscellany* published a short article by "Y" introducing "new psychology" (*xin xinlixue*), or "psychoanalysis" (*xinli jiexifa*), founded by Sigmund Freud. Introducing some of the basic distinctions between "unconscious" and "fore-conscious," the pseudonymous author also mentions some of the criticisms advanced by Freud's critics. In the same year, another more detailed introduction was published by the well-known philosopher Zhang Dongsun discussing Freud's innovative "talking cure."[10]

To assess the impact of psychoanalysis on Chinese writers entails confronting its promiscuous manifestations.[11] Freudian thought often took on incongruous forms of articulation in the understanding of Chinese writers. From the more familiar dream analysis to the popularized understanding of sex in handbooks on secrets of the bedroom chamber, Freud's reception in China was not gauged simply by quantifiable volumes of translation. Fragmented and sometimes even proverbialized appropriations of knowledge also facilitated his influence. As noted by one scholar, publication on Freud in China increased from 1920 and reached its highest volume in the mid-1930s, shortly before its decline with the official onset of the Second Sino-Japanese War (1937–45).[12] After the New Sensationalist writers brought the fusion of psychoanalysis and fiction to a new height in the 1930s, Freudian psychoanalysis did not undergo another literary revival until the Root-Seeking Movement in the 1980s.[13] With the outbreak of World War II, the focus of psychoanalytical study in China shifted from problems of individual sexuality to national and social issues.

Even though a rather incomplete record impedes our observation of the direct connection between Freud and Chinese intellectuals, it is clear that Chinese writers were captivated by psychoanalytical interpretations of sexuality and their implications for the importance of individual desire in relation to sociality. In 1922, Lu Xun experimented with what he later remembered as an abortive attempt to give a psychoanalytical framework to his retelling of the story of creation by the woman goddess in Chinese mythology. Distracted by an article in the newspaper that he happened to read in the middle of writing, Lu Xun was unable to continue his project with the seriousness he had originally intended. The next time Lu Xun discussed Freudian psychoanalysis was two years later in 1924 and with much more critical distance. Armed with the analysis of the Japanese literary critic Kuriyagawa Hakuson, Lu Xun found grounds for rejecting the theory of the libido in favor of a more general sense of vital force.[14] This is a theory based on Henri Bergson's notion of élan vital, which Kuriyagawa synthesized into his theory of creative origins in *Symbol of Angst*. Lu Xun's translation, which superseded two previous Chinese versions, was widely read by intellectuals of different ideological persuasions. Yu Dafu, for example, explicitly lists this book as a reference in the postscript to his important piece on literary criticism, "Life and Art." [15]

The fascination with the psychoanalytic conception of sexuality remained unabated among Chinese writers up to the War of Resistance. Lu Xun himself continued to speak of Freud until as late as 1935, a year before Lu Xun's death. Other writers also took great interest in how psychoanalytic explanations of sexuality might reorient literary criticism in a more modern critical perspective. In his 1935 review of the biography of late Qing courtesan Sai Jinhua, who was mythologized as a national heroine who sold her body to save the nation, Yu Dafu uses Freudian analysis to support the speculation that the male characters with whom the female protagonist were involved died from physical exhaustion due to her extraordinary sexual appetite. [16] Interestingly, reflecting this fascination with sexual prowess and masculinity, Yu Dafu's own writings frequently focus on men who are emasculated or weakened by sexually threatening women. Indeed, as we will see, Yu Dafu's engagement with Freud on the literary register plays out a much more complex relation between literature and national identity. Guo Moruo, as another example, explicitly acknowledges the use of Freudian dream analysis in his narrative technique. Written in 1922, "Late Spring" was Guo Moruo's attempt to deal with the ambivalence and unconscious guilt of a married man who feels sexual attraction for a nurse caring for his sick friend. [17] The fantasy and the punishment it incurs culminate in a dream in which, modeled on Euripides' *Medea*, the wife kills their two sons before losing her own sanity.

Guo Moruo's conceptual as opposed to terminological appropriation of dream analysis reveals much more than an unequivocal acceptance of Freudian psychoanalysis. He deployed Freudian psychoanalysis at a time when discussions of the importance of the unconscious served as discursive capital in reevaluating the complexity of modern cultural China. The task Guo took upon himself was how to render Freudian psychoanalysis in terms accessible to common sense in the context of Chinese culture, so utterly different from Freud's Vienna. A key statement Guo makes in "Criticism and Dreams" demonstrates this point. [18] After summarizing what various Western psychoanalysts have said about dream analysis, Guo shifts to his own culturally specific context: "To borrow an even simpler phrase, [dream analysis] is what we in a proverbial saying call 'what we think during the day, we dream at night.' This saying basically exhausts the fundamental principles of the psychoanalytical school on dream analysis." [19] Only at this moment, when Guo sheds the plumage of Freudian terminology and offers a "native" understanding of dream analysis, does the epistemological shift in this act of cultural appropriation become apparent. Difference, rather than the logic of equivalence, underlies the moment of cultural encounter in this act of translation.

The different contexts in which Chinese writers used the idea of masochism, for example, offer one way of looking at this basic epistemological problem. The term "masochism" in its English original occurs at least twice in Guo Moruo's writings, once in 1921 and again in 1924. At the time, there were controversies over the vernacular (*baihua*) movement—a language reform that sought to change written classical Chinese into the more accessible vernacular form—between those like Guo himself and traditional scholars who refused to compromise classical Chinese for the sake of promoting mass literacy. For Guo and many of his contemporaries, the vernacular-language reform was indispensable to China's modernizing process. Because the opponents to the movement, as Guo saw it, would rather keep the learning processes as painful as possible than to spread the benefits of literacy to all, he called them pathological antiquarians who "pierce [themselves] with needles to the point of bleeding" in order to feel a certain pleasure.[20] Furthermore, Guo asserts, they want to impart their own "masochism"—which Guo translates as "passive sadism" (*beidongde yinnuekuang*)—to others as "active sadism" (*zhudongde yinnuekuang*).[21] Strikingly, Yu Dafu's 1922 story "Endless Night"—which we will examine shortly—eroticizes precisely such a scene of piercing oneself with needles as masculine masochism. Masochism, however, was not always translated as passive sadism, a choice clearly taken from the Japanese translation. Another Chinese writer, Zhou Zuoren, translated it as "self-torment" (*ziku*), locating the agency of torture as oneself.[22]

The word *masochism* derives from the name of the nineteenth-century Austrian writer Leopold von Sacher-Masoch (1835–95) and was formally first recognized as a pathology by Richard von Krafft-Ebing (1840–1902). One German-Japanese dictionary defines *Masochismus* as an abnormality (*biantai*) or licentious disorder (*yinluanzheng*) in sexual love (*xing ai*) where one's degradation or abjection (*quru*) is sought at the hands of someone else.[23] *Sadism*, in turn, is suggested as the antonym of *masochism*: the only difference between the two lies in the direction of the act. From the Chinese translations, which are clearly taken from the Japanese—*beinuedaikuang* (and its shorter version *beinuekuang*), *shounuelian*, *beinuedai yinluanzheng*, and *beinueai*—we see that the predominant trait of the illness lies in its passivity, to-be-done-to, to-be-subjected-to (*bei, shou*). Whereas Western psychoanalytical literature has documented the distinguishing trait of passivity in masochism, the Japanese gloss specifies the agency of this act of degradation as someone of the opposite sex (*yixing*).

This gender specification, made in a parenthetical remark, survived its transport back into Chinese on at least one occasion. A 1939 comprehensive English-Chinese dictionary published by the influential Commercial Press glossed *masochism* as an abnormal state of sexual desire in which one derives pleasure from suffering the mistreatment (*nuedai*) or harm inflicted by someone of the opposite sex.[24] Although this etymological transport shows the complexity of translating masochism across cultures, it also reveals assumptions about opposite-sex perversions. Whether male masochism involves male or female agency to complete its drama of punishment is a question that takes us beyond the lexical level and into the realm of a literary culture of male suffering.

Pleasure in Pain

As the most ostensible attribute of masochism expressed in Chinese literature from the May Fourth period, the search for pain always implicates male masochists in a laboriously theatrical process. Texts written by women writers that have been described in similar ways express the experience of pain in a very different manner.[25] Surprisingly, maleness is often voiced as uncertainty, lack of confidence, and the desire to be exposed in one's frailty. Masochism becomes an indissociable constituent of male subject formation and of the masculinity that defines it.

Yu Dafu's 1922 short story "Endless Night" (Mangmangye) gives an intimate glimpse into this psychic figuration. A young man in his midtwenties leaves Shanghai for a teaching job in an unnamed province.[26] His lover is unable to go with him, leaving him alone and desolate in an unfamiliar town. Further adding to his distress, the school turns out to be a battleground between warlord politics and local corruption, recruiting students to carry out the retaliations. A different problem, however, preoccupies the protagonist, Yu Zhifu. We learn that his sexual drive is "twice as strong as in other people."[27]

This hyperbolic affirmation of masculine sexuality, however, appears blatantly incongruous with all the sexual or potentially sexual episodes in the story. For instance, when the protagonist spends a whole night with someone, we learn that they actually "conversed" the entire night. Physical love and spiritual friendship are for the most part confused until one realizes that the most felicitous sexual act in the story occurs in a dream from which the protagonist awakes and finds that "he is holding himself there."[28] Yet even that almost accomplished solitary act remains uncertain, for in the dream they too only "conversed." After he so enthusiastically and desperately sought out a brothel, he again reverted to holding a conversation. For whatever reason the protagonist shies from pleasure, he does not hesitate to seek pain. Indeed, the two seem inextricably bound:

> He immediately takes out the used needle and handkerchief he had swindled. Sitting down at the table, he covers his mouth and nose with these two precious objects. He takes a deep breath inhaling their fragrance. Then he suddenly notices the mirror standing on the table, and wants to reflect every one of his present movements into it. Taking hold of it, he looks at his own silly expressions. Yet he feels that this used needle has not yet been appropriately used. Struck dumb, he stares into the mirror for a couple of minutes. Then he violently pricks his cheek with the needle. Suddenly, a drop of blood rolls like a coral bead down his face, already turning partly red and white from excitement. He wipes it away with the handkerchief and sees yet another round moist drop rolling down the face in the mirror. He watches the blood-stained face in the mirror and looks down at the dark red trace on the handkerchief. Sniffing the fragrance still lingering on the used cloth and needle, he thinks of the mannerism of their owner and feels a kind of pleasure seeping through his whole body. Not much later, the lights went out. Afraid that the pleasure he's enjoying is about to be interrupted, he sits without stirring in the dark room, coveting that demented pleasure.[29]

Despite the ostensible mania, one does not fail to notice the detailed control with which the protagonist stages this moment. Contrary to its appearance of thoughtless abandonment, this scene is punctuated with precise moments of self-reflection, a remarkable reflexivity that reveals the subject's exercise of intent. The protagonist repeatedly arrests himself in the ritualized act of self-mutilation. More important and gratifying than the act of inflicting pain on oneself is the sight of the suffering self. As he takes a couple of minutes to examine himself in the mirror after executing each step of the ritual, the seemingly irrational enigma of this scene takes on a reason of its own. The subject decides at every juncture the way in which his own suffering will unfold.

Far from submitting to pain, the protagonist turns his suffering into the culminating embodiment of his will, as he demonstrates his mastery over a most convincing reenactment of his own abjection. Relishing each movement in the scene of self-mutilation, he meets his own requirements of exactitude and "appropriateness." As both the administrator and the victim of suffering, he presides over the event with inviolable sovereignty, while maintaining the jurisdiction over the way in which he suffers. In light of this careful, ritualized preparation leading up to the scene of self-mutilation, we begin to see the contour of the masochist. His enjoyment lies in not pain itself but, rather, the reproduction of that pain in a most dutiful observance to the letter of the law. Thereby perverting authority with pleasure, he turns its juridical force into voluntary ascription.

Even though "Endless Night" received scathing critiques from readers as well as critics, there were sympathetic voices. In a review published shortly after the story, Mao Dun speaks favorably of "Endless Night."[30] What endears the protagonist to his readers, Mao claims, is his own acknowledged inability to renounce a life of sin. In direct response to those who criticized "Endless Night" for its male protagonist's failure to give up his decadent ways with alcohol and women, Mao Dun defends the story's good intentions. The opponents claim that such a display of the utter lack of will would only lead China's youth to misconceptions of sexuality and thus have a negative influence on them. Su Xuelin, a female critic often dismissed for her extreme and personalized style of attack, calls Yu Dafu the embodiment of "satyriasis."[31] She takes issue specifically with the needle scene, the realism of which she questioned. How can this kind of laughable and exaggerated behavior, she asks, be realistic for the average man unable to release his sexual urge?

In response, Yu Dafu published what he called an "apology" for "Endless Night" three months after its appearance in print.[32] Prompted by the overwhelming number of letters from readers, he offered to address their objections. The chief complaint appears to have been the thematization of "unethical sexual desires" that, to those concerned with the infancy of the development of New Literature in modern China, not only corrupted youth but also furnished the movement's opponents with ammunition.[33] According to another group of critics, Yu should have refrained from advertising "depraved sexual desires" and "inciting young people to descend into the bestial world of homosexual love," if only out of a sense of shame.[34] In response to the latter criticism, which Yu saw as an attack on his person, he fiercely defended himself, disclaiming any autobiographical source for the fictional protagonist.

Although Yu returns again and again in his literary career to wrestle with his critics on the issue of conflating the author with his character, his clarification does very little to address the meaning of homosexuality in "Endless Night."[35] Instead, he subsumes the question under the more general issue of artistry. As with his critics, the issues he takes up do not dispute the sexual constitution of masculinity itself, but rather confirm the premise of a prodigal masculinity consistent with heterosexuality. Even though he quickly counters accusations of improper behavior, the impropriety Yu defends never transgresses the bounds of heterosexuality and only reasserts it by way of hyperbolic expression.

Later, Yu Dafu revealingly refers to "Endless Night" as a work written at a time when the combination of "seeing the decline of one's own country" and "suffering the humiliation of being in a foreign country" inflicted on him a feminized grief like that suffered by "a new young widow after the loss of her master."[36] The period Yu Dafu describes coincides with the time of his study in Japan. His best-known piece, "Sinking," was written only a year before "Endless Night." The famous last lines of the story spoken by the Chinese protagonist studying in Japan express a sense of nationalism spurred by the humiliation of his failed sexual venture with a corpulent Japanese prostitute.[37] Although Yu's critics claimed that his writings distracted young people from the exigencies of national survival by dwelling on narcissistic sexual indulgence, his works actually boldly root the experience of nationalism in the psychic foundation of sexuality. The endangered nation needs to be saved in much the same way that a shattered masculine identity attempts to survive. And this survival ostensibly depends on the woman, in whose hands his sexual destiny unfolds.

Upon feeling his insuppressible "bestial instinct," the protagonist in "Endless Night" puts on "Chinese clothing" before setting out in the middle of the night to search for sexual gratification.[38] In a later episode in a brothel, the protagonist dons foreign clothes and speaks English as he evades the prostitute's simple question of whether he is Chinese.[39] His allegiance to Chineseness is, strangely, suspended in Western language and clothing. Significantly, this disavowal of national identity usually occurs in conjunction with failed sexual encounters. With each renewed quest for sexual gratification, the protagonist enjoys not only the thrill of his "depraved" behavior but also the subversion of Chinese identity. On the verge of giving up the task altogether after hours of fruitless search, the protagonist spots a small cigarette and foreign goods shop where a young female shopkeeper makes the final calculation of the day's sales:

"What would you like to buy?"
He first buys a few cigarettes, and then glances at her. In his eyes, her looks are rare for a merchant woman. She is actually quite commonplace. Yet her figure is petite and chic, and her clothes are pretty modish. So he finds her attractive enough. Like a hungry dog, he stares for a minute or two before asking her,
"Do you sell needles?"
"You mean sewing needles?"
"Yes, but I want one that's been well-used. It would be best if, after you sell a new one to me, I can exchange the new one for your used one."
The woman smiles and asks, "Are you using it for heating medicine?"
He answers evasively, "Uh yes, yes. How did you know?"
"There's always some prescription like that in folk medicine."
"Indeed, indeed. The needle is actually pretty easy to get, but there's still one thing that's difficult to obtain."
"What's that?"

"A women's used handkerchief. Since I'm here all alone without friends, it's impossible to find. I've actually given up on the idea altogether."

"Will this do?" As she asks, the woman takes out a used handkerchief made from foreign cloth from her pocket.

Upon seeing this, his heart starts to pound. Flushed, he says, "If you agree to let me have it, I would be willing to buy a top-quality one and trade you for it."

"Please just take it. There's no need for the exchange."[40]

After the strenuous efforts he put into searching for the properly low woman, the protagonist anticlimactically conducts a rather business-like transaction. He solicits a barter exchange rather than her affection. Indeed, the preparations are meticulous. The acquisition of the two "precious objects" (*baowu*, i.e., the handkerchief and the needle) in itself is worthy of an elaborately planned pilgrimage. Like a "hungry dog," we are told, the protagonist stumbles through town, looking for "the lowliest woman" befitting the ownership of these objects. The object of his urge is precisely "this sort of woman." The inauspicious onset of his nocturnal quest, marked by physically thwarted movements of falls and stumbles in the unfamiliar outskirts of the town, forebodes an even more infelicitous outcome. After hours of fruitless searching, he breaks down in an emotional reverie, longing in the end for a woman who, in her devotion to him, would redeem him through an "embrace with blood and tears." Contemplating suicide, the protagonist bemoans why this ungratified longing, which he already had to suffer during his earlier years in Japan, should continue to plague him in his own country.

Although the redemptive figure of the woman appears central to the protagonist's despair, her ultimate function is to facilitate the staging of a tactful evasion. The circuitous path of the protagonist's desire, far from simply taking the woman as its object, veers away from her. His staged scene requires her presence to the extent that she fulfills the condition of his quest for an object and testifies to the difficulty and ingenuity of that labor. She is made complicit in his drama insofar as she contributes, by virtue of her participation, to the credibility of its details and execution. The masochist needs her consent and, even more so, the chain of exchange she thereby agrees to set into motion. The "thoroughly used" quality of the objects she gives up signs her over, in that sense, to the masochist's fantasy as a substitute for the object of his fantasy. For the masochist, the feminine figure enables rather than exhausts the significance of the object.

The protagonist conducts his overly strenuous solicitation less for the sake of the objects themselves than for the sake of exerting a certain persuasive, narrative control over the transaction. He expends his efforts not merely toward the goal of acquisition but toward constructing her act of giving up as a sacrifice for him, a renunciation that then requires his compensation. Furthermore, this sacrifice can be compensated only by him, as he offers again and again to provide her with substitutes that are better and newer. This precondition of fetishism, however, is never fulfilled. As the woman, in the end, makes the handkerchief a gift rather than a sacrifice—"Please just take it. There's no need for the exchange"—she refuses his fetishistic fantasy.

The woman's nonparticipation in the male subject's fetishism, however, hardly prevents him from carrying it out. From the male masochist's point of view, to the extent he needs her involvement, she cannot be an autonomous other. Her otherness has already been accounted for in the masochist's fantasy as the other who must be persuaded and won over by his scheme. Limited in her claim to self-willed agency, she is not so much excluded from the scene as included for a specific purpose. Not coincidentally, the objects he seeks must be "used" (*yongshu*) or, more precisely, thoroughly used. He takes the object as the token of her exchange, substituting the woman in fulfilling his masochistic desire. The woman shopkeeper serves as an element in a more elaborate fantasy unexhausted by her presence alone. The fantasy uses her as a point of proliferation and repetition and takes that instrument of torture as the cruel consent of the tortures herself. The careful placement of the proper interlocutor and the appropriate objects point to an order of fantasy beyond the highly dramatized quality of the masochistic scene.

The problem with placing the feminine figure in the male subject's masochistic fantasy lies in the fact that we are never dealing with her presence without the contours of fantasy. By no means particular to "Endless Night," this complex invocation of the woman figure occurs throughout Yu Dafu's works. Often, her pronounced presence, especially through the exercise of a certain authority, serves only to stage diversions for the masochistic subject. In "The Past" (Guoqu), written five years later, the predominance of fantasy is inseparable from the male subject's voluntary servitude. Eager to please his mistress, the narrator tries to court her favor:

> If there should be occasions on which I disobey her commands, she would, without thinking twice, raise that plump tender hand and slap me right in the face. As for me, after enduring her reprimands, I would feel an inexpressible satisfaction. For the sheer reason of wanting to feel her beating again, I would sometimes disobey her commands on purpose, wanting her to come beat me or kick me in the loins with those pointy leather shoes. If either were not sufficiently exercised, I would intentionally cry out, "Doesn't hurt! It's not enough! Come try again! Hit me!" She would then, without reservation, raise her hand or foot to abuse me. Only when my cheeks are beaten red, or my loins completely sore and achy, do I then docilely obey her orders and do the things she wants me to do. On such occasions, [her sisters] would try to persuade her to stop and tell her not to go overboard. Yet I, the beaten, would solemnly beseech them not to interfere.[41]

The narrator does not shun any opportunity to accentuate his undignified role as a "hen" to the dominating "rooster," a position he willingly accedes to the woman, Number Two. Her authority, however, assumes a susceptibility to his prompting. Even though he expresses these provocations in the form not of command but disobedience, they guarantee the same outcome in accordance with the design of the masochist. For him, transgression locates the site of pleasure, evoked in every predictable instance of her administration of the punishment. The "inexpressible satisfaction" he then feels lies in not the mere act of beating but the fantasy that saturates the scene. Pleasure in pain superimposes fantasy on reality.

Appended to the masochistic fantasy, the woman fulfills the required role of the cruel mistress.[42] Despite all the tasks the narrator must undertake at the command of Number Two, her orders remain unexecuted until he gets what he wants. Only after he has received the beating does he "then docilely obey her orders and do the things she wants [him] to do."[43] Rather than give his obedience under the threat of possible punishment, he withholds it until the event of the punishment itself can be guaranteed. The aggressive penitent does not just demand his punishment but secures it through extortion.

Both the deployment of the woman shopkeeper as exchange value in "Endless Night" and the prominence given to the cruel mistress in "The Past" suggest that the formation of masculine identity and the confirmation it needs depend on the sacrifice of the woman to the conditions of sexual difference. However, our analysis should not end there. Masculinity's preference for masochism proves more complicated than the predictability of the former's demise. Although the scene of fetishistic exchange seems to corroborate the view that the foundation of masculinity is grounded in, rather than prior to, sexual difference, Yu Dafu's "Endless Night" in fact foregrounds the cruel mistress's intervention in a different story. Masculinity comes undone not during moments of its ostensible failings but in its prior exclusion of sameness.

The complex meaning of the masochist's triumph compels our inquiry into the direction not of logic but of necessity, of the masochist's compulsion to flee from what most intimately haunts him. While the protagonist painstakingly stages the scene of self-mutilation in "Endless Night," his controlled pauses indicate a certain self-mastery over his own suffering and thus destiny. However, beneath each composed instance of stopping the action, the protagonist reacts to another set of internal impulses. This pressure from within compels him to respond by reasserting self-control through pain. Just as the pleasure is derived from the stopping, from the interruptions that one makes in the face of a catapulting rush toward imposed punishment, the stopping itself seems to respond to a pressing internal anxiety, a paranoiac or guilty conscience that subsequently demands the reassertion of subjective control as relief. One recalls that it is always a kind of "urge" or "impulse" (*chongdong*), an unexplainable force beyond the protagonist himself, that goads him into pursuing his quest for ritualized punishment:

> As his tense state of mind relaxes, Zhifu's sexual urge, having been long dormant, slowly rekindles. Because of time and space, the memory of Wu Chisheng fades in his mind day by day. Thus what has risen in its place (*daici erxing*) and commands his total attention, is a desire which has simultaneously taken two directions. One is pure love, which he devotes to his young students. Another is an intermittent, irregular urge. When this urge acts up, he would become a wild beast without senses. Then, unable to suppress his sexual urge, he would have to go into town and on the streets, loiter in the poor country neighborhoods near the school, and steal a few glances at the women.[44]

Contrary to the ostensible quest for the cruel mistress, we discover in this passage that the "urge," which takes the form of a perversion, turns out to be a replacement for something else (*daici erxing*, that which has risen in place of), a former love that has "faded." It may be surprising to find out that this former love, Wu Chisheng, is a former male acquaintance. This detail barely stands out amid the narrative contrivance toward asserting the primacy of femininity as the object of the masochist's desire. The possibility of a same-sex object has been precluded from our view. Ironically, this preclusion also corroborates with the critical discourse surrounding Yu Dafu that received this episode of homosexuality with denunciation or denial.[45] The ostensibly heterosexual content of the masochistic scene—replete with a sexualized female object—itself is not only successfully conveyed by the literary artifice but also affirmatively interpreted by its critics. In fact, the trajectory of the perversion delineates not an anomaly within the scheme of heterosexuality but a departure from a secret same-sex attachment. The perversion of masochism is a swerve away from rather than toward deviance.

Beating the Nation

The compulsion behind the masochist's elaborate scheme of expiation and subversion holds the key to our understanding of the phenomenon of literary masochism in Chinese writers such as Yu Dafu and Guo Moruo. Its complexity, the mix of pleasure with grief, suggests that seeking pleasure in pain in fact expresses a displaced relation of loss or dysfunctionality. It resignifies something else, a relation not ostensibly present in the scene of masochism but tangentially mentioned as a side remark. If we think of this restructuring as taking precedence over what it resignifies, then masochism becomes an apt mode of psychic expression for disguising and refiguring relations of pain. Modality, in this sense, is the hidden logic of masochism. In fact, embedded in the masochistic narrative of the private pains of the distressed male suitor are the national pains of a "Chinese" identity. Psychoanalytical narratives of male masochism can also disguise confessions to national shame, metaphorized as not only a loss of assured sexual identity but also a humiliated national consciousness.

Yu Dafu's first attempt at a novel, five years after "Endless Night," crystallized into the 1927 piece *Lost Sheep* (Miyan). A critic at the time lamented the failure of the novel to meet general expectations that advertisements had already helped produce four or five years prior to its appearance. The author, according to the critic, was rather unsuccessful and squandered his energy on unnecessary disguises and disclaimers. But Yu Dafu was apparently not the only male writer at the time perceived to suffer this kind of artistic decline. Guo Moruo, the critic notes, has also been producing some rather crude and awkward fiction writings. His "Donna Carméla," completed in August 1924, revealed a similar kind of narrative failure as seen in "Endless Night" and "The Past."[46] Guo's story, however, wallows in a more outrageous kind of failure. In this story, dealing with the male protagonist's desire for a woman he never comes to know, we are made to engage, through the constant second-person address, his fantasy of the Japanese candy girl, whom he "baptizes" as the Spanish temptress:[47]

> Did you know, friend, that Spanish women are the most vicious? I read somewhere that there was a man who once asked a young Spanish woman to marry him. She wouldn't accept his proposal until after she had lashed him with a horsewhip twenty-five times. As the man willingly bared his back for her, she stopped after the twenty-fourth lash. Trembling to endure the last whip, he was already anticipating the joy of love afterwards. But the twenty-fifth whip never came. Without it, the woman would not agree. His back was already streaked with blood, but the woman, tossing the whip to one side, walked off. Such are the ways of Spanish women! I don't think there has been anyone like her in our culture. Even though I baptized her [the Japanese candy girl] with Spanish rites, I believe that she will not be like the Spanish woman! But, ah, friend! I have already suffered her invisible twenty-four lashes! I threw away my dignity for her! My spirit and body languished for her! I've thrown away my career and family. Even now I still don't know what she's thinking. I'm desperately seeking the beauty of an undying illusion. I long for the twenty-fifth lash! If only I could hear her say "I love you," I would be happy with death![48]

Most likely inspired by his reading and translation of the works of the Spanish writer Vicente Blasco Ibáñez (1867–1928), Guo chose the Spanish temptress for her unrelenting cruelty.[49] As the second-person addressee of the protagonist, the reader cannot help turning into his confidant, the loyal audience of his confession of the desire for punishment. Throughout the

story, the protagonist refers to himself as "Mephistopheles" and "the cru-
cified," the transgressor and the martyr.[50] His repentance seems unmis-
takable, even convincing. His audience, though intimately addressed as his
confidant, is charged with the duty to recriminate him, to hold the very
whip that he consecrates as the prerogative of the woman. For the masochist, the flight from the secrecy of guilt gives him the freedom of action,
despite the fact that he perceives its impetus as a source of displeasure.

It is not surprising that the protagonist never receives the twenty-fifth
stroke, for, in that unreserved prostration before the punishment, he obtains
the respite he seeks. For the time being, anticipation frees him from the privacy of self-torment. The judgment lies in the hand of another, the "you,"
the "friend." The temporal duration sustained by the masochist himself in
his pious anticipation appears redeemable by punishment. That possibility of
redemption sustains not the truth or falsity of the transgression but the
promise of restitution.

The underlying anxiety of the protagonist's imagined scene with the
Spanish temptress is not revealed to us until later. Despite his often-professed
desire to get close to her, he never manages to move beyond the realm of
fantasy. Having never spoken to the Japanese woman, he finally discloses the
reason for this abstention in a stammer: "I want to talk to her, but we never
speak somehow. She is shy and so am I. And I'm afraid that she knows I'm
Chinese. I'm afraid my Japanese is bad. . . . I want to write her. . . . I'm afraid
she knows I'm Chinese."[51]

The protagonist's desire does not find easy articulation in what he claims
he wants. In every instance of his "wanting" to do something, be it to talk
or write to Donna Carméla, he avoids carrying it out. Fixated on her hand-
writing as though it encrypts the solution to his torment, he steals her correspondence and feels jealous rage at someone else writing her. The protagonist never manages to communicate with her in any direct way. We find,
instead, its renunciation or avoidance. He repeatedly utters his fear that she
would find out that he is "Chinese," as though without her knowing, he
would otherwise succeed in masquerading as Japanese.

His anxiety hides an inability to acknowledge his willingness to readily
forgo his own Chinese identity for that of a Japanese. Although the focal
point of this anxiety concentrates on what the other, Donna Carméla, might
know about him, the importance of her judgment is only secondary. The
possibility of her knowledge merely gives pretext for the protagonist's self-
recrimination, in turn making possible his exteriorization of guilt over the
secret of his national preference. He admits to his national identity only under the condition that such knowledge entail punishment. Transposed onto
the register of illicit romance, the confession of national shame seeks relief

in a confession of guilty love. What Donna Carméla might know about the protagonist's identity participates in rather than determines the complex process of his identification.

One of the events that the protagonist witnesses, after all, is the celebration of the Japanese victory over Russian naval forces during the Russo-Japanese War of 1904–5. This marks a crucial turning point for Asia at which Japan, having defeated China only ten years earlier, wins recognition as a world power, an event as ambivalent for the Chinese as much as it is cause for victorious identification. The Japanese victory brings to the fore the possibility of redeeming the Sick Man of East Asia, while at the same time recalling China's defeat in the Sino-Japanese War and, with that, China's failure to match Japanese modernization. Against this backdrop, the protagonist's suppression of his Chinese identity in confrontation with a Japanese woman carries an additional significance. Much like Yu's male protagonists, Guo's character requires a female interlocutor to express his ambivalence. Relying on the female other to condemn or affirm, to expose or console, the male protagonist poses his identity as a question in hope of confirmation. The alternative scenario—having a male interlocutor—proves devastating. This is made abundantly clear in another story, "Hard Road Traveling" (1925), in which the imposture of Chineseness is this time revealed in all its powerless dejection.

Looking for a reasonable place to rent on a very limited budget in a small Japanese town, the protagonist, Aimou, approaches the mistress of a grand house who is renting out three rooms. When asked to leave his address, Aimou hurriedly makes up a Japanese name, only to quickly realize that, even if she were to send a reply of consent, it would never reach him under the false name. Just as he is about to leave, the husband enters the room. Though donning only a casual bathrobe, Aimou recognizes the intimidating demeanor of a military man. As the husband glances up and down at him with his "fierce eyes," Aimou feels exposed of his fraud, as the Japanese man asks whether he is from Shanghai or Korea, which also shares a colonized status. Aimou dejectedly admits that he is a "Chinese student studying abroad" (*Zhongguo liuxuesheng*), and the mistress lets out a cry of shock and asks in contempt, "Oh, Chinaman (*zhinaren*)?"[52]

She immediately finds an excuse to reject the housing request. Aimou regrets having come and, even more, having falsified his name, which made him look even more despicable in the eyes of the Japanese. Walking home embittered and resentful, he feels as though the pleasure seekers on the beach were mocking him in their merriment. He imagines that, beneath their laughter, they were calling him the homeless *zhinaren* not even worthy of seeking shelter in empty houses guarded by dogs in their masters' absence:

"Zhinaren, Zhinaren, aimlessly wandering zhinaren!"[53] As the feeling of injury and humiliation overwhelms him, Aimou voices a rebuttal:

> Japanese, Japanese, you ungrateful Japanese! What has China ever done to you to invite your contempt? Even just in the way you say the three words, "zhinaren," more than demonstrates your extreme disgust. The way you crinkle your nose when you utter the word "zhi" and the way you prolong the pause at the end of that nasal tone, "na"—ah! Are you even aware of the origin of the word "zhina"? During the Qin dynasty, you were still barbarians, perhaps still gnawing on coconuts in the South Pacific! Ah, you ungrateful Japanese! I did not falsify my name out of envy for your civilization. I falsified my name to protect myself against your connivances! Your imperialism may have succeeded, but your conscience is dead. You are quick to say that you're "misunderstood," and you love to say that other people's justified defense against you is unfounded. Oh, you arrogant Japanese! How profound is your intent that it's even worthy of others' misunderstanding? . . . Don't think that other people are fools! Repent![54]

The interpellation that begins this speech follows exactly the formulation by which Aimou had imagined himself addressed by the beachgoers. Deflecting the insult, Aimou turns an imaginary address into his own response to the Japanese, doubling the internal dialogue. He hastens to defend his embarrassing falsification as a strategy against imperialism and reverses his guilt into its culpability. In the final injunction for Japan's penitence, he vindicates his own confession to guilt by indicting the graver crime of imperialism. Investing the guilty with the power of grievance and suffering, the act of falsification itself becomes a victim's testimony to the powers oppressing him. His attempt at deception is itself explained away as an effect of imperialism compelling him to feel inferior as a Chinese and pass himself off as Japanese. He realizes only later that the imposture defeats the purpose because, under a falsified name, he could never legally rent the place anyway. His falsification for the purpose of gaining access thus becomes itself an exclusionary act.

Interestingly, Guo Moruo wrote a short scholarly article almost ten years later commenting on Japan's use of *zhina* for China. In a special issue of the journal *Wind of the Universe* (Yuzhou feng) on Japan and the Japanese, Guo Moruo reflected on the Japanese attitude toward the Chinese. Although *zhina* in itself bears no derogatory connotations, Guo pointed out that "when the word comes from the mouth of a Japanese, it sounds more demeaning than the word 'Jew' out of a European's mouth."[55] Perhaps it is this enunciation of contempt that he was trying to capture in the crinkling of the nose and elongated nasal pause that Aimou endured in his fantasy of self-persecution.

"Hard Road Traveling" is one of a number of Guo's short stories featuring Aimou, a Chinese student studying in Japan whose name also happens to be what Guo's close friends sometimes called him.[56] The intensification of nationalistic sentiments among students abroad has been a well-known fact since the late Qing.[57] The first radical revolutionary journals, such as *Tide of Zhejiang, The World of Hubei Students,* and *Jiangsu,* were founded by Chinese students in Japan. The experience, however, made a particular impact on the young writers who would later become members of the Creation Society. Writers such as Guo Moruo, Yu Dafu, Cheng Fangwu, Zhang Ziping, Tian Han, Zheng Boqi, Tao Jingsun, and He Wei spent on the average 10.4 years in Japan as Chinese exchange students. This is in stark contrast to the older figures of the May Fourth period, such as Lu Xun, Hu Shi, Xu Zhimo, Xu Dishan, Wen Yiduo, Li Jinfa, Bing Xing, Hong Shen, Liang Shiqiu, Lin Yutang, Liu Bannong, Li Jieren, Li Jianwu, and Qian Xuantong, whose time abroad was only 4.1 years on average.[58] In a letter to his parents, the poet Wen Yiduo, who studied Western art in Chicago and was in America from 1922 to 1924, remarked that "only the students abroad know the bitter hardships of being Chinese."[59]

Wen's poems succinctly convey the centrality of perceived humiliation in summoning one's affinity to the nation.[60] As far back as *An Unofficial History of Studying in Japan* (Liudong waishi, 1907), one of the earliest literary accounts of the experience of Chinese students in Japan, the encounter was fraught with mixed feelings of admiration and resentment.[61] Continuing this tradition, the most prominent example in May Fourth literature belongs to Yu Dafu's "Sinking," in which a similar scene of imagined insult spurs an ambivalent passion of loving and hating the nation.[62] As Yu's young twenty-one-year-old male protagonist reproaches himself for missing an opportunity to start a conversation with two Japanese girls, he immediately turns his self-accusations into an insult directed at himself. He convinces himself that the reason they did not pay him any attention was that he was a *zhinaren*:

> Oh, you fool! Even if they seemed interested, what are they to you? Isn't it quite clear that their ogling was intended for the three Japanese? Oh, the girls must have known! They must have known that I am a "Chinaman"; otherwise why didn't they even look at me once? Revenge! Revenge! I must seek revenge against their insult. . . . China, O my China! Why don't you grow rich and strong? I cannot bear your shame in silence any longer![63]

Conflating sexual rejection with his national identity, the protagonist turns to China as both the explanation and possible redemption for his personal grievances. National shame reflects the nation's defeat, but it traces more intimately to an inability to affirm one's masculinity. The weight of the nation's humiliation bears on the certainty of masculinity, which can be posited only as a question or under falsification. It is not national humiliation that wreaks havoc on masculine identity. The failure of masculinity as a viable identity leaves its imprint on the allegiance to the nation, a bondage professed as a burden rather than pride. In this way, the protagonist's call for revenge parallels Aimou's call for Japan's repentance. The power of humiliation lies in its justification for revenge. In the name of national humiliation, masculinity claims the possibility of redemption. The link between the nation and the individual is forged in the indebtedness to guilt and its expiation.

Although Yu's "Sinking" occupies a unique position in the formation of modern Chinese literature, its canonical status cannot adequately reflect its participation in, rather than representation of, a literary culture of confession and shame. The language of despair and guilt pervaded the writings of male intellectuals. Zheng Boqi's lesser-known short story "The Very First Lesson" (Zuichu zhi ke) was published in the same year as "Sinking." Pingzhou, a young Chinese student attending the first year of school in Japan, encounters the jeers of his fellow students. Even the teacher joins in the effort of humiliating by asking whether he's Korean or "Chinese." Rather than referring to him as *zhinaren*, the teacher uses an equally insulting designation, *Qingguoren*, which means "person of the Qing":

> Upon hearing this, Pingzhou was inevitably incensed. He's not upset by "Korean"; *Qingguoren* is what's unbearable. When he first came to Tokyo and was looking for the Chinese embassy, he had to ask several people where to find the embassy of Republic of China. No one replied, until finally he swallowed his pride and asked, "Where is the Zhina embassy?" Then someone asked him, "You mean the Qingguo embassy? It's just on top of the hill." At the time, Pingzhou didn't quite clearly hear "Shinkoku." As he was still trying to figure it out, all the people around him had already dispersed. With no other choice, he walked uphill three or five steps, before suddenly realizing "Yes, Shinkoku, shinkoku, *Qingguo, Qingguo*, baka [*sic*]! These sons of bitches! I don't believe that you bastards don't even know *zhina*. Baka, Chinksho [*sic*]!" . . . he immediately wanted to stand up and argue with the teacher, but he forced down his anger. "I am a citizen of the Chinese Republic (*Zhonghua minguo ren*)," he calmly replied. "What? Chinese Republic (*Zhonghua minguo*)? How come I've never heard of it? You sure it's not *Zhina*?" The teacher asks, throwing over a glance of contempt. Everyone in the room burst out laughing.[64]

Pingzhou submits to the hierarchy of national designations only to find his own proper *Zhonghua minguo ren* unrecognized. Overlooking the offense in being called a Korean in view of Korea's connotation as a Japanese colony, he concedes to referring to China, as the Japanese would derogatorily, as *Zhina*. Yet he finds his concession again inadequate to deflect the insult in *Qingguoren*, a much-contested designation in the late Qing because it equated the Chinese people with a dynasty ruled by the Manchus and, at the same time, excluded the possibility of recognizing China as a modern sovereign state.

Encapsulating this historical contention in the scene of a Japanese classroom—one can hardly forget Lu Xun's famous decapitation slide show, which also took place in a classroom during his study in Japan and subsequently prompted him to save the nation through literature—Zheng shows the different levels of insults embedded in the Japanese address of the Chinese. In this way, his treatment differs significantly from Guo Moruo's and Yu Dafu's thematization of national humiliation. Whereas Pingzhou seizes every opportunity to tell his friends about this experience, Guo's and Yu's protagonists are much more covetous of the privacy of humiliation. Yu's character writes it down in a diary, whereas Guo's protagonist largely carries on an interior monologue. Even the event of being recognized as a *zhinaren* is something the protagonists themselves psychologically anticipate before being found out. Whereas Pingzhou exteriorizes his humiliation, thereby faulting the Japanese as the ones solely responsible, Guo's and Yu's protagonists incorporate it as part of a complicated structure of producing a masculine identity premised on failure.

Reflecting on what he had learned as his very first lesson in Japan, Pingzhou sums up the experience as "studying books from the western ocean, while suffering the abuse of the eastern sea" (*du de xiyang de shu, shoude shi dongyang de qi*).[65] The additional aggravation and insult of studying in an imperialist Japanese setting compound the demeaning necessity of having to study Western knowledge. Interestingly, this succinct formulation was not a product of literary inventiveness. Zheng actually borrowed the phrase from a letter Guo Moruo wrote in 1920 to Zong Baihua, whom he would not actually meet until 1925 but with whom Guo exchanged an important set of correspondence. These letters reveal the centrality of confession and expiation in the self-perception of May Fourth male intellectual culture.

Guilt and Expiation

Composed in the period just before the founding of the Creation Society, *Trefoil Collection* contains a series of twenty letters exchanged between Guo Moruo, Zong Baihua, and Tian Han during January to March 1920. At the time, Guo was studying medicine at Kyūshū Imperial University in Fukuoka, Tian Han was in Tokyo, and Zong was working in Shanghai as the editor of *Learning Lamp*, the supplement to *New Current Affairs* (Shishi xinbao). Guo and Zong had already been in correspondence prior to that regarding Guo's various submissions to *Learning Lamp*, and Zong later introduced Tian Han to Guo. In these letters they discussed topics as varied as philosophy, aesthetics, marriage, love, and literature. The descriptions of personal affairs were often interspersed with quotations from German philosophers and English poets. The letters were as deeply personal, with Guo and Tian discussing their own relationships and marriages, as they were visionary in describing these young writers' artistic aspirations.

The title *Trefoil* (Sanyeji) is taken from the German *Kleeblatt*, used to symbolize the friendship between the three young intellectuals. In his preface, Tian stated his hope that the collection would inspire the kind of "Werther fever" that Goethe's novel had for German youths. The volume of letters did not disappoint and became a sensation for young Chinese people who felt their personal concerns voiced by these young writers' private writings. In his preface, Zong stated that the primary issue they wanted to tackle was the institution of marriage: freedom of choice in matters of love, arranged marriages, true love in arranged marriages, and the question of responsibility arising from the conflict between arranged marriages and love out of free will. As for Guo, he chose his preface with cogency by simply quoting a verse from Goethe's *Faust*.

Even though the three writers have somewhat different impressions of what this collection represents, they all agree on the importance of the epistolary form of open confessions. "Wearing one's liver and exposing one's gall," Tian writes, "the expressed thoughts are written with the utmost seriousness and sincerity."[66] Taking it a step further, Zong feels that the collection, more than merely confessional, also asks for the reader's adjudication in considering the issues put forth.[67] It is not often easy, however, to distinguish the issues the three writers discuss from the impassioned language they use, as their requests for one another's literary advice also ask for exonerations in personal matters. From the very first letters, the conveyance of personal guilt through the vehicle of Western literary personas discloses the mutual borrowings between literary aesthetics and subjective posturing. For example, responding to Zong's letter praising him for possessing lyrical genius and encouraging him to perfect his "poet character," Guo feels compelled to disclose his unworthiness. After listing a dazzling array of figures whom he aspires to emulate—Percy Bysshe Shelley (1792–1822), Qu Yuan (c. 340–278 BCE), Cai Wenji (Han dynasty, 202 BCE–220 CE), Li Bai (701–62), Du Fu (712–70), Alighieri Dante (1265–1321), John Milton (1608–74), Johann Wolfgang von Goethe (1749–1832), Oscar Wilde (1854–1900), Saigyō (1118–90), Matsuo Bashō (1644–94), and Rabindranath Tagore (1861–1941)—Guo cannot help but reveal his dark secret:

> Brother Baihua, I'm afraid you don't yet fully know what kind of person I am. You say I have lyrical genius, that I have no way of knowing. But my character

is indeed rotten to the core. I feel more fallen than Oliver Goldsmith, more frustrated than Heinrich Heine, and more decadent than Baudelaire. When I read your words "poet character," I started to cry. . . . I'm not even worthy of an "amoeba." . . . In short, Baihua, I'm not a "person." I'm damaged. I'm not worthy to be the one you "respect." I wish I could, like a phoenix, set to fire the remnants of my physical form, while singing a mournful song, and be reborn.[68]

The excessive quality of this urgent plea may put one off, as it has many critics who prefer to overlook this somewhat self-indulgent phase of Guo's literary development.[69] However, the gesture of excessive self-demeaning circuitously enables a sense of self-validation. As though making his audience more amenable with suspense, Guo does not yet explain what makes him so fallen and despicable. Whatever it is, it seems to elevate his "poet character" the more he disparages himself. More fallen, frustrated, and decadent than the formidable Western literary figures he summons, Guo, in professing his having committed egregious crimes, does anything but devalue the confessor. The measure of "genius" seems directly proportional to his "self-degradation." Through his passionate confessions, we are led to be moved by, rather than condemn, his sins.

In fact, the self-flagellating tone does not last long, as Guo immediately moves on to a discussion of the founding of genius. He distinguishes between two types of genius: linear and concentric. The first kind is bestowed with a specific gift that requires ever so careful and rigorous refinement, whereas the second kind takes in all that surrounds him and his brilliance is matched only by his versatility. In Guo's opinion, there are only two examples of the latter category, Goethe and Confucius, and he also seems to imply his own membership.

As is well known, Guo was heavily invested in pantheism at the time.[70] His choice of a quotation from *Faust* in lieu of a preface more than testifies to his aesthetic leaning. However, the discussion of genius in relation to the sincerity of confession carries a long-standing significance. The focus on the question of genius has precedents in the late Qing, when intellectuals were questioning China's failure to produce its own Napoleon, Washington, or Columbus. The ethnic or national marker "Chinese," however, is now subsumed under a general rubric of individual genius, disguised in aesthetic and poetic language. Among other things, the inquiry into the disposition of the "genius" legitimates a kind of borrowed persona as something original and creative. Zong's response to Guo's penitent letters acknowledges this practice in an interesting way: "You are sincere in your penitence, a drive to strive for the better. Your sin is only the Mephistopheles in you. You have cultivated—from the works of Rousseau and Tolstoy—a sincere, true spirit and the courage for repentance. This is something to be happy about. From this one can tell that western literature has this positive feature, which is not something possessed by eastern literary arts."[71]

The figure of the penitent somehow enables a transposition from Tolstoy or Rousseau's confessor to the guilty genius. The ethnic marker of the Chinese is reintroduced after all in the comparison of Western with Eastern literary arts. The guilty is not only redeemed but also praised for his "sincerity," measured by the degree to which he can persuade his audience of his penitence. At the same time, this also marks a moment of forging a new kind of literary aesthetics that, Zong believes, had not been a part of Chinese literary sensibilities. The courage for repentance reveals the true spirit. The more one repents, the truer this original spirit appears. As if to put it to narrative practice, the name "Mephistopheles" returns in Guo's "Donna Carméla" as one of the male protagonist's remorseful self-namings. The drama of penitence somehow does not observe the distinction between fiction and personal correspondence, as it is no longer the content of a certain narrative but the very mode in which narratives about the masculine self become possible.

As it turns out, Guo's conscience suffers from the fact that he had begun a relationship with a Japanese woman while he was still married. He met Sato Tomiko while she was a nurse tending a sick friend of Guo's at the time. Guo's own marriage was prearranged, and he soon moved in with Sato, whom he also called "Anna." Although he had intended for it to have been a purely spiritual relationship, physical passion quickly ensued. Guo did not at first relate the details of his "sins" to Zong. In the meantime, Zong had put Tian in touch with Guo. Independent of the confession being played out in the correspondence between Zong and Guo, Tian's first letter adds a different flair to the articulation of guilt. Claiming that he treasures above all else people who are "sincere," Tian relates to Guo a story of someone who once tried to befriend Tian but was discouraged by Tian himself to do so:

> If you want to get to know me, I'm merely a "juvenile delinquent," far from the "model youth Tian Han" idealized in your mind. It's better that you don't know me. The fact that I'm no good already pains me. If you were to see through my true element and thereby destroy your own illusion, that will bring you pain. And I would further reproach myself. If you don't deem unworthy this "juvenile delinquent," then I ask you to please come often to instruct me and set me straight. That way, you won't be disappointed and I won't be ashamed.[72]

Not to be outdone in unworthiness, Guo's reply is equally rife with a passion for guilt:

> My own crime has erected an insurmountable wall between us. What I've related to Baihua about my person is only the distant peaks barely visible through the evening clouds. I now regret not having completely and unreservingly confessed

to my despicable parts. My "romantic" nature ruined me; it led me to cleverly disguise myself, deceiving both myself and others. Baihua was victimized by my beguilement! . . . allow me to discard those clouds and remove my mask. I shall introduce you to my naked self and love. . . . I thought god took pity on me, having lost a dear friend, and gave me a demure companion to compensate my loss. . . . I asked her to sacrifice her life at the hospital and move to Fukuoka with me. . . . Ah, Brother Shouchang [Tian Han]! I ended up having been too confident in my own tender, weak soul! Not long after we moved in together, my soul ended up failing miserably! My Anna was damaged by me! . . . Having written all this, I feel like an inmate on death row waiting for the death penalty. You said you wanted to make one's character public (*renge gongkai*), I almost have a character too shameful to be publicized. You say you're a juvenile delinquent, I am simply the essence of sin. . . . Would you want to be a brother to someone like me? Am I worthy to be your brother? Please make haste and announce my death sentence![73]

On one level, Guo and Tian refer to particular instances of their unworthiness, which they feel necessary to reveal as a token of their sincerity toward one another. The self-undercutting accusations serve an apparently more lofty purpose of moral rectitude. The exchange reflects no more than a humble way of expressing their mutual admiration. Beyond the bonds of friendship and intimacy between literary men, however, confessions operate in conjunction with the literary on a different level. Underlying both men's accounts of themselves is a strongly professed fear of imposture. Unlike the literary treatment of imposture as a problem of national identities, however, here the notion provides currency for accessing unconditional recognition. Professing to his own delinquency, Tian is not at all trying to discourage his interlocutor's sympathy. Far from hiding a true self to be ashamed of, Tian discloses the terms by which it will be recognized. At the risk of destroying his own idealized illusion, the addressee is asked to endanger himself in the knowing. Suspending all judgments by which the unworthy will be adjudicated, the interlocutor enters into a relation in which the only stance to take is that of the sympathizer and, in many ways, co-conspirator.

Appropriately enough, Guo responds in just that way. Not only does he share in the guilt of imposture but he claims that his disguise has been even more insidiously successful than Tian's "juvenile delinquent." He has deceived, much as his protagonists have attempted to do with the women in their lives, someone as innocent as Zong, whom he "victimized" and who has shown nothing but the utmost faith in him. The parallel between the innocent male interlocutor and the equally dedicated female figure is as striking as it is puzzling. Because both rapports are motivated by guilt and implicated in a drama of exposure, their roles in the narrative of repentance seem to contribute to the perpetuation of the penitent's confession. With the legitimating act of repentance, the guilty now exhibits himself in all his nakedness. But that is in fact what he has been doing all along with tenacity and resilience. Indeed, indispensable to his self-reproach is an audience.

Trefoil was published two months after the letters were completed. A public venue seems to have always been part of the desired reception, as Guo sent both Tian's letter and his response to Tian to Zong, allegedly on the newfound conviction that he must bare all his sins to Zong as well. Zong published the letter in *Learning Lamp* in February. The next time he writes Guo, he asks for his forgiveness for publishing his letters without consent. Guo, however, insists that he has nothing to begrudge Zong for, because the publication was "more than what he could have hoped for," for he "often reproached [himself] for not having the genius of Augustine, Rousseau, and Tolstoy, and the ability to write a naked 'confession' and declare [his] faults to the world."[74]

Communal Intimacies

The way in which penitence is enacted, performed, and even insisted upon underlies a self-inventing literary persona as well as a genuine mode of building a community. Self-exposure ensures intimacy among its male constituents. There exists little distinction between a self-conscious aesthetic posturing and the literary experience. For all their regrets and insistence on being left alone, Tian and Guo are not looking to punish themselves with an incommunicable burden of conscience. On the contrary, this is what brings them together, a mutually recognized and sympathized unworthiness. In both letters, the beseeching quickly turns into a welcoming of new friendship, a new confidant who forgoes the authority to judge only because he himself is guilty of a greater moral decline.

Open confession, in the form of "making public one's character," is an interesting phenomenon alongside May Fourth's penchant for first-person narratives and the diary and epistolary forms. From Lu Xun's seminal "Diary of a Madman" to Ding Ling's "Miss Sophie's Diary," as well as lesser-known pieces by Lu Yin and Zhang Ziping, the desire to confess one's true guilt seems to attribute shame to the nature of human frailties. At the same time, however, the demonstrative aspect of these confessions also creates a certain gratification in tireless self-exposure. It becomes productive of a particular mode of self-expression that survives its own self-denunciation. Confessions of failure, sexual or national, continually privilege the self as the point of reference, even if the guilty ostensibly leaves his fate in the hands of an other.

Whereas the woman figure is often present in confessional narratives as the redeemer or punisher, *Trefoil* is a series of penitent writings circulated within a community of literary men. The exaggerated language of culpability and eagerness for judgment extends beyond masochistic, fictional narratives and resurfaces as the very terms of self-perception for male writers. Just as the protagonists of Yu Dafu or Guo Moruo beg for death at the hands of their cruel mistresses, the writers themselves appeal to one another in the same language of guilt and exoneration. The distinction between private and public writings dissolves in the form of confession, which moves easily between literary persona and personal identity, excess and redemption.[75]

Confession to failures thrives on the possibility of exteriorizing personal pain. In the same way that it obfuscates the line between literary masochism and personal correspondence, it also escapes the distinction between private suffering and national distress. This is perhaps one of the distinguishing and persistent features of the modern narrative of the self in these masochistic narratives that emerges resiliently, however repeatedly defeated, under the imperatives of desire, sexuality, and sacrifice.

A literary consideration demonstrates the intricate workings of the felt need for trauma in the individual. It also opens for consideration the possibility of a cultural trauma relying on a similar but projected notion of objectless suffering. More than merely relieving oneself of inner torments, masochistic confessions gesture toward a communal sense of bondage and expiation. In the range of possible forms of cultural survival, none can do without the preservation of an insurmountable anguish that resounds in the minds of individuals and binds them to a national community. Whether this stems from the individual's recognized torment or perceived national dejection does not alter the power of suffering in summoning a nation to claim its own epoch of affliction. In the final chapter, we shall see how the notion of suffering itself comes to be consecrated as an aesthetic as well as a political experience. Thus laying claim to a national community of pain, suffering becomes that encapsulating feature of the modern epoch that brings together the self in agony with the nation in peril.

CHAPTER 7

Kumen, *Cultural Suffering*

A PROFOUND SENSE of suffering, unease, and affliction permeated social, political, and cultural life in the 1920s and 1930s. The expression of masochism and melancholia in first-person literary narratives reveals part of an increasingly encompassing sentiment regarding the destiny of modern Chinese literature. Indeed, the cultural project of literary modernity relies on the same vision of exaltation and despair as national survival. The nation's failure resounds intimately with one's own, a nexus that, according to different persuasions of literary criticism from that period, should be addressed in literature. One way of understanding this fraught relationship between self and society is to parse it in terms of the ideological content of literary trends in the 1920s and 1930s, such as realism, naturalism, Romanticism, or New Sensationalism.[1] The dilemmas expressed in literary ideologies, however, were only symptomatic of the underlying sentiment of cultural malaise itself. Questions such as what constitutes literary genius, whether great Chinese works are on par with those by Western masters, or whether Chinese literary modernity is distinctive, were asked with a poignant awareness of deficiency.

The idea of cultural discontent in this period has been considered so indisputable that it has failed to stimulate critical inquiry. No one would contest the fact that Chinese intellectuals and writers faced great uncertainty regarding their nation's destiny and their own roles in it during these decades of transition. Even less would one cast doubt upon the degree of torment these individuals proclaimed in their struggle with the project of nation building. This profound sense of uncertainty and suffering, however, has in significant ways become the productive condition of both nation and culture building in China. Torment itself has enabled the formation of a regenerative cultural identity protected from destruction and sustained in suffering. A peculiar "mood" accompanied the building of literary and cultural modernity. This sentiment did not merely confine itself to a period of political and social introspection but also provided the central impetus for the revolutionary passion necessary for patriotic resistance in the Second Sino-Japanese War. The mood for this embrace of failure was *kumen*.

The Appeal of Affliction

Kumen—variously translated as "suffering," "agony," "mental anguish," or "depression"—was a term with great discursive capital in the 1920s and 1930s. Suffering displayed the emotion of literary modernity. Encompassing the nation's demise as well as the individual's tormented sexual identity, suffering provided the common framework in which both the self and nation could be expressed. Kumen, however, has a broader range of meaning than mere suffering and depression. Even within the category of suffering, the meaning of kumen appears rather ambiguous, as it wavers between individual and cultural, bodily and psychological desires. This is evident in Yu Dafu's "Sinking," one of the earliest modern literary usages of kumen:

> The weather was now getting milder, and the grass was turning green under the influence of warm breezes. The young shoots in the wheat fields near the inn were growing taller inch by inch. With all nature responding to the call of spring, he too felt more keenly the urge (kumen) implanted in him by the progenitors of the human race. Unflaggingly, he would sin every morning underneath his quilt. He was ordinarily a very self-respecting and clean person, but when evil thoughts seized hold of him, numbing his intellect and paralyzing his conscience, he was no longer able to observe the admonition that "one must not harm one's body under any circumstances, since it is inherited from one's parents." Every time after committing the crime, he felt bitter remorse and vowed not to transgress again. But, almost without exception, the same visions appeared before him vividly, at the same time the next morning. All those descendants of Eve he would normally meet in the course of the day came to seduce him in all their nakedness, and the figure of a middle-aged *madman* appeared to him ever more tempting than that of a virgin. Inevitably, after a hard struggle (kumen) he succumbed to temptation. Thus once, twice, and this practice became a habit. Quite often, after committing the crime, he would go to the library to look up medical references on the subject. They all said without exception that this practice was most harmful to one's health. After that his fear increased.[2]

In the first instance in this passage, kumen substitutes for the desire to procreate, an "urge" passed down from the protagonist's ancestors. This sexual urge does not turn into a crime until it materializes in the act of masturbation, an event he subsequently reflects on as a transgression. However, the knowledge of guilt had already insinuated itself before the execution of the act. Sexual desire implies this prior recognition of guilt and criminality. For the protagonist, simply the awareness of physical desire predicates itself on the idea of sin as a kind of suffering and torment. The "urge" (kumen) he feels is inseparable from the act of masturbation. It not only anticipates the crime but also shares in its illicit relief. In this way, kumen embodies corpo-reality within the contour of psychological torment.

Ku, meaning "bitter," and *men*, a kind of suppressed melancholy, denote a sealed enclosure. Whereas *ku* implies a state of hardship or agony, its attachment to *men* is less transparent in meaning. We are not certain what torments the subject in his state of kumen, for *men* somehow mutes the ex-pression of suffering. On the one hand, kumen describes a state of incapac-itation from expression, as though barred from making a proper address to the outside world. On the other hand, it also demarcates an interior space of the subject that is precluded from view, an inner life removed from external scrutiny.[3] The second use of kumen in the passage suggests that conflict con-stitutes the main drama of this internal life. The protagonist's "hard struggle" presumably stems from his unspeakable sin, a struggle that finds relief only in a temporary indulgence in criminality.

Whereas in the first instance kumen hints at masturbation, in the second it aligns itself with moral conscience. Kumen seems to indicate a pivotal condition in which desire and the struggle against it are simultaneously ex-perienced. Its appeal as a description of a suffering both profound and irrec-oncilable was, however, not limited to Yu Dafu's stories, which were often considered the romanticist confessions of a prodigal figure brimming with self-indulgence and sentimentality. Lu Yin, often noted as a female counter-part to Yu Dafu, used kumen to gesture toward a kind of unconsummated female intimacy. In works such as "Lishi's Diary" (Lishi de riji) and "Some-one's Grief" (Huoren de bei ai), kumen denoted the condition particular to the torments of female sexual identity.[4]

Kumen in fact has a broader appeal than mere sentimental self-deprecation. Mao Dun and Ye Shengtao, both champions of realist fiction, favored the term in their works as well. In their usage of the term, kumen encompassed a sense of social suffering that included while exceeding indi-vidual affliction. This extension of suffering into the social found resonance with authors interested in directing literature away from the individual and toward the masses. "A Woman" (Yige nüren, 1928) by Mao Dun, for in-stance, uses kumen in the context of the New Woman. "A Woman" focuses on the consequences of oppressive social expectations on a young woman's life. It refers to this experience as the "kumen of modern women."[5] The fe-male protagonist, Qionghua, falls prey to a society that provides little space for a woman's independence. Her persistent ideals and aspirations finally end in her tragic death. Clearly, for Mao Dun, kumen is the effect of externally imposed prescriptions from which one struggles to free oneself. His preoccupation with the New Woman, also evident in his other stories, such as "Creation," leads him to understand this mood in terms of the discontent of gender.[6] Kumen, in this case, is led away from the subject's interior torment and directed at a larger social criticism.

In a similar way, Ye Shengtao uses kumen to capture the suffering of individuals at the hands of historical forces. "Night" (Ye, 1927) focuses on the mind of an old woman whose son and daughter-in-law are illegally executed by the secret police. Left to care for her grandson, she awaits confirmation of their deaths from her brother. Meanwhile, she agonizes over a question about justice that the political turmoil and violence around her fail to answer:

> Like her brother, she doesn't understand what was going through the heads of her son and daughter-in-law. But she does know very well that they are not of the same kind as those convicts with murderous looks and brutality in their voices. Why it is that they end up being treated as if they were the same is a question she has recently been brooding over. This has caused her much torment (kumen). But no one has given her an answer.[7]

From the simple view of the old woman, the deaths of her grandson's parents are incomprehensible. As a political sacrifice, her family has been torn apart, ending in her son's death and the orphaning of the infant. In Ye's text, kumen mirrors the consequence of political affliction, to which the common masses fall victim. It is enlarged to encompass the suffering brought about by forces unsympathetic to the individual. Far from being the private grievances of individuals, kumen becomes a generalized affliction that reflects more a social than a psychological torment. Instead of sympathizing with particular individuals, one sees, rather, the larger historical context that necessitates, however regrettably, their tragedies. We are alerted to the fact of suffering only to aestheticize its implications for a grander historical moment. Through the suffering of individuals, one is to extrapolate the general condition of an epoch.

To writers and intellectuals increasingly politicized toward class revolution in the 1920s and 1930s, this double sense of kumen, as both individual and societal torment, suggests a powerful way of reconciling literary artistry with social reality. Literary criticism was increasingly steered toward a more socialist agenda in an effort to bring literature closer to the masses. The kind of critical energy this project commands was evident in the ideological battles between the Creation Society and the Literary Association beginning in the early 1920s. The debate over whether literature should be not only unrestrained artistry but also responsible for social reform continues to dominate the twentieth century.[8]

It is important to recall, however, that in the early 1920s, May Fourth literature did not quite develop according to the dictates of Liang Qichao's 1902 vision of new fiction. Lu Xun's madman, Yu Dafu's self-flagellating protagonist, Ding Ling's tormented Sophie, and Mao Dun's New Woman, were, first and foremost, explorations of modern self-consciousness. Subsequent questions as to whether this was socially responsible were moralized attempts to redirect this fundamentally individualistic preoccupation. The idea of depicting real suffering as an antidote to a New Literature dominated by the narcissism of first-person narratives became the task of intellectuals and writers. Suffering was claimed as the exclusive prerogative of socially productive literature. One recalls that Hu Shi's programmatic address on the direction of New Literature specifically opposed "groaning without illness" (*wubing shenyin*) and reserved the power of affliction exclusively for serious literature.[9] The assumption here is that pointless whining about one's sexual or personal discontent destroys the proper solemnity of social anguish. However, the task of making suffering a socially useful expression did not entail abandoning the notion of individual suffering either. In 1933, when intellectual attention increasingly turned to the masses, Yu Dafu, for example, redefined kumen in a sense surprisingly different from its literary figuration in his earlier works:

> The most important thing about New Fiction is that it must relinquish the small "I" of former times in exchange for a greater "I" which can represent the masses of the world. One must take the individual's emotion of an instant and expand it into a cumulative sentiment of an epoch, a class. The kind of life story told in fiction of former times focuses primarily on the age of purity which was taken as the richest period in one's lifetime. Romance novels about love triangles or even quadrangles and novels about desire which seek to arouse the sexual appetite belong to such a genre. Fiction now, however, cannot be this way. To represent life, one must put one's finger on what is most important in life. To depict kumen, one must focus on depicting the kumen of life which is far more important than sexual kumen. Libido is not all there is to life. In a person's lifetime, there are innumerable important things that happen apart from the intercourse between men and women.[10]

Emptying kumen of its sexual content, Yu favors a kind of literature with greater resonance to the hardship of life. Although undeniable, sexual kumen is now placed in the service of the discontent at the foundation of life. Of course, no one could fail to notice that Yu rejects as much of his own literary past as he does old fiction. Significantly, he lifts kumen from the literary imagination to encompass what plagues the Chinese intellectuals in a historical moment of a cultural crisis.

In a similar way, literary critics of different orientations take kumen as the condition for the birth of Chinese literary modernity. Somehow, the severity of suffering promises a new birth and even health. The Marxist critic Qian Xingcun (A Ying), for instance, praises Yu Dafu for his "very healthy expression of the illness of an era," an era characterized by kumen.[11] Qian even specifies the various kinds of kumen facing modern life, including social and economic hardships. He maps out a succession of these kumens in the order of sexuality, society, and economy. In a remarkable trajectory, each stage is superseded by the next in a teleological progression. Kumen not only encapsulates sexual torment but also provides the impetus for revolution. Despite his Marxist teleological tendency to subsume sexual kumen under the grander project of revolution, Qian's argument does not succeed in disengaging the sexual from the political. It reveals, rather, the evocative force of sexual torment in the making of revolutionary passion.

Although its appeal cannot be limited to the sexual torment that occasioned its literary genesis, kumen includes the kind of suffering for which sexual desire is responsible. Its wide applicability lies in its articulation of a struggle against desire in general. An increasingly complex view of artistry in literary criticism reflects this attempt to deepen the notion of suffering as something particular to China's social and national struggle. Zheng Boqi, for example, the noted critic from the Creation Society, proposes that kumen itself is precisely what distinguishes Chinese literary modernity. He further uses it to separate modern Chinese literature from the Western literary conventions that have informed much of its modern style. Using kumen to distinguish a "Chinese" literary modernity, he remarks:

> China in the 1920s is just at the beginning of a great transformation. Everything has declined from the stability of thousands of years into a state of agitation. It is impossible to say whether what has been affected the most is the status of intellectuals or the livelihood of the petit bourgeois. . . . Poets, novelists, scholars, literati, the so-called petit bourgeois class, and the intellectual class are now embarking on the path of terror and anxiety. They do not have the "leisure" of Balzac to write about the *comédie humaine*. What they sense, first and foremost, is the instability of their own lives and the falling status of their position in society. The more honest those writers are to themselves, the more poignant is this realization. Hence their works are all the more objective. The reason that, in our present literary scene, this kind of objective work is so few and far between is precisely due to this lack. People often say that there are two reasons why literary works fail to be objective. The first is that the author's own experiences are limited. The second is that the author's perceptive powers lack depth. Of course, both of these explanations are irrefutable. However, the most important reason

is still the epoch in which the author lives. If this were late nineteenth-century France, Zola's Realism could certainly take our literary scene by a storm. If this were Russia in the 1900s, then Chekhov's hopelessness and detachment could surely also strongly influence our style.[12] But that is not the case. *Our epoch is an epoch of kumen.* It is an era of agitation, resistance, and outcry. In an era like this, we must absolutely reject objectivity and ask instead for pure subjectivity.[13] (emphasis added)

This view of literature sheds important light on the issue of Western literary influences. For Zheng, the determining factor in the significance of Western literature resides in China's own mode of reception. He points out that for realism, or any literary orientation, to have the effect one would admire in the Western context, one's own historical context would essentially have to pose an equivalence. Yet, he emphasizes, that is precisely never the case. The epochal moment in which China finds herself is one of suffering and agitation. Hence, its need for realism must differ radically from what Western realism can offer.

Zheng also points out that kumen necessarily envelops those who seek to give it expression. Artists' own perceptive powers do not hold the key to their expressive potential. More important is their responsiveness to what already manifests itself around them, the pervasive and undeniable mood of anguish that extends into the lives of the common people. In this way, Zheng seems to suggest that authors carry no importance in their creations. If anything, the propensity of the epoch determines both the authors and their work. However, Zheng takes a step back to assert that writers must not compromise their subjective views, for they also particularize and express in them the kumen permeating the world they live in. Interestingly, kumen returns to occupy a deeply subjective mood. The author becomes a symptom of suffering. In this way, Qian's idea of the author as the "healthy" embodiment of a diseased era is less paradoxical than it seems. If the author himself is not distanced from kumen, then he is necessarily an expression of it. Thus, he is not privy to what determines kumen, for his very authorship is predicated on his inability to reflect on what constitutes kumen.

Perhaps out of this very necessity of absolute immersion, writers and intellectuals seldom discuss kumen as such in literary or cultural discourse. Yet, as though proving its ineffable presence, kumen surfaces in every discussion. In his preface to the *Compendium of Modern Chinese Literature*, Mao Dun acknowledges kumen as the dominating mood among writers and readers alike up to the May Thirtieth Incident of 1925. In connection with the anti-British and anti-Japanese strikes in Shanghai, the event brought intellectuals to a turning point.

Members of the Creation Society, for instance, relinquished the idea of "art for art's sake" and proclaimed, instead, their embrace of revolutionary literature. In his review of the first decade of New Literature, Mao Dun distinguishes between two literary approaches to life.[14] The rationalist view sought reason rather than emotion. It proposed deepening abstractions with substance and finding the right "prescription" to remedy China's ills. The other approach moved from the emotions to the senses, from the abstract to the material. Thus, a cycle of suffering and hesitation (*kumen panghuang*) and the need for the excitement it engenders were born. Even though the rationalist view amounted only to a detached and weakened realism, Mao Dun asserts, the more volatile and emotional response intoxicated the young people. Thus, kumen and panghuang dominated the entire literary scene. Even though on the surface people make some distinction between detached cynicism and hedonistic indulgence, underneath lies the same suffering and uncertainty. Thus, a literature that was supposed to resolve itself by walking toward change at the crossroads, Mao Dun observes, ended up pacing back and forth in hesitation.

In contradistinction to Zheng Boqi, however, Mao Dun did not believe that the period of kumen would continue exerting its influence over the mood of revolutionary China. For him, the writers' inability to gain a more profound insight into their historical context bespoke the barrenness of their lives. This lack of involvement, in turn, manifested itself in the sterility of their literature. Despite his prognosis of kumen's transient appeal, however, neither was Mao Dun prepared to abandon the force of kumen for the kind of literature he wanted to espouse. Kumen remains the passion, however tormented, behind the intellectuals' sympathy for the masses. In fact, the suffering of the masses in part becomes an extension and enlargement of the inner conflict intellectuals could not resolve in sensing their own crisis of diminishing relevance.

For the intellectuals, kumen represented the propensity of an era. Its appearance always assumed a certain transparency, even though it never had a fixed definition. Kumen could be a social, cultural, political, economic, or literary condition. Covering a wide spectrum of distress from inhibition to inexpressibility, it was deeply subjective, yet also the only way to be objective. The last thing the writer should do, according to Zheng, is to abandon his subjective voice in trying to achieve an objective narration. "Pure subjectivity" holds the ultimate objectivity to which one can aspire. In this view, kumen involves anything and everything. Without having to be attached to any particular object, it comes to define an epoch. In many ways, Mao Dun also shares this conviction. Despite his effort to confine kumen to a period of political and social irresolution, the notion of suffering nonetheless sustains his vision of how to access more ambitiously a historical reality greater than the artist himself. To get at this desired kind of realism, suffering always stood for that truer object demanding that the writer exceed his own subjective experience.

Thus, as a versatile articulation of Chinese literary modernity, kumen was not a kind of literature or ideology but a "mood" giving everything a distinct inflection. A belief in suffering as the appropriate condition drives the conviction that China has a modern epoch proper to itself. Western realism would not take effect in China unless refracted through the lens of kumen. Thus, defining Chinese literary modernity prescribes a task not so much of manifesting the modern as searching for a mode in which to experience modernity.

In this way, kumen bespoke a particular problem for the intellectuals. Even though kumen was attempted as a diagnostic notion encompassing the greater social reality of cultural malaise, it was specifically the loss of purpose among intellectuals that brought on their interest in kumen. Zheng Boqi discussed kumen as if it were a kind of literary aesthetic enveloping both the author and his world, but it was most tangible as a crisis sensed within intellectual circles.

Kumen was not a kind of mental anguish belonging to a particular epoch but, in a strange way, that primal mode of operation in which intellectuals found the artistic and literary expressions befitting the historical era, which Zheng called an "epoch" (*shidai*). Extrapolated from their sense of loss and agony, kumen authorizes the mood proper to modern consciousness. Intellectuals' felt disorientation from their fallen status thus turns into the solution itself. Their unease becomes the source through which they can still be useful in that era. Kumen no longer manifests the contradictions of their private anxieties but pronounces the universal mood for an entire epochal transformation. Zheng's remark that intellectuals experienced, first and foremost, their own discomfort in a changing cultural milieu proves more central to the question of kumen than he would admit. He does reveal, however, that kumen is privileged with a sense of inescapable objectivity. By stating that the more an author confronts his own kumen, the more poignant becomes his insight, Zheng confirms the relevance of intellectual labor to a changing cultural world that threatens its very continuance. Kumen lends legitimacy to the literary preoccupation with the self and thus validates the torment of interior life as the ineluctable symptom of the modern era.

Symbol of Angst

The preoccupation with suffering as the only access to social truth was not merely the writers' vision of the political. In one way, kumen was the suffering they wanted to believe had originated from the outside, the social reality they so much wanted to access. Individual psychic torment could be legitimated to partake in a larger cultural anguish. In another way, however, kumen was consciously embraced as something intrinsic to artistry. Kumen captured the intellectuals' contemporary sense of unease, which they then displaced onto societal, cultural, and political problems. Yet kumen remains a fundamentally artistic, romanticist, and narcissistic investment in the vision of creation. What was originally the condition that literature sought to express became the effect it aimed to achieve. Kumen promises literary artistry, only if the writer or creator suffers enough during the process of creation.

Thus claiming a very specific place in the intellectuals' and writers' conception of themselves, it remains something in which writers heavily invest their romanticist identities. But the vision that suffering deepens in direct proportion to great art had greater ambitions. Kumen was considered a universal sentiment of the angst that plagues the modern consciousness. To understand how this was a reflection on the condition of modernity, Western or Chinese, one needs to turn to a familiar though little-understood episode in Chinese literary history, involving intellectuals' fascination with a translated treatise on kumen.

Kuriyagawa Hakuson (1880–1923), largely forgotten today, was a Japanese cultural and literary critic who taught Western literature at Kyoto University. He is now best known in Chinese literary studies for his collection *Kumon no shōchō*, which Lu Xun translated into Chinese as *Kumen de xiangzheng* (Symbol of angst) in 1924. The well-noted connection between Lu Xun's interest in Kuriyagawa's works and his knowledge of Freudian psychoanalysis, however, has been accompanied by little analysis. Beyond an act of translation, *Symbol of Angst* facilitated conceptions of suffering as a validation of great art in modern Chinese literary criticism. The translation of this text into Chinese is as much a displacement of Western theories of evolution and creation as it is a reinvention of torment. It had long been held that the theory of evolution had dominated intellectual thought since Yan Fu's translation of Thomas Huxley's *Evolution and Ethics*. However, the fascination with kumen also led writers and intellectuals to aspire to a mystical view of regeneration and evolution that was deeply indebted to failure.

Kumon no shōchō was never intended by its author to be published in its present form. The title was taken from an earlier essay Kuriyagawa had published in the Japanese journal *Kaizō*, a leading progressive journal that started after World War I and was read by Chinese intellectuals.[15] According to his student Yamamoto Shūji, who made the editorial decisions, Kuriyagawa had intended to incorporate this earlier essay into part of a larger project. Yamamoto thus thought it appropriate to take its title for the whole.[16] By the time Lu Xun decided to translate it, two other translations already existed. One of these, by Feng Zikai, was published as part of the Literary Research Association Book Series; the other was a translation of the third chapter, published in *Eastern Miscellany* around the same time that Lu Xun's version appeared.[17] What Lu Xun apparently did not know was that an earlier translation of the first two chapters had already appeared in *Learning Lamp* (Xuedeng) as early as 1921.[18]

Symbol of Angst is a treatise on the fundamentals of literary aesthetics. At the core, it privileges a deeply subjective relation to artistic creation and appreciation over a deterministic approach. Kuriyagawa absorbs into his thinking various debates stemming from the contexts of German and English Romanticism and philosophy. Because Kuriyagawa had taught English literature and literary criticism, his premise is heavily influenced by literary trends in Western thought. Yet he is reluctant to wholly identify with any of their articulations, such as Henri Bergson's élan vital, Nietzsche's notion of the instinct, Schopenhauer's will to power, Bernard Shaw's "life force," or Bertrand Russell's "impulse." Among the lesser-known figures he invokes are the English mystic poet Edward Carpenter (1844–1929), with his idea of the "cosmic self," and the German poet Nikolaus Lenau (1802–50), with his notion of Weltschmerz. Seeing in all these philosophical and literary works the attempt to grasp at something more originary than rational thought, something that underlies life itself, Kuriyagawa sets out to identify the source of all creative energy that drives humankind to higher and higher expressions.

Of the four parts, the first, "The Theory of Creation," is the most complete. Kuriyagawa begins his treatment on the symbol of kumen with a symbolic image: "Where iron and stone collide, sparks of fire leap out; where the torrent is blocked by a boulder, a rainbow appears in the spattering foam. Under the collision of two different forces, the kaleidoscope of a beautiful and dazzling life and the myriad of living come into being."[19] This initial metaphor serves as the basis for all subsequent attempts to explain kumen in Kuriyagawa's treatise. Kumen, in fact, is never defined. We are given images of conflict and strife, but never a precise articulation of its constitution. At times, Kuriyagawa explains kumen as a contributing factor to psychic trauma. Other times, he describes it as psychic trauma itself.[20] It is a "reaction" to "action," we are told. Kumen unleashes that creative energy, the explosiveness, danger, and underlying destructiveness threatening the basis of civilization that we call society.[21] For Kuriyagawa, our desire for self-expression, which arises from the extreme suffering of kumen, covers anything from the instinct to survive, the impulse to play, religious faith, lofty aspirations, the desire to know, and the ambition for conquest.[22] It is an impulse toward not any specific goal but the expression that would be the precondition of any realization.

Among other things, kumen is also a prerequisite to absolute freedom. Only under censorship and oppression can one imagine and desire with passion unconditional liberation. However, Kuriyagawa hastens to add, the two forces whose clash gives rise to kumen are not easily dichotomized into the categories of individual and society. The conflict also exists within the individual as a fundamental contradiction. The "human" at once embodies the demonic and the divine, the narcissistic and the altruistic. In fact, Kuriyagawa asserts, the force that wishes to break through the obstacle and the force of the obstacle itself are one and the same thing. As the oppression increases, so does the explosiveness and destructiveness. Without oppression, Kuriyagawa believes, there can be no energy in life.

Thus, Kuriyagawa suggests, kumen both participates in an opposition and absorbs this opposition into itself. No real exteriority lies outside kumen, for its experience implies this external opposition as an inner tension. Hidden in the opposition between oppression and life is the equivalence that life *is* oppression. There is no opposition to escape but a tension to be preserved. Kuriyagawa shifts from talking about kumen as a required state for higher liberation to universalizing it as the very substance of life itself. The importance of oppression lies in less its imposition from the outside than its centrality to inner desire. Kuriyagawa seems to be pointing at kumen's indispensability to the experience of creativity, a condition he grasps with more confidence than he could the state of creation itself.

The order of necessity he outlines operates, in fact, in the reverse. Rather than the state of suffering desiring its liberation, the state of liberation covets the bondage. Even though Kuriyagawa speaks of artistic creation as the absolute state of freedom, he also underscores the fact that artistry holds its greatest potential when most restrained. Lacking a precise definition in Kuriyagawa's conception, kumen encompasses all sources of life that react to the denial of expression. Thus it is, in Kuriyagawa's synthesis, both Bergson's idea of élan vital and Freud's notion of repressed dream content; it is Milton's lost paradise as well as the Weltschmerz of the German poetic and philosophical imagination. The symbol of kumen stands in for all that seeks to give expression to the kind of "psychic trauma" constituting the condition of life.

Kuriyagawa intends the lack of specificity in his generalizing conception. He is neither convinced of nor satisfied with theories of life and creation that gave primacy to certain aspects of human activity or motivation over others.

He takes a particular liking, however, to Bergson's notion of élan vital and the primacy of intuition. Born in the year that Darwin's *The Origin of Species* was published, Henri Bergson (1859–1941) became one of the most influential French philosophers in the early decades of the twentieth century, only to dwindle in status after the Second World War.[23] Much like Kuriyagawa Hakuson, Bergson is little studied today. His perhaps most widely read book, *Creative Evolution* (1907), received the Nobel Prize for Literature in 1927, a fact that also accounted for its popularity among the Chinese intellectual elite.[24] Against mechanism and finalism, Bergson proposed a theory of life force, élan vital, that places the experiential limits of the human soul beyond the determined finitude inscribed in the premise of Darwin's theory of evolution and causality.

A proponent of an almost mystical and religious view of the spirit, Bergson argues for a primordial and generative energy unspecified in its nature but marked by its impulsion. Drive in the pure sense, it tends toward no goal, as though pulled by a necessity exterior to itself, but is in fact compelled by its own raison d'être to express itself as an impetus. There are different ways in which this impetus can then be utilized, but that teleology does not define the substance of this energy. It is rather the result that unintentionally follows from the event of the impulsion. Thus, evolution must be grasped as a movement rather than a series of accomplished positions. The mobility remains indivisible, for it does not reflect an accumulation of discrete increments according to some blueprint, even though one is trained to think against this intuition of fluidity and analyze evolution as a series of changes. The diversity thus engendered from evolution marks not a necessity of adaptation but a process of self-generating change, responding first and foremost to this impetus within.

Bergson's notion of creative evolution challenges Darwin's view of natural selection. Species, in his view, do not change in order to compete with one another; they are rather pushed to continually evolve on their own according to their own necessities. Each response to the necessity, in turn, generates a different need that is specific to the way the species has evolved. The process continuously renews itself without a terminal point. It carries a movement that responds to its own impetus to travel rather than to the logic of reaching any particular destination.

Bergson's notion of creative evolution, therefore, places the emphasis on individuals' own initiative to change rather than on pitting one against the other. The appeal of Bergson to the likes of Kuriyagawa Hakuson may perhaps be best understood in the translator's preface to the 1919 Chinese edition of *Creative Evolution*:

The theory of the various stages of evolution, as explained by Spencer and Darwin, is no more than using the creed of "struggle for existence, survival of the fittest" to forcibly attribute coherent meaning to the various loose details throughout history after the fact of evolution. In actuality, the ones competing for survival may not be those selected by nature, and those who survive may not be the fittest. Each species has its own basic instinct, its own drive for absolute freedom, and its own circumstance for continuation. Because the required circumstances are different, we have diversity among living things. Where humans are at now is not won from vanquishing other living things. The superman of the future will not have evolved because he had vanquished the humans. The instinct of life is extraordinarily rich and the parameters of its freedom are immense. The realm of creation is also expansive. The myriad living things all have their own circumstances for advancement. They do not harm each other, nor do they make concessions towards one another.[25]

If one compares this view of evolution to Yan Fu's translation of *The Origin of Species*, one can see that the cultural and intellectual preoccupation in the 1920s and 1930s has certainly changed in significant ways. The appeal of an explanation of evolution based not on the inevitability of struggling against outsiders but on the notion of a self-driven impulse for life cannot be underestimated. The power held by those who are superior, in this view, does not reflect the legitimacy of might. Domination merely occupies one moment in the continual flow of life energy. Those who are subjugated, by the same logic, cannot be judged as weak, for they too are progressing along the trajectory befitting their own life force. The espousal of a creative, innovative, and self-regenerating evolution is discussed as a process of all humankind, but the generalization of life's impetus clearly addresses the particular concerns of the Chinese intellectuals. If power does not equate superiority, or subjugation inferiority, then a national destiny is not forged by the strife between nations but, rather, propelled by its own inner necessity. The distinction between inferiority and superiority, as concerning China's national strength, becomes less relevant than one's conviction that it is all part of a due course. Because the required condition for unleashing life's vital force varies, one's transformation does not ultimately rely on fulfilling a goal or achieving a state. The mobility of the instinct of life is itself a directional force, however that direction realizes itself.

In Kuriyagawa's synthesis of Bergson's élan vital, the expansive force of life, as that which conjoins all life and humans, takes on an additional dimension. In his "Theory of Appreciation," Kuriyagawa also presents the so-called common content of life as the basis on which aesthetic appreciation cannot help coming into existence. Life force is seen as a "Great Life" in which we all take part. Any expression of individual contains this universality. Whether ancient or modern, Eastern or Western, we share in this common humanity, even if we do not see it at first. The moment of realization always occurs in the instant of self-reflection. Readers discover, through the writer's symbolism of his own desire for expression, their part in this larger content of life. The literary work speaks to the reader, even as it expresses the writer's inner thoughts. Because of the suggestiveness and stimulus of the symbolization, literature ingeniously leads the readers into a hypnotic state and takes them to a realm of illusions and fantasies, the world of dreams. In this absolute realm of pure creation, readers come to recognize the content of their own lives.

For Kuriyagawa, then, the writer need not strive for an objectivity restricted to the understanding of the intellect. Rather, the writer must reach deep into the reservoir of his suppressed impulses in order to tap into the stream of life. However, this reservoir of life's vital energy is preconditioned by suffering. The promise of life resides in its barred expression. Here, Kuriyagawa supplements Bergson's unbridled, explosive force of vitality with the then relatively unknown theory of the unconscious. For Kuriyagawa, Freud's notion of repressed dream content offers the dimension of suffering appropriate for explaining the genesis of artistic creations.

Although he gives credit to psychoanalysis, Kuriyagawa received with much skepticism the assertion that sexual libido is the primary driving force behind people's aspiration for sublime works of literature. For him, the impulse that drives humans is more sublime than what sexual desire can encompass. Instead, he finds Freud's most useful contribution in the theory of dreams. Quoting a case study, which actually comes from a lecture Freud gave at Clark University in Massachusetts in December 1908, Kuriyagawa finds the idea of repressed dream content most appropriate to his view on life's vital force. Lumping together psychoanalytical notions of "preconscious," "unconscious," and "conscious," Kuriyagawa asserts that what he means by the symbol of kumen is no other than the "content of life." Shared by all humans on a fundamental level, this common content lifts out of symbolism, by which Kuriyagawa means any linguistic artifice erected to convey suggestion, the power to evoke rather than inform. Symbolism is an abstraction of a greater content of life as universality. Inducing in the reader a state of self-reflection, literature, in this way, seeks to find a point of resonance in its addressee such that readers can discover their own participation in this reservoir of intuition rather than intellect.

Kuriyagawa's knowledge of Freud was limited to the latter's early works on dream interpretation.[26] Yet he gleaned much from early Western studies attempting to approach literature from a psychoanalytical perspective, such as Albert Mordell's *The Erotic Motive in Literature* (1919), I. H. Coriat's *The Hysteria of Lady Macbeth* (1912), Alexander Harvey's *William Dean Howells:*

A Study of the Achievement of a Literary Artist (1917), Axel Johan Uppvall's *August Strindberg: A Psychoanalytic Study* (1920), and Wilfred Lay's *H. G. Wells and His Mental Hinterland* (1917). It is likely that Kuriyagawa came across Uppvall's work during his visit to Clark University, where he met the reputable psychoanalyst G. Stanley Hall (1844–1924), as *August Strindberg* was a dissertation written under Hall's supervision. Hall was the founding president of the American Psychological Association (1892) who was responsible for inviting the then relatively unknown Sigmund Freud to introduce his views on abnormal psychology in his first lecture series in America.[27]

Kuriyagawa disagrees with Freud's premise, as expressed in his study of Leonardo da Vinci, that all creative impulses are sublimated libidinal desires deflected from their original, prohibited objects. He suggests, in place of Freud's "sexual desire," employing "interest" in the analysis as a way of broadening the definition of the creative impulse to encompass life's principle of survival.[28] One lives through the interminable and repetitive experience of kumen, a process of struggle. Displacing Freud's emphasis on the development and organization of erogenous zones on the infant's body with a more general notion of survival, Kuriyagawa gives a different narrative:

> Life is combat. From the first day we are born onto the earth—no, at the very first moment, we already experience the agony of battle. Is not the infant's physical being a continuous struggle against hunger, disease, heat and cold? Leaving aside the ten [sic] peaceful months of sleeping in the mother's womb, one's life as an "individual being" begins only after leaving the mother's body. The agony of struggle, therefore, will have become an inevitability. Is not that cry, simultaneous with one's birth, the first outcry of suffering? Is that cry, which has only just met the stimuli from the external world upon leaving the safe harbor of the maternal womb, the battle cry of he who has come into the front line of life? Or the first cry of agony? Or the congratulatory cry for those who enjoy their lives on earth? These questions aside, that primordial cry can be considered to be identical in essence to art on a certain level of meaning. Thus, to dispel hunger, the child restlessly seeks the mother's breast. After feeding, one sees the beautiful smile on its angelic, peaceful face. Both the restlessness and smile are the lyrical poetry and art of humanity. The more vibrant the child, the louder its cry. Without this sound or this art, there awaits only death.[29]

The more painful the struggle, the more heightened the desire to live. Kuriyagawa further emphasizes that the symbolism to which he refers is not restricted to French symbolism but extends more generally to the sublimation of repressed experiences.[30] Furthermore, the repressed content is not, as the term would suggest, exhausted by the psychoanalytical view of sexual repression. Rather, it applies to any experience of inhibited desire. Kuriyagawa's maneuver away from the sexual underlies the larger significance of kumen. Psychoanalysis was considered to be a legitimate Western science at the time. It gave an appealing system of rationalization to explain the human unconscious, a task that from its inception was subjected to the difficulty of translating the unconscious into conscious discourse. In an attempt to steer away from the sexual, Kuriyagawa was restoring to the foundation of psychic conflict the sanctity of creative imagination. He did not think a cure for "psychic trauma" would be appropriate or even desirable. For him, it was the generative condition of artistic expression.

Kuriyagawa's appeal to an entire generation of May Fourth writers was significant. The influence his works had on Tian Han, for example, the founder of modern drama and a Creation Society member, can be easily seen in Tian's 1920 essay on New Romanticism.[31] He had personally visited Kuriyagawa while was studying in Japan and even asked Guo Moruo to accompany him. From Lu Xun's diary, we know that he was translating *Kumon no shōchō* at the same time he was writing *Wild Grass* (Yecao). Even though it took him only nineteen days to translate it, *Kumen de xiangzheng* was to have a profound impact on the artistic and psychological formation of *Wild Grass*.[32] Pieces from this collection of prose poetry were often written in conjunction with chapters of *Symbol of Angst*.[33] Lu Xun not only recommended *Symbol* for reading at a lecture he gave in 1927 but he himself had also taught it in 1925.[34] As late as 1933, he lamented that he had not seen the likes of Kuriyagawa in recent years.[35]

Lu Xun never met or read Kuriyagawa before the latter's death in the Kanto earthquake in September 1923, nor is there evidence to suggest that the Japanese scholar was familiar with Lu Xun's works. Lu Xun's knowledge of his biography is limited. Other than where Kuriyagawa was schooled, his foot amputation, and a general idea of his travels, Lu Xun knew him only through his works.[36] A year after Lu Xun translated *Symbol of Angst*, he also translated and published some of Kuriyagawa's articles from *Out of the Ivory Tower*. Lu Xun also included a partial translation of Kuriyagawa's "Walking Towards the Crossroads," which resonates with the title of his own later collection, *Panghuang* (Hesitation, wandering), written between March 1924 and November 1925. Indeed, Kuriyagawa's writings captured for writers such as Lu Xun the hesitation and uncertainty suffered by the "modern" consciousness. Discussions and references to the dilemma of modern China often use the image of a "crossroads" (*shizi jiekou*) as a metaphor for intellectual crisis. Lu Xun's short story collection, *Panghuang*, resonates with this notion of not knowing the right path to take.

Scholars who acknowledge the Japanese critic's influence on Lu Xun often credit Kuriyagawa with providing Lu Xun a knowledge of Freudian psychoanalysis. Writers such as Guo Moruo and Lu Xun dallied with psychoanalysis in their literary writings only to abandon it quickly afterward upon realizing its limitations. Lu Xun's process of writing one of his *Old Tales Retold*, "Nüwa," a literary experiment with psychoanalysis, was interrupted because of his own skepticism regarding the primacy of sexuality. However, Freudian psychoanalysis as absorbed into Kuriyagawa's idea of kumen clearly had much more appeal to Lu Xun. Kumen enabled the conceptualization of a kind of suffering transcending sexual or personal distress. It promised a broader vision of torment, offering Lu Xun a way of rejecting the sexual premise of psychoanalysis. Prompted by the 1933 New Year's issue of *Eastern Miscellany* featuring readers' responses to a call for submissions on dreams and ideals for the future, Lu Xun gave his most overt and lengthy objection to Freud's theory of sexuality. In a language strikingly similar to Kuriyagawa's own discussion of birth as the originating moment of kumen, Lu Xun found a way to challenge the predominance of sexuality in "On Dreams":

> In the columnist's "Thoughts After Reading," he used Freud's ideas to advance the notion that "authentic" dreams "express each individual's deep secret without carrying any societal function." Freud thinks that repression is the basis of dreams. But why are people repressed? This would then have to do with norms and habits of society. . . . However, Freud probably had a pocket full of change and too much food, and thus didn't feel the hardship of keeping fed. That's why he focused only on the libido. There are many who, being from the same background, would enthusiastically applaud in agreement with him. As he has told us himself, the reason daughters love their fathers and sons their mothers, is related to sexuality. Yet soon after babies are born—regardless of whether they are male or female—they all pucker their lips and turn their heads back and forth. Is that because they want to kiss someone of the opposite sex? No, everyone knows that it's because they want to be fed![37]

Dissatisfied with the all-encompassing sexual explanation for human discontent, Lu satirically offers an eating metaphor in its place. For him, sexuality is less a repression in need of therapeutic enlightenment than one of the many sacrifices people have to make as a matter of course. Freud serves as a convenient stand-in object for Lu Xun's sarcasm, for Lu Xun was both reacting against and sympathizing with the political pretensions of Chinese intellectual life. On this particular occasion, his dismay was prompted by *Eastern Miscellany*'s publication of various prominent figures' personal ideals and visions regarding the future.[38]

The editor had asked for submissions under two categories: depictions of a future China and dreams of a personal future. The latter category was encouraged to be as visionary as possible because, the editor explains, it was of a fantastic nature and required no restraints of realism. Among the prominent figures who replied were high-profile intellectuals and writers. For a future China, the female writer Xie Bingying looked forward to a realm of great union without national, racial, or class boundaries. Ba Jin, in a more pessimistic vein, saw no future for China. Quoting what he had written in a short story, he remarked, in a way strikingly similar to concerns voiced by eugenicists over premature racial aging, that China had become decrepit with old age and that even its youth was fragile and weak. Zhang Kebiao, the editor of *Shidai huabao* (Pictorials of the times), thought that only a dream vision would do away with distinctions such as nationalism. Ye Shengtao modestly hoped that everyone would stay fed and have jobs. Lao She, in the same way, made his point by underscoring that dreams have nothing to do with keeping people from starvation. Mao Dun noted his own humble effort in merely trying not to dream but to recognize reality. Shi Zhecun, member of *Les Contemporains*, expressed what he thought was the dream shared by every average citizen: to go to a foreign country without being held in contempt and to be able to fearlessly spit out "foreign devil!" at a Westerner on Chinese soil. The intertwining of utopian visions and national vengeance marks, once more, the conjunction between individual hopes for a better life and the national desire for stronger sovereignty. As for more humble and practical aspirations, the secret desires ranged anywhere from better pay to having a flushing toilet in every household.

For the editor, the responses to the vision of a better China sketch out the general intellectual atmosphere at the time. In his editor's postscript, he states that all these ideals are part of the secret hope that China may encompass this world without boundaries.[39] Even though the respondents seem to reject the idea of nationhood, that does not mean that they do not love the nation. It is because their hope for a future China is so great, he observes, that only a utopian world can embody such an ideal.

For Lu Xun, however, these dreams for the future reveal only the intellectuals' concern with their immediate gains. Few, he jeers, were actually propagating a vision for the future without interest for their own rice bowls. These respondents said what they thought was appropriate to their status and reputation. For that reason, although many harbored hopes for a realm of great union—a notion harking back to the optimistic visions of late Qing reformers and even adapted by Zhang Jingsheng in his "society of beauty"— few could imagine the political terror and persecution that would necessarily precede it. Indeed, Lu Xun remarks, those who truly endeavor to realize the vision of a future China are those who are not merely talking but doing something about it. Of course, he says with deeper sarcasm, one need not feel embarrassed about prioritizing one's rice bowl. At a time when the preoccupation with libido treats pillow talk as public conversation, one need not be embarrassed about admitting to the pressing need for food. In the end, whatever has been unabashedly expressed as dreams for the future, Lu

Xun comments, are still waking dreams. One pretends to take relief in the fact that censorship is being lifted. However, even in relating their true feelings, they still speak in observance of the appropriate political slogans. For this reason, Lu Xun remarks, the editor has failed miserably in his task.

Interestingly, this episode, which brought in Freudian psychoanalysis as a convenient object of critique, reveals the competing stakes in envisioning a new China. Lu Xun, in many ways, also expresses a vision of future China. For him, however, this vision is not possible without a sober critique, exposing the kind of pretense that lies at the root of China's ills. Although on this occasion his critique aims at his fellow intellectuals and writers, the method belongs to his usual practice of self-dissection. The purpose is to confront the illness in others and, at the same time, to share in that discomfort itself as what plagues China. Unlike the editor, Lu Xun imagines a better China not through utopian ideals but through their annihilation. Annoyed with his colleagues' vision of China, he detests the cowardice in writers who would not speak truthfully about the nation they live in. Lu Xun's vision was not set in the future but fixed on the suffering of the present, a suffering of terror and persecution that for him reflected most honestly the condition of China.

This more basic preoccupation with suffering, rather than psychoanalytical explanations of sexuality, underlies Lu Xun's interest in Kuriyagawa and his idea of kumen. Even though Kuriyagawa primarily articulates the sublimation of agony as the ecstasy of artistic and literary creation, the appeal of suffering as a primal condition carried greater resonance for Chinese intellectuals. It was what they felt within themselves and what they struggled to exteriorize as a political, social, and universal experience. This struggle both entails an emotional difficulty or intellectual dilemma and involves a graphic form of pain for its expression. This preoccupation with excavating the kumen within their intimate sense of self is most compellingly expressed in a remarkable comment Lu Xun made in explaining his personal attraction to Kuriyagawa Hakuson's works:[40]

> In translating this book, my purpose was not to expose another's faults in order to bring gratification to the Chinese. China cannot afford the ambition of exploiting others' crises, nor do I feel it incumbent upon me to poke fun at the weaknesses of another nation. Yet as I watch (*pangguan*) him [Kuriyagawa] whip himself, it is as if I feel the pain on my own body. Then, however, it is as though I am suddenly relieved by a sedative. Those who live in ancient and festering countries . . . feel a certain pain, like a boil. Those who have never had one or had it cut away probably wouldn't know this. Otherwise, they would understand that the pain of its removal brings far more pleasurable relief than the pain of enduring it. I supposed this is the so-called "extreme pleasure" (*tongkuai*). This is

precisely what I wish to use to first awaken that pain and then impart this "extreme pleasure" to other people suffering the same illness.[41]

As announced from the onset, Lu Xun takes no pleasure in the sight or exposure of another's pain, another's humiliation. The position of the spectator affords him neither gratification nor interest. Yet we can only take Lu Xun to mean a certain kind of spectatorship still assured of its distance from the object, for he immediately uses the same visual metaphor to present a very different kind of experience, one that participates in the object's pain by "watching from the side" (*pangguan*). It is not that this participation contributes to producing the other's pain but that it experiences the pain as though it were the subject's own. In fact, the distance between subject and object is dissolved in a moment of desiring pain for oneself, the certitude of which offers Lu Xun the purging effect of the "sedative."

At this point, Lu Xun has identified with what he perceives as Kuriyagawa's relentless self-laceration. He then forces this identification onto others who supposedly "suffer from the same illness." Through this identification Lu Xun legitimates himself as the proper administrator of the pain. At the same time, he justifies the pain as an inevitability, as a future disaster, displaced from the individuals themselves. Although the interiorization of pain is necessary for Lu Xun to feel it—"as if the pain were felt on my body"—this substitutive identification is then taken as an illness to which all others *already* suffer. It is only at the time of the sore's removal, Lu Xun continues, that the people suffering from it will understand that "the pain of its removal brings far more pleasurable relief than the pain of enduring it." Thus, not only does Lu Xun explicitly distinguish between pleasurable and unpleasurable pain but it is only with pain that he can then "impart this 'painful pleasure' to other people."

This desire to bring to others the pain of the experience as a certain kind of enlightenment in many ways encapsulated the elitist intellectual conceit, the critique of which would later be used to dethrone the May Fourth Movement. Kuriyagawa's notion of taking intellectual aspirations and tasks out of the protected environment of the ivory tower could not have spoken more poignantly to Lu Xun's sardonic but tormented humor. Kuriyagawa's critique of the lack of resolve of the Japanese in committing themselves to pragmatic action would have pierced the minds of many Chinese writers. Equally significantly, Kuriyagawa's critique of the Japanese could only have had such relevance for the Chinese intellectuals because the latter were embroiled in their own conviction of the failed project of intellectual modernity. Kuriyagawa fulfills, as seen earlier with Arthur Smith, Lu Xun's relentless imperative of China's self-dissection. Interestingly, amid this painful embrace of failure, what Lu Xun hopes for is the regeneration of China. In his translator's preface to *Kumen de xiangzheng*, he takes the capacity for artistic creation as a reflection of the spirit of an age and, more specifically, of China.[42] He laments that China's current condition gives rise to no great art, because China's spirit is in a state of atrophy. Kumen, in a paradoxical way, provides the regeneration for this state of decline. Suffering becomes the path to triumph. And it is this intertwinement between pain and triumph, individual suffering and national spiritual regeneration, that is embodied in the visual representation Lu Xun chose for kumen.

Embodying Kumen

Lu Xun first met the young artist Tao Yuanqing in 1924 through Xu Qinwen, his longtime friend. Lu Xun did not record this acquaintance until five months later, by which time he had become impressed with the struggling young artist's work and asked him to design the cover for *Kumen de xiangzheng*.[43] Tao, who was trained in traditional brush painting, worked for the famous publishing house of the Shanghai newspaper *Shibao* (Current affairs) and was in charge of design for *Xiao Shibao* (Little current affairs). At that time, *Shibao* had affiliations with the Youzheng Publishing House. Through that connection, Tao had access to Di Chuqing's collection of Japanese and Indian art, which he absorbed into his own style.[44] After working for *Shibao*, Tao became interested in Western oil painting and further developed its influence into his work. Lu Xun, whose interest in art and particularly woodblock prints is well known, shared many of Tao's views on art and its social purpose. Tao designed other covers for Lu Xun's collections, such as *Panghuang* and *Fen* (Grave). He also did Lu Xun's favorite portrait of himself as well as the cover design for his translation of Kuriyagawa Hakuson's *Out of the Ivory Tower*. Unfortunately, their collaboration lasted only four years. Tao died in 1928, shortly after starting to teach at the Hangzhou West Lake National Art School. Lu Xun donated three hundred dollars to help build a small memorial for him at West Lake and took it upon himself to publish a collection of Tao's works.

Lu Xun did much to help the young artist with his career, including arranging an exhibition of his works in 1925.[45] At the time, Lu Xun commented on Tao's style as "using innovative form and color to depict his own world, while still harboring within himself the soul China has always had, that is, its national and racial character."[46] Lu Xun's opinion was unchanged at Tao's next exhibition in 1927. Yet this time he reveals the deeper affinity he shares with the young artist. People in China today, Lu Xun notes, are indeed in a state of kumen, due to a sense of belatedness felt by youths born into an ancient civilization. While new ways of thinking appropriate to the new epoch overwhelm them from all sides, they realize that they themselves are still imprisoned in an ancient cell. Thus, Lu Xun continues, they wake, struggle, rebel, and want to take part in global tasks. Whereas artists, Lu Xun observes, have rebelled against, severed themselves from, and remolded nature, art historians abandoned traditional criteria of aesthetic appreciation. Thus, they praise the murals in the tombs of Egyptian pharaohs and extol the intricate designs carved into African sword handles. This leads them to the false conclusion that they must return to the prison of the past. For this misconceived reason, they can only accept with reservations the bold strides ventured by new artists. As a result, Lu Xun states, we are held back and end up in a double cell.

For Lu Xun, Tao's art, however, resolves this double bind. Both inside and out, he has moved with the current of new ways of thought in the world, yet he has not lost China's racial character. Lu Xun makes a parallel between art and literature by pointing out that there are those who object to the use of "European syntax" in modern literature. They would harshly and sarcastically criticize those who use European forms by pointing out what a pity it is that these people have not managed to grow a white skin or high noses. However, Lu Xun points out, precisely because their skins are ultimately not white and their noses still flat despite their Western affectations, they have become the oddities ostracized in China today. Tao, however, claims to be neither wholly Europeanized nor traditionally Chinese. Although he uses new colors and forms, he is still Chinese on the inside. Only those who have any real ambition to join in the pursuit of global tasks, Lu Xun remarks, can begin to appreciate his art.

Lu Xun's remarks are revealing. He sees kumen as a struggle between Western and Chinese modernities. Yet this struggle neither affirms nor discounts the desirability of Western modernity. The struggle itself compels the expression of a distinct Chinese identity. Even though Lu Xun still largely equates worldliness with westernization, he talks about the global as something to be excavated from within as well. It is that irreducible Chineseness, defined as a racial and national essence, that cannot be effaced, however much one tries. It perseveres regardless of the form one uses. Thus Tao, precisely because he mixes Western with traditional Chinese style, expresses what is peculiar to the Chinese, a tension that can only be called a modern Chinese identity. This, for Lu Xun, constitutes the task of world literature, an enterprise global in form but Chinese in character. However, it is important to note, Lu Xun's notion differs in significant ways from Zhang Zhidong's well-known call in 1898 for "Chinese as essence, westernization as application." Nor is the characteristically Chinese he identifies a true racial essence in the way Pan Guangdan problematically defined it. For Lu Xun, "Chineseness" is a sedimented identity constituted between westernization and the failure to create that semblance. Failure in this sense, however, is not predicated on the certainty of a successful version of modernity, as would be implied in westernization. Rather, it removes Chinese modernity from the necessity of tracing itself to Western inspirations. The consciousness of that failure provides the foundation for the Chinese character and thus creates its own modern national and racial identity.

In this way, as the "un-Chinese" expression of Chinese racial character, Tao's art embodies what Lu Xun deems as the necessary kumen of an epoch of modernity and globalization. Extraordinarily, the agony once restricted to the individual's sexual torment and an aesthetics of creation looms as the desired condition of the modern Chinese race and nation. In this way, the cover of kumen itself expresses both the artistic torment of the individual and the suffering proper to an epoch.

According to Xu Qinwen, the design for *Kumen de xiangzheng* is "a half-naked woman with long, black hair who licks the fork's sharp tip through her bright, red lips" (see Figure 7.1).[47] This "desolately plush" cover was not prescribed by Lu Xun, but he was immediately taken with Tao's design when he first saw it. Xu's account gives the woman a more voluntary and pleasurable reading. However, other critics have interpreted this design in a more abject way as a woman's tongue pierced by the fork, an interpretation that emphasizes the side of pain and violence.[48] Yet, upon closer inspection, one sees the woman holding the fork with her foot in an unforced manner. As though pulling it toward her with her toes, she leans into it, with a calm and satisfied expression on the part of her face that is visible to the viewer. The contour of the other side of her face dissolves into a circular, jagged, and discontinuous line that forms a womblike structure enveloping her body. Escaping commentators' notice, however, is the placing of the trident and the foot holding it, both of which are outside this unity, thus complicating the question of whether the apparent bliss enjoyed within can be separated from the proximity of, and desire for, abjection.

Interestingly, in *Kumon no shōchō*, Kuriyagawa gives a similarly ambivalent description of artistic creation itself. He draws an analogy between childbirth and the agonizing experience of artistic creation. Interspersed with phrases in English, this passage deserves to be quoted in full:

> At first, this concretized "image" lives within the artist. Like pregnancy in its inception, the fetus is only in its embryonic form as a "conceived image," or what western aestheticians call an unshaped fetus, or "abortive conception." Already conceived, it cannot fail to be given birth to. Thus the artist, compelled by this

徴象的悶苦

譯迅魯　著村白川廚

FIGURE 7.1 Book cover design for Lu Xun's translation of Kuriyagawa Hakuson's
Kumon no shōchō. Artist: Tao Yuanqing, 1924.
Source: Shanghai People's Fine Arts Publishing Company (Shanghai renmin meishu
chubanshe), Shanghai.

internal, irrefutable demand for "self-expression or self-externalization," experiences the pangs of birth. An artist's birth pains are spent on how to take what exists inside, shape it into the sensory phenomena of natural life, and project it into the external world; or how to construct a sensible, completely unified world in itself. As with mothers, the artist shares his own blood and carves out his own soul and flesh, in order to give birth to a new creation.[49]

Enclosed within her own agony, reminiscent of Kuriyagawa's analogy of giving birth, the woman on Lu Xun's cover is surrounded by dark red shapes strangely evocative of the failure of self-externalization, of "aborted conceptions." It was because of the bloody redness of these indistinguishable, "unshaped" forms that Lu Xun regretted the first publication, which was unable to run it in color.[50] For Kuriyagawa, the completion of this "self-externalization" coupled with agony affords the artist "pleasure" and "joy," much as the mother is rewarded with the joy of having given birth to a child. The sublimating analogy with motherhood, however, hardly conceals the underlying violence at work in Kuriyagawa's conception of the creative impulse. Although artistic creation is born under the pressure of external pain, it is also impossible without the reproduction of pain. As a condition, the experience of pain accompanies and enables the joy of self-externalization.

In this light, pain figures as a part of and not exterior to the subject's attempt to extricate himself or herself from its constraints. Even though Kuriyagawa identifies society as the main opposition to individual expression, this subjective act of poesis already internalized the antagonism as its enabling tension. Its absence would deprive the joy of sublimation and self-expression of certainty. In the act of externalization, the violence turns inward against oneself. The self-torturing process of the artist curiously parallels the feminine moment of birth giving in both Kuriyagawa's and Lu Xun's visualization of kumen.[51] Beneath the surface of celebrating motherhood, however, one detects in Kuriyagawa's account the possibility of feminine failure, an "abortive conception." Just as the greater the pain, the greater the triumph of creation, so does the threat of self-degradation increase with the possibility of self-affirming joy.

Lu Xun's chosen cover design spawned at least one imitation. The symbol of kumen was adapted into the cover design for a book on revolutionary literature.[52] According to Lu Xun, the trident was taken directly from *Symbol of Angst*. However, rather than pierce the woman's tongue, it props up the hammer symbol taken from the Soviet flag. This awkward combination, Lu Xun remarks, can neither pierce nor strike and is as useless and mundane as the literary works contained in the collection. However, Lu Xun's disapproval neglects something more significant about the notion of kumen. Even revolution was taking on the idea of kumen as representative of its own exigency. Kumen has broken out of the confines of sentimentality and decadence in art and literature. It no longer pivots on the mere discontent of gender or inarticulation of social dissatisfaction. The idea of suffering has found a rationalizing way out. Revolution provides the new rallying point around which kumen can at last find a substituting solution in the survival of the nation.[53]

The epochal feel of malaise finds an explanation for its ailment. The nation is to be the promise of salvation. However, discussions of revolutionary literature, despite the newfound euphoric passion, cannot help resorting to the language of kumen. In Guo Moruo's essay on revolution and literature, he argues that the more strongly the author can express his inner experience of oppression, the more universally this expression will encompass the social reality of the epoch.[54] In this language strongly evocative of Zheng Boqi's description of literature during the kumen epoch, Guo considers it the task of revolutionary literature to express individual as well as collective failure. However, instead of kumen, he insists on the desire of revolution as the answer to oppression. Failure becomes the prerequisite of revolution. It is also the sustaining sentiment of revolutionary passion. As Guo puts it, unaware of the reversible logic embedded in the rhetoric of failure, "Before the revolution succeeds, all acts of resistance must end in failure."[55] In this way, failure becomes the only driving certainty of revolution. Without suffering, there is no conviction in the nation's survival.

Ideas about revolutionary literature as the literature of class suffering or kumen came to override all other dimensions of what had been largely felt as cultural kumen. The imperatives of a militantly defended nationhood superseded personal and psychological aspects of torment and suffering. Revolutionary literature was referred to as a literature that depicted the kumen of the proletariat, a new articulation that challenged previous notions of oppression in literature. The vision of revolution, however, remains profoundly indebted to the failure embodied by the epochal feel of kumen. It could neither deny nor leave behind the kind of passion generated in suffering. Even less could it sever itself from the profound sense of failure that enabled and still continues to incite articulations of the modern epoch.

The Emergence of Culture in Failure

IT IS DIFFICULT to understand how cultural and national identities would embrace failure as a way of building cultural confidence. Even though contemporary examples from other parts of the world attest to the fact that the Chinese case is by no means unique, one of the most compelling aspects of failure is the conviction that it is unique to oneself, who alone can both defy and return from the precipice of annihilation. No other civilization could be confronted with the same despair, for it reflects the greatness from which one has fallen and, for that reason, must be exceptionally engendered. In this way, failure achieves that distinct prerequisite of nationalism that perhaps no other positivistic definition can compel, the recognition of a singular destiny that is the foundation of sovereign thinking.

This unexpected emergence of sovereignty disquiets the mind from easy presuppositions about enjoyed cultural plenitude. It also forces us to consider the condition of failure as an enabling possibility for a vital social existence. The period of nation building in China, from the late 1890s throughout the 1930s, presents such a challenge. Beneath the surface of modernity and enlightenment lies an unabated restlessness expressed as passionate discontent with the self and nation. The experience of imperialism produced a self-doubt that eventually became a parasitic mode in which one both resisted and reformulated that experience. The ambition to nationhood and, more important, to power and dominance, rested on a foundation of despair, further stimulating the desire for fulfillment and, ultimately, revenge and the affirmation it brings.

From the late Qing intellectuals' attempts to establish the yellow race's relevance to the progress of world civilization, to the May Fourth generation's privileging of suffering, *kumen*, as the determining mood of an epoch, the building of modern cultural and national consciousness in China encompasses a logic of failure, a resilience founded on the very embrace of defeat. This rhetoric by which subjugation is rationalized as the very possibility of menace relies on the powerful appeal of redeeming an image of humiliation.

Perhaps nothing attests more to this commemoration than the fact that China's present "national humiliation day," a "day of national defense education," is yet to have a designated date. The reason behind this law, passed by the Chinese legislature in April 2001, is to promote patriotism and national defense construction. The hope is to "spur the younger generation to aspire for a greater China" by incorporating national defense education into current curricula.[1]

The proper day of infamy, however, has been the subject of much disagreement. Some proposed September 7, the day on which China was forced to sign the Boxer Protocol in 1901. Others suggested July 7 or September 18, dates marking watershed events in the Japanese aggression against China in World War II. Refreshed by the embassy bombing in 1999, the spy plane incident in 2001, and the controversy over Japanese textbooks that expunged accounts of Japanese war atrocities, lawmakers said that the trauma suffered by the Chinese people in the past one hundred years is "far from being healed."

Indeed, the question is whether we want healing in a world of injured nationalisms. What would be the prerequisite conditions for satisfactory restitution, and whose conscience, as opposed to someone's history of suffering, does it alleviate? Or is the possibility of restoration of sovereignty the very ideality that should be undone? In a world contrary to healing but paradoxically highly conscientious of "ethics" and responsibility, one can hardly afford to dismiss as derivative or passive an agency that finds a way to make meaning from the ruins of survival. Instead of looking to a future where ideals such as self-determination, freedom, and democracy—concepts without consensus in practice—would find their universal embodiment, it would be worthwhile to examine how, in the absence of success, a commitment to failure provides meaningful registers of agency.

The discourse of redress, be it international, social, or racial, can prolong a structure of guilt rather than address atrocities. Mourning and penitence, as marked by commemorative speeches on past atrocities, have replaced the urgency of prevention and its accompanying task of better understanding different cultural imperatives and complex modalities of national identity.[2] Humiliation, despite its dishonorable beginnings, has inaugurated a productive condition for national and cultural identity in China in the twentieth century. Created by more than a century of foreign domination—coined as the "century of humiliation" (*bainian guochi*)—but reabsorbed into a nationalistic narrative of cultural resilience, the example of China's nation-building process carries great implications for any consideration of sovereignty, agency, and identity in literary, transcultural, or historical contexts defined by power and resistance.

My use of "failure" is intended to map a different order of critique for literary and cultural studies. Approaches toward opening new critical terrain for comparative and cross-cultural analysis have concerned themselves with the challenge of dominant narratives in which other narratives may take part, but fail to effect a fundamental revision. A well-trodden path is to expose the shortcomings of ideology such that it proves neither impervious nor invincible to the voices of alterity. To this end, empires of imperialism are exposed in their fragile sense of self-worth that is reimposed in a compulsive fashion as the problem of an other in need of colonial rectification. Fantasies of dominance are projected and exchanged as mixed pleasures and neurotic fixations. We also see terms once applied to the colonized returned to the colonizers themselves. The primitivism and abjection of the dispossessed are, in this way, relocated to the center of colonial confidence as anxiety and melancholy. Much critical effort has gone into disclosing universal values—language, norms, or institutions—as negotiated and contested categories settled by might rather than intuited through reason.

Although all these are part of the story of colonial encounters, they do not fundamentally shift the frame of analysis such that they can break the pattern of arguing against the disadvantage of a cultural and temporal belatedness. Even if framed as a constructive intervention, such critical stances remain on the defense, resorting to the same language they try to defy. Despite the often admitted quandary of reproducing the logic of domination while attempting to challenge it, this disclaimer barely veils the shortcomings that reflect underlying methodological and conceptual problems.

"Failure," in this way, argues for a different point of departure. Rather than rush to debunk and reinject plurality into universalisms, for instance, it takes universalism to its logical conclusion. Instead of deflating the imperialist image, it sees it in its fantasized plumage. Taken to its desired extreme, the absolute embodiment of power, as we have seen, is never attainable in its ideal form. In this way, failure builds itself on the impossible commitment to ideality. It considers how this impossible commitment engenders a different order of recognition parasitic to the aspirations of ideality and productive of a contrary sense of sovereignty. As a register of thought simultaneous with historical deprivation, feelings of inadequacy and confessions of national humiliation generate recuperative visions from a distressing reality. This self-reflection is parasitic, for it is unintended by the structure of domination but nonetheless contributes to its felicity. As J. L. Austin once unsuccessfully tried to exclude from his outline of the prerequisite conditions for performative language, "parasitism" is that extra, unsanctioned order of meaning generated by, but outside of, the proper rules of engagement.[3] Because this unsanctioned knowledge is illegal only from the point of view of a set of rules it has no need to observe in any case, once freed from this commitment, parasiticism describes the modality by which power is wielded by the particular instance of its exercise. Instead of desiring the place of the white man for his dominance, to paraphrase Fanon, one embraces one's dejection so as to enable a different, unprescribed ideality of the self to emerge.[4] Failure is a modality rather than an object. For that reason, it is also distinct from an absolute sense of failure, where the experience is no longer visionary but terminal.

Although I have analyzed "failure" as the specificity of defeated national culture and literary modernity in China, the conceptual orientation behind it suggests other trajectories of revising critical inquiries into culture and formations of knowledge. For instance, what are the possibilities for analyzing categories of self, text, and culture in the absence of ideality? Departing from the much-propagated notion of imagined communities, how do we establish a sense of commonality under the specters of unadorned selves? We might consider what unintended orders of knowledge reveal about the assumptions of establishing shared sensibilities across cultures, be it in contexts of conflict, contract, or peace. For instance, during the still underexamined cultural history of nineteenth-century China, during which time Western technology, revolutionary and liberal ideologies, and literature were translated en masse into Chinese, what fissures of miscomprehension were produced on this forced common ground? How is "reception," a long-stigmatized term for its implication of passivity, the accidental offspring of "imprecision," as translated Western discourses excite their Chinese audience under false impressions? As an extension of "failure," one might also probe questions of contemporary "worldliness" in the traffic of people, communities, labor, and things. For instance, how does the logic of absent allegiances, such as diasporic nationalisms and "homeland" in Southeast Asia, Australia, Europe, or the North America, reconfigure the conception of cultural nations, local identities, and cosmopolitanism?

The idea that the torment is far from over or that a national trauma can ever heal, alerts us to the fact that healing may not be what is sought after in the desire for sovereignty. We require new conceptions of how sovereignty as a political ideal or cultural practice has evolved and adapted apart from the colonial or imperialist context in order to evaluate new forms of its expression. Looking back on the development of modern Chinese nationalism and cultural identity from the late nineteenth through the first four decades of the twentieth century, one sees how the sense of injury resurfaces as reason for further "defense." No vengeance can wash away a memory that tenaciously holds on to the nation's destruction. As long as there is blame, directed at oneself or others, national memory can choose not to be at the mercy of history.

As an inquiry into China's nation-building project, *Failure* revises the way we understand representations of cultural distinctions and survivals. Taking China as a focal point, it reevaluates how one approaches the questions of culture, identity, and nation in contemporary critical and psychoanalytical inquiries. It proposes alternative considerations of the condition of abjection, subjugation, and dejection. Individuals' attachment to these states, usually considered preemptive of the meaningful exercise of autonomous agency, can in fact generate productive affirmations of one's identity. The appeal of suffering, furthermore, continues to bind individuals to the quest for collective identities. Even though the process of identification is fraught with the tension between individual and collective desires, it enables the preservation of a community in pain. *Failure* reconceptualizes the production of identity predicated not on idealized images of empowerment and plenitude but, rather, on their absence.

In this way, this book has redefined the way we understand the emergence of "Chineseness" in the modern period. The articulations of Chinese cultural and national identity relied on a self-awareness that thrived not on affirmation but on self-reproach and negativity. Considerations of Chinese cultural nationalism and literary modernity require this crucial distinction. The mode of failure motivates every search for that positive image of the self and the nation. As both a national identity and cultural specter, "Chineseness" underscores the centrality of failure in the possibility of resilience.

Reference Matter

Notes

CHAPTER ONE

1. "China Demands End to War in Iraq," *Far Eastern Economic Review* (04.03.2003).

2. The sentiment of national injury was deep and pervasive among the Chinese populace. In the city of Nanjing, McDonald's and Kentucky Fried Chicken closed to avoid being the targets of such outrage, and in Beijing the otherwise-popular Western fast-food restaurants were boycotted. However, amid all this outrage and sense of injury, the slogan "Long live national sovereignty" reverberated through the crowds of the Chinese nation. United against aggression, the posterity of the Yellow Emperor was summoned to take national humiliation as occasion for striking down "hegemony" (*dadao baquan*).

3. For two contrasting focuses, see, for instance, Anthony Giddens, *The Nation-State and Violence* (Berkeley & Los Angeles: University of California Press, 1985); Anthony D. Smith, *The Ethnic Origins of Nations* (Oxford & New York: Blackwell, 1986).

4. David Rennie, "Chinese Feel Betrayed by 'Double Meanings,'" *The Daily Telegraph* (12.04.2001).

5. Elazar Barkan, *The Guilt of Nations: Restitution and Negotiating Historical Injustices* (Baltimore & London: Johns Hopkins University Press, 2000). For discussions of the question of redress and reconciliation, see, for example, Martha Minow, ed., *Breaking the Cycles of Hatred* (Princeton, NJ: Princeton University Press, 2002); Judith Butler, *Excitable Speech: A Politics of the Performative* (New York: Routledge, 1997).

6. Barkan, *Guilt of Nations*, p. 316.

7. The British newspaper *Observer* (10.17.1999), under collaboration with the Danish newspaper *Politiken*, reported that NATO deliberately bombed the Chinese embassy after discovering that the embassy was transmitting Yugoslav army communications. Although *The New York Times* (05.10.1999) noted early on—three days after the incident—that the event was "portrayed in China as deliberate," it later consistently referred to the incident as the "accidental bombing of the Chinese embassy." Other American newspapers such as the *Washington Post* and *USA Today* vehemently denied the possibility. Canada's *Globe and Mail* (10.18.1999)—along with

the *Times of India* (10.18.1999), *Irish Times* (10.18.1999), and the *Sydney Morning Herald* (10.18.1999)—ran the complete story covered by Reuters news agency. The CIA soon took the blame. George Tenet, the director, admitted to intelligence failure, even though the exact source of this failure—whether it was the use of an outdated map provided by the National Imagery and Mapping Agency or faulty relay of corrective measures upon its discovery—is unclear. See "Director of Central Intelligence Statement on the Belgrade Chinese Embassy Bombing House Permanent Select Committee on Intelligence Open Hearing" (07.22.1999), a document available from http://www.cia.gov. The equally uncomfortable question rests with why the Chinese embassy was rebroadcasting Yugoslav radio signals. See also John Sweeney, Jens Holsoe, and Ed Vulliamy, "Nato Bombed Chinese Deliberately," *The Guardian* (10.17.1999); Bryan Bender, "Embassy Bombing Report to Reveal Targeting Flaws," *Jane's Defense Weekly* (02.06.1999); Steven Pearlstein, "NATO: Bombs Aimed in Error," "Bombing Q & A," *Washington Post* (05.08.2000); Martin Kettle, "CIA Takes Rap for Embassy Attack," *The Guardian* (04.10.2000); Bo Wen, "Why Does the US Always Bring Disgrace to Itself?" *People's Daily* (05.26.1999).

8. See Ian Buruma, "The Joys and Perils of Victimhood," *The New York Review of Books* (04.08.1999); Orville Schell, "Prisoners of Its Past," *Salon.com* (6.08.1999).

9. Schell, "Prisoners of Its Past."

10. See Kwame Anthony Appiah, "The Multiculturalist Misunderstanding," *The New York Review of Books* (10.09.1997) and his *The Ethics of Identity* (Princeton, NJ: Princeton University Press, 2005). The autobiographical "I" is often the temporary convergence of presumed ethnic root, belongingness in nostalgia, and appropriation of authenticity. See Patricia J. Williams, *The Alchemy of Race and Rights: Diary of a Law Professor* (Cambridge, MA: Harvard University Press, 1991).

11. Historians and political scientists have recently begun to emphasize the distinctive mark of humiliation and memory in modern Chinese nationalism. Paul Cohen argues that it is the amnesia of humiliation that invites continual political remobilization of the humiliation narrative in historical memory. Peter Gries and William Callahan, on the other hand, examine the preeminence of humiliation in a political culture saturated with remembrances. This study, in contrast, rather than seeing humiliation as an isolated phenomenon of nationalism, analyzes it in a broader cultural context in which humiliation relies on other forms of passion for failure. Together, these different notions of injury help sustain humiliation as a kind of cultural power that wants not only to right a wrong but also to aggressively advance its own entitlement. See Paul A. Cohen, "Remembering and Forgetting: National Humiliation in Twentieth-Century China," *Twentieth-Century China* 27.2 (Apr. 2002): 1–39; William A. Callahan, "National Insecurities: Humiliation, Salvation, and Chinese Nationalism," *Alternatives* 29 (2004): 199–218; Peter Hayes Gries, *China's New Nationalism: Pride, Politics, and Diplomacy* (Berkeley: University of California Press, 2004); Luo Zhitian, "National Humiliation and National Assertion: The Chinese Response to the Twenty-one Demands," *Modern Asian Studies* 27.2 (1993): 297–319.

12. The sentiment of humiliation bolsters some of the most violent forms of nationalism in the twentieth century. For example, one can hardly forget that in 1989, the one event Slobodan Milosevic commemorated in his launch of the Serb nation-

alist project was the Battle of Kosovo Polje of 1389, in which the Serb army was annihilated by the advancing Ottoman Empire. A parallel pattern can be found in modern Greek national identity. See Michael Herzfeld, *Cultural Intimacy: Social Poetics in the Nation-State* (New York: Routledge, 1997). For similar rhetoric on Hindu nationalism in the early twentieth century, see Chetan Bhatt, *Hindu Nationalism: Origins, Ideologies and Modern Myths* (Oxford & New York: Berg, 2001). For a thoughtful set of essays on the search for national identity without being able to rely on an organic sense of historical nationalism, see Christopher Jaffrelot, ed., *Pakistan: Nationalism Without a Nation?* (London & New York: Zed Books, 2002).

13. Lin Mohan and Wei Wei, eds., *Women tuoqi nazhong Zhongguo ren* (We spit on that kind of Chinese) (Lanzhou: Gansu renmin chubanshe, 1999), esp. pp. 262–311.

14. Kenneth Scott Latourette, *The Development of China* (Boston & New York: Houghton Mifflin, 1917), p. 236.

15. The sign on display was indeed a reproduction of the original sign, but the point of contention is whether an original existed that would have substantiated this claim against Western imperialism.

16. Historians who have studied this particular controversy, however, concluded that "Chinese and dogs not admitted" is, at its most credible, a conflation of two separate clauses on the park sign: one that limits the entry of Chinese in specific cases, such as servants accompanying their Western masters; and the other that forbids bringing dogs into the park, using bicycles, and plucking flowers. See, for example, Robert A. Bickers and Jeffrey N. Wasserstrom, "Shanghai's 'Dogs and Chinese Not Admitted' Sign: Legend, History and Contemporary Symbol," *The China Quarterly* 142 (June 1995): 444–66; Ye Xiaoqing, "Shanghai Before Nationalism," *East Asian History* 3 (June 1992): 33–52.

17. Lin and Wei, *Women tuoqi nazhong Zhongguo ren*, p. 263. This view reiterates the one expressed in the official newspaper, *Jiefang ribao* (Liberation daily). See Chen Youjie, "Buneng wanji lishi" (History must not be forgotten), *Liberation Daily* (06.07.1994), p. 1. See also Ye Qing, "Guanyu huaren yu gou bude runei de yixie lishi" (Some historical facts regarding "Dogs and Chinese not admitted"), *Guangming ribao* (06.13.1994), p. 3.

18. "Nation as failure" is to be distinguished from the current designation of "failed states" in international politics. "Failed states" refers to states as a political entities that have collapsed, resulting in social and economic disarray and, most likely, humanitarian catastrophes. Examples include Afghanistan, Somalia, Sierra Leone, and, most recently, Liberia. The Solomon Islands may perhaps be the first failed state in the Pacific. However, "failure" is here analyzed as a mode of nationalistic and cultural sensibility through which "nation" as an identity is experienced.

19. Lin and Wei, *Women tuoqi nazhong Zhongguo ren*, p. 262.

20. In this sense, I also do not consider memory the pivotal issue in nationalism, a platform that suggests that the preservation of the nation is possible because nation itself is worthy of this memorialization. Rather, we should examine how subjects come to be emotionally invested in the nation, a psychic process of which commemoration is but one consequence. Renan's notion of the nation remains faithful to the unquestioned sanctity naturally possessed by the nation, whereas it is that sanctity that, as I have suggested, must always already be in doubt for nationalism to

be possible. See Ernest Renan, "What Is a Nation?" in Homi Bhabha, ed., *Nation and Narration* (New York: Routledge, 1990), pp. 8–22.

21. A resurgence of this persistent quest for one's flaws in relation to the Chinese national character can be witnessed in not only Lu Xun studies but also ongoing intellectual discussions. For Lu Xun studies, see, for example, Zheng Xinsen, *Wenhua pipan yu guominxing gaizao* (Cultural critique and the reconstruction of the national character) (Shanxi: Shanxi renmin chubanshe, 1988); Bao Jing, ed., *Lu Xun "guominxing sixiang" taolun ji* (On Lu Xun's "National character") (Tianjin: Tianjin renmin chubanshe, 1982). For discussions of the Chinese national character in a broader cultural context, see, for example, Ouyang Lun, *Zhongguo ren de xingge* (The Chinese character) (Shanxi: Shanxi renmin jiaoyu chubanshe, 1989); Zhang Pingzhi and Yang Jinglong, *Zhongguo ren de maobing* (The quirks of the Chinese) (Beijing: Zhongguo shehui chubanshe, 1998); Lin and Wei, *Women tuoqi nazhong Zhongguo ren*; Jie Sizhong, *Guomin suzhi yousilu* (Worries over the national character) (Beijing: Zuojia chubanshe, 1998); Xu Xing and Xun Bu, eds., *Fanxing Zhongguo ren* (Reflecting on the Chinese) (Beijing: Zhongguo wenlian chuban gongsi, 1999); Sha Lianxiang, ed., *Zhongguo minzu xing* (The Chinese national character), 2 vols. (Beijing: Zhongguo renmin daxue chubanshe, 1989).

22. At least two other recent modern Chinese translations appeared in 1998 and 2005, respectively. See Yue Aiguo and Zhang Huayu, trans., *Zhongguo ren de xingge* (The Chinese character), 4th ed. (Hong Kong: Sanlian, 2000); Shu Yang, Shu Ning, and Mu Ti, trans. *Wenming yu louxi: dianxing de Zhongguo ren* (Civilization and crude habits: The typical Chinese) (Taiyuan: Shuhai chubanshe, 2004). A complete classical Chinese rendition was also published by Zuoxin she in Shanghai in 1903. See Lydia Liu, *Translingual Practice: Literature, National Culture, and Translated Modernity* (Stanford: Stanford University Press, 1995), p. 53.

23. This is a direct reference to a satirical work on the Chinese published in Taiwan in the mid-1980s. See Bo Yang, *Chouloude Zhongguo ren* (The ugly Chinese) (Taibei: Linpai chubanshe, 1985).

24. See Frank Dikötter, *The Discourse of Race in Modern China* (Stanford: Stanford University Press, 1992).

25. *Yousheng youyu* (superior birth, superior nurture) is used as a slogan for pre- and postnatal care in modern-day Shanghai. *Yousheng* (superior birth) was the translation used for *eugenics* in the 1920s and 1930s when racial engineering was contemplated as a viable solution for China's racial decline.

26. Tani E. Barlow, ed., *Gender Politics in China: Writing and Feminism* (Durham, NC: Duke University Press, 1993); Dai Jinhua and Meng Yue, *Fuchu lishi dibiao* (Emerging from the horizon of history) (Zhengzhou: Henan renmin chubanshe, 1989); Rey Chow, *Woman and Chinese Modernity: The Politics of Reading Between West and East* (Minneapolis: University of Minnesota Press, 1991).

27. See, for example, Christina Kelley Gilmartin, *Engendering the Chinese Revolution: Radical Women, Communist Politics, and Mass Movements in the 1920s* (Berkeley, Los Angeles, & London: University of California Press, 1995); Angela Zito and Tani E. Barlow, eds., *Body, Subject, & Power in China* (Chicago: University of Chicago Press, 1994).

28. For representative views, see Chen Peng-Hsiang and Whitney Crothers

Dilley, eds., *Feminism/Femininity in Chinese Literature* (Amsterdam: Rodopi, 2002); Amy D. Dooling and Kristina M. Torgeson, "Introduction," in Dooling and Torgeson, eds., *Writing Women in Modern China: An Anthology of Women's Literature from the Early Twentieth Century* (New York: Columbia University Press, 1998); Barlow, *Gender Politics in China*; Dai and Meng, *Fuchu lishi dibiao*; Chow, *Woman and Chinese Modernity*.

29. Bao Mi (Wang Lixiong), *Huanghuo* (Yellow peril), 3 vols. (Taibei: Fengyun shidai chuban youxian gongsi, 1991).

30. See "Chinese Premier Calls for Patriotism of Democracy, Science in SARS Fight," *Xinhuanet* (05.04.2003).

31. My concept of failure, however, does not merely point at the underside of the May Fourth project of modernity as plagued by a cultural anxiety over racial degeneration. This phenomenon, I believe, carries a more complex dialogue with national and cultural survival in which anxieties become productive as unobvious forms of self-recognition. For recent arguments about the literary decadence accompanying the enlightenment project in the early twentieth century, see Huang Qiaosheng, "Lu Xun, Bodelai ji shijibing" (Lu Xun, Baudelaire, and the illness of fin-de-siècle), in *Lu Xun yanjiu ziliao* (Research materials on Lu Xun) (Beijing: Zhongguo wenlian chuban gongsi, 1992), 23:131–44; Sun Lung-kee, "The Presence of the Fin-de-Siècle in the May Fourth Era," in Gail Hershatter et al., eds., *Remapping China: Fissures in Historical Terrain* (Stanford: Stanford University Press, 1996).

32. Many scholars of "third-world" literary, cultural, and gender studies have interpreted this critical stance as nonetheless a disguised form of universalism. See, for example, Chandra Mohanty, *Third World Women and the Politics of Feminism* (Bloomington: Indiana University Press, 1991); Rey Chow, *Writing Diaspora: Tactics of Intervention in Contemporary Cultural Studies* (Bloomington: Indiana University Press, 1993); Inderpal Grewal and Caren Kaplan, eds., *Scattered Hegemonies: Postmodernity and Transnational Feminist Practices* (Minneapolis: University of Minnesota Press, 1994); Elizabeth Abel, Barbara Christian, and Helene Moglen, eds., *Female Subjects in Black and White: Race, Psychoanalysis, Feminism* (Berkeley: University of California Press, 1997).

33. This problem, for example, can be seen in the continuing controversy surrounding Fredric Jameson's notion of "national allegory," which has sparked continual debates on the value of third-world literature, especially among those working in "area studies." At the core of the discussions is the problematic position of undercutting the merit of national literatures because they have lost their own voice in succumbing to the primacy of the Western academy in bearing the national or, as Rey Chow puts it, "ethnic marker." The cycle of indictment and guilt, however, does not end there. Another level of its perpetuation lies in the appointed responsibility of those working in minor literatures and area studies to participate, as the vigilant disenfranchised, in the enterprise of guilt naming. Without feeding into this project of Western guilt by launching critiques of new orientalisms, one risks not being political enough, the task that has been assigned to area studies as one of their primary contributions. One may well consider how national literatures are themselves built on a similar kind of hierarchization in their own "areas." For a recent discussion on

234 Notes to Pages 17–19

the problem of literary canons, see, for example, Linda Hutcheon and Mario J. Valdés, eds., *Rethinking Literary History* (Oxford: Oxford University Press, 2002). For recent treatments of global recognition and area studies, see Masao Miyoshi and H. D. Harootunian, eds., *Learning Places: The Afterlives of Area Studies* (Durham, NC: Duke University Press, 2002); Shih Shu-mei, "Global Literature and the Technologies of Recognition," *Publications of the Modern Language Association of America* 119.1 (2004): 16–30. For "national allegory," see, for example, Frederic Jameson, "Third-World Literature in the Era of Multinational Capitalism," *Social Text* 15 (Fall 1986): 65–88; Fredric Jameson, "A Brief Response," *Social Text* 17 (1987): 26–27; Aijaz Ahmad, "Jameson's Rhetoric of Otherness and the 'National Allegory,'" in Ahmad, *In Theory: Classes, Nations, Literatures* (London: Verso, 1992), pp. 95–122.

34. It would perhaps be useful to consider what set of circumstances allows for or bars that kind of forum of exposure and how that access to a speaking platform can coerce new complicities rather than free silences. For a glimpse into debates during the early formation of this diasporic canon, see a series of exchanges sparked by a mainland Chinese writer's view on Malayan Chinese literature between 1932 and 1936. For example, Fei Ming, "Difang zuojia tan" (On local writers), in Fang Xiu, ed., *Mahua xin wenxue daxi, 1919–1942* (Compendium on new Malaysian Chinese literature, 1919–1942) (Kuala Lumpur & Singapore: Popular Books, 2000), 1: 259–62; C Jun, pseud., "Difang zuojia jieshao de shangtui" (Reconsidering the introduction to local writers), pp. 263–65; Fei Ming, "Zongsuan shi wo paole yikuai 'difang zuojiatan' de zhuan" (Consider me having started a controversy over "local writers"), pp. 266–69; C Jun, "Xianweijing xia Fei Ming xiansheng de lilun de xicha" (Scrutinizing Mr. Fei Ming's theory under the microscope), pp. 270–74.

35. One of the recent critical orientations in "area studies," and Chinese studies in particular, is to reinvest the experience of modernity in third-world nations with the power of agency and self-invention. By examining the processes of cultural, visual, and linguistic exchange, scholars focus on the transformative role of appropriation. This enables the shift back to the "indigenous" as agency rather than passive recipient. For important recent studies, see, for example, Tang Xiaobing, *Chinese Modern: The Heroic and Quotidian* (Durham, NC: Duke University Press, 2000); Leo Ou-Fan Lee, *Shanghai Modern* (Cambridge, MA: Harvard University Press, 1999); Liu, *Translingual Practice.*

36. This assumption is particularly prominent in recent debates on race and ethnicity. See, for example, Amy Gutman, "Introduction," in Charles Taylor, *Multiculturalism: Examining the Politics of Recognition* (Princeton, NJ: Princeton University Press, 1994); Amy Gutman, "Responding to Racial Injustice," in Anthony Kwame Appia et al., *Color Consciousness: The Political Morality of Race* (Princeton, NJ: Princeton University Press, 1996). See also discussions in Nathan Glazer, *We Are All Multiculturalists Now* (Cambridge, MA, & London: Harvard University Press, 1997); Bhikhu Parekh, *Rethinking Multiculturalism: Cultural Diversity and Political Theory* (Cambridge, MA: Harvard University Press, 2000).

37. See, for example, Jerome Chen, *China and the West: Society and Culture, 1815–1937* (Bloomington: Indiana University Press, 1979); Maurice Meisner, *Li Ta-Chao and the Origins of Chinese Marxism* (Cambridge, MA: Harvard University Press,

1967); Lin Yusheng, *The Crisis of Chinese Consciousness: Radical Anti-traditionalism in the May Fourth Era* (Madison: University of Wisconsin Press, 1979).

38. In the existing literature on nationalism, the nation is taken as a sanctified entity that holds the promise of sovereignty and power; nationalism is taken as the sentiment espousing such an aspiration. Classic works on nationalism include Ernest Gellner, *Nations and Nationalism* (Oxford: Blackwell, 1983); Eric Hobsbawm, *Nations and Nationalism Since 1780* (Cambridge: Cambridge University Press, 1990); Eric Hobsbawm and Terence Ranger, eds., *The Invention of Tradition* (Cambridge: Cambridge University Press, 1983); Tom Nairn, *The Break-Up of Britain: Crisis and Neonationalism* (London: NLB & Verso Editions, 1977); Elie Kedourie, *Nationalism* (Oxford & Cambridge, MA: Blackwell, 1993); Giddens, *Nation-State and Violence*; Smith, *Ethnic Origins of Nations*; Benedict Anderson, *Imagined Communities: Reflections on the Origin and Spread of Nationalism* (New York: Verso, 1991).

39. See Lydia Liu, *The Clash of Empires: The Invention of China in Modern World Making* (Cambridge, MA: Harvard University Press, 2004).

40. See David Wang, *The Monster That Is History: History, Violence, and Fictional Writing in Twentieth-Century China* (Berkeley: University of California Press, 2004); C. T. Hsia, *A History of Modern Chinese Fiction* (Bloomington: Indiana University Press, 1999), esp. David Wang's "Introduction," vii–xxxv.

41. This applies, in particular, to works that attempt the subversion of precisely such a concession to subjugation. See discussions in Gayatri Chakravorty Spivak, "Can the Subaltern Speak?" in Cary Nelson and Lawrence Grossberg, eds., *Marxism and the Interpretation of Culture* (Urbana: University of Illinois Press, 1988), pp. 217–313; Gayatri Chakravorty Spivak, *In Other Worlds: Essays in Cultural Politics* (New York: Routledge, 1988); Homi Bhabha, ed., *Nation and Narration* (New York: Routledge, 1990); Homi Bhabha, *The Location of Culture* (London & New York: Routledge, 1994); Partha Chatterjee, *Nationalist Thought and the Colonial World: A Derivative Discourse* (London: Zed Books for the United Nations University, 1986); Partha Chatterjee, *The Nation and Its Fragments: Colonial and Postcolonial Histories* (Princeton, NJ: Princeton University Press, 1993); Ranajit Guha, *Dominance Without Hegemony: History and Power in Colonial India* (Cambridge, MA: Harvard University Press, 1997).

42. In the field of China studies, this is most visible in earlier scholarship that followed a model of Western impact / Chinese reception. For an outline of the conceptual development of historiography in the field up to the 1980s, see Paul A. Cohen, *Discovering History in China: American Historical Writing on the Recent Chinese Past* (New York: Columbia University Press, 1984); Q. Edward Wang, *Inventing China Through History: The May Fourth Approach to Historiography* (Albany: State University of New York Press, 2001). For a critique of dominant narrative modes that have structured our interpretations of the modern period, see Prasenjit Duara, *Rescuing History from the Nation: Questioning Narratives of Modern China* (Chicago: University of Chicago Press, 1995).

43. The problem of periodization is as perennial as it is tirelessly debated. And both sides maintain justifiable positions. However, just because problems of xenophobia, cultural assimilation, or questions of identity—be it Han, Hua, or Chinese—have existed prior to what we consider to be the modern era, those issues do

not exist in the same degree or configuration. And it is the specific ways in which people perceive their world and their role in it that determine each historical epoch and its sensibilities.

44. This is evident in the recent attention given to trauma, melancholy, and injury. See, for example, Wendy Brown, *States of Injury: Power and Freedom in Late Modernity* (Princeton, NJ: Princeton University Press, 1995); Cathy Caruth, *Unclaimed Experience: Trauma, Narrative, and History* (Baltimore, MD: Johns Hopkins University Press, 1996); Anne Cheng, *The Melancholy of Race* (New York: Oxford University Press, 2000); Wolf Lepenies, *Melancholy and Society*, trans. Jeremy Gaines and Doris Jones (Cambridge, MA: Harvard University Press, 1992); Naomi Schor, *One Hundred Years of Melancholy* (Oxford: Clarendon Press, 1996).

45. For two different views drawing from the psychoanalytical corpus, see Julia Kristeva, *Black Sun: Depression and Melancholia*, trans. Leon S. Rondiez (New York: Columbia University Press, 1989); Judith Butler, *The Psychic Life of Power: Theories in Subjection* (Stanford: Stanford University Press, 1992).

46. See Ashis Nandy, *The Intimate Enemy: Loss and Recovery of Self Under Colonialism* (Oxford & New York: Oxford University Press, 1983).

47. See James C. Scott, *Weapons of the Weak: Everyday Forms of Peasant Resistance* (New Haven, CT, & London: Yale University Press, 1985); Pierre Bourdieu, *Language & Symbolic Power* (Cambridge: Polity Press, 1991). See also nn. 33, 41, and 42.

48. In recent years, scholars have attempted to adapt the transcultural assumptions of studies of psychoanalysis to the analysis of race and its nation-specific sites. The binding premise predicates complicity and coercion as causing varying degrees of detriment to the sexualized subject. For compelling analyses, see, for example, Christopher Lane, ed., *The Psychoanalysis of Race* (New York: Columbia University Press, 1998); David L. Eng, *Racial Castration: Managing Masculinity in Asia America* (Durham, NC: Duke University Press, 2001); Kalpana Seshadri-Crooks, *Desiring Whiteness: A Lacanian Analysis of Race* (London & New York: Routledge, 2000); Claudia Tate, *Psychoanalysis and Black Novels: Desire and the Protocols of Race* (New York & Oxford: Oxford University Press, 1998).

49. The main issues in the politics of recognition are discussed in Gutman, in Taylor, *Multiculturalism*.

50. See, for example, Anderson, *Imagined Communities*, especially chapter 8, "Patriotism and Racism."

51. Indeed, as Michael Billig points out in an interesting book, the rape of the mother country is considered even worse than the rape of one's own mother. See Michael Billig, *Banal Nationalism* (London & Thousand Oaks, CA: Sage, 1995).

52. This is a prominent, though little analyzed theme in the works of Chinese writers such as Ding Ling, Mao Dun, Lu Yin, and Yu Dafu.

53. By this, I mean something quite distinct from Gellner's earlier statement that "it is nationalism which engenders nations." Gellner takes nationalism as a specifically modern phenomenon enabling the political entity of the nation. However, he ignores nationalism in the sense of a process of identification, a crucial distinction through which the incitement of individuals' desires makes possible that identity we call "nation." See Gellner, *Nations and Nationalism*, p. 55.

54. See Andrew Parker et al., eds., *Nationalisms & Sexualities* (London: Routledge, 1992); Bhabha, *Nation and Narration*. The exception to this approach is that of George Mosse, who argues that the social perceptions of sexuality are predicated on the imperatives of national unity. One of the shortcomings of Mosse's account is that categories of sexuality and nation are themselves not interrogated and are examined only in their effects, not their constitution. See Mosse, *Nationalism and Sexuality: Middle-Class Morality and Sexual Norms in Modern Europe* (Madison: University of Wisconsin Press, 1985). For an outline of some of the issues in the relationship between nationalism and sexuality, see Sam Pryke, "Nationalism and Sexuality: What Are the Issues?" in *Nations and Nationalisms* 4 (1998): 529–46.

55. See n. 44.

56. Sigmund Freud, "Mourning and Melancholia," in *The Standard Edition of the Complete Psychological Works of Sigmund Freud*, ed. and trans. James Strachey (London: Hogarth Press, 1953–74), 14:239–58.

57. Ibid., p. 247.

58. Ibid., pp. 239–58.

59. Consider how, in "Mourning and Melancholia," Freud's use of a metaphor displaces the articulation of this relational sense of the object. The "shadow of the object" falls upon the ego and becomes incorporated as the subject's own superego. In this way, the relation to the object is preserved, a relational displacement that itself can be spoken of only metaphorically as a "shadow" with a missing corporeality. The object creates the ostensible occasion of incorporation. Yet the relation structuring the object's significance to the subject endures as the most productive basis for the subject's reworking. Incorporated is less the object than one's relation to it. Freud himself remarks—without successfully resolving—the curious opacity the object of mourning has to the melancholic: "He knows *whom* he has lost but not *what* he has lost in him." The subject cannot reflect on this blind spot, because that lack of awareness plays a crucial role in the individual's ability to sever himself or herself from the object. It matters little that conflict and ambivalence figure into the melancholic's relation to the object, for his or her symptoms do not express the content of the conflict. Rather, they operate in the mode of ambivalence. Although the ambivalence remains unresolved and unknown, that opacity makes little difference in terms of its transposition into external symptoms.

60. For a very useful analysis of the object in this relational sense, see Nicolas Abraham and Maria Torok, *The Shell and the Kernel*, trans. Nicolas Rand (Chicago: University of Chicago Press, 1994).

61. See Theodor Reik, *Masochism in Sex and Society*, trans. Margaret H. Beigel and Gertrude M. Kurth (New York: New Grove Press, 1962); Gilles Deleuze, "Coldness and Cruelty," in Deleuze, *Masochism, an Interpretation of Coldness and Cruelty* (New York: Zone Books, 1991); Jean Laplanche, *Life and Death in Psychoanalysis*, trans. Jeffrey Mehlman (Baltimore, MD: Johns Hopkins University Press, 1976).

CHAPTER TWO

1. Earlier intellectual historians of this period have often posited the problem in the context of the ideological and philosophical traditions of imperial China. In this view,

the felt crisis in the late Qing is often seen as a historically bound problem in the structural conflict between tradition and modernity, individualism and nationalism, or nationalism and class. I am, however, interested in how the historically founded sense of "crisis" becomes a sustaining modality generating a position of reflection, as a different order of epistemology, across larger terrains of knowledge. See, for example, Lin, *Crisis of Chinese Consciousness*; Meisner, *Li Ta-Chao*; Hao Chang, *Chinese Intellectuals in Crisis: Search for Order and Meaning, 1890–1911* (Cambridge, MA: Harvard University Press, 1971). For a recent study that makes an important departure from this interpretation, see Theodore Huters, *Bringing the World Home: Appropriating the West in Late Qing and Early Republican China* (Honolulu: University of Hawaii Press, 2005).

2. The imminent partition of China was widely reported. For a sample of reports in leading reformist journals of the day, see, for example, "Lun guafen zhina" (On partitioning China), *Xiangbao* 51 (1898): 429–30, 52 (1898): 441–42; "Lun huangzhong jianglai zhi huo" (On the future peril of the yellow race), *Qingyibao* 13 (1899): 796; "Lun guafen Zhongguo zhi liuyan" (On the rumor of partitioning China), *Waijiaobao* 113 (1905): 116–18; Ruo Nan, "Gao jiaomin" (Telling the people of faith), *E shi jingwen* (01.04.1904); "Xulun" (A preface), orig. pub. in *Hubei xueshengjie*, collected in Zhang Nan and Wang Yenzhi, eds., *Xinhai geming qian shinianjian shilun xuanji* (A selection of contemporary views in the ten years before the Revolution of 1911), 5 vols. (Beijing: Sanlian, 1960), 1.1:434–43; "Jiaoyu hui wei mintuan zhi jichu" (Education will be the foundation of civil community), orig. pub. in *Jiangsu*, collected in Zhang and Wang, *Xinhai*, 1.2:547–51; "Xin Zhongguo zhi shaonian" (The youth of New China), "Guafen Zhongguo zhi yuandongli" (The catalyst force for China's partition), orig. pub. in *Juansheng*, collected in Zhang and Wang, *Xinhai*, 2.1:567–72; "Lun lixian yu waijiao zhi guanxi" (On the relationship between constitutionalism and diplomacy), orig pub. in *Waijiaobao*, collected in Zhang and Wang, *Xinhai*, 2.2:575–77; Yi xian (Sun Zhongshan), "Zhina baoquan fenge helun" (A composite view on preserving and partitioning China), orig. pub. in *Jiangsu*, collected in Zhang and Wang, *Xinhai*, 1.2:597–602. The imminent danger of partitioning was at the same time expressed in a language with which the population readily sympathized. The format was often much more casual in the traditional style of storytelling or folk songs. See, for example, "Shishi wenda" (Questions and answers on contemporary affairs), *Zhongguo baihuabao* 2 (1903): 67–73; "Xingmengge" (A song for waking from a dream), *Anhui suhuabao* 8 (1904): 33–40.

3. Benjamin A. Elman, "Naval Warfare and the Refraction of China's Self-Strengthening Reforms into Scientific and Technological Failure," *Modern Asian Studies* 38.2 (2003): 283–326.

4. See, for example, Chen, *China and the West*; Guy S. Alitto, *The Last Confucian: Liang Shu-ming and the Chinese Dilemma of Modernity* (Berkeley: University of California Press, 1979).

5. For discussions of the theory of evolution in China, see Benjamin Schwartz, *In Search of Wealth and Power: Yen Fu and the West* (Cambridge, MA: Harvard University Press, 1964); James Reeve Pusey, *China and Charles Darwin* (Cambridge, MA: Harvard University Press, 1983).

6. Yan Fu, "Yuanqiang" (On strength), in Wang Shi, ed., *Yan Fu ji* (Yan Fu collection), 5 vols. (Beijing: Zhonghua shuju, 1986), 1:18.

7. For an excellent treatment of national consciousness as awakening, see John F. Fitzgerald, *Awakening China: Politics, Culture, and Class in the Nationalist Revolution* (Stanford: Stanford University Pres, 1996).

8. "Guozi jie" (An explication of the word *guo*), *Jingye xunbao* 7 (1906): 7–10; "Guojia lun" (On nation), *Jingye xunbao* 12 (1908): 11–14, 14 (1909): 5–8.

9. There was also much discussion of how the "little I" (*xiaowo*) should be sacrificed for the "greater I" (*dawo*). The chosen framework for understanding the collective is always centered on the subjective "I," but it is defined in terms of selflessness rather than selfishness.

10. Yichi, "Shuo aiguo" (Talking about loving the nation), *Anhui suhuabao* 14 (1904): 1–4.

11. However, in contrast to his earlier glorification, Yue Fei, along with another southern Song figure much celebrated in the twentieth century, Wen Tianxiang, was recently demoted by the ruling Communist Party. Yue Fei's bloody campaigns against the northern people have lost their particular flair of heroism, as these former "barbarians" are part of the "Chinese" today. Wen, known for his fight against the Mongols that culminated in his capture and execution, has also lost his relevance to the current policy of promoting official harmony among the fifty-five ethnic minorities. The Education Ministry, which issued official secondary school curricula instructing that Yue Fei would no longer be celebrated as a national hero, thought that the category of national heroes should be reserved for those who fought against real foreigners, such as the Dutch or Japanese, as opposed to Central Asian nomadic groups. See "Age-Old Nationalist Hero Gets a Demotion in China: Beijing Decides That a 12th Century General Long Revered for His Loyalty Is No Longer P.C.," *Los Angeles Times* (02.04.2003).

12. See Fang Shi, "Lun xue guochou yi xianli guochi" (In order to avenge national hatred one should first encourage national humiliation), *Dongfang zazhi* 1.4 (1904): 65–67.

13. "Guochi tu 1: Jiangjun beikun" (Portrait of national humiliation 1: A general in captivity), *Anhui suhuabao* 13 (1904). There were six such portraits published in three issues, 13–15 (1904).

14. In Shanghai, other varieties of portraits of national humiliation were circulated: "Mingchitu" (Portrait of understanding shame) and "Guochi yuefen pai" (National humiliation monthly cards). By 1897, a "Learning Society of Knowing Shame" (*Zhichi xuehui*) had been established in Beijing. See reports in *Jingzhong ribao* (1904); Zong Shishou, "Zhichi xuehui houxu" (Afterword to the Learning Society of Knowing Shame), *Shiwubao* 42 (1897): 2761–64; Liang Qichao, "Zhichi xuehui xu" (Preface to the Learning Society of Knowing Shame), *Shiwubao* 40 (1897): 2705–7.

15. "Guochi tu 2: Baojiao shouru" (Portrait of national humiliation 2: Bound feet humiliated), *Anhui suhuabao* 13 (1904).

16. See, for instance, "Daci dabei jiuku jiunan aiguo xinjing" (Heart mantra of great benevolence and compassion, saving one from hardship and trouble, and loving the nation), *Hangzhou baihuabao* 22 (1903): 1–2; "Mianxue ge" (Song for encouraging learning), *Anhui suhuabao* 17 (1904): 2. "Mianxue ge" also appears as "Xingshi ge" (Song of awakening the world), *Cuixinbao* 3 (1904): 1.

17. See, for instance, "Mingchi pian" (Understanding shame), *Jingye xunbao* 1 (1906): 15–18, 2 (1906): 11–18; "Wangchi" (Forgetting shame), *Buren* 4 (1913): 1–7.

18. See, for instance, "Waiwu pian" (An essay on humiliation from the outside), *Tongzi shijie* 32 (1903): 1–7.

19. Yong Li, "Lun paiwai buyi you xingji" (On how it is inappropriate to leave traces when rejecting the foreign), *Dongfang zazhi* 3.12 (1907): 227–29; Jun Jian, "Wenming de paiwai yu yeman de paiwai" (Civilized and barbaric ways of rejecting the foreign), *Jingye xunbao* 5 (1906): 13–16.

20. Yu Yi, "Minzu zhuyi lun" (On ethnonationalism), *Zhejiangchao* 1 (1903): 1–8, 2 (1903): 11–23, 5(1903): 25–32.

21. Liang Qichao, *Xin dalu youji* (Travels in the New World), in Yang Gang and Wang Xiangyi, eds., *Liang Qichao quanji* (The complete works of Liang Qichao), 10 vols. (Beijing: Beijing chubanshe, 1999), 2:1217–22.

22. See Huang Jie, "Huang Shi: Zhongzushu" (Yellow history: A book on race), *Guocui xuebao* 1 (1905): 1–10, 2 (1905): 1–10. "Huang Shi" continues with other subheadings in 3 (1905): 1–10, 4 (1905): 1–9, 5 (1905): 1–10, 6 (1905): 1–10, 7 (1905): 1–5, 8 (1905): 1–5, 9 (1905): 1–5; Liu Shipei, *Rangshu* (Book on expulsion), in Liu, *Liu Shenshu xiansheng yishu* (The posthumous works of Lu Shipei) (Nanjing: Jiangsu guji chubanshe, 1997). The National Essence School, to which both Huang Jie and Liu Shipei belonged, was strongly influenced in this regard by the work of French historian Terrien de Lacouperie (1845–94). See Lacouperie, *Western Origins of the Early Chinese Civilization* (Osnabrück, Germany: Zeller, 1966). A discussion of this can be found in Dikötter, *Discourse of Race*, pp. 119–23. For a detailed treatment of the theory of racial origins in the context of the discussions on the difference between "Chinese" (*hua*) and "barbarians" (*yi*), see Tang Wenquan and Luo Fuhui, *Zhang Taiyan sixiang yanjiu* (A study of the thought of Zhang Taiyan) (Wuchang: Huazhong shifan daxue chubanshe, 1986), pp. 47–63.

23. See, for instance, Gu Yin, "Tuihua lun" (On degeneration), *Dongfang zazhi* 1.11 (1904): 256–59; Gu Yin, "Bo tuihua lun" (Against the theory of degeneration), *Dongfang zazhi* 1.11 (1904): 259–62; "Lun tianyan yu mingyun" (On evolution and fate), *Dongfang zazhi* 4.9 (1907): 168–72; "Lun datong pingdeng zhi shuo bu shiyong yu jinri zhi Zhongguo" (On why principles of equality and great harmony are not appropriate when applied to China today), *Dongfang zazhi* 1.12 (1904): 301–2; "Zhu huangzhong zhi jiangxing" (Well wishes for the imminent rise of the yellow race), *Dongfang zazhi* 1.1 (1904): 13–15; "Lun Zhongguo ren tianyan zhi shen" (On the advanced state of the evolution of the Chinese), *Dongfang zazhi* 2.1 (1905): 24–26; "Zuijin zhi youlie tan" (Recent discussions on superiority and inferiority), *Dongfang zazhi* 1.8 (1904): 174–77.

24. For an illustration of the use of Darwinian evolution for the purpose of propagating the "yellow peril" in American media around the same time, see plate 75, "Darwin's Theory Illustrated—the Creation of Chinaman and Pig," in Philip P. Choy, Lorraine Dong, and Marlon K. Hom, eds., *Coming Man: 19th Century American Perceptions of the Chinese* (Hong Kong: Joint Publishing, 1994), p. 111.

25. See Zou Rong, *The Revolutionary Army*, trans. John Lust (The Hague & Paris: Mouton, 1968); Zhang Binglin, "Bo Kang Youwei shu" (A letter disputing Kang

Youwei), orig. pub. in *Subao*, collected in Zhang and Wang, *Xinhai*, 1.2:752–63. Also see, for example, Zhida, "Baoman yu paiman" (Protecting and discriminating against the Manchus), orig. pub. in *Tianyibao*, collected in Zhang and Wang, *Xinhai*, 2.2:915–16; "Shi chouman" (Defining hatred against the Manchus), orig. pub. in *Subao*, excerpt collected in Zhang and Wang, *Xinhai*, 1.2:678–80. See also Pamela Crossley's discussion in Crossley, *A Translucent Mirror: History and Identity in Qing Imperial Ideology* (Berkeley: University of California Press, 1999).

26. In 1881, Alexander II of Russia was assassinated by a group called the People's Will. After a period of reaction, the Socialist-Revolutionary Party (agrarian socialists) started assassinating high government officials again at the start of the twentieth century. Articles on Russian Nihilism include Yuan Sun, "Luxiya xuwudang" (The Russian Nihilist Party), orig. pub. in *Jiangsu*, collected in Zhang and Wang, *Xinhai*, 1.2:565–70; "Xuwudang" (The Nihilist Party), orig. pub. in *Subao*, collected in Zhang and Wang, *Xinhai*, 1.2:696–98. See also Arif Dirlik, *Anarchism in the Chinese Revolution* (Berkeley: University of California Press, 1991); Don Price, *Russia and the Roots of the Chinese Revolution 1896–1911* (Cambridge, MA: Harvard University Press, 1974); Peter Zarrow, *Anarchism and Chinese Political Culture* (New York: Columbia University Press, 1990); Mary Backus Rankin, *Early Chinese Revolutionaries: Radical Intellectuals in Shanghai and Chekiang, 1902–1911* (Cambridge, MA: Harvard University Press, 1971).

27. Zou Rong, *Gemingjun* (Revolutionary army), collected in Zhang and Wang, *Xinhai*, 1.2:663. A similar polarizing formula was advanced regarding the Japanese, "Riren rong Zhongguo ru" (The glory of the Japanese is the shame of the Chinese).

28. Recently, scholars have begun to revise this long-held view of Manchu's Sinification. Contrary to what has long been endorsed in narratives of Chinese nationalism, the process of cultural assimilation was much more complicated and cut both ways. For three excellent studies, see Mark C. Elliott, *The Manchu Way: The Eight Banners and Ethnic Identity in Late Imperial China* (Stanford: Stanford University Press, 2001); Edward Rhoads, *Manchus & Han: Ethnics Relations and Political Power in Late Qing and Early Republican China, 1861–1928* (Seattle: University of Washington Press, 2000); Pamela Crossley, *Orphan Warriors: Three Manchu Generations and the End of the Qing World* (Princeton, NJ: Princeton University Press, 1990).

29. See Zhang Taiyan, "Paiman pingyi" (An even assessment of ostracizing the Manchus), in Zhang and Wang, *Xinhai* 3:45–52.

30. Zou Rong, *Zou Rong ji qi gemingjun* (Zou Rong and his *The Revolutionary Army*), ed. Sichuan congshu bianji weiyuanhui (Taibei: Zhongxi dazi fanyishe, 1978). For an English translation, see John Lust, trans., *The Revolutionary Army: A Chinese Nationalist Tract of 1903* (The Hague & Paris: Mouton, 1968).

31. See Chen Tianhua, *Chen Tianhua ji* (Chen Tianhua collection) (Shanghai: Zhongguo wenhua fuwuhui, 1946).

32. W. E. B. Du Bois made a similar point regarding the black and white races. See discussion in Appiah, *In My Father's House.*

33. For a long discussion on the significance of "perished nations" as those subjected to foreign rule, see San Ai, "Wangguo pian" (A treatise on perished nations), *Anhui suhua bao* 8 (1904): 1–4, 10 (1904): 1–4, 13 (1904): 1–4, 15 (1904), 17 (1904): 1–4, 19 (1904): 1–4.

34. Kang Youwei, *Datongshu* (The book of the great union), collected in Zhu Weizheng, ed., *Kang Youwei datonglun liang zhong* (Kang Youwei's view on the great union: Two kinds) (Hong Kong: Sanlian shudian, 1998). There has been much dispute over the exact period of composition of *Datongshu*. Here I follow the date given by Liang Qichao, which has become the standard. For a discussion on dating, see Zhu, "Daoyan: Cong *Shili gongfa quanshu* dao *Datongshu*" (An introduction: From *The complete work on pragmatic principles and public dictates* to *The book of the great union*), in Zhu, *Kang Youwei datonglun liang zhong*, pp. 13–15.

35. Kang, *Datongshu*, p. 167.

36. The title of this section is "Qu zhongjie tong renlei" (Abolishing racial boundaries and uniting humankind). See ibid., pp. 170–78.

37. Ibid., p. 168.

38. Ibid., p. 173.

39. The passage in Chinese is as follows: "renlei pingdeng, renlei datong, ci gu gongli ye. Ran wu zhi buqi, wu zhi qing ye." See ibid., p. 171.

40. Ibid., p. 171.

41. Ibid., p. 176.

42. See Zhu, "An introduction," in *Kang Youwei datonglun liang zhong*, p. 15. Liang Qichao, Kang's disciple who later became one of the most important reformers of the late Qing, gives 1901–2 as the date of publication. Another scholar, Li Sizheng, believes, however, that Kang had started writing the first part in 1884, when he was twenty-seven years old, during the French invasion of Guangzhou. The first draft of the first part, *Principles of Humankind* (Renlei gongli), was seen only by his disciples in 1885. By the time of the Reform Movement of 1898, Kang showed twenty-odd chapters to his friend, a Japanese intellectual named Inukai Tsuyoshi (1855–1932). Kang later also gave a copy of the book to German missionary Richard Wilhelm, who included it in his book *Zhongguo jingshen* (1926), which was translated into English as *Soul of China* (1928).

43. Kang, *Datongshu*, p. 21.

44. "Xi boshi xinzhu Renwen yiben" (Regarding a new work, *The Origin of Species* by a western scholar), *Shenbao* (1873). Darwin was introduced as "Dawen." In the same year, the Jiangnan Arsenal's Translations Division published a Chinese translation of Charles Lyell's *Elements of Geology* (Dixue qianshi) by Daniel Jermore MacGowan. Discussed in this work is not only the Darwinian notion of evolution but also Lamarckian theory, which argues that acquired characteristics, such as impressions made on the pregnant mother, can be inherited. Lamarck's theory became one of the most discussed tenets in the development of Western eugenics.

45. John Fryer, an English entrepreneur in China, also introduced Darwin in his journal, *Gezhi huibian* (Compendium of science), 6 (1891). For a list of Chinese translations beginning in the early 1900s, see R. B. Freeman, "Darwin in Chinese," *Archives of Natural History* 13 (1986): 19–24; P. J. P. Whitehead, "Darwin in Chinese: Some Additions," *Archives of Natural History* 15 (1988): 61–62. For a very important essay on Fryer's involvement with early modern Chinese fiction, see Patrick Hannan, "The New Novel Before the New Novel: John Fryer's Fiction Contest," in Lydia H. Liu, Judith T. Zeitlin, and Ellen Widmer, eds., *Writing and Materiality in China: Essays in Honor of Patrick Hanan* (Cambridge, MA: Harvard University Press, 2003), pp. 317–24.

46. Liang Qichao, "Yu Yan youling xiansheng shu" (Letter to Mr. Yan Youling [Yan Fu]), collected in Liang, *Yinbingshi heji* (Collated edition of ice drinking studio), 12 vols. (Beijing: Zhonghua shuju, 1989), 1:106–11.

47. Outside Western Europe, however, eugenics was adopted for purposes of nationalism as well. See Nancy Leys Stepan, *"The Hour of Eugenics": Race, Gender, and Nation in Latin America* (Ithaca & London: Cornell University Press, 1991); Mark B. Adams, ed., *The Wellborn Science: Eugenics in Germany, France, Brazil, and Russia* (New York & Oxford: Oxford University Press, 1990): 110–52; Maria Bucur, *Eugenics and Modernization in Interwar Romania* (Pittsburgh, PA: University of Pittsburgh Press, 2002). Also see Chapter 4.

48. Kang, *Datongshu*, p. 175.

49. *Geguo zhonglei kao* (An investigation into the races of various nations) was first serialized in *Xiangxuebao* during 1897–98, nos. 15–27. The following discussion is based on the text collected in Chen Shanwei, ed., *Tang Caichang nianpu changbian* (An expanded chronology of Tang Caichang), 2 vols. (Hong Kong: Zhongwen daxue chubanshe, 1990), 1:351–403.

50. Chen, *Tang Caichang nianpu changbian*, 1:351. Tang saw Yan Fu's article in the newspaper *Hanbao*. What he saw was apparently the unrevised version of "Yuanqiang" (On strength), which first appeared in the Tianjin newspaper *Zhibao* (03.04–09.1895). When the Shanghai newspaper *Shiwubao* also wanted to publish this article in 1896, Yan Fu asked for a ten-day extension in order to complete his revision, yet his final version, which contains more than 50 percent additional characters, was never published. See his letter to Liang Qichao, collected in Yan Fu, *Yan Fu ji*, 5:513–15.

51. In addition, he relied on *Wanguo tongjian* (A composite history of myriad nations), translated by Devello Zelotos Sheffield (1841–1913); the pioneer of atlases in China, Xu Jiyu's (1795–1873) *Yinghuan zhilue* (A brief history of the ocean circuit); and the Book of Genesis from the Old Testament. Xiong Yuezhi lists *The Book of Dates* as the original English title. However, it must have been some version of John Blair's *Chronological and Historical Tables*, which underwent several revisions and expansions. See Xiong Yuezhi, *Xixue dongjian yu wanqing shehui* (The rise of Western learning in the East and late Qing society) (Shanghai: Renmin chubanshe, 1994), p. 539. The Chinese sources are primarily drawn from historical works such as *Jinshu* (History of Jin) and *Tongdian* (Encyclopedic history of institutions). *Jinshu*, edited by Fang Xuanling (578–648), was the standard history of the Jin dynasty. Its compilation began in 644 and was presented to the throne in 646. *Tongdian*, compiled by Du You (735–812) and completed in 801, was used as a reference work for administering institutions.

52. These are the titles of two chapters in Darwin's *Origin of Species*. Tang used "hasten" (*ji*), whereas Yan Fu used the character "compete" (*zheng*).

53. Tang, *Geguo zhonglei kao*, p. 352. Yan Fu's racial order is slightly different, with the reds preceding the blacks, and the whites usually mentioned before the yellows.

54. See also Dikötter's pioneering work, *Discourse of Race*.

55. Tang, *Geguo zhonglei kao*, p. 398.

56. Ibid., p. 398.

57. Ibid., p. 400.

58. Even though Chinese observers recognized the plight of colonized races as their own, they nonetheless asserted that they stood out from all the rest of this third-world imaginary, thus erecting a different hierarchy of their own within the category of oppressed peoples. Cf. Rebecca Karl, *Staging the World: Chinese Nationalism at the Turn of the Twentieth Century* (Durham, NC: Duke University Press, 2002).

59. See Tang Xiaobing, *Global Space and the Nationalist Discourse of Modernity* (Stanford: Stanford University Press, 1996).

60. Liang Qichao, "Lun Zhongguo zhi jiang qiang" (On China's imminent rise), *Shiwubao* 31 (1897): 2075.

61. See Stephen Jay Gould, *The Mismeasure of Man: The Definitive Refutation to the Argument of the Bell Curve* (New York & London: Norton, 1981).

62. This revisits the event of the Sino-Japanese War of 1894–95, to which Liang makes reference in his various essays on national survival. For Chinese intellectuals at the time, China's defeat in the war delivered the unambiguous message that China lacked not only the military power but also the political capacity to survive in the modern world. China, after all, had for centuries held Japan in contempt as a vassal state. Formerly referred to as the kingdom of dwarfs, Japan demonstrated during the Meiji period an enviable ability to modernize with greater speed and success than China. To master such a trauma, the Chinese used an argument of reconciliation to explain the turn of events. Liang was not alone in making such an attempt. In 1897, Zhang Binglin propagated the alliance between the Chinese and the Japanese as a racial affinity that must not be betrayed by Japan's rise to power. See Zhang Binglin, "Lun yazhou yi ziwei chunchi" (On how Asia would do well by maintaining the alliance between the teeth and lips), *Shiwubao* 18 (1897): 1177–79. Similar arguments of persuasion, as I later point to, resurfaced with renewed urgency after Japan's victory in the Russo-Japanese War of 1904–5.

63. Liang Qichao, "Zhongguo renzhong zhi jianglai" (On the future of the Chinese race), *Qingyibao* 19 (1899): 1183–92.

64. Liang, "Zhongguo renzhong zhi jianglai," p. 1184.

65. Ibid., p. 1186.

66. Ibid., p. 1185.

67. See Wang Gungwu, *The Chinese Overseas: From Earthbound China to the Quest for Autonomy* (Cambridge, MA: Harvard University Press, 2000); Philip A. Kuhn, *The Homeland: Thinking About the History of Chinese Overseas* (Canberra: Australia National University, 1997); Adam McKewon, *Chinese Migrant Networks and Cultural Change: Peru, Chicago, Hawaii, 1900–1936* (Chicago: University of Chicago Press, 2001); Madeline Y. Hsu, *Dreaming of Gold, Dreaming of Home: Transnationalism and Migration Between the United States and South China, 1882–1943* (Stanford: Stanford University Press, 2000).

68. There was much discussion of whether the Chinese possessed the spirit of adventure and exploration. See, for example, Zhuang You, "Guomin xin linghun" (The soul of the new citizen), *Jiangsu* 5 (1903): 1–9; "Guohun pian" (On the national soul), *Zhejiangchao* 1 (1903): 1–17; Wulaisheng (Sir Bum), "Wo xianmin maoxian xingzhi zhi yiban" (About the trait of adventurousness in our forefathers), *Fubao* 5 (1906): 59–63; Baihua daoren (The vernacular Taoist), "Zuo baixing de si-

xiang ji jingshen" (The thought and spirit of the common folks), *Zhongguo baihuabao* 4 (1903): 1–6.

69. Liang, "Zhongguo renzhong zhi jianglai," p. 1188.

70. Observations of Chinese social and hygienic habits figure prominently into both Western and Chinese conceptions of the Chinese national characteristics. See Chapter 4.

71. For an interesting article on why the notion of equality is inappropriate for China, see "Lun datong pingdeng," 301–2. See n. 23.

72. Zhuo Dai (Xu Zhuodai), "Fengehou zhi wuren" (Our people after the partition), *Jiangsu* 8 (1903): 19–20, 9–10 (1903): 1–16.

73. Guazi, "Mingri zhi guafen" (Tomorrow's partition), *Jiangsu* 7 (1903): 1–10.

74. It was actually Wei Yi, Lin Shu's collaborator, who first came across Stowe's novel and, after reading it, introduced it to Lin, who then agreed to the translation project. See Wei Yi's preface to *Heinu yu tian lu* (A record of the black slaves lamenting, "Heaven!"), collected in A Ying, ed., *Wanqing wenxue congchao: xiaoshuo xiqu yanjiu juan* (A collection of late Qing literature: Fiction and drama) (Beijing: Zhonghua shuju, 1960), pp. 279–80.

75. This is likely Lin Shu's translation for the original English title, *Uncle Tom's Cabin, or, Life Among the Lowly*. A facsimile of this 1852 cover can be found in Harriet Beecher Stowe, *Uncle Tom's Cabin*, ed. Elizabeth Ammons (New York: Norton, 1994), p. xii.

76. Lin Shu and Wei Yi, trans., *Heinu yu tian lu* (A record of the black slaves lamenting, "Heaven!") (Beijing: Shangwu yinshuguan, 1981), p. 1.

77. For an interesting study on how Lin Shu handles Western references, see Martha P. Y. Cheung, "The Discourse of Occidentalism? Wei Yi and Lin Shu's Treatment of Religious Material in Their Translation of *Uncle Tom's Cabin*," in David Pollard, ed., *Translation and Creation: Readings of Western Literature in Early Modern China, 1840–1918* (Philadelphia: Benjamins Publishing, 1998): 127–50.

78. See "Liyan" (Preface), in Lin and Wei, *Heinu yu tian lu*, p. 2.

79. See Liang Qichao, "Zhi wu xingshi shu: Lun meiguo huagong liu shi" (A letter to Ambassador Wu: Six matters regarding the Chinese laborers in America), *Zhixinbao* 14 (1897): 3–4; 15 (1897): 1–2.

80. In the few years before and during the same year as Lin Shu's preface, articles on the Chinese laborers were readily available, especially in Liang Qichao's, *Qingyibao*. Liang himself reported extensively on the situation during his travels in America. See, for example, "Meibao lun zhinaren yizhu" (American newspaper on Chinese immigration), *Qingyibao* 22 (1899): 1408–9; "Huaren kukuang" (The bitter hardships of the Chinese), *Qingyibao* 59 (1900): 3771–72; Yan Jinrong, "You tanxiangshan riji" (Diary from travels to Hawaii), *Qingyibao* 96 (1901): 6001–04; 97 (1901): 6063–68; Zili guomin, "Meiguo nuedai huaren bugaowen" (A public notice on Americans' ill-treatment of the Chinese), *Qingyibao* 90 (1901): 5657–65; 92 (1901): 5771–78; 93 (1901): 5831–32; 99 (1901): 6177–80.

81. Lin Shu, "Ba" (Postscript), in Lin and Wei, *Heinu yu tian lu*, p. 206.

82. For a similar observation, see Xue Zhuo, "Lin Shu qianqi yishu sixiang guankui" (A glimpse into the thinking in Lin Shu's early translations), in Xue Suizhi and Zhang Juncai, eds., *Lin Shu yanjiu ziliao* (Research materials on Lin Shu) (Fujian: Fujian renmin chubanshe, 1983), pp. 387–99.

83. See Lin Shu, "'Yishuo yuyan' erti" (Two prefatory remarks on *Aesop's Tales*), as collected in A Ying, *Wanqing wenxue congchao*, pp. 199–204, esp. p. 202.

84. Ibid., p. 202.

85. Ibid., p. 204.

86. Lin Shu, "'Wuzhongren' xu" (Preface to *People in the mist*), in A Ying's *Wanqing wenxue congchao: xiaoshuo xiqu yanjiu juan*, p. 232.

87. Ibid., p. 232.

88. Sun Jilin, "Lin Shu he Wei Yi" (Lin Shu and Wei Yi), in Wei Weiyi, ed., *Lin Shu Wei Yi heyi xiaoshuo quanji chongkan houji* (Afterword to the re-publication of the Complete collection of fiction jointly translated by Lin Shu and Wei Yi) (Taibei: Wei Weiyi, 1990), pp. 42–47.

89. Ibid., p. 44.

90. Ling Shi, "Du *Heinu yu tian lu*" (Reading *A record of the black slaves lamenting, "Heaven!"*), *Juemin* (Awakened citizen), 7 (1904): 29–32. Also see Xingshi (Awakened lion), "Ti *Heinu yu tian lu* hou" (After *A record of the black slaves lamenting, "Heaven!"*); Huiyun, "Du *Heinu yu tian lu*" (Reading *A record of the black slaves lamenting, "Heaven!"*); Jinyi, "Du *Heinu yu tian lu*" (Reading *A record of the black slaves lamenting, "Heaven!"*). All three are collected in A Ying's *Wanqing wenxue congchao: xiaoshuo xiqu yanjiu juan*, p. 591.

91. Ling, "Du *Heinu yu tian lu*," p. 29.

92. Ibid., p. 31.

93. Ibid., p. 32.

94. For discussions of early modern drama and drama societies in China, see, for example, Fan Boqun, ed., *Zhongguo jinxiandai tongsu wenxueshi* (A history of popular literature in late imperial and modern China), 2 vols. (Nanjing: Jiangsu jiaoyu chubanshe, 2000); Jia Zhifang, ed., *Zhongguo xiandai wenxue shetuan liupai* (The schools of modern Chinese literary societies), 2 vols. (Jiangsu: Jiangsu jiaoyu chubanshe, 1989); Fan Boqun and Zhu Donglin, eds., *Zhongwai wenxue bijiaoshi 1898–1949* (A history of Chinese and international comparative literature), 2 vols. (Nanjing: Jiangsu jiaoyu chubanshe, 1993); Wei Shaochang, ed., *Zhongguo jindai wenxue daxi: Shiliao suoyin ji* (Great compendium of late imperial Chinese literature: An index of historical sources), vols. 29, 30 (Shanghai: Shanghai shudian, 1996).

95. A Ying, ed., *Wanqing wenxue congchao: chengwai wenxue yiwen juan* (A collection of late Qing literature: Translations of foreign literature) (Beijing: Zhonghua shuju, 1960), 1:2–3.

96. "Chunliushe yanyibu zhuanzhang" (Statement of purpose for the performance department of Spring Willow Society) (1906), collected in A Ying, *Wanqing wenxue congchao: xiaoshuo xiqu yanjiu juan*, pp. 635–38.

97. From 1906 to 1915, Spring Willow Society performed eighty-one plays. A number of them were the society's own creations; others were translated or adapted from Western novels and classical Chinese tales. There were also those with program notes but no scripts. See Jia, *Zhongguo xiandai wenxue shetuan liupai*, 2:896–915.

98. See Wei, *Zhongguo jindai wenxue daxi*, 29:167–70.

99. Lü Bing, *Dongjing meng* (Tokyo dreams) (Shanghai: Zuoxinshe, 1909), chap. 8.

100. Tian Han, "Tan 'Heinu hen'" (About "The hatred of the black slaves"),

Tian Han quanji (The complete works of Tian Han), 20 vols. (Shijiazhuang: Huashan wenyi chubanshe, 2000), 16:477–92.

CHAPTER THREE

1. Jack London, "The Unparalleled Invasion" (1906), in Dale L. Walker, ed., *Jack London: Fantastic Tales* (Lincoln & London: University of Nebraska Press, 1998): 117–18.

2. Ibid., p. 116.

3. See Ma Tailai, "Lin Wei fanyi yinyuan" (The coming about of Lin Shu and Wei Yi's collaboration in translation), in Wei Weiyi, ed., *Lin Shu Wei Yi heyi xiaoshuo quanji chongkan houji* (Afterword to the re-publication of the Complete collection of fiction jointly translated by Lin Shu and Wei Yi) (Taibei: Wei Weiyi, 1993), pp. 12–29.

4. Ma Tailai attributes this in part to the restricted number of copies published. See ibid., p. 14.

5. Michael Haberlandt, *Völkerkunde* (Ethnology), trans. J. E. Loewe (London: Ballantyne Hanson, 1900).

6. Lin, trans., *Minzhongxue* (Ethnology), 2 vols. (Beijing: Beijing daxuetang guanshuju, 1903), 1:1–2.

7. Ibid., p. 3.

8. Yan Fu, "On strength," in *Yan Fu ji*, 1:9. Yan uses "the mind, moral, and essence of the people" (*minzhi minde minqi*).

9. See Haberlandt, *Völkerkunde*, p. 57; Lin, *Minzhongxue*, 1:27.

10. See, for instance, Haberlandt, *Völkerkunde*, p. 67; Lin, *Minzhongxue*, 1:32.

11. Lin Shu, *Minzhongxue*, 2:4.

12. Haberlandt, *Völkerkunde*, p. 87.

13. "Xieleihen" (Traces of bloody tears), *Hubei xuesheng jie* 5 (1903): 1–9.

14. Ibid., pp. 2–3.

15. Ibid., pp. 6–7.

16. See, for example, "Feilibin wangguo canzhuang ji lue" (A record of the horrendous circumstance of the perished nation Philippines), *Cuixinbao* 1 (1904): 1–6.

17. Xiamin, "*Feiliebing waishi* zixu" (An unofficial history of the Philippines), in Chen Pingyuan and Xia Xiaohong, eds., *Ershi shiji Zhongguo xiaoshuo lilun ziliao 1897–1916* (Theoretical materials of Chinese novels in the twentieth century 1897–1916) (Beijing: Beijing daxue chubanshe, 1989), p. 129.

18. Ziyouhua, *Ziyou jiehun* (Freedom of marriage), in *Zhongguo jindai xiaoshuo daxi* (Compendium of China's early modern literature) (Nanchang: Baihua wenyi chubanshe, 1991), pp. 105–286.

19. Apart from the thinly veiled allegory of geographical names, the text also makes a syntactical error in its title in mistaking "freedom of marriage" for "free marriage."

20. Gao Chuiwan, "Guanyu 'Ziyou jiehun' erti" (Two verses on *Freedom of marriage*), in A Ying, *Wanqing wenxue congchao: xiaoshuo xiqu yanjiu juan*, p. 574.

21. Another example is the novel by Yisuo, *Huang Xiuqiu* (Jilin: Jilin wenchi chubanshe, 1985). The title of the novel as well as the name of the female protago-

nist, Huang Xiuqiu, means "yellow embroidered earth." For an interesting discussion of this novel, see Hu Ying, *Tales of Translation: Composing the New Woman in China, 1898–1918* (Stanford: Stanford University Press, 2000), chap. 4.

22. For a discussion of the presence of "yellow peril" in American fiction, see William F. Wu, *The Yellow Peril: Chinese Americans in American Fiction 1850–1940* (Hamden, CT: Archon, 1982). For a treatment of "yellow peril" in film, see Gina Marchetti, *Romance and the "Yellow Peril": Race, Sex, and Discursive Strategies in Hollywood Fiction* (Berkeley: University of California Press, 1993).

23. For a detailed treatment of political discussions of the yellow peril in Europe and America, see Heinz Gollwitzer, *Die Gelbe Gefahr: Geschichte eines Schlagworts. Studien zum imperialistischen Denken* (Gottingen: Vandenhoeck & Ruprecht, 1962). For a collection of useful primary data, such as Wilhelm II's correspondence with Tsar Nicholas, translated into Chinese, see Lu Pu and Zhang Zhenkun, eds., *"Huanghuo lun" lishi ziliao xuanji* (Selected historical documents on the history of the "yellow peril") (Beijing: Zhongguo shehui kexue chubanshe, 1979). For a discussion of images of the "yellow peril" in film from this period, see Marchetti, *Romance and the "Yellow Peril."*

24. See Gordon A. Craig, *Germany, 1866–1945* (New York & Oxford: Oxford University Press, 1978). The following discussion is partly based on Gollwitzer, and Lu Pu and Zhang Zhenkun.

25. For Knackfuss's background, see Christa Stolz, *Hermann Knackfuss: Monographie über e. im 19. Jahrhundert in Wissen geborenen Künstler* (Wissen, Germany: Verlag G. Nising, 1975).

26. See Gollwitzer, *Die Gelbe Gefahr*, p. 207. This sketch was also seen by the Chinese, as it was apparently reprinted in *Waijiaobao*. See "Dehuang shouhui Huanghuo tu sheben" (German kaiser's hand-sketch of the "yellow peril"), *Waijiaobao* 113 (1905).

27. Gollwitzer, *Die Gelbe Gefahr*, p. 207.

28. D. C. Boulger, "Bogey of Yellow Peril," *Nineteenth Century and After* 55 (1904): 30. There were many other articles published in American journals, such as *Munsey's Magazine, Overland Monthly, Contemporary Review*, and *Chautauquan*, as well as in newspapers. See, for example, F. Brinkley, "Japan, The Yellow Peril, a Bogey," *Munsey's Magazine* 31 (1904): 818; T. B. Wilson, "So-Called Yellow Peril," *Overland Monthly* 45 (1905): 133; O. Eltzbacher, "The Yellow Peril," *Nineteenth Century and After* 55 (1904): 910.

29. For a recent discussion, see Efraim Karsh and Inari Karsh, *Empires of the Sand: The Struggle for Mastery in the Middle East 1789–1923* (Cambridge, MA: Harvard University Press, 1999), p. 106. For speculation on the visual source of the idea of the "Sick Man of East Asia," see Larissa N. Heinrich, "Handmaids to the Gospel: Lam Qua's Medical Portraiture," in Lydia Liu, ed., *Tokens of Exchange: The Problem of Translation in Global Circulations* (Durham, NC, & London: Duke University Press, 1999).

30. *Jingzhong ribao* was originally titled *E shi jingwen* (Alarming news on Russian affairs). It was published by the Association of Comrades Resisting Russia (Dui e tongzhi hui), which was established in December 1903 by Liu Shipei, Cai Yuanpei, and others. The publication was in response to Russian troops moving into the

Fengtien Province in preparation for the Russo-Japanese War and reported primarily on the crisis in Manchuria. After the war broke out in 1904, the journal was renamed *Jingzhong ribao* and reported on the war. See also n. 41.

31. See, for example, "Zhongguo shuairuo fei Riben zhi fu shuo" (China's decline is not a blessing for Japan), *Dongfang zazhi* 1.10 (1904): 231–33.

32. See Chapter 2.

33. "Lun riben yan tangren wenhua" (On Japan's lineage from Tang culture), *Waijiaobao* 79 (1904): 463–66; also in *Dongfang zazhi* 1.4 (1904): 73–75. Page references to *Waijiaobao* are taken from *Waijiaobao huibian* (Collation of *Waijiaobao*), 33 vols. (Taibei: Guangwen shuju, 1964).

34. Part of this cowardice was also identified as the result of the lack of military, or Bushido, spirit in late imperial China. See Liang Qichao, *Zhongguo zhi wushidao* (China's Bushido spirit) (Shanghai: 1904). See also "Lun Zhongguo zhi qiantu ji guomin yingjin zhi zeren" (On the future of China and the responsibilities its citizens should fulfill), *Hubei xuesheng jie* 3 (1903): 319–30; Chong You, "Lun Zhongguo minqi zhi keyong" (On the use of Chinese people's essence), *Dongfang zazhi* 1.1 (1904): 5–7; "Ai tongbao zhi jiang wang" (On the imminent death of our fellow citizens), *Jingzhong ribao* (10.03.1904). This is also reprinted in *Dongfang zazhi* 1.12 (1904): 295–98.

35. "Lun Zhongguo zeren zhi zhong" (On the weight of China's responsibility), *Dongfang zazhi* 1.1 (1904): 3–5.

36. Ibid., p. 5.

37. There are many examples of this kind of attempt to elevate China's status by emphasizing its "responsibility" to the world. A similar argument can be seen, for example, in "Lun Zhongguo ren duiyu shijie zhi zeren" (On Chinese responsibility to the world), *Waijiaobao* 65 (1903): 391–94.

38. Sun Yat-sen also used the idea of the Chinese as truly the most peace-loving people in the world to advance the notion that China's success will not be that of a nationalism but rather of a globalism in the interest of humankind. See Sun, "Minzu zhuyi: Di si jiang" (Nationalism: Fourth lecture), in Sun, *Sanmin zhuyi* (Three people's principles), in Zhongyang dangshi shiliao bianzuan weiyuanhui, ed., *Guofu quanji* (The complete works of the nation's founding father), 6 vols. (Taibei: Zhongguo Guomingdang zhongyang weiyuanhui, 1973), 1:42–44.

39. This article, originally published in the Japanese newspaper *Jiji shinbo* (05.02.1902), was translated and reprinted in *Waijiaobao*. See "Fei tongzhong tongwen" (Not of the same race and culture), *Waijiaobao* 12 (1902): 105–9. Cf. Ding Fengjia, "Zhongri erguo tong zai yazhou tong wei huangzhong you tongshi yu oumei tongshang er qiangruo xuanshu zhi ci qi gu he yu?" (Why is it that China and Japan, both in Asia and both members of the yellow race who simultaneously have commercial dealings with Europe and America, differ so greatly in their strengths and weaknesses?), *Dongfang zazhi* 1.4 (1905): 11–15.

40. For a collection of selected primary journalistic sources on the yellow peril, see Lu and Zhang, "*Huanghuo lun.*" This collection does not, however, include discussions of the "yellow peril" published in *Jingzhong ribao* (03.14.1904), (03.16.1904), (03.17.1904), (03.18.1904), (03.19.1904).

41. *Jingzhong ribao* initially began as a monitor on Russian ambitions to expand in

northeastern China. In February 1904, it was renamed to adapt to the new circumstances of imperialism in general and stopped publication in March 1905. Part of its new mission was to "cultivate the quality of national citizens and resist pressure from the outside." Contributors included Cai Yuanpei, Liu Shipei, Zou Rong, Tao Chengzhang, and Chen Duxiu. *Waijiao bao* (*Waijiaobao*) was established in January 1902 by Shanghai's Commercial Press. Cai Yuanpei, Ma Yuzao, and Yan Fu contributed to its translations. The journal had a primary focus on promoting "civilized xenophobia" in order to fulfill the duty of keeping out aggressors. It stopped circulation in January 1911. See also n. 30.

42. Discussion on the threat posed by the yellow race in France began in the 1890s with the warning from Kaiser Wilhelm II. I examine here, however, primarily those warnings coinciding with the Russo-Japanese War. For an earlier French discussion translated into Chinese in 1898, see, for example, "Huangzhong wuhai yu baizhong lun" (The yellow race poses no harm to the white race), trans. Pan Yan, *Changyanbao* (10.20.1898): 20–33. Pan's translation is based on an article published in what is translated as *Zhongfa xin huibao* (Collation of Sino-French news) 30 (1898). See also "Pinglun Zhongguo" (Assessing China), *Lingxuebao* 1 (01.20.1898): 14–15. This translation is based on an article published in *Revue des deux mondes*, translated as *Liangqiu yue pingbao* (Twin globe monthly). According to a report in *Jingzhong ribao*, there was apparently also a book published in France around 1904 on Japan and the yellow peril. See "Zoujin fei huanghuo shuo" (Against the report of "yellow peril"), *Jingzhong ribao* (07.31.1904).

43. As another way of pointing out Russia's culpability, the notion of the "white peril" was also advanced in Chinese and Japanese media. Discussions on the "white peril" continued to appear in Chinese journals well into the 1910s. See, for example, "Lun baihuo"(On the white peril), *Jingzhong ribao* (05.05.1904); "Lun Yingelusaxun huo" (On the Anglo-Saxon peril), *Waijiaobao* 83 (1904): 659–60; "E huo" (The Russian peril), *Jingzhong ribao* (02.05.1904); "Lun baihuo" (On the white peril), *Waijiaobao* 122 (1905): 193–202; "Baihuo shi" (The history of the white peril), *Dongfang zazhi* 10.3 (1913): 13–23. For other discussions of the yellow peril, see, among others, "Huanghuo lun" (On the yellow peril), *Dongfang zazhi* 9.2 (1912): 40–44; "Zhen huanghuo lun" (On the real yellow peril), *Dongfang zazhi* 10.4 (1913): 15–22; "Huangbai zhongzu zhi jingzheng" (The competition between the yellow and white races), *Liumei xuesheng jibao* 1 (1914): 1–2; "Lishi shang huangbai liangzhong zhi jingzheng" (The competition between the yellow and white races in history), *Dongfang zazhi* 3.13 (1906): 248–50; "Ri E kaizhan yu Zhongguo zhi guanxi" (The opening of the war between Russia and Japan and its relation to China), *Jiangsu* 8 (1904): 1377–83.

44. "Lun huanghuo" (On the yellow peril), *Waijiaobao* 83 (1904): 567–80. There are three installments of this article. The following discussion is based on the second. For other articles that express British views on the yellow peril, see, for example, "Lun huanghuo shuo zhi bu zu xin" (On the lack of evidence for the warning of the "yellow peril"), *Jingzhong ribao* (07.21.1904); "Lun huanghuo" (On the yellow peril), *Waijiaobao* 72 (1904): 487–94; "Lun huanghuo" (On the yellow peril), *Waijiaobao* 80 (1904): 545–51; "Lun huanghuo" (On the yellow peril), *Waijiaobao* 103 (1905): 27–

29; "Lun Riben yu De zhi jinqing" (On the recent relations between Japan and Germany), *Waijiaobao* 100 (1905): 129–31; "Lun Zhongguo zhi qiantu" (On the future of China), *Waijiaobao* 125 (1905): 223–28; "Lun huangzhong zhi jiang xing" (On the imminent rise of the yellow race), *Waijiaobao* 268 (1909): 319–36.

45. For Japanese articles on the yellow peril translated into Chinese, see, among others, "Huangzhong zhi cunwang" (The survival of the yellow race), *Qingyibao* 52 (1900): 3361–63; "Huanghuo yuce" (The prediction of the "yellow peril"), *Jiangsu* 1 (1903): 103–7; "Lun E De miyue" (On the secret Russo-German treaty), *Waijiaobao* 100 (1905): 127–28; "Lun guafen Zhongguo zhi liuyan" (On the rumor of partitioning China), *Waijiaobao* 113 (1905): 116–18; "Lun huanghuo" (On the yellow peril), *Waijiaobao* 90 (1904): 665–68; "Lun huangzhong zhi zhonghe" (On the yellow race's burden), *Waijiaobao* 157 (1906): 235–38; "Lun huanghuo zhi shuo buhe yu xueli" (On the illogicality of the "yellow peril"), *Jingzhong ribao* (07.23.1904).

46. "Lun huanghuo" (On the yellow peril), *Waijiaobao* 83 (1904): 579.

47. "Lun Zhongguo zhi qiantu" (On the future of China), *Waijiaobao* 125 (1905): 228.

48. Huang Zunxian, "Xuan jun ge" (Song of victorious troops), in Zhong Xianpei, Guang Lin, Xie Hua, and Wang Songtao, eds., *Huang Zunxian shixuan* (A selection of Huang Zunxian's poetry) (Guangdong: Guangdong renmin chubanshe, 1994), p. 181. Cf. Noriko Kamachi, *Reform in China: Huang Tsun-hsien and the Japanese Model* (Cambridge, MA: Council on East Asian Studies, Harvard University, 1981), p. 141.

49. "Lun 'huanghuo' zhi shuyu huaren" (The "yellow peril" belongs to the Chinese), *Waijiaobao* 200 (1908): 401–5. For other American views that reappeared in Chinese journals and newspapers, see, for example, Xianxiansheng, "Lun Zhongguo jiang xing" (On China's imminent rise), *Waijiaobao* 114 (1905): 119–25; "Lun huanghuo" (On the yellow peril), *Waijiaobao* 97 (1904): 711–15.

50. "Lun 'huanghuo' zhi shuyu huaren," p. 405.

51. Gu Yin, "Bian huanghuo zhi shuo" (Arguing against the "yellow peril"), *Dongfang zazhi* 2.2 (1905): 32–35. For other original articles in Chinese, see, for example, "Lun huanghuo" (On the yellow peril), *Dongfang zazhi* 1.2 (1904): 34–36; "Du xiren huanghuo shuo ganyan" (Thoughts after reading Westerners' views on the "yellow peril"), *Waijiaobao* 204 (1908): 325–28.

52. "Science fantasy," aptly chosen by David Wang to distinguish the genre of science fiction in late Qing China, emphasizes the element of the fantastic as linked with the cultural imagination. See David Der-wei Wang, *Fin-de-Siècle Splendor: Repressed Modernities of Late Qing Fiction, 1849–1911* (Stanford: Stanford University Press, 1997).

53. Gaoyang bucaizi (The untalented from Gaoyang), "Dian shijie" ("Electrical world"), *Xiaoshuo shibao* 1 (1909): 1–58.

54. Ibid., p. 3.

55. Ibid., p. 6.

56. Ibid., p. 9.

57. Ibid., p. 18.

58. Ibid., p. 41. This is a recurring theme in futuristic fiction and treatises on so-

cial utopia. In the 1920s, "Dr. Sex" Zhang Jingsheng proposes a similar measure for curbing sexual desires in propagation of the society based on beauty. Kang Youwei also recommends medication for reproductive regulation. See Chapters 2 and 5.

59. See Chapter 1.

60. Biheguan zhuren (Master of the sapphire lotus house), *Xin jiyuan* (New century) (Shanghai: Xiaoshuolin chubanshe, 1908). For a synopsis as well as discussion, see Wang, *Fin-de-Siècle Splendor*; Liu Delong, "Wanqing zhishi fenzi xintai de xiezhao" (A portrait of the mind-set of late Qing intellectuals), *Mingqing xiaoshuo yanjiu* (Study of Ming and Qing fiction) 32 (1994): 92–98. See also Chen Pingyuan, "Zhongguo xiaoshuo shi lun" (On the history of fiction in China), in Chen, *Chen Pingyuan Zhongguo xiaoshuo shi lunji* (Collected essays by Chen Pingyuan on the history of fiction in China), 3 vols. (Shijiazhuang: Hebei renmin chubanshe, 1997), 3:1671–1717.

61. Biheguan zhuren, *Xin jiyuan*, p. 23.

62. Ibid., p. 3.

63. Ibid., pp. 216–18.

64. Ibid., p. 78.

65. Qi Youzi, *Ku xuesheng* (The suffering student), in Wang Jiquan et al., eds., *Zhangguo jindai xiaoshuo daxi* (Compenium of China's early modern fiction), 80 vols. (Nanchang: Baihua wenyi chubanshe 1993), 54: 127–75.

66. See, for example, "Zuijin zhi youlie tan," pp. 174–77; "Lun Zhongguo ren tianyan zhi shen," pp. 24–26; Lin Yongxuan, "Lun ershi shiji guoji jingzheng shengbai zhi zong yuanyin ji Zhongguo yu shijie shang zhi weizhi" (On the outcome of international competitions in the twentieth century and China's position in the world), *Dongfang zazhi* 4.8 (1907): 39–51.

67. Yugong (Old fool), "Zhongguo zhongzu cunwang wenti" (The survival question for the Chinese race), *Zhenhua wuri dashiji* 31 (1907): 1–8; 32 (1907): 1–10; 33 (1907): 1–8; 34 (1907): 1–10; 35 (1907): 1–10; 37 (1907): 1–11; 38 (1907): 1–8; 39 (1907): 1–8; 40 (1907): 1–9; 43 (1907): 1–10; 44 (1907): 1–8; 47 (1907): 1–9; 49 (1907): 1–8; 50 (1907): 1–8; 51 (1907): 6–13.

68. On the other side of this argument is the self-assuring view arguing that the Chinese are in fact much farther along than other races in the scheme of evolution. If anything, the problem China faces is that it had already gone through the stages of development long ago, leaving little else to be accomplished. This is the source of their inertia; heaven's favoritism spoiled the Chinese with the best conditions for life and culture. cf. n. 66.

69. For this reason, humiliation suffered at the hands of Westerners is considered instructive for promoting this sense of pride. For example, in "Waiwu pian," pp. 1–7, the author states that humiliation at the hands of outsiders could only strengthen the Chinese national character. The stronger the force of humiliation, the stronger is the resistance. One must endure hardships and surpass obstacles before finding the will to persist. Humiliation is the precursor of constructive reflection. Thus, humiliation from outsiders serves as the "lethal weapon" for strengthening Chinese citizens. See Chapter 2, n. 18. Another article published in *Dagongbao*, "Wairen qingwu Zhongguo duoyou Zhongguo zizhao shuo" (On how foreigners' contemptuous treatment of China is largely brought about by the Chinese themselves) (06.11.1904), laments that China's complete inadequacy in dealing with unequal treaties justifiably calls for the contempt of the Western powers. The resulting humiliation and continued

transgression, the author emphasizes, is induced by the Chinese themselves, because they refused to give up the conviction that they still possess the cultural greatness they once had. The perils of a great tradition verging on extinction are blamed on the bearers of that tradition; they have failed to transmit it. This article is reprinted in *Dongfang zazhi* 1.8 (1904): 161–78.

CHAPTER FOUR

1. See Vera Schwarcz, *The Chinese Enlightenment: Intellectuals and the Legacy of the May Fourth Movement of 1919* (Berkeley: University of California Press, 1986); Chow Tse-Tsung, *The May Fourth Movement: Intellectual Revolution in Modern China* (Cambridge, MA: Harvard University Press, 1964).

2. Although recently developed scholarship on eugenics in China sheds light on its role in the development of modern science on sexuality and reproduction, little has been said about the specific cultural significance it has for the imperatives of nation building and westernization. See Frank Dikötter, *Imperfect Conceptions: Medical Knowledge, Birth Defects, and Eugenics in China* (New York: Columbia University Press, 1998); Dikötter, *Discourse of Race*; Yuehtsun Juliette Chung, *Struggle for National Survival: Eugenics in Sino-Japanese Contexts, 1896–1945* (New York: Routledge, 2002).

3. See, for example, Havelock Ellis, *The Task of Social Hygiene* (Boston: Houghton Mifflin, 1912); Paul Bowman Popenoe, *Applied Eugenics* (New York: Macmillan, 1918). Because of its association with World War II, most scholarship on eugenics in Europe focuses on Nazi Germany. For an account of an earlier phase of racial hygiene in Germany in relation to its policy toward colonies and imperialism, see Pascal Grosse, *Kolonialismus, Eugenik und bürgerliche Gesellschaft in Deutschland 1850–1918* (Frankfurt/Main: Campus Verlag GmbH, 2000). For comparisons outside the familiar framework of European and American eugenics from the perspective of nationalism, see, for example, Adams, *Wellborn Science*; Stepan, *"The Hour of Eugenics"*; Bucur, *Eugenics and Modernization*.

4. For example, see Chatterjee, *Nationalist Thought and the Colonial World*; Chatterjee, *Nation and Its Fragments*; Guha, *Dominance Without Hegemony*; Gellner, *Nations and Nationalism*; Anthony D. Smith, *Theories of Nationalism* (London: Duckworth, 1983).

5. For example, see Lu Shoujing, "Chuanzhong gailiang xinxueshuo zhi yiban" (The school that propounds the new view of improving the inheritance of race), *Zhonghua xuesheng jie* 4 (1916): 1–8; Jie You, trans., "Youshengxue qianshuo" (A brief introduction to eugenics), *Yiban* 1 (1929): 35–59. See also the following three notes. The new focus on racial improvement can in part be traced to earlier interests in hygiene and general health in the early 1900s. For earlier articles, see, for example, "Guangbu weisheng shuji yi qiang zhonglei shuo" (On circulating books on hygiene in order to strengthen the race), *Dongfang zazhi* 1.8 (1904): 177–78; "Weisheng lun" (On hygiene), *Dongfang zazhi* 2.8 (1905): 156–57; Charles Benedict Davenport, *Heredity in Relation to Eugenics* (Renzhong gailiangxue), trans. Chen Shoufan (Shanghai: Shangwu yinshuguan, 1919); Chen Changheng and Zhou Jianren, *Jinhualun yu shanzhongxue* (Evolution and eugenics) (Shanghai: Shangwu yinshuguan, 1923).

6. Major works in the Western language were introduced in one capacity or an-

other. Figures such as Havelock Ellis, August Weissmann, Ernst Haeckel, and Alfred Ploetz were quite familiar to the Chinese eugenicist circle. However, the Chinese translations were often edited quite freely at the discretion of the translator. It was often noted that the translator was the editor as well. Some of these works were even composites of several Western works. See, for example, Chen Shoufan, ed. and trans., *Renzhong gailiangxue* (The study of racial improvement) (Shanghai: Shangwu yinshuguan, 1919); Wang Xinming, *Yousheng wenti* (Havelock Ellis's *Problems in eugenics*) (Shanghai: Shangwu yinshuguan, 1924); Hua Rucheng, *Youshengxue ABC* (Eugenics ABC) (Shanghai: Shijie shuju, 1929). Paul Popenoe's popular textbook, *Applied Eugenics*, was also partly translated by Pan Guangdan. Eight out of the twenty chapters in the book appeared in his *Yousheng Yuanli* (The fundamental principles of eugenics) (Shanghai: Guanchashe, 1949).

7. See, among others, Zhang Junjun, *Zhongguo minzu zhi gaizao* (The reconstruction of the Chinese race) (Shanghai: Zhonghua shuju, 1936); Zhang Junjun, *Zhongguo minzu zhi gaizao xubian* (Sequel to *The reconstruction of the Chinese race*) (Shanghai: Zhonghua shuju, 1937); Zhang Junjun, *Minzu suzhi zhi gaizao* (The improvement of racial essence) (Chongqing: Shangwu yinshuguan, 1943); Pan Guangdan, *Renwen shiguan* (A view of the history of man and letters), collected in *Minguo congshu* (Books from the Republican period), 50 vols. (Shanghai: Shanghai shudian, 1989), 1.20; Chen Da, *Renkou wenti* (The problem of overpopulation) (Shanghai: Shanghai shudian, 1989).

8. See, for example, Hua Lu, "Minzu yi laolema?" (Is the race already old?), *Dongfang zazhi* 19.23 (1922): 1–2; Zhou Jianren, "Geren yu zhongzu de shuailao" (The decrepitude of the individual body and race), *Dongfang zazhi* 19.10 (1922): 42–48; Jian Meng, "Minzu zhi shuaitui" (Racial decline), *Dongfang zazhi* 18.21 (1921): 1–3; Tong Runzhi, "Zhongguo minzu de zhili" (The intelligence of the Chinese race), *Dongfang zazhi* 26.3 (1929): 67–76.

9. See, for example, Jian Meng, "Meidu shi zhongzu shuaitui de yuanyin" (Syphilis is the cause of racial decline), *Dongfang zazhi* 19.7 (1922): 85–86; Gen Zhimin, "Jiehe zhi yufang" (The prevention of tuberculosis), *Yishi yuekan* 5 (1924): 1–5, 9 (1924): 1–4, 10 (1924): 1–6. Opponents to the view of racial degeneration argue that, on the contrary, China is in the prime of its youth, brimming with energy and renewed vigor. Journals that espouse the more positive view—racial degeneration as a problem that can be remedied—name themselves accordingly. See, for example, *Shaonian Zhongguo* (Adolescent China) and *Huanian* (Golden era). In a different context, Laura Engelstein points out that the Russian medical and social inquiry into syphilis around the turn of the century became a way of controlling women rather than the disease. See Engelstein, *The Keys to Happiness: Sex and the Search for Modernity in Fin-de-Siècle Russia* (Ithaca, NY: Cornell University Press, 1992). In contrast, the association of syphilis with the "illnesses of civilization" in the Chinese context had less to do with women than with westernization. "Civilization *wenming*" in the sense we think of it today was a relatively new term at the time, fraught with the idea of Western democracy.

10. For articles on racial improvement in medical journals as well as articles emphasizing the importance of medical science to China's national strengthening, see, for example, Yu Desun, "Minzhong zhi gailiang" (The improvement of race),

Yiyaoxue 12 (1930): 7–12, 1 (1931): 39–46; Hai Huo, "Yixue yu shehui zhi guanxi" (The relationship between medical science and society), *Dongfang zazhi* 2.4 (1905): 7–10; Gu Yin, "Lun Zhongguo qiantu yu yixue zhi guanxi" (On the relationship between China's future and medical science), *Dongfang zazhi* 2.6 (1905): 107–14; Liang Boqiang, "Yixue shangde Zhongguo minzu—hanzu—zhi yanjiu" (The study of the Chinese race—the Han race—in medical science), *Dongfang zazhi* 23.13 (1926): 87–100.

11. See Dikötter, *Discourse of Race*, chaps. 1, 2.

12. Wu Zhenzi, "Women wei shenmo yao yanjiu youshengxue?" (Why should we study eugenics?), *Xuesheng zazhi* (Student magazine) 9 (1928): 33.

13. Eugenics as a national movement is also expressed by Pan Guangdan in *Yousheng gailun* (A general outline of eugenics), collected in *Minguo congshu*, 1.20:1–259. *Yousheng gailun* was also republished separately by Shanghai shudian in 1989.

14. Wu, "Women wei shenmo yao yanjiu youshengxue?" p. 34. Wu's "Realm of Great Union" (*datong zhi jing*) harks to the utopian world of human community expressed in Kang Youwei's *Datongshu* (The book of the great union). See Chapter 2.

15. Zhou Jianren, "Shanzhongxue de lilun yu shishi" (The theory and practice of eugenics), in Chen and Zhou, *Jinhualun yu shanzhongxue*, pp. 75–76.

16. Youze pifu, *Zhongguo xianzai de bujiufa* (The present remedy for China) (N.p., 1915). The pseudonym "Youze pifu" itself is a reworking of the following: "The rise or death of all that is under heaven is the responsibility of every rustic" (*tianxia xing-wang pifu youze*), which was frequently invoked at this time to emphasize the imperative of national survival.

17. This was one of the important formulations for national consciousness in the late Qing, as it can be found as early as Zou Rong's tract, *The Revolutionary Army*.

18. For martial arts manuals from this period, see, for example, *Guoshu daquan* (Complete encyclopedia of martial arts), ed. Zhongyang jiji xuehui (Shanghai: Shanghai quanshu yanjiu hui, 1929); *Guoshu daguan* (A comprehensive view of martial arts), eds. Chen Tiesheng, Tang Hao, and Lu Weichang (Shanghai: Zhenmin bianji hui, 1929). For an interesting account of nation saving, sports, and calisthenics during this period, see Andrew D. Morris, *Marrow of the Nation: A History of Sport and Physical Culture in Republican China* (Berkeley: University of California Press, 2004).

19. See Fu Shaozeng, *Zhongguo minzuxing zhi yanjiu* (A study of Chinese national character) (Beiping: Beiping wenhua xueshe, 1929), pp. 95–106.

20. See Gao Huaichuan, *Zhongguo minzu de bingyuan ji zhiliaofa* (The source of illness and treatment for the Chinese race) (Shanghai: Minzhi shuju, 1929), pp. 154–56.

21. Zhou Jianren, *Lun youshengxue yu zhongzu qishi* (On eugenics and racial discrimination) (Shanghai: Sanlian, 1948).

22. Ibid., pp. 68–69.

23. What Zhou may not have known was that Charles Darwin worked as an unpaid naturalist on the British survey rather than on the military vessel bound for South America. Because of Darwin's apparently belatedly recognized susceptibility to seasickness, the naturalist did as much survey on land as possible. His famous observations on Galápagos are from this period (1831–36).

24. In addition, articles on eugenics in relation to evolution, women, family, and racial engineering can be found in a variety of journals, such as *Dongfang zazhi*

(Dongfang zazhi), *Funü zazhi* (The ladies journal), *Xuesheng zazhi* (Student magazine), and *Minduo* (People's bell), as well as in journals that deal exclusively with or feature special sections on the topic, such as *Yousheng yuekan* (Eugenics monthly) and *Huanian* (Golden era).

25. For example, see Hua Rucheng, *Youshengxue ABC*. According to the publisher's preface, this belonged to a series of "ABC" books designed as college textbooks. For the translation of Davenport, see Chen Shoufan, *Renzhong gailiangxue*. See n. 6.

26. For a recent account of Pan's activities while studying in America, see Ye Weili, *Seeking Modernity in China's Name: Chinese Students in the United States, 1900–1927* (Stanford: Stanford University Press, 2001).

27. Pan Quentin, "Eugenics in China: A Preliminary Survey of the Background," *The Eugenical News* 11 (1923): 101–10.

28. Ibid., p. 101.

29. Ibid., p. 109.

30. Pan Guangdan, "Minzu yuanqi pian" (On the primary essence of race), *Yousheng yuekan* 5 (1931): 8. The immediate impetus to Pan's exasperated call is the fighting between the Guomindang and the CCP, as well as the Japanese invasion of Manchuria, which occurred in the two months before the completion of this article.

31. Ibid., p. 6.

32. The emphasis on the importance of the essence of a people was already stated in Pan's 1925 work, "Ershi nianlai shijie zhi yousheng yundong" (Eugenics movements in the world in the past twenty years), in *Yousheng gailun*, collected in *Minguo congshu*, 1.20:111–56. The "incitement of people's essence," it is there argued, is a precondition for nationalism. Without healthy bodies, a stable *minqi* cannot be cultivated. Without a stable "essence," people will not be able to effectively organize themselves politically.

33. "'Huanian' jie" (Explaining the meaning of "huanian"), *Huanian* 1 (1926): 3. In accordance with this advocacy of China's youthfulness, Pan launched the journal *Huanian* (Golden era), which includes a supplement on eugenics, "Yousheng fukan" (Eugenics supplement), to which Pan continues to contribute after *Yousheng yuekan* was discontinued.

34. Ibid.

35. See Li Jinghan's preface in Pan Guangdan, *Minzu texing yu minzu weisheng* (National characteristics and racial hygiene), collected in *Minguo congshu*, 1.20:1–25.

36. Pan Guangdan, "Minzu yuanqi pian pan guandang," p. 8. Also in *Renwenshi guan* (A view of the history of human letters), in *Minguo congshu*, 1.20:201–14.

37. See Lu Xun, "Zixu" (Preface to *Nahan*), in *Lu Xun quanji* (Complete works of Lu Xun), 16 vols. (Beijing: Renmin chubanshe, 1981), 1:415–20. Also see Fitzgerald, *Awakening China*.

38. See Arif Dirlik, "The Ideological Foundations of the New Life Movement: A Study in Counterrevolution," *Journal of Asian Studies* 4 (1975): 945–80; Lloyd E. Eastman, *The Abortive Revolution: China Under Nationalist Rule, 1927–1937* (Cambridge, MA: Harvard University Press, 1974).

39. See Hao Chang, *Chinese Intellectuals in Crisis: Search for Order and Meaning* (Berkeley: University of California Press, 1987); Charlotte Furth, ed., *The Limits of*

Change: Essays on Conservative Alternatives in Republican China (Cambridge, MA: Harvard University Press, 1976).

40. Chiang Kai-shek, *Xin shenghuo yundong gangyao* (Outline of the New Life Movement) (Shanghai: Zhonghua shuju, 1936).

41. "Sizhe xiang lianguan, fa yu chi, ming yu lian, xing yu yi, and xing zhi yu li, xiangxu xiangcheng, queyi bu ke" (The four principles continue into one another, released by shame, illuminated by integrity, conducted in righteousness, and embodied in propriety. They depend on and constitute one another. Not one can be lacking.), in *Xin shenghuo yundong gangyao*, p. 14.

42. See Nayan Shah, *Contagious Divides: Epidemics and Race in San Francisco's Chinatown* (Berkeley: University of California Press, 2001).

43. This maneuver would seem to recast current debates on universalism in which universalism is often criticized as Western particularism disguised. What has not been adequately addressed is how, as in the case of China, particularism also requires that "universalism"—Western or not—maintain its disguise so as to make it possible to transcend even the universal.

44. Pan Guangdan, "Kangzhan de minzu yiyi," in *Yousheng yu kangzhan* (Eugenics and the War of Resistance) (Chongqing: Shangwu yinshu guan, 1944), pp. 67–72.

45. Ibid.

46. See preface in Ellsworth Huntington, *The Character of Races as Influenced by Physical Environment, Natural Selection and Historical Development* (New York: Scribner's, 1927), p. vii.

47. Some of this correspondence is translated and included in the appendix of Harvey M. Lindquist, "Arthur Henderson Smith: A Study in Ambivalence" (Master's thesis, Harvard University, 1962).

48. Smith was known as someone quite familiar with the Chinese culture and often took it upon himself to explain one culture to the other. For an interesting reference to his reputation, see "Jinri yang guizi yiri sheng mingjun" (Today the foreign devil, tomorrow the sagely discerning ruler), *Anhui suhuabao* 6 (1904): 39–40.

49. For a detailed discussion of the background and impact of Arthur Smith's work, see Lydia Liu, *Translingual Practice*, pp. 51–60.

50. Pan Guangdan, *Minzu texing yu minzu weisheng* (National characteristics and racial hygiene), in *Pan Guangdan wenji* (Pan Guangdan collection), 14 vols. (Beijing: Beijing daxue chubanshe, 1995), 3:22. This appears also in *Minguo congshu*.

51. This evaluation, of course, is made against the background of Lamarckian influence in hereditary studies that consider the environment a more decisive factor than genes. The literature on this in Western languages is immense. For two representative books, see Daniel J. Kevles, *In the Name of Eugenics: Genetics and the Uses of Human Heredity* (Cambridge, MA: Harvard University Press, 1995); Gould, *Mismeasure of Man*.

52. Pan, *Minzu texing yu minzu weisheng*, p. 23.

53. Ibid., p. 6.

54. Pan Guangdan, "Xihua dongjian ji Zhongguo zhi yousheng wenti" (The rise of westernization in the East and the problem of eugenics in China), in *Yousheng gailun* (An overview of eugenics), collected in *Minguo congshu*, 1.20:29–63.

55. Ibid., p. 62.

56. Pan Guangdan, "Tan 'Zhongguo benwei'" (On "Sino-centrism"), in *Minzu texing yu minzu weisheng*, pp. 44–46.

57. See Pan Guangdan, "Riben Deyizhi minzuxing zhi bijiao de yanjiu" (A comparative study of Japanese and German characteristics), in Pan Naimu, ed., *Xunqiu Zhongguo ren weiyu zhi dao: Pan Guangdan wenxuan* (In search of the way of adaptation for the Chinese: Selected works of Pan Guangdan), 2 vols. (Beijing: Guoji wenhua chuban gongsi, 1997), 1:49–99.

58. See "Chinese Characteristics," *The Spectator*, no. 3324 (03.12.1892): 374–75.

59. According to Pan's daughter, Pan Naimu, Pan was the only official member in the society, a fact that reemphasizes Chinese eugenics' ideological rather than institutional significance in the expression of cultural anxieties. This is from an interview I conducted with Ms. Pan in Beijing in the summer of 2000.

60. See Lu Xun, "E guo yiben *A Q zhengzhuan* xu" (Preface to the Russian translation of *The story of Ah Q*), in *Lu Xun quanji*, 7:81–87.

61. Fang Bi (Mao Dun), "Lu Xun lun" (On Lu Xun), *Xiaoshuo yuebao* 18.11 (1927): 37–48, esp. p. 46. Also see Zhang Mengyang, *A Q xinlun: A Q yu shijie wenxue zhongde jingshen dianxing wenti* (A new interpretation of Ah Q: Ah Q and the problem of spiritual archetype in world literature) (Xi'an: Shanxi renmin jiaoyu chubanshe, 1996), p. 22.

62. Also see Qian Xingcun's noted essay, "Siqule de A Q shidai" (The bygone days of Ah Q), in Chen Shuyu, ed., *Lu Xu lunzheng ji* (Collection of debates over Lu Xun), 2 vols. (Shanghai: Zhongguo shehui kexue chubanshe, 1998), 2:1029–36; Changpai, "Xiegei sile de A Q" (A letter to the dead Ah Q), in Chen, *Lu Xun lunzheng ji*, 2:1075; Zhu yan, "A Q yu Lu Xun" (Ah Q and Lu Xun), in Chen, *Lu Xun lunzheng ji*, 2:1076–78; Qingjian, "A Q shidai meiyou si" (Ah Q's days are not gone), in Chen Shuyu, ed., *Shuobujin de A Q: wuchu buzai de hunling* (The inexhaustible Ah Q: A spirit everywhere) (Beijing: Zhongguo wenlian chuban gongsi, 1997), pp. 260–61.

63. See, for example, *A Q: qishi nian* (Ah Q: Seventy years), Peng Xiaoling and Han Aili, eds., (Beijing: Beijing shiyue wenyi chubanshe, 1993); Zhang Mengyang, *A Q xinlun*; Shao Bozhou, *"A Q zhengzhuan" yanjiu zongheng tan* (A comprehensive discussion of the study of the *Story of Ah Q*) (Shanghai: Shanghai wenyi chubanshe, 1989).

64. See Zhang Mengyang, "Lu Xun yu Shimisi de *Zhongguo ren qizhi*" (Lu Xun and Smith's *Chinese characteristics*), *Lu Xun yanjiu niankan* (Annual publication on Lu Xun studies) 2 (1980): 208–17.

65. See Lydia Liu, *Translingual Practice*, p. 51. Liu also cites what appears to be the first translation of Smith's work into classical Chinese published in Shanghai in 1903. Neither Lu Xun, Pan Guangdan, nor Zhang Mengyang is apparently aware of the existence of this early translation. See Liu, *Translingual Practice*, p. 53.

66. In this sense, it is useful to refer to an earlier article on Arthur Smith's *Chinese Characteristics* that puts it in the context of American middle-class Protestant culture and the contradictions in Smith's approach to China's Christianization as a "native" informant. See Charles W. Hayford, "Chinese and American Characteristics:

Arthur H. Smith and His China Book," in Suzanne W. Barnett and John K. Fairbank, eds., *Christianity in China: Early Protestant Missionary Writings* (Cambridge, MA: Harvard University Press, 1985).

67. *Zhinaren*, or *shinajin* in Japanese, was used by the Japanese as a derogatory address for the Chinese. *Shina* is taken from the Sanskrit rendering of *Qin*, from Qin dynasty (221–206 B.C.). For a detailed treatment in English, see Joshua Fogel, "The Sino-Japanese Controversy over *Shina* as a Toponym for China," in Fogel, *The Cultural Dimension of Sino-Japanese Relations: Essays on the Nineteenth and Twentieth Centuries* (Armonk, NY: Sharpe, 1995), pp. 66–76; Satō Saburō, "Nihonjin ga Chūgoku o *Shina* to yonda koto ni tsuite no kōsatsu" (A study of the Japanese use of *shina* for China), in Satō, *Kindai Nitchū kōshōshi no kenkyū* (Studies in the history of modern Sino-Japanese relations) (Tokyo: Yoshikawa kōbunkan, 1984), pp. 25–66; Guo Moruo, "Guanyu Ribenren duiyu Zhongguo ren de taidu" (About the Japanese attitude toward the Chinese), *Yuzhou feng* (Wind from the universe) 25 (Sept. 1936): 19–20.

68. Lu Xun, *Lu Xun quanji*, 3:326–27.

69. Lu Xun, *Lu Xun quanji*, 6:266–69.

70. Ibid., p. 266. Lu Xun refers here not to the English original but to the Japanese translation, published in 1896, six years after Smith had begun publishing it as a series of essays in *North China Daily News*. It is uncertain whether Lu Xun had actually read the Japanese translation and, even less likely, the English original.

71. This is a reference made to what Lu Xun had earlier commented on regarding conclusions reached in Yasuoka Hideo's *Chinese Characteristics*. See Lu Xun, "Mashangzhi riji" (Subchapter to instant diary) (07.02.1926), *Lu Xun quanji* 3: 325–28.

72. See Lu Xun's letter to Tao Kangde, no. 331027, in *Lu Xun quanji*, 12: 245–46.

73. For a similar point made specifically about Lu Xun and the Japanese, see Jiang Xiaoling, trans., "Qingmo liuxuesheng: Lu Xun yu Zhou Zuoren" (Students abroad during the late Qing: Lu Xun and Zhou Zuoren), *Lu Xun yanjiu yuekan* (Lu Xun studies monthly) 6 (1996): 43–55.

74. See Liu, *Translingual Practice*, pp. 51–53.

75. Lu Xun, *Lu Xun quanji*, 3:326.

76. Ibid., 6:266. Uchiyama Kanzō was a Japanese writer who had lived in China since 1913 and owned a bookstore in Shanghai that Lu Xun, Guo Moruo, Yu Dafu, and Tian Han often visited. His book, translated into Chinese as *Wenhua shenghuo xiade zhen Zhongguo* (The real China behind a living culture), shows strong sympathy and respect for the Chinese. Lu Xun warns, however, that for the Chinese to be overwhelmed by his words with a sense of pride would indeed be a mistake. The Chinese must, instead, continue to disclose their own weaknesses and improve themselves. See Xiao Meng and Lin Li, eds. and trans., *Sanzhi yanjing kan Zhongguo: Ribenren de pingshuo* (Looking at China through three lenses: Japanese assessments) (Beijing: Zhongguo shehui chubanshe, 1997).

77. Another critic raises the interesting question of why Lu Xun, if he had taken such an interest in *Chinese Characteristics*, did not embark on a Chinese translation

himself, as was normally the case when he felt strong enough about what he encountered in foreign literature. See Sun Yu, "He 'Zhongguo ren qizhi' chuban" (Congratulating the Publication of *Chinese Characteristics*) *Lu Xun yanjiu yuekan* 5 (1996): 52. In fact, the first complete Chinese translation of Arthur Smith's *Chinese Characteristics* did not appear until 1995, under the collaborative efforts of Zhang Mengyang and Wang Lijuan, as *Zhongguo ren de qizhi* (Chinese characteristics) (Lanzhou: Dunhuang wenyi chubanshe, 1995). Another translation by Qin Yue appeared in 1999 under the title *Zhongguo ren de suzhi* (Chinese characteristics) (Shanghai: Xuelin chubanshe, 1999). Two other translations were published in 2000 and 2004, respectively. See Chapter 1, n. 22.

78. Lu Xun, *Lu Xun quanji*, 1:493–94.

79. Lu Xun, "Chule xiangya zhi ta: houji" (Out of the ivory tower: Postscript), in *Lu Xun quanji*, 10:240. See Chapter 7.

80. Lu Xun, "Xie zai 'Fen' houmian" (Postscript to the collection "Grave"), in *Lu Xun quanji*, 1:282–87.

81. See Chapter 1.

82. Hao Huazhong, *Zhongguo ren de wuxing* (The Chinese capacity for enlightenment) (Shenyang: Liaoning renmin chubanshe, 1997), p. 227.

83. Xiang Tuijie, *Zhongguo ren xingge sumiao* (A sketch of the Chinese character) (Harbin: Beifang wenyi chubanshe, 1988), p. 3.

84. See, for example, titles published in the series Xianhua Zhongguo ren (Chatting about the Chinese), such as *Zhongguo ren de qipai* (The comportment of the Chinese) (Shenyang: Liaoning renmin chubanshe, 1997), *Zhongguo ren de jihui* (The taboos of the Chinese), and *Zhongguo ren de youxian* (The leisure of the Chinese). The last two titles were advertised as part of the series, though I have not seen them. Another series, which has published to date fourteen books on the various aspects of the Chinese, is Zhongguo ren de xinli (The psychology of the Chinese), with titles such as *Zhongguo ren xinfu guan* (The Chinese view of happiness). The lectures from the television series *Mantan minzuxing yu xiandaihua* (Conversing about racial character and modernity) were published as *Huashuo Zhongguo ren: Mantan minzuxing yu xiandaihua* (Talking about the Chinese: Conversing about racial character and modernity), ed. Zhongyang renmin guangbo diantai lilunbu (Central People's Broadcast Network Theory Division) (Beijing: Beijing gongye daxue chubanshe, 1992).

85. For other works dealing with the problem of the Chinese national character or spirit, see Xiao Junhe, *Huahunlun* (Soul of China), 3 vols. (Harbin: Heilongjiang jiaoyu chubanshe, 1995); A Liao, *Zhongguo ren de wonang* (The cowardice of the Chinese) (Beijing: Xinhua shudian, 1997); Wang Ling, Wei Kaifeng, and Wang Caimei, *Huanghe, Huangtudi, Yanhuang Zisun* (Yellow river, yellow earth, the children of Shennong) (Beijing: Zhongguo shudian, 1991); Yang Zhongming, *Xunzhao Zhongguo ren de zixin* (Searching for the confidence of the Chinese) (Changsha shi: Hunan wenyi chubanshe, 1999); Zeng Shiqiang and Liu Junzheng, *Jiedu Zhongguo ren* (Decoding the Chinese), 3 vols. (Beijing: Zhongguo gongren chubanshe, 2001); Ren Jiantao, *Cong zizai dao zijue: Zhongguo guominxing tantao* (From self-ease to self-awareness: An inquiry into the Chinese national character) (Xi'an: Shanxi renmin chubanshe, 1992).

86. Lu Xun, "Zhongguo ren shiqu liao zixinxinle ma?" (Have the Chinese lost their sense of confidence?), in *Lu Xun quanji*, 6:117–19.

87. "Mashang zhi riji" (Instant diary), in *Lu Xun quanji*, 3:333.

88. Lu Xun, "Suiganlu: 38" (Spur of the moment record: 38), in *Lu Xun quanji*, 1:312–14.

CHAPTER FIVE

1. On the classification of physical illnesses as testimony to modernity and progress in China, see, for instance, Mary P. Sutphen and Bridie Andrews, eds., *Medicine and Colonial Authority* (London & New York: Routledge, 2003); Ruth Rogaski, *Hygienic Modernity: Meanings of Health and Disease in Treaty-Port China* (Berkeley: University of California Press, 2004); Bridie Andrews, "Tuberculosis and the Assimilation of Germ Theory in China, 1895–1937," *Journal of the History of Medicine and Allied Sciences* 52 (Jan. 1997): 114–57.

2. At the time, Belgium was holding the Exposition universalle et internationale in Ghent (1913), which Zhang attended. There was a recruitment for a two-year program in gardening at a Belgian institution, but because his fellowship was for studying in France, Zhang gave up the idea. Zhang remembers this with regret on many occasions throughout his life. This detail in his student career will prove significant later. See Zhang's "Wo xuele xie shenmo?" (What did I learn? in his autobiography, *Fushen mantan* (Banters of a floating life), collected in *Zhang Jingsheng wenji* (Collected works of Zhang Jingsheng), 2 vols. (Guangzhou: Guangzhou chubanshe, 1998), 2:43.

3. See Charles Leary, "Sexual Modernism in China: Zhang Jingsheng and 1920s Urban Culture," Diss. (Cornell University, 1994). Leary's study is the most detailed treatment of Zhang Jingsheng's life and work to date.

4. See Li Hongkuan, "Fu: Zhongguo xing jiaoyu de qianqu—Zhang Jingsheng" (Appendix: The pioneer of China's sex education—Zhang Jingsheng), in *Zhang Jingsheng wenji*, 2:448–53.

5. This led Pan Guangdan to publish a series of articles on the role of the sex educator. See "'Xin Wenhua' yu jia kexue—bo Zhang Jingsheng" (*New Culture* and fake science—a rebuttal to Zhang Jingsheng), "Xing jiaoyuzhe de zige wenti" (The problem of the qualification of the sex educator), and "Biantai xingli yu shehui zhi an" (Abnormal psychology and order in society), all collected in Pan's *Yousheng gailun*, in *Minguo congshu*, 20:241–59.

6. By "third kind of fluid," Zhang refers to the Bartholin's gland, which can produce something like female ejaculate. See Zhang Jingsheng, *Di sanzhong shui yu luanzhu ji shengji de dian he yousheng de guanxi—youming Meide xingyu*) (The third kind of fluid and the relationship between eugenics and the electricity of vitality and the female egg—also titled Sexual desire based on beauty) (Shanghai: N.p., 1927). The heated exchange between the eugenicists and Zhang is treated in detail by Chung. See Chung, "Struggle for National Survival: Chinese Eugenics in a Transnational Context, 1896–1945," Diss. (University of Chicago, 1999).

7. See the unauthorized reprint in *Xing zazhi* 2 (1927). In the same volume is also an article written under the pretext of a serious inquiry into the nature of Zhang's third kind of fluid. See Qian Qian, "A study of the third kind of fluid," *Xing zazhi* 2 (1927): 3–8.

8. Wen Yiduo, "*Shijing* de xingyu guan" (The libido theory in *Book of odes*), in Sun Dangbo and Yuan Jianzheng, eds., *Wen Yiduo quanjii* (The complete works of Wen Yiduo), 12 vols. (Wuhan: Hubei chubanshe, 1993), 3:169.

9. See K. S. Tchang (Zhang Jingsheng), "Les Sources antiques des théories de J.-J. Rousseau sur l'éducation," Thèse de Doctorat d'Université (University of Lyon, 1919); Zhang Jingsheng, trans., *Chanhuilu* (Confessions) (Shanghai: Shijie shuju, 1931).

10. Pan Guangdan, "'Xing boshi' bei kong" ("Dr. Sex" sued), *Huanian* 2.35 (1933): 682–83.

11. See Meng Yu, "Wo suo zhidao de Zhang Jingsheng" (The Zhang Jingsheng I know) (11.20.1968), in *Zhang Jingsheng yu Xing Shi* (Zhang Jingsheng and *Sexual histories*) (Hong Kong: Tao zhai shuwu, 1970). This is a compilation of newspaper articles on Zhang Jingsheng from 1957 to 1970 on file at Cornell University.

12. Peng Xiaoyan, "Xing qimeng yu ziwo de jiefang: 'Xing boshi' Zhang Jingsheng yu wusi de seyu xiaoshuo" (Sexual enlightenment and self-liberation: Dr. Sex Zhang Jingsheng and pornographic fiction of the May Fourth), in *Chaoyue xieshi* (Transcending realism) (Taibei: Lianjing, 1993), pp. 117–38.

13. Zhang Jingsheng, *Meide renshengguan* (A way of life based on beauty), in *Zhang Jingsheng wenji*, 1:38.

14. Ibid., p. 44.

15. Zhang Jingsheng, *Meide shehui zuzhifa* (Organizational principles of a society based on beauty), in *Zhang Jingsheng wenji*, 1:215.

16. Ibid., pp. 48–49.

17. Ibid., pp. 79–83.

18. See Kai Chi, "Shenmo shi 'shenjiao'?" (What is spiritual communion?), *Xin nüxing* 1.3 (1926): 189–93.

19. See Zhou Zuoren, "Gouyan tongxing: Er" (Correspondence from *The studio of bitter rain gathering on the eaves*), *Chenbao fukan* (08.27.1924), vol. 2. The letter is also included in Chen Zishan and Zhang Tierong, eds., *Zhou Zuoren jiwaiwen* (Uncollected works of Zhou Zuoren), 2 vols. (Haikou: Hainan guoji xinwen chuban zhongxin, 1995), 1:603–5.

20. Zhang, *Meide shehui zuzhifa*, p. 142.

21. Ibid., p. 238.

22. Ibid., p. 204.

23. Zhang, *Meide renshengguan*, p. 55. For a treatment of fetal education in traditional China and its relation to eugenics, see Dikötter, *Discourse of Race*.

24. Zhang, *Meide renshengguan*, p. 55.

25. Zhang Jingsheng claims to have advocated the use of contraception in 1921, a year before the visit of Margaret Sanger to China and her birth-control campaigns. He complains that no one at the time supported his view and that it was even attacked. Yet with Sanger's visit, the critics immediately embraced the idea, praising her while denouncing Zhang. Zhang laments that this difference in treatment was due to the fact that, in his words, Sanger was an American woman and he, a Chinese man. See *Meide renshengguan*, p. 81.

26. *Meide shehui zuzhifa*, p. 156.

27. Ibid., p. 157.

28. Ibid., pp. 184–92.

29. Ibid., p. 219.

30. Zhang's equal emphasis on punitive and psychological discipline presents a scenario quite different from the one advanced by Foucault, for whom the power wielded by one's psychic life was never a point of comfortable admission. See, among others, his interviews collected in Colin Gordon, ed., *Power / Knowledge: Selected Interviews & Other Writings, 1972–1977* (New York: Pantheon Books, 1980); Lawrence D. Kritzman, ed., *Politics, Philosophy, Culture: Interviews and Other Writings, 1977–1984* (London & New York: Routledge, 1990); Graham Burcell, Colin Gordon, and Peter Miller, eds., *The Foucault Effect: Studies in Governmentality* (Chicago: University of Chicago Press, 1991).

31. Zhang, *Meide shehui zuzhifa*, pp. 219–21.

32. Ibid., p. 221.

33. Such debates are largely between environmental determinists—Lamarckians who hold that environmental rather than genetic factors play the ultimate decisive role in the individual—and scholars of heredity, who believe in genetic determination independent of the social environment. This debate is also carried on among Chinese eugenicists and population specialists. See Ru Song, "Ping youshengxue yu huanjinglun de lunzheng—Pan Guangdan, Zhou Jianren, Sun Benwen zhuren yijian de qingsuan" (An assessment of the debates over eugenics and environmental determinism—taking stock of the opinions of Pan Guangdan, Zhou Jianren, Sun Benwen, et al.), *Ershi shiji* 1 (Feb. 1931): 57–124.

34. Pan Guangdan, "Funü jiefang xinlun: jieshao yingren Pushi shi de xueshuo" (New view on women's liberation: An introduction to the work of British scholar Meyrick Booth), *Yousheng yuekan* 3 (1931). This is also collected in Pan's *Renwenshi guan*, pp. 181–99.

35. Another article on the same topic was published by Zhang Xiruo, "Zhishi funü yu yousheng wenti" (Educated women and the problem of eugenics), *Huanian* 18 (1935): 346–48.

36. *Funü zazhi* (The ladies journal) published a number of special issues dealing with specific issues facing women in modern times, such as love, marriage, and new sexual morality. The issues on sexual morality were later edited by Zhang Xichen and Zhou Jianren and published in *Xin xing daode taolunji* (Discussions on new sexual ethics) (Shanghai: Kaiming shudian, 1936).

37. Pan Guangdan, "Xihua dongjian ji Zhongguo zhi yousheng wenti" (The rise of westernization in the East and the problem of eugenics in China), in Pan, *Yousheng gailun*, pp. 58–59.

38. Pan, "Funü jiefang xinlun," p. 190.

39. Zhou Jianren is interested, however, more in the biological sciences in general, as can be seen in his writings. Unlike that of Pan Guangdan, Zhou's orientation is much less specifically eugenic. He does not so much advocate Chinese eugenics as reiterate the principles of Western eugenics.

40. Zhou Jianren, "Du 'Zhongguo zhi yousheng wenti'" (Reading *The problem of eugenics in China*), in Pan, *Yousheng gailun*, pp. 95–110.

41. Zhou Jianren, "Funü yu shehui" (Women and society), *Funü zazhi* 9 (1921): 1–6.

42. Zhou Jianren, "Jiating shenghuo de jinghua" (The evolution of family life), *Funü zazhi* 5 (1921): 1–5.

43. See, for example, Liu Kang and Tang Xiaobing, eds., *Politics, Ideology, and Literary Discourse in Modern China: Theoretical Interventions and Cultural Critique* (Durham, NC: Duke University Press, 1993); Ellen Widmer and David Der-wei Wang, eds., *From May Fourth to June Fourth: Fiction and Film in Twentieth-Century China* (Cambridge, MA: Harvard University Press, 1993); Lydia Liu, "The Female Body and Nationalist Discourse," in Grewal and Kaplan, *Scattered Hegemonies*; Tani Barlow, "Theorizing Woman: *Funü, Guojia, Jiating*," *Genders* 10 (Spring 1991): 132–60. For more recent works, see n. 72.

44. For a recent exception to this focus on femininity in gender studies, see, for instance, Zhong Xueping, *Masculinity Besieged? Issues of Modernity and Male Subjectivity in Chinese Literature of the Late Twentieth Century* (Durham, NC: Duke University Press, 2000); Susan Brownell and Jeffery N. Wasserstrom, eds., *Chinese Femininities / Chinese Masculinities: A Reader* (Berkeley: University of California Press, 2002).

45. For example, see Barlow, *Gender Politics in Modern China*; Lu Tonglin, ed., *Gender and Sexuality in Twentieth-Century Chinese Literature and Society* (Albany: State University of New York Press, 1993).

46. David Der-wei Wang, *Fictional Realism in Twentieth-Century China: Mao Dun, Lao She, Shen Congwen* (New York: Columbia University Press, 1992), chap. 3, esp. pp. 77–89.

47. Yun Fang, "Xin funü suo yinggai chanchude jizhong liegenxing" (Some negative characteristics that the "New Woman" should get rid of), *Funü zazhi* 6.9 (1920): 3–8. For other articles dealing with reforming specific aspects of the female character, see, for example, Xu Shiheng, "Jinhou funü yingyou de jingshen" (The spirit women should have from here on), *Funü zazhi* 6.8 (1920): 13–18; Yanbing, "Funü yundong de yiyi he yaoqiu" (The significance and demand of a women's movement), *Funü zazhi* 6.8 (1920): 1–6; Pei Wei, "Jiefang de funü yu funü de jiefang" (Liberated women and women's liberation), *Funü zazhi* 5.11 (1919): 1–6.

48. Yun Fang, "Xin funü suo yinggai chanchude jizhong liegenxing," p. 4.

49. Just as the notion of a decayed national character extends into the inquiry into women's undesirable characteristics, female negative traits are also translated into the illnesses of youths. See, for example, Gong Baosun, "Xiandai qingnian zhi bingtai yu jiuji" (The illness of modern youths and its remedy), *Xuesheng zazhi* 6 (1930): 11–15; Se Lu, "Funü zhi jiefang yu gaizao" (The liberation and reconstruction of women), *Funü zazhi* 12 (1919): 3–7; Xu Shiheng, "Jinhou funü yingyou de jingshen," pp. 13–18.

50. Mao Dun, "Xie zai 'ye qiangwei' de qianmian" (Preface to *Wild roses*), in Sun Zhongtian and Zha Guohua, eds., *Mao Dun yanjiu ziliao* (Research materials on Mao Dun), 3 vols. (Beijing: Zhongguo shehui kexue chubanshe, 1983), 2:11–14.

51. See David Der-wei Wang, *Fictional Realism*, chap. 3.

52. Mao Dun, "Chuangzao" (Creation), collected in *Zhongguo xiandai xiaoshuo jingping: Mao Dun juan* (A selection of modern Chinese fiction: Mao Dun) (Shanxi: Shanxi renmin chubanshe, 1995), p. 86.

53. Ibid., p. 88.

54. Ibid., p. 89.

55. Ibid., p. 96.

56. Ibid., p. 99.

57. This case was particularly important in revealing the concept of lesbianism as a social and psychological crime in Republican China. Cf. Deborah Tze-lan Sang, *The Emerging Lesbian: Female Same-Sex Desire in Modern China* (Chicago: University of Chicago Press, 2003). Perhaps more significantly, the homicide was also important for reinforcing Pan's view that an understanding of China's social ills required psychological studies of sexual tendencies as perversions. Pan reported this with great interest in his biweekly journal, *Huanian*, in 1932. See "Zaiti Tao Liu dusha an" (Again on the Tao and Liu homicide case of jealousy), *Huanian* 5 (1932): 82–83; "Wudu you ou de tongxingjian sha an" (Not an isolated case of same-sex homicide), *Huanian* 11 (1932): 205–6; "Zhi bujiangli" (Only being unreasonable), *Huanian* 18 (1932): 347–48; "Liangfeng qingshu" (Two love letters), *Huanian* 23 (1932): 445–46; "Zailun Tao Liu an de diaocha buzu" (Again on the insufficient investigation into the case of Tao and Liu), *Huanian* 26 (1932): 504–5; "Jingshen bing zhuanjia lai hua" (A specialist on psychopathology comes to China), *Huanian* 1 (1934): 2–3.

58. Pan, "Zhi bujiangli," pp. 347–48.

59. Pan, "Wudu you ou de tongxingjian sha an," p. 205.

60. Pan, "Zhi bujiangli," p. 348.

61. At the time, Pan was also concerned with youth's tendency to commit suicide and the usually accompanying condition of excessive sentimentalism.

62. The fascination with women's literature, genuine or fabricated by male intellectuals themselves, follows a long literati tradition. The female tragic fate often coincides with male writers' self-perception. The play on female persona can be witnessed already in *Chuci* (Lyrics of Chu) (third century B.C.).

63. Pan Guangdan, "Feng Xiaoqing: Yijian yingnian zhi yanjiu" (Feng Xiaoqing: A study of narcissism), in Pan Naigu and Pan Naihe, eds., *Pan Guangdan xuanji* (Selected works of Pan Guangdan), 4 vols. (Beijing: Guangming ribao chubanshe, 1999), 1:1–67.

64. Ibid., p. 88.

65. It is often argued that Xiaoqing was the concoction of male poets who tried to voice their discontent with their lack of recognition through a tragic woman figure. This was also a way of having their own poetry read, under a false but sensationalized female authorship. See Ellen Widmer, "Xiaoqing's Literary Legacy and the Place of the Woman Writer in Late Imperial China," *Late Imperial China* (June 1992): 111–53.

66. Widmer, "Xiaoqing's Literary Legacy," p. 153. This is, of course, a tribute to the most well-known tragic heroine in Chinese literature, Lin Daiyu, in the eighteenth-century novel *Dream of the Red Chamber*, whose famous flower burial mirrors her own ephemeral existence.

67. Pan, "Feng Xiaoqing: Yijian yingnian zhi yanjiu," p. 27.

68. For studies of female literary traditions in China, see Tan Zhengbi, *Zhongguo nüxing wenxue shihua* (A history of women's tradition in China) (Tianjin: Baihua wenyi chubanshe, 1984); Widmer, "Xiaoqing's Literary Legacy," pp. 111–53; Paul S. Ropp, *Banished Immortal: Searching for Shuangqing, China's Peasant Woman Poet* (Ann

Arbor: University of Michigan Press, 2001); Wilt L. Idema and Beata Grant, *The Red Brush: Writing Women of Imperial China* (Cambridge, MA: Harvard University Asia Center, 2004).

69. See Ropp, *Banished Immortal.*

70. Pan, "Feng Xiaoqing: Yijian yingnian zhi yanjiu," p. 19.

71. Ibid., p. 30.

72. For recent studies of feminism and women's literature in China, see Tani E. Barlow, *The Question of Women in Chinese Feminism* (Durham, NC: Duke University Press, 2004); Chang Shuei-May, *Casting Off the Shackles of Family: Ibsen's Nora Figure in Modern Chinese Literature, 1918–1942* (New York: Peter Lang, 2004); Sally Taylor Lieberman, *The Mother and Narrative Politics in Modern China* (Charlottesville & London: University Press of Virginia, 1998); Hu Ying, *Tales of Translation: Composing the New Woman in China, 1899–1918* (Stanford: Stanford University Press, 2000); Wendy Larson, *Women and Writing in Modern China* (Stanford: Stanford University Press, 1998); Dooling and Torgeson, *Writing Women in Modern China*; Chen and Dilley, *Feminism / Femininity in Chinese Literature*; Rey Chow, *Primitive Passions: Visuality, Sexuality, Ethnography, and Contemporary Chinese Cinema* (New York: Columbia University Press, 1995); Shen Ying, ed., *Ershi shiji Zhongguo nüxing wenxue shi* (A literary history of women's writing in the twentieth century) (Tianjin: Tianjin renmin chubanshe, 1995); Megan Marie Ferry, "Chinese Women Writers of the 1930s and Their Critical Reception," Diss. (Washington University, 1998). Hu Ying brings to light a refreshing set of materials from the still little-known period of the late Qing that dates the modern "New Woman" to the turn-of-the-century literature. Lieberman makes an interesting examination of physical maternity in the writings of male and female writers from the 1920s and 1930s.

73. See Dooling and Torgeson, "Introduction," in their edited volume, *Writing Women in Modern China.*

74. Tani Barlow, for instance, demonstrates how the female body in Ding Ling's fiction maintains a narrative resistance to its conflation with national trauma as rape. Lydia Liu, in a convincing analysis of Xiao Hong's *Field of Life and Death*, reverses the referential framework for reading women's bodily experience in terms of the rise and fall of the nation by anchoring the nation's narrative in the female body. Interestingly, both accounts seek to divorce nation from the female body as a way of countering a literary historiographical practice of subsuming the female experience under the imperatives of masculinity and nationalism. See Barlow, ed. and trans., "Introduction," in *I Myself Am a Woman: Selected Writings of Ding Ling* (Boston: Beacon Press, 1989); Lydia Liu, *Translingual Practice.*

75. See Barlow, *Gender Politics*; Liu, *Translingual Practice*; Tani Barlow and Angela Zito, eds., *Body, Subject, & Power in China* (Chicago & London: University of Chicago Press, 1994); Dai Jinhua and Meng Yue, *Fuchu lishi dibiao* (Emerging from the horizon of history) (Zhengzhou: Henan renmin chubanshe, 1989).

76. The following discussion is based on Howard Goldblatt's translation of *Market Street: A Chinese Woman in Harbin* (Seattle: University of Washington Press, 1986).

77. See Lydia Liu's analysis of Xiao Hong's *Field of Life and Death* in *Translingual Practice*, chap. 7.

78. Just before their life in Harbin, Xiao Hong was recovering from giving birth out of wedlock to a child she had to give up for adoption. Her life with Xiao Jun was also very tumultuous, as she was often subjected to his physical and emotional abuse. Both events left a significant imprint on *Market Street*. See Luo Binji, *Xiao Hong xiaozhuan* (Small biography of Xiao Hong) (Shanghai: Jianwen shudian, 1947).

79. Howard Goldblatt. "Translator's Introduction," in *Market Street*, p. xvi.

80. Goldblatt, *Market Street*, p. 48.

81. Ibid., pp. 21–22.

82. Ibid., p. 45.

83. Ibid., p. 51.

84. See *Xiao Hong yanjiu* (Studies of Xiao Hong), ed. Beifang Luncong bianjibu (Editorial department of discussion series of the North) (Harbin: Harbin shifan daxue beifang luncong she, 1983).

85. The following discussion is based on Tani Barlow's translation. See *I Myself Am a Woman*.

86. See, for example, Chang Shuei-May, *Casting Off the Shackles of Family*.

87. Barlow, "I Myself," p. 51.

88. Ibid., p. 52 (my translation is slightly modified from Barlow's).

89. Ibid.

90. Ibid., p. 54.

91. Ibid., pp. 58–59.

92. Ibid., p. 55.

93. Ibid., p. 62.

94. Ibid., p. 62.

95. Ibid.

96. Ibid., p. 72.

97. Ibid., p. 74.

98. See Deborah Tze-lan Sang, *Emerging Lesbian*; Larson, *Women and Writing in Modern China*, esp. pp. 85–130.

CHAPTER SIX

1. See Guo's "Zhi Zhang Ziping" (01.24.1921) (Letter to Zhang Ziping), in Huang Chunhao, ed., *Guo Moruo shuxinji* (Collection of Guo Moruo's correspondence), 2 vols. (Beijing: Zhongguo shehui kexue chubanshe, 1992), 1:192.

2. By contrast, Zhang Ziping, another writer at the time known for his graphic descriptions of sexual indulgences and tormented love affairs, was never quite "repatriated" back to political-literary historiography.

3. For a history of psychology in China, see, among others, Yang Xinhui, ed. *Xinlixue tongshi* (A complete history of psychology), 5 vols. (Jinnan: Shandong jiaoyu chubanshe, 2000); Zhao Liru et al., eds., *Xinlixue shi* (A history of psychology) (Beijing: Tuanjie chubanshe, 1989); Yan Guocai, *Zhongguo xinlixue shi* (A history of psychology in China) (Hangzhou: Zhejiang jiaoyu chubanshe, 1998); Ye Haosheng, *Laoji fenti: Xinlixue yidai zongshi Gao Juefu* (Old steed galloping forth: The master of a generation of psychology, Gao Juefu) (Nanjing: Nanjing daxue chubanshe, 2000). For discussions of Freudian psychoanalysis and modern literature in China in par-

ticular, see, for instance, Yu Fenggao's pioneering work, *"Xinli fenxi" yu Zhongguo xiandai xiaoshuo* ("Psychoanalysis" and modern Chinese fiction) (Beijing: Zhongguo shehui kexue chubanshe, 1987); Shih Shu-mei, *The Lure of the Modern: Writing Modernism in Semicolonial China, 1917–1937* (Berkeley: University of California Press, 2001); Lin Jicheng, "Fuluoyide de xueshuo zai Zhongguo de chuanbo, 1914–1924" (The dissemination of Freudian theory in China, 1914–1924), *Ershiyi shiji* 4 (Apr. 1991): 20–31; Sun Naixiu, *Fuluoyide yu ershi shiji Zhongguo zuojia* (Freud and twentieth-century Chinese writers) (Taibei: Yeqiang chubanshe, 1999), *Fuluoyide yu Zhongguo xiandai zuojia* (Freud and modern Chinese writers) (Taibei: Yeqiang chubanshe, 1995); Zhang Jingyuan, *Psychoanalysis in China: Literary Transformations, 1919–1949* (Ithaca, NY: Cornell East Asian Series, Cornell University Press, 1992); Zhang Ying, *Jingshen fenxixue shuping* (A narrative assessment of psychoanalysis) (Shenyang: Liaoning daxue chubanshe, 1986), pp. 126–33.

4. Dengzhou Society of Letters in Shandong Province apparently already had "xinglingxue" as part of their curriculum after becoming an academy in 1876, three years before Yan became director of St. John's University. Apart from a schedule of classes published in 1891, however, no written record is available. See Yang Xinhui, *Xinlixue tongshi*, 2:105–12.

5. Ibid.

6. See Kang Youwei's *Riben shumu zhi* (A catalog of Japanese books), in *Kang Youwei quanji* (Complete works of Kang Youwei), ed. Jiang Yihua, 3 vols. (Shanghai: Shanghai guji chubanshe, 1992), 3:655–57.

7. For a discussion on how Nishi's contribution of new terms made a significant impact on the Japanese and Chinese languages, see Morioka Kenji, *Kindai go no seiritsu: Meijiki go ihen* (The evolution of modern language: The vocabulary of the Meiji era) (Tokyo: Meiji shoin, 1969), pp. 158–81, esp. pp. 175–76. Also see Wolfgang Lippert, "Language in the Modernization Process: The Integration of Western Concepts and Terms into Chinese and Japanese in the Nineteenth Century," in Michael Lackner, Iwo Amelung, and Jochim Kurtz, eds., *New Terms for New Ideas: Western Knowledge and Lexical Change in Late Imperial China* (Leiden, The Netherlands: Brill, 2001), pp. 57–66.

8. Some scholars believe that with the knowledge of Nishi's translation of Haven's work after 1897, Chinese preferred to use *xinlixue* to designate "psychology." However, as the case in question shows, doubled efforts in translation often happen as a result of the lack of knowledge of other translations. The linguistic landscape of translated terms in late Qing and early Republican periods was much more promiscuous and took a longer time to settle. One example is Protestant missionary Devello Zelolos Sheffield's *Xinlingxue*, which was published fourteen years after Kang Youwei's catalog in 1911 by North China Union College Press. As is clear from Sheffield's English preface, *xinlingxue* is used as a translation of "psychology." I located a copy of this book in the Harvard Yenching Library's Rare Book Room. See Devello Z. Sheffield, *Xinlingxue* (Mind spirit study), trans. Guan Guoquan (Beitongzhou: Gonglihui yinziguan, 1911). Similarly, four of the known five Chinese translations of Freud's works published before 1949 bear no relation to the more than twenty Japanese translations of Freud that appeared between 1929 and 1936. See Zhang Jingyuan, *Psychoanalysis in China*, p. 40.

9. According to Zhang Jingyuan, five of Freud's works were translated into Chinese by 1949: *Introductory Lectures on Psychoanalysis* (trans. by Gao Juefu from English), *An Autobiographical Study* (trans. by Zhang Shizhao from German), *Group Psychology and the Analysis of the Ego* (trans. by Xia Fuxin from Japanese), *The Interpretation of Dreams* (trans. by Zhang Jingsheng from French or English), and *New Introductory Lectures on Psychoanalysis* (trans. by Gao Juefu from English). Four of these five translations bear no relation to existing Japanese translations of Freud, more than twenty of which were produced between 1929 and 1936. Commentaries on Freud's thought, however, arrived earlier. Articles by "Y" and Zhang Dongsun, both from 1920, are among the earliest I have come across. Another article by Qiu Shan appeared in 1921: "Fulude de yinyishi shuo yu xinli" (Freud's theory of the unconscious and psychology), *Dongfang zazhi* 18.14 (1921): 41–50. Other criticisms of Freud introduced to the Chinese audience include those of Barbara Lowe, *Psychoanalysis: A Brief Account of the Freudian Theory* (New York: Harcourt, Brace, 1921) (*Fuluote xinli fenxi*, trans. Zhao Yan [Shanghai: Commercial Press, 1927]); D. H. Bonus, *How to Psychoanalyze Yourself* (Zizhi zhishu, trans. Hao Yaodong, 1925); John Carl Flugel, "Theories of Psychoanalysis" (Jiexinshu xueshuo, trans. Chen Derong, 1934); Wilhelm Reich, "Dialektischer Materialismus und Psychoanalyse," and W. Jurinetz, "Psychoanalyse und Marxismus" in *Criticisms of Psychoanalysis* (*Jingshen fenxixue pipan*, trans. Yu Xinyuan [Shanghai: Xinken shuju, 1936]); Reuben Osborn, *Freud and Marx: A Dialectic Study* (*Jingshen fenxi yu weiwu shiguan*, 2nd ed., Shanghai: Shijie, 1949; 1st ed., 1940); W. Fritche, "Freudianism and Art" ("Jingshen fenxi xue yu yishu," trans. Hu Qiuyuan, *Dushu zazhi* 6 [1932]); Zhou Qiying, trans., "Fuluoyite zhuyi yu yishu," *Wenxue yuebao* (06.10.1932). See Zhang Jingyuan, *Psychoanalysis in China*, p. 14, fn. 29.

10. Y, pseud., "Foluote xinlixue zhi yiban" (The school of Freud's new psychology), *Dongfang zazhi* 22 (1920): 85–86; Zhang Dongsun, "Lun jingshen fenxi" (About psychoanalysis), *Minduo* 5 (1920). I have not seen Zhang's article. The sources of translation often varied, from those in popular renditions to those in specialized journals. For example, an article by Qiu Shan, "Ximeng pian" (On elucidating dreams), appeared in *Dongfang zazhi* 13.12 (1916): 6–14. This was translated from an article published four years earlier in the popular American literary and political journal *McClure's Magazine*, "The Marvels of Dream Analysis," 40.1 (1912): 113–19. The author, H. Addington Bruce, was among the first to popularize psychology before World War I. I thank Leo Lee for providing these materials.

11. The only direct historical encounter between Freud and Chinese intellectuals is a letter Freud wrote to Zhang Shizhao on May 27, 1929. The letter was apparently in response to one from Zhang. Unfortunately, that earlier letter to Freud has not been found. In Freud's letter, he welcomes Zhang's idea of an intercultural exchange in the form of either introducing psychoanalysis to China or contributing an article to the psychoanalytical journal *Imago* that would evaluate the hypotheses regarding archaic forms of expression as manifested in the Chinese language. See Zhang Jingyuan, *Psychoanalysis in China*, pp. 5–6; Yu Fenggao, *"Xinli fenxi" yu Zhongguo xiandai xiaoshuo*, pp. 35–37.

12. Zhang Jingyuan, *Psychoanalysis in China*, pp. 5–6.

13. For an interesting study of the New Sensationalists and their engagement

with the project of modern subjectivity, see Shih, *Lure of the Modern*. See also Sun Naixiu, *Foluoyide yu ershi shiji Zhongguo zuojia*.

14. See Chapter 7.

15. See "'Shenghuo yu yishu' shuhou" (Postscript to "Life and art"), in Yu Dafu, *Yu Dafu wenji* (The works of Yu Dafu), 12 vols. (Hong Kong: Sanlian shudian, 1982), 7:160.

16. See, for example, *Miyang* (Lost sheep), in *Yu Dafu wenji*, 2:1–93.

17. Guo Moruo, "Canchun" (Late spring), in *Moruo wenji* (Moruo collection), 17 vols. (Hong Kong: Sanlian shudian, 1957), 5:13–28.

18. "To footnote one's own story is already a most uneconomical task to begin with. Yet even a bird has to sing to its death just to please its mate. One might do well here to imitate the bird's cry," from Guo, "Piping yu meng" (Criticism and dreams), in *Guo Moruo quanji: wenxue bian* (The complete works of Guo Moruo: Literature), 20 vols. (Beijing: Renmin chubanshe, 1986), 15:238.

19. "Criticism and Dreams," in *Guo Moruo quanji*, 15:236.

20. See Guo Moruo, "Gushu jinyide wenti" (The problem of translating the classics into vernacular), in *Guo Moruo quanji*, 15:164–65.

21. Apart from winning intellectual and literary interests, psychoanalytical concepts were also incorporated into the arsenal for launching personal attacks and disagreements in China's usually sardonic and lively intellectual life. Zhang Shizhao, for instance, cites Freud's concept of the unconscious as a way of describing his opponent's gross oversight in argumentation. See Zhang Shizhao (Gutong), "Zaida Zhihui xiansheng" (Replying once more to Mr. Wu Zhihui), *Jiayin zazhi* 27 (1926): 6–12, esp. p. 10.

22. See Chong Mi, "'Chenlun'" (Sinking), in Chen Zishan and Wang Zili, eds., *Yu Dafu yanjiu ziliao* (Research materials on Yu Dafu), 2 vols. (Tianjin: Tianjin renmin chubanshe, 1982), 2:305.

23. German-Japanese dictionaries were often consulted in compilations of German-Chinese dictionaries. See "Zur Einführung" in Hellmut Wilhelm, ed., *Deutsch-Chinesisches Wörterbuch* (Shanghai: Max Nößler, 1945).

24. See Huang Shifu et al., eds., *Zonghe Yinghan dacidian* (A comprehensive English-Chinese dictionary) (Shanghai: Commercial Press, 1937).

25. See Chapter 5.

26. Yu Dafu, "Mangmangye" (Endless night), in *Yu Dafu wenji*, 1:116–146.

27. Ibid., p. 142.

28. Ibid., p. 128.

29. Ibid., pp. 133–34.

30. See Mao Dun, pseud. Sun, "'Chuangzao' gei wode yinxiang" (My impressions of *Creation*), in Chen and Wang, *Yu Dafu yanjiu ziliao*, 2:308–9.

31. See Su Xuelin, "Yu Dafu lun" (On Yu Dafu), in Chen and Wang, *Yu Dafu yanjiu ziliao*, 2:381–92.

32. To the stylistic criticism, Yu notes with appreciation that he agrees that the "sincerity" with which he wrote "Sinking" is missing in this particular work, which he composed in one night. He laments that, at the time, he was "swimming in cesspool of Shanghai," mired in the hardship of professional as well as of private life.

Indeed, Yu concedes that "[he] has recently felt that he is no longer as sincere as before." What exactly is lamented in the loss of "sincerity" (*shuaizhen*), however, is unclear. Directing their comments at the explicit sexual content in Yu's story, five or six readers denounced Yu for inciting young students to descend into the "bestial" world of homosexual love. Defending himself against this injustice, Yu protests that one should not take the protagonist as the author himself. He further emphasizes that he meant only to describe what he saw as a "tendency" in modern youths rather than to promote a certain behavior. See "'Mangmangye' fabiao zhi hou" (Notes after the publication of "Endless Night"), in *Yu Dafu wenji*, 5:124.

33. Ibid., p. 124.

34. Ibid., p. 125.

35. For discussions on the problem of authorship and autobiography in Yu Dafu, see, for example, Michael Egan, "Yu Dafu and the Transition to Modern Chinese Literature," in Merle Goldman, ed., *Modern Chinese Literature in the May Fourth Era* (Cambridge, MA: Harvard University Press, 1977), pp. 309–24; Shu Yunzhong, "The Cost of Living Up to the Demand of Autobiographical Fiction: An Analysis of the Interaction Between Yu Dafu's Fiction and His Life," *Tamkang Review* 1 (Fall 2002): 57–75.

36. From "Chanyu dubai" (A monologue amidst remorse—a substitute preface to "A collection of remorse"), in *Yu Dafu wenji*, 7:249–52.

37. The following quotation is taken from "Sinking," in Joseph S. M. Lau and Howard Goldblatt, eds., *The Columbia Anthology of Modern Chinese Literature* (New York: Columbia University Press, 1995): 68–69:

> How could I have gone to such a place? I really have become a most degraded person. But it's too late for regrets. I may as well end my life here, since I'll probably never get the kind of love I want. And what would life be without love? Isn't it as dead as ashes? Ah, this dreary life, how dull and dry! Everyone in this world hates me, mistreats me, even my own brother is trying to push me off the edge of this world. How can I make a living? And why should I stay on this world of suffering. . . . Oh China, my China, you are the cause of my death! . . . I wish you could become rich and strong soon! Many, many of your children are still suffering.

38. Yu, "Mangmangye," p. 131.

39. Ibid., pp. 143–44.

40. Ibid., pp. 132–33.

41. "Guoqu" (The past), in *Yu Dafu wenji*, 1:377.

42. Unlike what Gilles Deleuze has claimed in his analysis of masochism, maternal supremacy is not affirmed without simultaneously restricting the capacity of her authority. For the same reason, the masochist's execution of disavowing the paternal function and creating a new definition of man under the maternal sign brings about only a limited success. I discuss the theoretical implications of masochism at length elsewhere. See my "Perversions of Masculinity: The Masochistic Male Subject in Yu Dafu, Guo Moruo, and Freud," *Positions: East Asia Cultures Critique* 8.2 (Fall 2000): 269–316.

43. Yu, "Guoqu," p. 377.
44. Yu, "Mangmangye," p. 130.
45. Yu, "'Mangmangye' fabiao zhi hou," pp. 121–26.
46. "Geermeiluo guniang" (Donna Carméla), in *Guo Moruo quanji*, 9:205–38.
47. Ibid., p. 214.
48. Ibid., pp. 213–14.
49. Guo read the 1924 Japanese translation of *La Moja Desnuda*.
50. Western figures of suffering and redemption, from the sacrifice of Christ to the self-torment of Faust, and even the penitence of Rousseau, have been employed in Chinese writers' imagination of modern selfhood. See Jiang Zheng, *Rende jiefang yu yishu de jiefang: Guo Moruo yu Gede* (Liberating the man and liberating art: Guo Moruo and Goethe) (Jilin: Shidai wenyi chubanshe, 1991). For a different perspective on the reception of Nietzsche in China, see Raoul David Findeisen, "Die Last der Kultur: Vier Fallstudien zur chinesischen Nietzsche-Rezeption," *Minima Sinica* 2 (1989): 1–42, 1 (1990): 1–40.
51. Guo, "Geermeiluo guniang," p. 230.
52. *Zhinaren* (person of Zhina) calls to mind the derogatory connotation of *Shina*, which is believed to have been originally a Sanskrit rendering of "Qin dynasty," but has since the late nineteenth-century become an insulting designation used by the Japanese in reference to the National Republic of China (established in 1911). This issue stirred much heated debate, an issue Guo Moruo himself revisited in a 1936 article published in the literary journal *Yuzhou feng*. See Fogel, "The Controversy over *Shina*," in Fogel, *Cultural Dimension of Sino-Japanese Relations*. Guo Moruo, "Guanyu Ribenren duiyu Zhongguo ren de taidu," pp. 19–20.
53. Guo Moruo, "Xinglunan" (Hard road traveling), in *Guo Moruo quanji*, 9:308.
54. Ibid., pp. 309–10.
55. Guo Moruo, "Guanyu Riben ren duiyu Zhongguo ren de taidu," pp. 19–20.
56. Soon after the May Fourth Incident in 1919, Guo and other Chinese students studying in Japan formed Xiashe, an organization for transmitting information on anti-Chinese sentiments in Japan in correspondence with what was happening at home. During this time, Guo wrote two anti-Japanese and anti-imperialist essays revisiting the issue of Japan and China's cultural and racial affinity. See Guo Kaizhen (Guo Moruo), "Tongwen tongzhong bian" (On "same culture, same race") and "Dizhi rihuo zhi jiujing" (The real situation with the boycott of Japanese goods), both collected in Zhongguo Guo Moruo yanjiu xuehui "Guo Moruo yanjiu" bianjibu, ed., *Guo Moruo yanjiu* (Studies of Guo Moruo) (Beijing: Wenhua yishu chubanshe, 1989), 2:307–25.
57. See, for example, Sanetō Keishū, *Zhongguo ren liuxue Riben shi* (History of Chinese students in Japan), trans. Tan Ruqian and Lin Qiyan (Hong Kong: Zhongwen daxue chubanshe, 1982); Paula Harrell, *Sowing Seeds of Change: Chinese Students, Japanese Teachers, 1895–1905* (Stanford: Stanford University Press, 1992); Ye Weili, *Seeking Modernity in China's Name*.
58. See Wei Jian, "Chuangzaoshe xianxiang" (The phenomenon of Creation Society), in Zhongguo Guo Moruo yanjiu xuehui "Guo Moruo yanjiu" bianjibu (China's Guo Moruo research society "Guo Moruo" editorial department), ed., *Guo*

Moruo yanjiu (Guo Moruo research) (Beijing: Wenhua yishu chubanshe, 1998), 12:260.

59. Wen Yiduo, letter no. 74 (Nov. 1923), in *Wen Yiduo shuxin xuanji* (A selection of Wen Yiduo's letters) (Beijing: Renmin wenxue chubanshe, 1986), p. 173.

60. See, for example, "Faxian" (Discovery) and "Qidao" (Prayer) from *Sishui* (Dead water) collection, in *Wen Yiduo quanji*, 1:126–67.

61. Buxiaosheng (1889–1957), *Liudong waishi* (An unofficial history of studying in Japan), 3 vols. (Nanchang: Baihuazhou wenyi chubanshe, 1991).

62. The reversion of sexual love to patriotism also figures prominently in the writings of female writers. For example, Lu Yin's "Yige qingfu de riji" (Diary of a mistress) ends with a mistress abandoning her unfruitful affair with the resolution to serve the country. It is interesting to reflect on what this relationship to the nation—taking it as one's lover—entails, because *qingren*—meaning a lover rather than spouse at this time—usually falls out of the purview of legitimacy. See Lu Yin, *Lu Yin xiaoshuo quanji* (Complete fiction works of Lu Yin), ed. Guo Junfeng and Wang Jinting, 2 vols. (Chanchun: Shidao wenyi chubanshe, 1997), 1:407–25.

63. Yu, "Sinking," in Lau and Goldblatt, *Columbia Anthology of Modern Chinese Literature*, p. 48. See also Kirk Denton's interesting essay, "The Distant Shore: The Nationalist Theme in Yu Dafu's 'Sinking,'" *Chinese Literature: Essays, Articles, and Reviews* 14 (Dec. 1992): 107–23.

64. Zheng Boqi, "Zuichu zhi ke" (The very first lesson), in Zheng Boqi wenji bianwei hui, ed., *Zheng Boqi wenji* (Zheng Boqi collection) (Xi'an: Shanxi renmin chubanshe, 1988), pp. 581–82.

65. Zheng, "Zuichu zhi ke," p. 584.

66. Tian Han, "Xu" (Preface), *Sanyeji* (Trefoil), in *Guo Moruo quanji*, 15:3–4.

67. Zong Baihua, "Xu" (Preface), *Sanyeji*, in *Guo Moruo quanji*, 15:5.

68. "Guo Moruo to Zong Baihua," *Sanyeji*, in *Guo Moruo quanji*, 15:18–19.

69. Cf. Jiang Zheng, "Renwen zhuyi de lanmanshi juexing" (The romantic awakening of humanism), in *Guo Moruo yanjiu*, 7:96–113; Feng Xianguang, "Lun *Sanyeji* de wenhua jiazhi yishi" (On the consciousness of cultural values in *Trefoil*), in Zhongguo Guo Moruo yanjiuhui, ed., *Guo Moruo yu dongxi wenhua* (Guo Moruo and Eastern and Western cultures). (Beijing: Dangdai Zhongguo chubanshe, 1998), pp. 335–48.

70. For a discussion, see Chen Yongzhi, "Guo Moruo fanshen lun sixiang de fazhan guocheng" (The development of Guo Moruo's pantheistic thinking), in Wang Xunzhao, Lu Zhengyan, and Lin Minghua, eds., *Guo Moruo yanjiu ziliao* (Research materials on Guo Moruo), 3 vols. (Beijing: Zhongguo shehui kexue chubanshe, 1986), 2:45–66.

71. "Zong Baihua to Guo Moruo," *Sanyeji*, in *Guo Moruo quanji*, 15:70.

72. "Tian Han to Guo Moruo," *Sanyeji*, in *Guo Moruo quanji*, 15:36.

73. "Guo Moruo to Tian Han," *Sanyeji*, in *Guo Moruo quanji*, 15:39–42.

74. Ibid., p. 45. In a letter to Chen Jianlei, Guo suggests that he read *Trefoil* if he wishes to know more about his "naked self" (chichi luoluo de wo). Guo even offers to send him a copy. See "Zhi Chen Jianlei" (07.26.1920) (Letter to Chen Jianlei), in Huang, *Guo Moruo shuxinji*, 1:173.

75. For a study of privacy in modern Chinese literary culture, see Bonnie Mc-Dougall, trans., *Love-Letters and Privacy in Modern China: The Intimate Lives of Lu Xun and Xu Guangping* (Oxford & New York: Oxford University Press, 2002).

CHAPTER SEVEN

1. For important works in this regard, see, for example, David Der-wei Wang, *Fictional Realism*; Marston Anderson, *The Limits of Realism: Chinese Fiction in the Revolutionary Period* (Berkeley: University of California Press, 1990); Leo Ou-Fan Lee, *The Romantic Generation of Modern Chinese Writers* (Cambridge, MA: Harvard University Press, 1973).

2. This translation, with slight modifications, is taken from Lau and Goldblatt, *Columbia Anthology of Modern Chinese Literature*, p. 55.

3. The idea that there is a part of the protagonist's psychological struggle protected from view is particularly interesting in view of the fact that Yu Dafu's protagonists are held to be exhibitionists.

4. See Lu Yin, "Lishi de riji" (Lishi's diary), in Guo and Wang, *Lu Yin xiaoshuo quanji*, 1:45–55; "Huoren de bei ai" (Someone's grief), in Guo and Wang, *Lu Yin xiaoshuo quanji*, pp. 30–44.

5. Mao Dun, "Yige nüxing" (A woman), in *Mao Dun quanji* (The complete works of Mao Dun), 33 vols. (Beijing: Renmin wenxue chubanshe, 1984), 8:53.

6. See Chapter 5 for a discussion of "Creation."

7. Ye Shaojun, "Ye" (Night), in Zhao Jiabi, ed., *Zhongguo xin wenxue daxi 1927–1937: Xiaoshuo ji, 1* (Compendium of modern Chinese literature: Short stories, vol. 1) (Shanghai: Shanghai wenyi chubanshe, 1984), p. 108.

8. See Rao Hongjing et al., eds. *Chuangzao she ziliao* (Research materials on Creation Society), 2 vols. (Fuzhou: Fujian renmin chubanshe, 1985); Marián Gálik, *The Genesis of Modern Chinese Literary Criticism 1917–1930* (London: Curzon Press, 1980); Anderson, *Limits of Realism*; Wang Xiaoming, ed., *Wenxue yanjiu hui pinglun ziliao xuan* (A selection of discussions on Literary Research Association), vol. 1 (Shanghai: Huadong shifan daxue chubanshe, 1986).

9. Hu Shi, "Some Modest Proposals for the Reform of Literature," in Kirk A. Denton, ed., *Modern Chinese Literary Thought: Writings on Literature, 1893–1945* (Stanford: Stanford University Press, 1996): 123–39.

10. Yu, "Guanyu xiaoshuo de hua" (A few words about fiction), in Zhejiang Literary Publishing House, ed., *Yu Dafu wenlun ji* (Yu Dafu's literary criticism) (Hangzhou: Zhejiang wenyi chubanshe, 1985), p. 453. This is part of Yu Dafu's *Duancanji* (Maimed collection).

11. Qian Xingcun, "*Dafu daibiao zuo* houxu" (Postscript to "Dafu's representative works"), in Chen Zishan and Wang Zili, eds., *Yu Dafu yanjiu ziliao* (Research materials on Yu Dafu) (Hong Kong: Sanlian, 1986), p. 34. *Dafu daibiao zuo* (Dafu's representative works) was originally published in 1928.

12. Zheng was apparently not aware of the fact that Chekhov was active as a writer before 1900. However, he could have been referring to the period he thought had witnessed Chekhov's most significant impact.

13. Zheng Boqi, "Reviewing 'Hanhuiji,'" in Chen and Wang, *Yu Dafu yanjiu ziliao* (Research materials on Yu Dafu) (1986), p. 17.

14. Mao Dun, "Zhongguo xin wenxue daxi: xiaoshuo yiji—Daoyan" (Preface to *Compendium of modern Chinese literature: Fiction*, vol. 1), in Wang Xiaoming, *Wenxue yanjiu hui pinglun ziliao xuan*, 1:13.

15. The same journal, *Kaizō*, also featured a special issue in 1927 exploring the various manifestations of kumen—from sexual to economic—in Japanese society. See *Kaizō* 9 (1927): 1–70.

16. See Yamamoto Shūji's "Houji" (Postscript) to Lu Xun's translation, *Kumen de xiangzheng*, in *Lu Xun yiwenji* (A collection of Lu Xun's translations), 17 vols. (Beijing: Renmin wenxue chubanshe, 1959), 3:90–91.

17. Feng Zikai, trans., *Kumen de xiangzheng* (Symbol of angst) (Shanghai: Shangwu yinshuguan, 1925).

18. This was brought to Lu Xun's attention by a reader in 1925. See Lu Xun, "Guanyu *Kumen de xiangzheng*" (About *Symbol of angst*), in *Lu Xun quanji* (1981), 7:243–47. The same translator, Chongyun, also translated at least two other essays by Kuriyagawa, "Bingde xingyu yu wenxue" (Perverse libido and literature), *Xiaoshuo yuebao* 5 (1925): 1–9, and "Wenyi yu xingyu" (Literature and libido), *Xiaoshuo yuebao* 5 (1925): 1–4.

19. Lu Xun, trans., *Kumen de xiangzheng* (Symbol of angst) (Tianjin: Baihua wenyi chubanshe, 2000), p. 3. All subsequent quotations are from this edition.

20. Ibid., pp. 13, 45, 81.

21. Ibid., p. 31.

22. Ibid., pp. 5–6.

23. For the controversies surrounding Bergson's works, see, for example, R. C. Grogin, *The Bergsonian Controversy in France 1900–1914* (Calgary: University of Calgary Press, 1988); Frederick Burwick and Paul Douglass, eds., *The Crisis in Modernism: Bergson and the Vitalist Controversy* (Cambridge & New York: Cambridge University Press, 1992).

24. Henri Bergson, *Creative Evolution*, trans. Arthur Mitchell (Mineola, NY: Dover Publications, 1998).

25. Zhang Dongsun, trans., "Preface," *Chuanghualun* (Creative evolution), 2 vols. (Shanghai: Shangwu yinshuguan, 1919). Bergson's *Le Rire* was also translated into Chinese in 1921. See Zhang Wentian, trans., *Xiao zhi yanjiu* (A study of laughter) (Shanghai: Shangwu yinshuguan, 1923).

26. Kuriyagawa makes reference to Freud's *Die Traumdeutung* and *Eine Kindheitserinnerung des Leonardo da Vinci* in his footnotes.

27. See Axel Johan Uppvall, *August Strindberg: A Psychoanalytical Study with Special Reference to the Oedipus Complex* (Boston: Gorham Press, 1920).

28. Lu Xun, *Kumen de xiangzheng*, p. 19. Arthur Schopenhauer's *Die Welt als Wille und Vorstellung* (The world as will and idea) has no doubt influenced Kuriyagawa's conception of "interest."

29. Ibid., pp. 44–45.

30. Ibid., p. 51.

31. See Tian Han, "Xin luoman zhuyi ji qita" (New Romanticism and others),

in *Shaonian Zhongguo* 12 (1920). This can also be found in *Tian Han quanji* (The complete works of Tian Han), 20 vols. (Shijiazhuang: Huashan wenyi chubanshe, 2000), 14:157–90.

32. See *Lu Xun quanji* (1981), 14:515–17.

33. Lu Xun's translation, apart from the one I am citing, can also be found in *Lu Xun quanji* (Hong Kong: Wenxue yanjiushe, 1973) 3:3–89. Appended to the main text is a translation of Maupassant's "Xianglian" (The necklace) by Chang Weijun. Xu Shoushang helped with the English translations. The first two chapters appeared in installments in *Chenbao fuxi* (Morning news supplement) between October 1 and 31, 1924. The entire translation was first published in March 1925 in the *Weiming congkan* (Nameless books) series, marketed by Beijing Daxue Xinchaoshe (Beijing University New Tide Society) and later published by Beixin Shuju (Beixin Publishers).

34. See Chen Ma, *Goutong yu gengxin: Lu Xun yu Riben wenxue guanxi fawei* (Communication and renewal: An inquiry into Lu Xun's relationship to Japanese literature) (Beijing: Zhongguo shehui kexue chubanshe, 1990); letter from Xu Guangping, *Lu Xun quanji* (1981), 11:86.

35. Letter to Tao Kangde, no. 331102 (11.02.1933), in *Lu Xun quanji* (1981), 12:251–52.

36. A year after he translated *Symbol of Angst*, Lu Xun translated and published a selected number of Kuriyagawa's articles from *Out of the Ivory Tower*. See *Chule xiangya zhi ta* (Out of the ivory tower), in *Lu Xun quanji* (1973), 13:155–381. "Theory on Gaming" ("Youxilun") bears relevance to chapter 1, section 3 (On force of repression) in *Symbol*. Lu Xun also included a partial translation of Kuriyagawa's "Walking Towards the Intersection," which resonates the title for his own later collection, *Panghuang* (Hesitation, wandering), written between March 1924 and November 1925. One may well argue that for Lu Xun, "panghuang" indeed captures this "modern" state of mind.

> East or west, south or north? Forward towards the new, or back towards the old? Go towards where the spirit urges, or towards where the body desires? Looking to the left and to the right, not knowing where to turn at the intersection—this, indeed, is the state of the modern mind. "*To be or not to be, that is the question*" . . . Some people say that modern thought has walked into a blind alley. But it has not at all. It is only standing at the crossroads. There are many roads to take.

37. "Tingshuomeng" (About dreams), in *Lu Xun quanji* (1981), 4:469.

38. Cai Yuanpei, "Xinnian meng" (Dreams for the new year), *Dongfang zazhi* 30.1 (1933): 1–83.

39. See the journalist's "Duhougan" (Afterthoughts), *Dongfang zazhi* 30.1 (1933): 79–83.

40. See "Chule xiangya zhita: houji" (Out of the ivory tower: Postscript), in *Lu Xun quanji* (1981), 10:240.

41. Ibid., p. 243.

42. See Lu Xun, "*Kumen de xiangzheng yinyan*" (Prefatory remarks to *Symbol of angst*), in *Lu Xun quanji* (1981), 10:232.

43. See Xu Qinwen, "Lu Xun he Tao Yuanqing" (Lu Xun and Tao Yuanqing), in *Xin wenxue shiliao* (Historical documents on New Literature) 1 (1979): 70–85.

44. Di Chuqing (d. 1921), or Di Baoxian, was one of the exiled reformers in Japan who consorted with Tan Sitong and Tang Caichang during the 1898 Reform. He later founded *Shibao* (Times newspaper) and was a supporter of constitutionalism. He was immersed in Buddhist studies and had an extensive private collection of Eastern art and calligraphy.

45. See Lu Xun's preface to the catalog in Zhang Guangfu, ed., *Lu Xun meishu lunji* (A collection of Lu Xun's views on art) (Yunnan: Xinhua shudian, 1982), pp. 44–45.

46. See Lu Xun's "Dan Tao Yuanqing jun de huihua zhanlan shi wo suo yao shuode jijuhua" (A few words I want to say at Mr. Tao Yuanqing's art exhibition), in Zhang, *Lu Xun meishu lunji*, p. 46.

47. Xu Qinwen, "Lu Xun and Tao Yuanqing," p. 72.

48. See Gu Nong, "Lu Xun yu *Kumen de xiangzheng*" (Lu Xun and *Symbol of angst*), in *Lu Xun yanjiu ziliao* (Research materials on Lu Xun) 13 (1980): 235–54.

49. Lu Xun, *Kumen de xiangzheng*, p. 33.

50. See Lu Xun's letters to Xu Qinwen, no. 78 (09.30.1925) and no. 79 (11.08.1925), in Renmin wenxue chubanshe, ed., *Lu Xun shuxin ji* (Lu Xun's correspondence), 2 vols. (Beijing: Renmin wenxue chubanshe, 1976), 1:74–77.

51. Leo Lee makes an interesting connection between Lu Xun and the visualization of femme fatales. See Leo Lee, "Lu Xun yu xiandai yishu yishi" (Lu Xun and modern art consciousness), in *Tianwuzhong de nahan* (Voices from the iron house) (Hong Kong: Sanlian shudian, 1991), pp. 222–48.

52. See Lu Xun, "Xianjinde xin wenxue de gaiguan" (The outlook of current new literature) (1929), in *Sanxianji*, in *Lu Xun quanji* (1981), 4:133–37.

53. Lu Yin's short story "Diary of a Mistress" poignantly captures this elision from individual sexual distress to national salvation, as a mistress renounces her private feelings for a man and vows to take the nation as a lover. See "Yige qingfu de riji," in *Lu Yin xiaoshuo quanji*, 1:407–25. See Chapter 6, n. 62.

54. See Guo Moruo, "Geming yu wenxue" (Revolution and literature) (1926), in Zhongguo shehui kexue yuan wenxue yanjiu suo xiandai wenxue yanjiushi (Chinese Academy of Social Sciences: Institute for Literary Studies–Modern Literature Research Group), ed., *"Geming wenxun" lunzheng ziliao xuanbian* (Selections of materials on the debates over "Revolutionary literature"), 2 vols. (Beijing: Renmin wenxue chubanshe, 1981), 1:1–12.

55. Ibid., p. 7.

CONCLUSION

1. See *Renmin ribao* (People's daily newspaper) (04.28.2001).

2. One only needs to recall former president Bill Clinton's speech at the official opening of the Holocaust Memorial Museum in Washington, D.C., in 1993 with the words, "The evil represented in this museum is incontestable, but as we are its witness so must we remain its adversary in the world in which we live." It was only

a year later that Rwandan genocide was allowed to happen as a result of UN peace-keeping troops pulling out.

3. J. L. Austin, *How to Do Things with Words* (Cambridge, MA: Harvard University Press, 1962).

4. Frantz Fanon, *Wretched of the Earth* (New York: Grove Press, 1963).

aide jinhua	愛的進化	beinueai	被虐愛
aiguo	愛國	beinuedai yinluan-zheng	被虐待淫亂症
aiguo aizhong zhi xin	愛國愛種之心	beinuedaikuang	被虐待狂
aiguo baozhong	愛國保種	bianjing	變精
aiguo baozhong zhi xin	愛國保種之心	biantai	變態
		bianxiang de xingli	變相的性力
Aimou	愛牟	bingtai	病態
Anhui suhuabao	安徽俗话报	bingtai zizun	病態自尊
Ba Jin	巴金	bu jianquande min-zuxing	不健全的民族性
Bai Wei	白薇		
baihua	白話	buduojiang	不惰漿
bainian guochi	百年國恥	bujianquande biao-shi	不健全的表示
bairen zhimin zhi di	白人殖民之地		
		bupasi	不怕死
Bankoku tsūten	萬國通典	*Buren*	不忍
baoqian	抱歉	Bushido	武士道
baowu	寶物	Cai Wenji	蔡文姬
beidongde nue-daikuang	被動的虐待狂	Cai Yuanpei	蔡元培
		"Canchun"	殘春
beidongde yin-nuekuang	被動的淫虐狂	changtai	常態
		Changyanbao	昌言報

Chen Duxiu	陳獨秀	"Dian Shijie"	電世界
Chen Jianlei	陳建雷	Dianwang	電王
Chen Tianhua	陳天華	Ding Ling	丁玲
Chenbao fukan	晨報副刊	*Dongfang zazhi*	東方雜志
Cheng Fangwu	成仿吾	*Dongjing meng*	東京夢
chi	恥	dongya bingfu	東亞病夫
chichi luoluo de wo	赤赤裸裸的我	Dongyinguo	東陰國
chongdong	衝動	du de xiyang de shu, shoude shi dongyang de qi	讀的西洋的書 受的是東洋 的氣
chou e	醜惡		
chousha	仇殺	Dui e tongzhi hui	對俄同志會
Chu	楚	*E shi jingwen*	俄事警聞
"Chuangzao"	創造	e zhong	惡種
chuli	儲力	*Ershi nian mudu zhi guaixianzhuang*	二十年目睹之 怪現狀
chunchi xiangyi	唇齒相依		
Chunliushe	春柳社	*Ershi shiji*	二十世紀
Chunyangshe	春陽社	fa	發
Cuixinbao	萃新报	fanxing	反省
dadao baquan	打倒霸權	fei kexue	非科學
Dagongbao	大公报	"Fei tonzhong tongwen"	非同種同文
daici erxing	代此而興		
daixia	帶下	Feng Xiaoqing	馮小青
daoqian	道歉	Feng Zikai	豐子愷
datong shijie	大同世界	"Fengehou zhi wuren"	分割候之吾人
datong zhi shi	大同之世		
Dawen	大蘊	fubai de laoda guo ren	腐敗的老大 國人
"Dehuang shouhui Huanghuo tu sheben"	德皇手繪黃禍 圖攝本		
		Fubao	復報
		Funü zazhi	婦女雜誌
Deng Shi	鄧實	gailiang renzhong	改良人種
Dengzhou	登州	ge	戈
deyu zhiyu tiyu	德育智育體育	*Geguo zhonglei kao*	各國種類考
Di Chuqing	狄楚青	*Gemingjun*	革命軍
		Gezhi huibian	格致彙編

gongli	公理	Huang Zhiqiang	黃之強
guanmeiju	官媒局	Huang Zhisheng	黃之盛
guizhong	貴種	Huang Zunxia	黃遵憲
guo	國	*Huanian*	華年
Guo Moruo	郭沫若	*Hubei xuesheng jie*	湖北學生界
guochi	國恥	hunhe renzhong	混合人種
guochi yuefen pai	國恥月份牌	hunyin zhesi xue	婚姻哲嗣學
guocui	國粹	huoli	活力
Guocui xuebao	國粹學報	"Huoren de beiai"	或人的悲哀
guohun	國魂	Inoue Enryō	井上円了
guojia	國家	Inukai Tsuyoshi	犬養毅
guomin	國民	ji	己
guominxing	國民性	ji	記
Hangzhou baihuabao	杭州白話報	ji zicun	急自存
hanjian	漢奸	jia	家
hanren qiang man-ren wang	漢人強滿人亡	*Jiading tucheng ji lue*	嘉定屠城記略
		jian	賤
He Shuangqing	賀雙卿	*Jiangsu*	江蘇
he tongzhong yi yizhong	合同種異異種	*Jiayin zazhi*	甲寅雜誌
		Jiji shinpō	時事新報
heinu	黑奴	jingbian	精變
Heinu shoubi ji	黑奴受逼記	jingcunli	競存力
Heinu yu tian lu	黑奴籲天錄	jingshen de yun-dong	精神的運動
Hu Shi	胡適		
hua	華	jingshen shengli	精神勝利
Hua Rixing	華日興	*Jingye xunbao*	競業旬報
huang	黃	jiuchadui	糾察隊
Huang Huo	黃禍	jiuguo	救國
Huang Jie	黃節	jixian	己限
Huang Shi	黃史	juexing	覺醒
Huang Shibiao	黃士表	jueyuji	絕欲劑
Huang Xiuqiu	黃繡球	jun	君
Huang Zhenqiu	黃震球	*Kaizō*	改造

Kang Youwei 康有為

"Kangzhan de min- 抗戰的民族
zu yiyi" 意義

kexue 科學

kexue xiaoshuo 科學小說

Ku xuesheng 苦學生

Kumen de xiang- 苦悶的象征
zheng

kumen panghuang 苦悶彷徨

Kumon no shōchō 苦悶の象徴

kuozhangli 擴張力

Kuriyagawa Hakuson 廚川白村

Langhua 郎華

Lao Can youji 老殘游記

Lao She 老舍

Li Bai 李白

Li Dazhao 李大釗

Li Jianwu 李健吾

Li Jieren 李劼人

Li Jinfa 李金發

Li Jinghan 李景漢

Li Xishuang 李息霜

li yi lian chi 禮義廉恥

liang 良

Liang Qichao 梁啓超

Liang Shiqiu 梁實秋

Liang Shuming 梁漱溟

Liaozhai zhiyi 聊齋誌異

liegenxing 劣根性

liexing 劣性

liezhong 劣種

liezhong zhiren 劣種之人

Lin Shu 林紓

Lin Yutang 林語堂

Ling Jishi 凌吉士

Ling Shi 靈石

Lingxuebao 嶺學報

"Lishi riji" 麗石日記

Liu Bannong 劉半農

Liu E 劉鶚

Liu Rushi 柳如是

Liu Shipei 劉師培

Liu Wenru 劉文如

Liudong waish 留東外史

Liumei xuesheng 留美學生季報
jibao

lixiang xiaoshuo 理想小說

liyisi 禮儀司

lu 錄

Lu Xun 魯迅

Lu Xun yanjiu nian- 魯迅研究年刊
kan

Lu Xun yanjiu yue- 魯迅研究月刊
kan

Lu Xun yanjiu ziliao 魯迅研究資料

Lu Yin 盧隱

maiguonu 賣國奴

"Mangmangye" 茫茫夜

maoxianxing 冒險性

Matsuo Bashō 松尾芭蕉

Mei Guangdi 梅光迪

Meide renshengguan 美的人生觀

Meide shehui zu- 美的社會組
zhifa 織法

meishu 美術

meiwai 媚外

meizhi 美制

meizhong	美種	Okamoto Kansuke	岡本監輔
Miao	苗	paiman	排滿
mieguo	滅國	paiwai	排外
Minduo	民鐸	pangao	攀高
Ming Qing xiaoshuo yanjiu	明清小說研究	pangguan	旁觀
		Panghuang	彷徨
mingchitu	明恥圖	pingmin jieji	平民階級
"Mingri zhi guafen"	明日之瓜分	Pingzhou	屏周
minli	民力	Qian Xingcun (A Ying)	錢杏村 (阿英)
minli minzhi minde	民力民智民德		
minqi	民氣	Qian Xuantong	錢玄同
minxin	民心	Qin	秦
minzhong	民種	Qingguoren	清國人
Minzhongxue	民種學	qingrenzhi	情人制
minzu	民族	qingsha	情殺
minzu jingshen	民族精神	*Qingyibao*	清議報
Minzu texing yu minzu weisheng	民族特性與民族衛生	qizhi	氣質
		Qu Yuan	屈原
minzuxing	民族性	"Qu zhongjie tong renlei"	去種界同人類
Miyang	迷羊		
Morioka Kenji	森岡建二	quan shijie zhuren weng	全世界主人翁
muwu	木屋		
muzha	木柵	quru	屈辱
nanyang secai	南洋色彩	renge gongkai	人格公開
nei	內	"Renlei gongli"	人類公理
neishifa	內食法	"renlei pingdeng, renlei datong, ci gu gongli ye. Ran wu zhi buqi, wu zhi qing ye"	人類平等人類大同此固公理也然物之不齊物之情也
Nishi Amane	西周		
nu	奴		
nuxing	奴性		
nüxing shizu de nüren	女性十足的女人		
		renzhong	人種
Nüzi shijie	女子世界	renzhong gailiang	人種改良
nüzu jiaoyu	女子教育	renzhong gailiang xue	人種改良學

Riren rong Zhong-guo ru 日人榮中國辱

Sai Jinhua 賽金花

Saigyō 西行

Sanyeji 三葉集

Satō Tomiko 佐藤富子

Shangshi jie 商市街

shanzhongxue 善種學

Shaonian Zhongguo 少年中國

shehui xiaoshuo 社會小說

shen biao qianyi 深表歉意

Shenbao 申報

shenbiao qianyi 深表歉意

shenjiaofa 神交法

Shi Pingmei 石評梅

Shi Zhecun 施蟄存

shidai 時代

Shidai huabao 時代畫報

shijie datong 世界大同

Shinrigaku 心理學

Shiwubao 時務報

shizi jiekou 十字街口

shounuelian 受虐戀

shuairuo yeman de minzu 衰弱野蠻的民族

shuaizhen 率真

shuzhongxue 淑種學

Situhuo 斯土活

Siyi biannianbiao 四裔編年表

Su Xuelin 蘇雪林

Subao 蘇報

suzhi 素質

Tan Sitong 譚嗣同

Tang Caichang 唐才長

Tangmu jiashi 湯姆家事

Tao Jingsun 陶晶孫

Tao Sijin 陶思瑾

Tao Yuanqing 陶元慶

Tian Han 田漢 (壽昌)

tian zhi aozi 天之傲子

tianxia xingwang pifu youze 天下興亡匹夫有責

tianxian 天限

Tianyibao 天議報

tianzhi 天職

tiao 條

tigao 提高

tiyu 體育

tongkuai 痛快

tongxingjian 同性姦

tongxinglian 同性戀

tongzhong 同種

tongzhong 通種

Tongzi shijie 童子世界

Uchiyama Kanzō 内山完造

wai 外

waihunzhi 外婚制

Waijiaobao 外交報

Wang Guowei 王國維

Wang Zhongsheng 王鐘聲

wangguo 亡國

wangguo yimin 亡國遺民

wangguo zhi min 亡國之民

wangguonu 亡國奴

Wanguo gongbao 萬國公報

Wei Yi 魏易

Weidi	韋第	xinde youzhong-	新的優種學
weiyu	位育	xue	
Wen Yiduo	聞一多	xing ai	性愛
wenming	文明	xing boshi	性博士
wenming bing	文明病	*Xing zazhi*	性雜誌
wenming xi	文明戲	*Xingshi*	性史
wenming zhi guo	文明之國	xingyu	性育
Wu Jianren	吳趼人	xingyu de jingli	性欲的精力
Wu Mi	吳宓	xinli jiexifa	心理解析法
Wu Zhihui	吳稚暉	xinlingxue	心靈學
wubing shenyin	無病呻吟	xinlixue	心理學
wujing tianze, shizhe	物競天擇適者	xinshang	欣賞
shengcun	生存	xiong jiujiu de wei	雄赳赳的偉
Xia	夏	zhangfu	丈夫
Xiangbao	湘報	Xiongyelü	匈耶律
"Xianglei"	湘累	Xiwei	西威
Xiangxuebao	湘學報	Xu Dishan	許地山
Xiao Hong	蕭紅	Xu Qinwen	許欽文
Xiao Shibao	小時報	Xu Shoushang	許壽裳
Xiaoshuo shibao	小說時報	Xu Zhimo	徐志摩
Xiaoshuo yuebao	小說月報	Xue Fucheng	薛福成
Xiashe	夏社	*Xuedeng*	學燈
Xie Bingying	謝冰瑩	*Xuesheng zazhi*	學生雜誌
Xieleihen	血淚痕	Yamamoto Shūji	山本修二
xin guomin	新國民	Yan Fu	嚴復
Xin Jiyuan	新紀元	Yan Yongjing	顏永京
xin nüxing	新女性	Yang Guowei	楊國威
Xin qingnian	新青年	*Yangzhou shiri ji*	揚州十日記
Xin wenxue shiliao	新文學史料	Yasuoka Hideo	安岡秀夫
xin xinlixue	新心理學	yazhouren de ya-	亞洲人的亞洲
Xin Zhongguo wei-	新中國未來記	zhou	
laiji		Ye Shengtao	葉聖陶
xinde taijiao	新的胎教	*Yecao*	野草

yeman	野蠻	Zhang Zhidong	張之洞
Yeqiangwei	野薔薇	Zhang Ziping	張資平
yeren	野人	*Zhejiangchao*	浙江潮
yi shi zhu xing	衣食住行	Zheng Boqi	鄭伯奇
yi yizhong	遺宜種	zhengzhi xiaoshuo	政治小說
"Yige nüren"	一個女人	*Zhenhua wuri dashi ji*	振華五日大事記
yihan	遺憾	*Zhibao*	直報
yinluanzheng	淫亂症	Zhichi xuehui	知恥學會
Yishi yuekan	醫事月刊	Zhina	支那
yixing	異性	zhinaren	支那人
yixinglian	異性戀	zhinaren nuli xingzhi	支那人奴隸性質
Yiyaoxue	醫藥學	zhinatong	支那通
yiyi zhiyi	以夷制夷	*Zhixinbao*	知新報
yongshou	用熟	zhiye	職業
youliangde zhongzi	優良的種子	*Zhongfa xin huibao*	中法新彙報
Yousheng fukan	優生副刊	*Zhongguo baihuabao*	中國白話報
yousheng youyu	優生優育	Zhongguo lao bingfu	中國老病夫
Yousheng yuekan	優生月刊	Zhongguo liuxue-sheng	中國留學生
"Youxilun"	游戲論	"Zhongguo zhi jiang qiang"	中國之將強
Youze pifu	有責匹夫	Zhonghua minguo ren	中華民國人
Yu Dafu	郁達夫	*Zhonghua xuesheng jie*	中華學生界
yuanqi	元氣	Zhongri qinshan	中日親善
yue	約	Zhou Jianren	周建人
Yue	越	Zhou Zuoren	周作人
yule	娛樂	Zhu Guangqian	朱光潛
Yuzhou feng	宇宙風	zhudongde yinnue-kuang	主動的淫虐狂
Zeng Qi	增奇	zhudongli	主動力
Zeng Xiaogu	曾孝古		
zeren	責任		
Zhang Binglin	章炳麟		
Zhang Dongsun	張東蓀		
Zhang Jingsheng	張競生		
Zhang Kebiao	章克標		

zijuexin	自覺心	zizhi	自治
ziku	自苦	zizhili	自治力
ziqi	自欺	Zong Baihua	宗白華
zixin	自信	Zou Rong	鄒容
zixiu	自修	"Zuichu zhi ke"	最初之課
Ziyou hua	自由花	zuzhi	組織
Ziyou jiehun	自由結婚		

Selected Bibliography

A Liao. *Zhongguo ren de wonang* (The cowardice of the Chinese). Beijing: Xinhua shudian, 1997.

A Ying, ed. *Wanqing wenxue congchao: chengwai wenxue yiwen juan* (A collection of late Qing literature: Translations of foreign literature). Beijing: Zhonghua shuju, 1960.

———, ed. *Wanqing wenxue congchao: xiaoshuo xiqu yanjiu juan* (A collection of late Qing literature: Fiction and drama). Beijing: Zhonghua shuju, 1960.

Abel, Elizabeth, Barbara Christian, and Helene Moglen, eds. *Female Subjects in Black and White: Race, Psychoanalysis, Feminism.* Berkeley: University of California Press, 1997.

Abraham, Nicolas, and Maria Torok. *The Shell and the Kernel: Renewals of Psychoanalysis.* Trans. Nicolas Rand. Chicago: University of Chicago Press, 1994.

Adams, Mark B., ed. *The Wellborn Science: Eugenics in Germany, France, Brazil, and Russia.* New York and Oxford: Oxford University Press, 1990.

Addington, Bruce, H. "The Marvels of Dream Analysis." *McClure's Magazine* 1 (1912): 113–19.

Agamben, Giorgio. *Homo Sacer: Sovereign Power and Bare Life.* Trans. Daniel Heller-Roazen. Stanford: Stanford University Press, 1998.

Ahmad, Aijaz. "Jameson's Rhetoric of Otherness and the 'National Allegory.'" In *In Theory: Classes, Nations, Literatures*, pp. 95–122. London: Verso, 1992.

"Ai tongbao zhi jiang wang" (On the imminent death of our fellow citizens). *Dongfang zazhi* 12 (1904): 295–98.

Alford, William P. *To Steal a Book Is an Elegant Offense: Intellectual Property Law in Chinese Civilization.* Stanford: Stanford University Press, 1995.

Alitto, Guy. *The Last Confucian: Liang Shu-ming and the Chinese Dilemma of Modernity.* Berkeley: University of California Press, 1979.

Althusser, Louis. *Lenin and Philosophy, and Other Essays.* New York: Monthly Review Press, 1971.

Anderson, Benedict. *Imagined Communities: Reflections on the Origin and Spread of Nationalism.* London and New York: Verso, 1991.

———. *The Spectre of Comparisons: Nationalism, Southeast Asia and the World.* London and New York: Verso, 1998.

Anderson, Marston. *The Limits of Realism: Chinese Fiction in the Revolutionary Period.* Berkeley: University of California Press, 1990.

Andrews, Bridie. "Tuberculosis and the Assimilation of Germ Theory in China, 1895–1937." *Journal of the History of Medicine and Allied Sciences* 52 (January 1997): 114–57.

Appiah, Kwame Anthony. *In My Father's House: Africa in the Philosophy of Culture.* New York and Oxford: Oxford University Press, 1992.

———. "The Multiculturalist Misunderstanding." *The New York Review of Books* (10.09.1997).

Appiah, Kwame Anthony, and Amy Gutman. *Color Conscious: The Political Morality of Race.* Princeton, NJ: Princeton University Press, 1996.

Arendt, Hannah. *The Human Condition.* Chicago: University of Chicago Press, 1958.

Auerbach, Erich. *Mimesis: The Representation of Reality in Western Literature.* Trans. Willard R. Trask. Princeton, NJ: Princeton University Press, 1968.

Austin, J. L. *How to Do Things with Words.* Cambridge, MA: Harvard University Press, 1962.

Bai Wei. *Beiju shengya* (Life of tragedy). Shanghai: Wenxue chubanshe, 1936.

Baihua daoren (The vernacular Taoist). "Zuo baixing de sixiang ji jingshen" (The thought and spirit of the common folks). *Zhongguo baihuabao* 4 (1903): 1–6.

"Baihuo shi" (The history of the white peril). *Dongfang zazhi* 10.3 (1913): 13–23.

Bakhtin, Mikhail. *The Dialogic Imagination: Four Essays.* Trans. Michael Holquist and Caryl Emerson. Austin: University of Texas Press, 1981.

Balakrishnan, Gopal, ed. *Mapping the Nation.* London and New York: Verso, 1996.

Bales, Kevin. *Disposable People: New Slavery in the Global Economy.* Berkeley and Los Angeles: University of California Press, 1999.

Bao Jing, ed. *Lu Xun "guomingxing sixiang" taolun ji* (On Lu Xun's "National character"). Tianjin: Tianjin renmin chubanshe, 1982.

Bao Mi (Wang Lixiong). *Huanghuo* (Yellow peril). 3 vols. Taibei: Fengyun shidai chuban youxian gongsi, 1991.

Barkan, Elazar. *The Guilt of Nations: Restitution and Negotiating Historical Injustices.* Baltimore and London: Johns Hopkins University Press, 2000.

Barlow, Tani E. *The Question of Women in Chinese Feminism.* Durham, NC: Duke University Press, 2004.

———, ed. *Formations of Colonial Modernity in East Asia.* Durham. NC: Duke University Press, 1997.

———, ed. *Gender Politics in China: Writing and Feminism.* Durham, NC: Duke University Press, 1993.

———, ed. and trans. *I Myself Am a Woman: Selected Writings of Ding Ling.* Boston: Beacon Press, 1989.

Barnett, Suzanne, and John Fairbank, eds. *Christianity in China: Early Protestant Missionary Writings.* Cambridge, MA: Council on East Asian Studies, Harvard University, 1985.

Bataille, Georges. *Visions of Excess: Selected Writings, 1927–1939.* Trans. Allan Stoekl. Minneapolis: University of Minnesota Press, 1985.

Befu, Harumi, ed. *Cultural Nationalism in East Asia: Representation and Identity.* Berkeley: Institute of East Asian Studies, University of California Press, 1993.

Benjamin, Walter. *Illuminations: Essays and Reflections*. New York: Schocken Books, 1968.

―――. *The Origin of German Tragic Drama*. London and New York: Verso, 1998.

―――. *Reflections: Essays, Aphorisms, Autobiographical Writings*. New York: Schocken Books, 1978.

Benveniste, Emile. *Problems in General Linguistics*. Trans. Mary Elizabeth Meek. Coral Gables, FL: University of Miami Press, 1971.

Bergson, Henri. *Creative Evolution*. Trans. Arthur Mitchell. Mineola, NY: Dover Publications, 1998.

Bersani, Leo. *The Freudian Body: Psychoanalysis and Art*. New York: Columbia University Press, 1986.

Bhabha, Homi. *The Location of Culture*. London and New York: Routledge, 1994.

―――, ed. *Nation and Narration*. New York: Routledge, 1990.

Bickers, Robert A., and Jeffrey N. Wasserstrom. "Shanghai's 'Dogs and Chinese Not Admitted' Sign: Legend, History and Contemporary Symbol." *The China Quarterly* 142 (June 1995): 444–66.

Biheguan zhuren (Master of the sapphire lotus house). *Xin jiyuan* (New century). Shanghai: Xiaoshuolin chubanshe, 1908.

Billig, Michael. *Banal Nationalism*. London and Thousand Oaks, CA: Sage, 1995.

Blanchot, Maurice. *The Infinite Conversation*. Trans. Susan Hanson. Minneapolis: University of Minnesota, 1993.

―――. *The Unavowable Community*. Trans. Pierre Joris. Barrytown, NY: Station Hill Press, 1988.

Bloom, Harold. *The Anxiety of Influence: A Theory of Poetry*. New York: Oxford University Press, 1973.

Blumenberg, Hans. *The Legitimation of the Modern Age*. Trans. Robert M. Wallace. Cambridge, MA: MIT Press, 1983.

Bo Yang. *Chouloude Zhongguo ren* (The ugly Chinese). Taibei: Linpai chubanshe, 1985.

Bol, Peter K. *"This Culture of Ours": Intellectual Transitions in T'ang and Sung China*. Stanford: Stanford University Press, 1992.

Boulger, D. C. "Bogey of Yellow Peril." *Nineteenth Century and After* 55 (1904): 30.

Bourdieu, Pierre. *Language & Symbolic Power*. Cambridge, UK: Polity Press, 1991.

―――. *Outline of a Theory of Practice*. Cambridge: Cambridge University Press, 1977.

Braester, Yomi. *Witness Against History: Literature, Film, and Public Discourse in Twentieth-Century China*. Stanford: Stanford University Press, 2003.

Brown, Wendy. *States of Injury: Power and Freedom in Late Modernity*. Princeton, NJ: Princeton University Press, 1995.

Brownell, Susan, and Jeffery N. Wasserstrom, eds. *Chinese Femininities / Chinese Masculinities: A Reader*. Berkeley: University of California Press, 2002.

Bu Guanghua. *Guo Moruo yanjiu xinlun* (New perspectives on Guo Moruo). Beijing: Shoudu shifan daxue chubanshe, 1995.

Bucur, Maria. *Eugenics and Modernization in Interwar Romania*. Pittsburgh, PA: University of Pittsburgh Press, 2002.

Buruma, Ian. "The Joys and Perils of Victimhood." *The New York Review of Books* (04.08.1999).

Burwick, Frederick, and Paul Douglass, eds. *The Crisis in Modernism: Bergson and the Vitalist Controversy.* Cambridge and New York: Cambridge University Press, 1992.

Butler, Judith. *Precarious Life: The Powers of Mourning and Violence.* London and New York: Verso, 2004.

———. *The Psychic Life of Power: Theories in Subjection.* Stanford: Stanford University Press, 1992.

Buxiaosheng. *Liudong waishi* (An unofficial history of studying in Japan). 3 vols. Nanchang: Baihuazhou wenyi chubanshe, 1991.

Cai Yuanpei. *Cai Yuanpei jiaoyu lunji* (A collection of Cai Yuanpei's views on education). Ed. Gao Pingshu. Changsha: Hunan jiaoyu chubanshe, 1987.

Callahan, William A. "National Insecurities: Humiliation, Salvation, and Chinese Nationalism." *Alternatives* 29 (2004): 199–218.

Cao Xueqin. *Hongloumeng* (Dream of the red chamber). 3 vols. Taibei: Lianjing, 1991.

Caruth, Cathy. *Unclaimed Experience: Trauma, Narrative, and History.* Baltimore: Johns Hopkins University Press, 1996.

Certeau, Michel de. *Heterologies: Discourse on the Other.* Trans. Brian Massumi. Minneapolis: University of Minnesota Press, 1986.

Chai Shaowu. *Zhongguo bisheng* (China will certainly win). Shaoxing: Kangzhan jianguoshe, 1938.

Chang Hao. *Chinese Intellectuals in Crisis: Search for Order and Meaning, 1890–1911.* Cambridge, MA: Harvard University Press, 1971.

———. *Liang Ch'i-ch'ao and Intellectual Transition in China, 1890–1907.* Cambridge, MA: Harvard University Press, 1971.

Chang Shuei-May. *Casting Off the Shackles of Family: Ibsen's Nora Figure in Modern Chinese Literature, 1918–1942.* New York: Peter Lang, 2004.

Chatterjee, Partha. *The Nation and Its Fragments: Colonial and Postcolonial Histories.* Princeton, NJ: Princeton University Press, 1993.

———. *Nationalist Thought and the Colonial World: A Derivative Discourse.* London: Zed Books for the United Nations University, 1986.

Cheah, Pheng. *Spectral Nationality: Passages of Freedom from Kant to Postcolonial Literatures of Liberation.* New York: Columbia University Press, 2003.

Chen Changheng and Zhou Jianren. *Jinhualun yu shanzhongxue* (Evolution and eugenics). Shanghai: Shangwu yinshu guan, 1923.

Chen Huidao. *Kang Youwei Datongshu yanjiu* (A study of Kang Youwei's *The book of the great union*). Guangdong: Guangdong renmin chubanshe, 1994.

Chen Ma. *Goutong yu gengxin: Lu Xun yu Riben wenxue guanxi fawei* (Communication and renewal: An inquiry into Lu Xun's relationship to Japanese literature). Beijing: Zhongguo shehui kexue chubanshe, 1990.

Chen Peng-Hsiang and Whitney Crothers Dilley, eds. *Feminism / Femininity in Chinese Literature.* Amsterdam: Rodopi, 2002.

Chen Pingyuan. *Chen Pingyuan Zhongguo xiaoshuo shi lunji* (Collected essays by Chen Pingyuan on the history of fiction in China). 3 vols. Shijiazhuang: Hebei renmin chubanshe, 1997.

Chen Pingyuan and Xia Xiaohong, eds. *Ershi shiji Zhongguo xiaoshuo lilun ziliao 1897–1916* (Theoretical materials of Chinese novels in the twentieth century 1897–1916). Beijing: Beijing daxue chubanshe, 1989.

Chen Shanwei, ed. *Tang Caichang nianpu changbian* (An expanded edition of the chronology of Tang Caichang). 2 vols. Hong Kong: Zhongwen daxue chubanshe, 1990.

Chen Shoufan, ed. and trans. *Renzhong gailiangxue* (The study of racial improvement). Shanghai: Shangwu yinshu guan, 1919.

Chen Shuyu, ed. *Lu Xu lunzheng ji* (Collection of debates over Lu Xun). 2 vols. Shanghai: Zhongguo shehui kexue chubanshe, 1998.

———, ed. *Shuobujin de A Q: wuchu buzai de hunling* (The inexhaustible Ah Q: A spirit everywhere). Beijing: Zhongguo wenlian chuban gongsi, 1997.

Chen Song, ed. *Wusi qianhou dongxi wenhua wenti lunzhan wenxuan* (Debates on Eastern and Western cultures before and after the May Fourth period). Beijing: Zhongguo shehui kexue chubanshe, 1989.

Chen Tianhua. *Chen Tianhua ji* (Chen Tianhua collection). Shanghai: Zhongguo wenhua fuwuhui, 1946.

Chen Tiesheng, Tang Hao, and Lu Weichang, eds. *Guoshu daguan* (A comprehensive view of martial arts). Shanghai: Zhenmin bianji hui, 1929.

Chen Xiaomei. *Occidentalism: A Theory of Counter-Discourse in Post-Mao China.* Oxford: Oxford University Press, 1995.

Chen Zishan and Wang Zili, eds. *Yu Dafu yanjiu ziliao* (Research materials on Yu Dafu). 2 vols. Tianjin: Tianjin renmin chubanshe, 1982.

Chen, Jerome. *China and the West: Society and Culture, 1815–1937.* Bloomington: Indiana University Press, 1979.

Chen, Yu-shih. *Realism and Allegory in the Early Fiction of Mao Dun.* Bloomington: Indiana University Press, 1986.

Cheng, Anne. *The Melancholy of Race.* New York: Oxford University Press, 2000.

Cheung, Martha P. Y. "The Discourse of Occidentalism? Wei Yi and Lin Shu's Treatment of Religious Material in Their Translation of *Uncle Tom's Cabin.*" In David Pollard, ed., *Translation and Creation: Readings of Western Literature in Early Modern China, 1840–1918,* pp. 127–50. Philadelphia: Benjamins Publishing, 1998.

Chiang Kai-shek. *Xin shenghuo yundong gangyao* (Outline of the New Life Movement). Shanghai: Zhonghua shuju, 1936.

Ching, Leo T. S. *Becoming "Japanese": Colonial Taiwan and the Politics of Identity Formation.* Berkeley: University of California Press, 2001.

Chong You. "Lun Zhongguo minqi zhi keyong" (On the use of Chinese people's essence). *Dongfang zazhi* 1.1 (1904): 5–7.

Chow, Rey. *Ethics After Idealism: Theory, Culture, Ethnicity, Reading.* Bloomington: Indiana University Press, 1998.

———. *Primitive Passions: Visuality, Sexuality, Ethnography, and Contemporary Chinese Cinema.* New York: Columbia University Press, 1995.

Chow Tse-Tsung. *The May Fourth Movement: Intellectual Revolution in Modern China.* Cambridge, MA: Harvard University Press, 1964.

Choy, Philip P., Lorraine Dong, and Marlon K. Hom, eds. *Coming Man: 19th Century American Perceptions of the Chinese.* Hong Kong: Joint Publishing, 1994.

Chua, Amy. *World on Fire: How Exporting Free Market Democracy Breeds Ethnic Hatred and Global Instability*. New York: Doubleday, 2003.

Chung, Yuehtsun Juliette. *Struggle for National Survival: Eugenics in Sino-Japanese Contexts, 1896–1945*. New York: Routledge, 2002.

"Chunliushe yanyibu zhuanzhang" (Statement of purpose for the performance department of Spring Willow Society). In A Ying, ed., *Wanqing wenxue congchao: xiaoshuo xiqu yanjiu juan* (A collection of late Qing literature: fiction and drama), pp. 635–38. Beijing: Zhonghua shuju, 1960.

Cohen, Paul A. *Discovering History in China: American Historical Writing on the Recent Chinese Past*. New York: Columbia University Press, 1984.

———. "Remembering and Forgetting: National Humiliation in Twentieth-Century China." *Twentieth-Century China* 27.2 (April 2002): 1–39.

Cohen, Paul A., and Merle Goldman, eds. *Ideas Across Cultures: Essays on Chinese Studies*. Cambridge, MA: Harvard University Press, 1990.

Craig, Gordon A. *Germany, 1866–1945*. New York and Oxford: Oxford University Press, 1978.

Crossley, Pamela. *A Translucent Mirror: History and Identity in Qing Imperial Ideology*. Berkeley: University of California Press, 1999.

"Daci dabei jiuku jiunan aiguo xinjing" (Heart mantra of great benevolence and compassion, saving one from hardship and trouble, and loving the nation). *Hangzhou baihuabao* 22 (1903): 1–2.

Dai Jinhua and Meng Yue. *Fuchu lishi dibiao* (Emerging from the horizon of history). Zhengzhou: Henan renmin chubanshe, 1989.

Davenport, Charles Benedict. *Heredity in Relation to Eugenics* (Renzhong gailiang-xue). Trans. Chen Shoufan. Shanghai: Shangwu yinshu guan, 1919.

De Lauretis, Teresa. *Technologies of Gender: Essays on Theory, Film, and Fiction*. Bloomington and Indianapolis: Indiana University Press, 1987.

De Man, Paul. *Allegories of Reading: Figural Language in Rousseau, Nietzsche, Rilke, and Proust*. New Haven, CT, and London: Yale University Press, 1979.

———. *Blindness and Insight: Essays in the Rhetoric of Contemporary Criticism*. Minneapolis: University of Minnesota Press, 1983.

Debon, Günter, and Adrian Hsia, eds. *Goethe und China—China und Goethe*. Bern: Peter Lang, 1985.

Deleuze, Gilles. *Bergsonism*. Trans. Hugh Tomlinson and Barbara Habberjam. New York: Zone Books, 1991.

———. "Coldness and Cruelty." In *Masochism, an Interpretation of Coldness and Cruelty*. New York: Zone Books, 1991.

———. *The Logic of Sense*. Trans. Mark Lester. New York: Columbia University Press, 1990.

Denton, Kirk A. *The Problematic of Self in Modern Chinese Literature: Hu Feng and Lu Ling*. Stanford: Stanford University Press, 1998.

Derrida, Jacques. *Dissemination*. Trans. Barbara Johnson. Chicago: University of Chicago Press, 1983.

———. *Margins of Philosophy*. Trans. Alan Bass. Brighton, Sussex, UK: Harvester Press, 1982.

Dikötter, Frank. *The Discourse of Race in Modern China*. Stanford: Stanford University Press, 1992.

————. *Imperfect Conceptions: Medical Knowledge, Birth Defects, and Eugenics in China.* New York: Columbia University Press, 1998.

Ding Fengjia. "Zhongri erguo tong zai yazhou tong wei huangzhong you tongshi yu oumei tongshang er qiangruo xuanshu zhi ci qi gu he yu?" (Why is it that China and Japan, both in Asia and both members of the yellow race who simultaneously have commercial dealings with Europe and America, differ so greatly in strength and weakness?). *Dongfang zazhi* 1.4 (1905): 11–15.

Dirlik, Arif. *Anarchism in the Chinese Revolution.* Berkeley: University of California Press, 1991.

————. "The Ideological Foundations of the New Life Movement: A Study in Counterrevolution." *Journal of Asian Studies* 4 (1975): 945–80.

Dirlik, Arif, and Zhang Xudong, eds. *Postmodernism and China.* Durham, NC: Duke University Press, 1997.

Dooling, Amy D., and Kristina M. Torgeson, eds. *Writing Women in Modern China: An Anthology of Women's Literature from the Early Twentieth Century.* New York: Columbia University Press, 1998.

"Du xiren huanghuo shuo ganyan" (Thoughts after reading Westerners' views on the "yellow peril"). *Waijiaobao* 204 (1908): 325–28.

Duara, Prasenjit. *Rescuing History from the Nation: Questioning Narratives of Modern China.* Chicago: University of Chicago Press, 1995.

————. *Sovereignty and Authenticity: Manchuko and the East Asian Modern.* Lanham, MD: Rowman and Littlefield Publishers, 2003.

"E huo" (The Russian peril). *Jingzhong ribao* (02.05.1904).

Eastman, Lloyd E. *The Abortive Revolution: China Under Nationalist Rule, 1927–1937.* Cambridge, MA: Harvard University Press, 1974.

Elliott, Mark C. *The Manchu Way: The Eight Banners and Ethnic Identity in Late Imperial China.* Stanford: Stanford University Press, 2001.

Ellis, Havelock. *The Task of Social Hygiene.* Boston: Houghton Mifflin, 1912.

Elman, Benjamin A. "Naval Warfare and the Refraction of China's Self-Strengthening Reforms into Scientific and Technological Failure." *Modern Asian Studies* 38.2 (2003): 283–326.

Eng, David L. *Racial Castration: Managing Masculinity in Asia America.* Durham, NC: Duke University Press, 2001.

Engelstein, Laura. *The Keys to Happiness: Sex and the Search for Modernity in Fin-de-Siècle Russia.* Ithaca, NY: Cornell University Press, 1992.

Fan Boqun, ed. *Zhongguo jinxiandai tongsu wenxueshi* (A history of popular literature in late imperial and modern China). 2 vols. Nanjing: Jiansu jiaoyu chubanshe, 2000.

Fan Boqun and Zhu Donglin, eds. *Zhongwai wenxue bijiaoshi 1898–1949* (A history of Chinese and international comparative literature). 2 vols. Nanjing: Jiangsu jiaoyu chubanshe, 1993.

Fang Bi (Mao Dun). "Lu Xun lun" (On Lu Xun). *Xiaoshuo yuebao* 18.11 (1927): 37–48.

Fang Shi. "Lun xue guochou yi xianli guochi" (In order to avenge national hatred one should first encourage national humiliation). *Dongfang zazhi* 1.4 (1904): 65–67.

Fang Xiu, ed. *Mahua xin wenxue daxi, 1919–1942* (Compendium on new Malaysian

Chinese literature, 1919–1942). Vol. 1. Kuala Lumpur and Singapore: Popular Books, 2000.

Fanon, Frantz. *Black Skin, White Masks.* Trans. Charles Lam Markmann. New York: Grove Press, 1967.

——. *The Wretched of the Earth.* New York: Grove Press, 1963.

"Fei tongzhong tongwen" (Not of the same race and culture). *Waijiaobao* 12 (1902): 105–9.

Fei Xiaotong. *Meiguoren xingge* (The character of the Americans). Shanghai: Shenghuo shudian, 1947.

"Feilibin wangguo canzhuang ji lue" (A record of the horrendous circumstance of the perished nation Philippines). *Cuixinbao* 1 (1904): 1–6.

Felman, Shoshana. *The Literary Speech Act: Don Juan with J. L. Austin, or Seduction in Two Languages.* Ithaca, NY: Cornell University Press, 1983.

Feng Xianguang. "Lun *Sanyeji* de wenhua jiazhi yishi" (On the consciousness of cultural values in *Trefoil*). In Zhongguo Guo Moruo yanjiuhui, ed., *Guo Moruo yu dongxi wenhua* (Guo Moruo and Eastern and Western cultures), pp. 335–48. Beijing: Dangdai Zhongguo chubanshe, 1998.

Feng Zikai, trans. *Kumen de xiangzheng* (Symbol of angst). Shanghai: Shangwu yinshu guan, 1925.

Ferry, Megan Marie. "Chinese Women Writers of the 1930s and Their Critical Reception." Diss. (Washington University, 1998).

Feuerwerker, Yi-tsi Mei. *Ding Ling's Fiction: Ideology and Narrative in Modern Chinese Literature.* Cambridge, MA: Harvard University Press, 1982.

Findeisen, Raoul David. "Die Last der Kultur: Vier Fallstudien zur chinesischen Nietzsche-Rezeption." *Minima Sinica* 2 (1989): 1–42; 1(1990): 1–40.

Fitzgerald, John F. *Awakening China: Politics, Culture, and Class in the Nationalist Revolution.* Stanford: Stanford University Press, 1996.

Fogel, Joshua. *The Cultural Dimension of Sino-Japanese Relations: Essays on the Nineteenth and Twentieth Centuries.* Armonk, NY: Sharpe, 1995.

Foucault, Michel. *Discipline and Punish: The Birth of the Prison.* New York: Vintage, 1979.

——. *The Order of Things: An Archaeology of Human Sciences.* New York: Vintage Books, 1994.

——. "The Subject and Power." In Hubert L. Dreyfus and Paul Rabinow, eds., *Michel Foucault: Beyond Structuralism and Hermeneutics.* Chicago: University of Chicago Press, 1982.

Freeman, R. B. "Darwin in Chinese." *Archives of Natural History* 13 (1986): 19–24.

Freud, Sigmund. *The Standard Edition of the Complete Psychological Works of Sigmund Freud.* Ed. and trans. James Strachey. 24 vols. London: Hogarth Press, 1953–74.

Fu Shaozeng. *Zhongguo minzuxing zhi yanjiu* (A study of Chinese national character). Beiping: Beiping wenhua xueshe, 1929.

Furth, Charlotte, ed. *The Limits of Change: Essays on Conservative Alternatives in Republican China.* Cambridge, MA: Harvard University Press, 1976.

Gadamer, Hans-Georg. *Truth and Method.* New York: Continuum Publishing, 1995.

Gálik, Marián. *The Genesis of Modern Chinese Literary Criticism, 1917–1930.* London: Curzon Press, 1980.

Galton, Francis. *Hereditary Genius, an Inquiry into Its Laws and Consequences.* London: Macmillan, 1869.

Gang Yue. *The Mouth That Begs: Hunger, Cannibalism, and the Politics of Eating in Modern China.* Durham, NC: Duke University Press, 1999.

Gao Chuiwan. "Guanyu 'Ziyou jiehun' erti" (Two verses on *Freedom of marriage*). In A Ying, ed., *Wanqing wenxue congchao: xiaoshuo xiqu yanjiu juan* (A collection of late Qing literature: fiction and drama), p. 574. Beijing: Zhonghua shuju, 1960.

Gao Huaichuan. *Zhongguo minzu de bingyuan ji zhiliaofa* (The source of illness and treatment for the Chinese race). Shanghai: Minzhi shuju, 1929.

Gaoyang bucaizi (The untalented from Gaoyang). "Dian shijie" (Electrical world). *Xiaoshuo shibao* (Fiction times) 1 (1909): 1–58.

Gates, Henry Louis, Jr., ed. *"Race," Writing, and Difference.* Chicago: University of Chicago Press, 1986.

Gebauer, Gunter, and Christoph Wulf. *Mimesis: Culture, Art, Society.* Trans. Don Reneau. Berkeley, Los Angeles, and London: University of California Press, 1992.

Gellner, Ernest. *Nations and Nationalism.* Oxford: Blackwell, 1983.

Gen Zhimin. "Jiehe zhi yufang" (The prevention of tuberculosis). *Yishi yuekan* 5 (1924): 1–5; 9 (1924): 1–4; 10 (1924): 1–6.

Giddens, Anthony. *Modernity and Self-Identity: Self and Society in the Late Modern Age.* Stanford: Stanford University Press, 1991.

———. *The Nation-State and Violence.* Berkeley and Los Angeles: University of California Press, 1985.

Gilman, Susan. *Blood Talk: American Race Melodrama and the Culture of the Occult.* Chicago: Chicago University Press, 2003.

Gilmartin, Christina Kelley. *Engendering the Chinese Revolution: Radical Women, Communist Politics, and Mass Movements in the 1920s.* Berkeley, Los Angeles, and London: University of California Press, 1995.

Gilroy, Paul. *The Black Atlantic: Modernity and Double Consciousness.* Cambridge, MA: Harvard University Press, 1993.

Glazer, Nathan. *We Are All Multiculturalists Now.* Cambridge, MA, and London: Harvard University Press, 1997.

Goldblatt, Howard, trans. *Market Street: A Chinese Woman in Harbin.* Seattle: University of Washington Press, 1986.

Goldman, Merle, ed. *Modern Chinese Literature in the May Fourth Era.* Cambridge, MA: Harvard University Press, 1977.

Gollwitzer, Heinz. *Die Gelbe Gefahr: Geschichte eines Schlagworts. Studien zum imperialistischen Denken.* Gottingen, Germany: Vandenhoeck and Ruprecht, 1962.

Gong Baosun. "Xiandai qingnian zhi bingtai yu jiuji" (The illness of modern youths and its remedy). *Xuesheng zazhi* 6 (1930): 11–15.

Gould, Stephen Jay. *The Mismeasure of Man: The Definitive Refutation to the Argument of the Bell Curve.* New York and London: Norton, 1981.

Gourgouris, Stathis. *Dream Nation: Enlightenment, Colonization, and the Institution of Modern Greece.* Stanford: Stanford University Press, 1996.

Graham, Joseph F., ed. *Difference in Translation.* Ithaca, NY: Cornell University Press, 1985.

Grewal, Inderpal, and Caren Kaplan, eds. *Scattered Hegemonies: Postmodernity and Transnational Feminist Practices*. Minneapolis: University of Minnesota Press, 1994.

Gries, Peter Hayes. *China's New Nationalism: Pride, Politics, and Diplomacy*. Berkeley: University of California Press, 2004.

Grogin, R. C. *The Bergsonian Controversy in France 1900–1914*. Calgary: University of Calgary Press, 1988.

Grosse, Pascal. *Kolonialismus, Eugenik und bürgerliche Gesellschaft in Deutschland 1850–1918*. Frankfurt/Main: Campus Verlag GmbH, 2000.

Gu Hongming. *Zhongguo ren de jingshen* (The spirit of the Chinese people). Beijing: Beijing meiri xinwenhui, 1915.

Gu Nong. "Lu Xun yu *Kumen de xiangzheng*" (Lu Xun and *Symbol of angst*). *Lu Xun yanjiu ziliao* (Research materials on Lu Xun) 13 (1980): 235–54.

Gu Yin. "Bian huanghuo zhi shuo" (Arguing against the "yellow peril"). *Dongfang zazhi* 2.2 (1905): 32–35.

———. "Bo tuihua lun" (Against the theory of degeneration). *Dongfang zazhi* 1.11 (1904): 259–62.

———. "Lun Zhongguo qiantu yu yixue zhi guanxi" (On the relationship between China's future and medical science). *Dongfang zazhi* 2.6 (1905): 107–14.

———. "Tuihua lun" (On degeneration). *Dongfang zazhi* 1.11 (1904): 256–59.

Guang Sheng. "Zhongguo guomin xing jiqi ruodian" (The Chinese national character and its weakness). *Xin qingnian* 2.6 (1917): 495–505.

"Guangbu weisheng shuji yi qiang zhonglei shuo" (On circulating books on hygiene in order to strengthen the race). *Dongfang zazhi* 1.8 (1904): 177–78.

Guazi. "Minri zhi guafen" (Tomorrow's partition). *Jiangsu* 7 (1903): 1–10.

Guha, Ranajit. *Dominance Without Hegemony: History and Power in Colonial India*. Cambridge, MA: Harvard University Press, 1997.

Guibernau, Montserrat. *Nationalisms: The Nation-State and Nationalism in the Twentieth Century*. Cambridge, UK: Polity Press, 1996.

Gulick, Sidney L. *The White Peril in the Far East: An Interpretation of the Significance of the Russo-Japanese War*. New York: Fleming H. Revell, 1905.

Gunn, Edward. *Rewriting Chinese: Style and Innovation in Twentieth-Century Chinese Prose*. Stanford: Stanford University Press, 1991.

Guo Moruo. "Guanyu Riben ren duiyu Zhongguo ren de taidu" (About the Japanese attitude toward the Chinese). *Yuzhou feng* 25 (September 1936): 19–20.

———. *Guo Moruo quanji: wenxue bian* (The complete works of Guo Moruo: Literature). 20 vols. Beijing: Renmin chubanshe, 1986.

———. *Guo Moruo shuxinji* (Collection of Guo Moruo's correspondence). Ed. Huang Chunhao. 2 vols. Beijing: Zhongguo shehui kexue chubanshe, 1992.

———. *Moruo wenji* (Moruo collection). 17 vols. Hong Kong: Sanlian shudian, 1957.

"Guochi tu 1: Jiangjun beikun" (Portrait of national humiliation 1: A general in captivity). *Anhui suhuabao* 13 (1904).

"Guochi tu 2: Baojiao shouru" (Portrait of national humiliation 2: Bound feet humiliated). *Anhui suhuabao* 13 (1904).

"Guochi tu 3: Sougua caizhu" (Portrait of national humiliation 3: Fleecing the wealthy). *Anhui suhuabao* 14 (1904).

"Guochi tu 4: Zuoren weinu" (Portrait of national humiliation 4: Capturing people to become slaves). *Anhui suhuabao* 14 (1904).

"Guochi tu 5: Shunmin beichuo" (Portrait of national humiliation 5: Obedient people abused). *Anhui suhuabao* 15 (1904).

"Guochi tu 6: Kaoda wenren" (Portrait of national humiliation 6: Torturing the literati). *Anhui suhuabao* 15 (1904).

"Guohun pian" (On the national soul). *Zhejiangchao* 1 (1903): 1–17.

"Guojia lun" (On nation). *Jingye xunbao* 12 (1908): 11–14; 14 (1909): 5–8.

"Guozi jie" (An explication of the word *guo*). *Jingye xunbao* 7 (1906): 7–10.

Haberlandt, Michael. *Völkerkunde* (Ethnology). Trans. J. E. Loewe. London: Ballantyne Hanson, 1900.

Habermas, Jürgen. *The Philosophical Discourse of Modernity: Twelve Lectures.* Trans. Frederick G. Lawrence. Cambridge, MA: MIT Press, 1993.

Hai Huo. "Yixue yu shehui zhi guanxi" (The relationship between medical science and society). *Dongfang zazhi* 2.4 (1905): 7–10.

Hanan, Patrick. *Chinese Fiction of the Nineteenth and Early Twentieth Centuries: Essays.* New York: Columbia University Press, 2004.

Hao Huazhong. *Zhongguo ren de wuxing* (The Chinese capacity for enlightenment). Shenyang: Liaoning renmin chubanshe, 1997.

Haroontunian, Harry. *Overcome by Modernity: History, Culture, and Community in Interwar Japan.* Princeton, NJ: Princeton University Press, 2000.

Harrell, Paula. *Sowing Seeds of Change: Chinese Students, Japanese Teachers, 1895–1905.* Stanford: Stanford University Press, 1992.

Hayford, Charles. "Chinese and American Characteristics: Arthur Smith and His China Book." In Suzanne W. Barnett and John K. Fairbank, eds., *Christianity in China: Early Protestant Missionary Writings.* Cambridge, MA: Harvard University Press, 1985.

Heidegger, Martin. *Was heist Denken?* Frankfurt am Main, Germany: Vittorio Klostermann, 2002.

Heinrich, Larissa N. "Handmaids to the Gospel: Lam Qua's Medical Portraiture." In Lydia Liu, ed., *Tokens of Exchange: The Problem of Translation in Global Circulations*, pp. 239–75. Durham, NC, and London: Duke University Press, 1999.

Herzfeld, Michael. *Cultural Intimacy: Social Poetics in the Nation-State.* New York: Routledge, 1997.

Hevia, James L. *English Lessons: The Pedagogy of Imperialism in Nineteenth-Century China.* Durham, NC: Duke University Press, 2003.

Hinz, Hans-Martin, and Christoph Lind, eds. *Tsingtau: Ein Kapitel deutscher Koloniegeschichte in China 1897–1914.* Eurasburg, Germany: Edition Minerva, 1998.

Hirsch, Marianne, and Evelyn Fox Keller, eds. *Conflicts in Feminism.* New York and London: Routledge, 1990.

Hobsbawm, Eric. *Nations and Nationalism Since 1780.* Cambridge: Cambridge University Press, 1990.

Hobsbawm, Eric, and Terence Ranger, eds. *The Invention of Tradition.* Cambridge: Cambridge University Press, 1983.

Hocks, Michel. *Questions of Style: Literary Societies and Literary Journals in Modern China, 1911–1937.* Leiden, The Netherlands, and Boston: Brill, 2003.

Horkheimer, Max, and Theodor W. Adorno. *Dialectic of Enlightenment*. Trans. John Cumming. New York: Continuum Publishing, 1993.

Hsia Tsi-an. *The Gate of Darkness: Studies in the Leftist Literary Movement in China*. Seattle: University of Washington Press, 1968.

Hsia, C. T. *A History of Modern Chinese Fiction*. Bloomington: Indiana University Press, 1999.

Hsu, Madeline Y. *Dreaming of Gold, Dreaming of Home: Transnationalism and Migration Between the United States and South China, 1882–1943*. Stanford: Stanford University Press, 2000.

Hu Shi. "Some Modest Proposals for the Reform of Literature." In Kirk A. Denton, ed., *Modern Chinese Literary Thought: Writings on Literature, 1893–1945*. Stanford: Stanford University Press, 1996.

Hu Ying. *Tales of Translation: Composing the New Woman in China, 1899–1918*. Stanford: Stanford University Press, 2000.

Hua Lu. "Minzu yi laolema?" (Is the race already old?). *Dongfang zazhi* 19.23 (1922): 1–2.

Hua Rucheng. *Youshengxue ABC* (Eugenics ABC). Shanghai: Shijie shuju, 1929.

Huang Jie. "Huang Shi: zhongzushu" (Yellow history: A book on race). *Guocui xuebao* 1 (1905): 1–10; 2 (1905): 1–10.

Huang Qiaosheng. "Lu Xun, Bodelaier ji shijibing" (Lu Xun, Baudelaire, and the illness of fin-de-siècle). In *Lu Xun yanjiu ziliao* (Research materials on Lu Xun), 23: 131–44. Beijing: Zhongguo wenlian chuban gongsi, 1992.

Huang Zunxian. *Huang Zunxian shixuan* (A selection of Huan Zunxian's poetry). Ed. Zhong Xianpei, Guang Lin, Xie Hua, and Wang Songtao. Guangdong: Guangdong renmin chubanshe, 1994.

"Huangbai zhongzu zhi jingzheng" (The competition between the yellow and white races). *Liumei xuesheng jibao* 1 (1914): 1–2.

"Huanghuo yuce" (The prediction of the "yellow peril"). *Jiangsu* 1 (1903): 103–7.

"Huangzhong wuhai yu baizhong lun" (The yellow race poses no harm to the white race). Trans. Pan Yan. *Changyanbao* (10.20.1898): 20–33.

"Huangzhong zhi cunwan" (The survival of the yellow race). *Qingyibao* 52 (1900): 3361–63.

"Huaren kukuang" (The bitter hardships of the Chinese). *Qingyibao* 59 (1900): 3771–72.

Hung Chang-tai. *Going to the People: Chinese Intellectuals and Folk Literature, 1918–1937*. Cambridge, MA: Council on East Asian Studies, Harvard University, 1985.

Huntington, Ellsworth. *The Character of Races as Influenced by Physical Environment, Natural Selection and Historical Development*. New York: Scribner's, 1924.

Hutcheon, Linda, and Mario J. Valdés, eds. *Rethinking Literary History*. Oxford: Oxford University Press, 2002.

Huters, Theodore. *Bringing the World Home: Appropriating the West in Late Qing and Early Republican China*. Honolulu: University of Hawaii Press, 2005.

Huters, Theodore, and Tang Xiaobing, eds. *Chinese Literature and the West: The Trauma of Realism, the Challenge of the (Post) Modern*. Durham, NC: Asian / Pacific Studies Institute, Duke University, 1991.

Hymes, Robert P. *Way and Byway: Taoism, Local Religion, and Models of Divinity in Sung and Modern China.* Berkeley: University of California Press, 2002.

Idema, Wilt L., and Beata Grant. *The Red Brush: Writing Women of Imperial China.* Cambridge, MA: Harvard University Asia Center, 2004.

Inderpal, Grewal, and Caren Kaplan, eds. *Scattered Hegemonies: Postmodernity and Transnational Feminist Practices.* Minneapolis: University of Minnesota Press, 1994.

Irigaray, Luce. *Speculum of the Other Woman.* Trans. Gillian C. Gill. Ithaca, NY, and New York: Cornell University Press, 1985.

Iriye, Akira. *China and Japan in the Global Setting.* Cambridge, MA: Harvard University Press, 1992.

Jaffrelot, Christopher, ed. *Pakistan: Nationalism Without a Nation?* London and New York: Zed Books, 2002.

Jameson, Fredric. *The Political Unconscious: Narrative as a Socially Symbolic Act.* London: Routledge, 2002.

———. "Third-World Literature in the Era of Multinational Capitalism." *Social Text* 15 (Fall 1986): 65–88.

JanMohamed, Abdul R., and David Lloyd, eds. *The Nature and Context of Minority Discourse.* New York: Oxford University Press, 1990.

Jay, Martin. *The Dialectical Imagination: A History of the Frankfurt School and the Institute of Social Research, 1923–1950.* Berkeley and Los Angeles: University of California Press, 1996.

Jia Zhifang, ed. *Zhongguo xiandai wenxue shetuan liupai* (The schools of modern Chinese literary societies). 2 vols. Jiangsu: Jiangsu jiaoyu chubanshe, 1989.

Jia Zhifang, et al., eds. *Wenxue yanjiuhui ziliao* (Research materials on Literary Research Association). 3 vols. Zhengzhou: Henan renmin chubanshe, 1985.

Jian Meng. "Meidu shi zhongzu shuaitui de yuanyin" (Syphilis is the cause of racial decline). *Dongfang zazhi* 19.7 (1922): 85–86.

———. "Minzu zhi shuaitui" (Racial decline). *Dongfang zazhi* 18.21 (1921): 1–3.

Jiang Xiaoling, trans. "Qingmou liuxuesheng: Lu Xun yu Zhou Zuoren" (Students abroad during the late Qing: Lu Xun and Zhou Zuoren). *Lu Xun yanjiu yuekan* 6 (1996): 43–55.

Jiang Zheng. *Rende jiefang yu yishu de jiefang: Guo Moruo yu Gede* (Liberating the man and liberating art: Guo Moruo and Goethe). Jilin: Shidai wenyi chubanshe, 1991.

Jiang Zhiyou. *Zhongguo renzhong kao* (An inquiry into the Chinese race). Shanghai: Huatong shuju, 1929.

Jie Sizhong. *Guomin suzhi yousilu* (Worries over the national character). Beijing: Zuojia chubanshe, 1998.

Jinian Lu Xun 110 zhounian danchen xueshu taolun ji, ed. *Kongqian di minzu yingxiong: jinian Lu Xun 110 zhounian danchen xueshu taolun hui lunwen xuan* (An unprecedented national hero: Selected discussions from conference commemorating Lu Xun's 110th birthday). Xi'an: Shanxi renmin jiaoyu chubanshe, 1996.

"Jinri yang guizi yiri sheng mingjun" (Today the foreign devil, tomorrow the sagely discerning ruler). *Anhui suhuabao* 6 (1904): 39–40.

Jinyi. "Du *Heinu yu tian lu*" (Reading *A record of the black slaves lamenting, "Heaven!"*). In A Ying, ed., *Wanqing wenxue congchao: xiaoshuo xiqu yanjiu juan* (A collection of late Qing literature: Fiction and drama), p. 591. Beijing: Zhonghua shuju, 1960.

Johnson, Barbara. *The Feminist Difference: Literature, Psychoanalysis, Race, and Gender.* Cambridge, MA: Harvard University Press, 1998.

Johnson, David, Andrew Nathan, and Evelyn S. Rawski, eds. *Popular Culture in Late Imperial China.* Berkeley: University of California Press, 1985.

Jun Jian. "Wenming de paiwai yu yeman de paiwai" (Civilized and barbaric ways of rejecting the foreign). *Jingye xunbao* 5 (1906): 13–16.

Jusdanis, Gregory. *The Necessary Nation.* Princeton, NJ: Princeton University Press, 2001.

Kai Chi. "Shenmo shi 'shenjiao'?" (What is spiritual communion?). *Xin nüxing* 1.3 (1926): 189–93.

Kamachi, Noriko. *Reform in China: Huang Tsun-hsien and the Japanese Model.* Cambridge, MA: Council on East Asian Studies, Harvard University, 1981.

Kang Youwei. *Datongshu* (The book of the great union). In Zhu Weizheng, ed., *Kang Youwei datonglun liang zhong* (Kang Youwei's view on the great union: Two kinds). Hong Kong: Sanlian shudian, 1998.

———. *Kang Youwei quanji* (Complete works of Kang Youwei). Eds. Jiang Yihua and Wu Genliang. 3 vols. Shanghai: Shanghai guji chubanshe, 1992.

Karatani Kōjin. *Origins of Modern Japanese Literature.* Durham, NC: Duke University Press, 1993.

Karl, Rebecca E. *Staging the World: Chinese Nationalism at the Turn of the Twentieth Century.* Durham, NC: Duke University Press, 2002.

Karsh, Efraim, and Inari Karsh. *Empires of the Sand: The Struggle for Mastery in the Middle East 1789–1923.* Cambridge, MA: Harvard University Press, 1999.

Kedourie, Elie. *Nationalism.* Oxford and Cambridge, MA: Blackwell, 1993.

Kennedy, Randall. *Nigger: The Strange Career of a Troublesome Word.* New York: Pantheon, 2002.

Kevles, Daniel J. *In the Name of Eugenics: Genetics and the Uses of Human Heredity.* Cambridge, MA: Harvard University Press, 1995.

Kinkley, Jeffrey C. *Chinese Justice, the Fiction: Law and Literature in Modern China.* Stanford: Stanford University Press, 2000.

Kirby, William. *Germany and Republican China.* Stanford: Stanford University Press, 1984.

Kristeva, Julia. *Black Sun: Depression and Melancholia.* Trans. Leon S. Rondiez. New York: Columbia University Press, 1989.

Kubin, Wolfgang. "Der Junge Mann als Melancholiker: Ein Versuch zu Yu Dafu (1886–1945)." *Minima Sinica* 2 (1994): 15–33.

Kubin, Wolfgang, and Rudolf G. Wagner, eds. *Essays in Modern Chinese Literature and Literary Criticism.* Bochum, Germany: Herausgeber Chinathemen, 1982.

Kühl, Stefan. *Die Internationale der Rassisten: Aufstieg und Niedergang der internationalen Bewegung für Eugenik und Rassenhygiene im 20. Jahrhundert.* Frankfurt am Main, Germany: Campus Surkamp GmbH, 1997.

Kuhn, Philip A. *The Homeland: Thinking About the History of Chinese Overseas.* Canberra: Australia National University, 1997.

Kuriyagawa Hakuson. "Bingde xingyu yu wenxue" (Perverse libido and literature). *Xiaoshuo yuebao* (Short story monthly) 5 (1925): 1–9.

———. "Jindai de nian ai guan" (Recent outlook on love). *Fünu zazhi* 8.2 (1922): 7–12.

————. *Kuriyagawa Hakuson shū* (Kuriyagawa collection). 6 vols. Tokyo: Kuriyagawa Hakuson Shū Kankokai, 1924–25.

————. "Wenyi yu xingyu" (Literature and libido). *Xiaoshuo yuebao* 7 (1925): 1–4.

Lacan, Jacques. *Écrits*. Trans. Alan Sheridan. New York: Norton, 1977.

Lacapra, Dominick. *Writing History, Writing Trauma*. Baltimore, MD: Johns Hopkins University Press, 2001.

Lach, Donald F. *Asia in the Making of Europe*. 3 vols. Chicago and London: University of Chicago Press, 1965.

Lackner, Michael, Iwo Amelung, and Jochim Kurtz, eds. *New Terms for New Ideas: Western Knowledge and Lexical Change in Late Imperial China*. Leiden, The Netherlands: Brill, 2001.

Lacoue-Labarthe, Philippe. *Typography: Mimesis, Philosophy, Politics*. Ed. Christopher Fynsk. Stanford: Stanford University Press, 1998.

Lane, Christopher, ed. *The Psychoanalysis of Race*. New York: Columbia University Press, 1998.

Laplanche, Jean. *Life and Death in Psychoanalysis*. Trans. Jeffrey Mehlman. Baltimore: Johns Hopkins University Press, 1976.

Larson, Wendy. *Women and Writing in Modern China*. Stanford: Stanford University Press, 1998.

Latourette, Kenneth Scott. *The Development of China*. Boston and New York: Houghton Mifflin, 1917.

Lau, Joseph S. M., and Howard Goldblatt, eds. *The Columbia Anthology of Modern Chinese Literature*. New York: Columbia University Press, 1995.

Leary, Charles. "Sexual Modernism in China: Zhang Jingsheng and 1920s Urban Culture." Diss. (Cornell University, 1994).

Lee, Leo Ou-Fan. *The Romantic Generation of Modern Chinese Writers*. Cambridge, MA: Harvard University Press, 1973.

————. *Shanghai Modern*. Cambridge, MA: Harvard University Press, 1999.

————. *Voices from the Iron House: A Study of Lu Xun*. Bloomington: Indiana University Press, 1987.

Leonard, Jane Kate. *Wei Yuan and China's Rediscovery of the Maritime World*. Cambridge, MA: Council on East Asian Studies, Harvard University, 1984.

Lepenies, Wolf. *Melancholy and Society*. Trans. Jeremy Gaines and Doris Jones. Cambridge, MA: Harvard University Press, 1992.

Leutner, Mechthild. *Deutsch–chinesische Beziehungen vom 19. Jahrhundert bis zur Gegenwart: Beiträge des internationalen Symposiums in Berlin*. Ed. Kuo Heng yü and Mechthild Leutner. Munich, Germany: Minerva, 1991.

————, ed. *Musterkolonie Kiautschou: Die Expansion des Deutschen Reiches in China: deutsch-chinesische Beziehungen 1897 bis 1914: eine Quellensammlung*. Berlin, Germany: Akademie Verlag, 1997.

Levenson, Joseph. *Confucian China and Its Modern Fate: A Trilogy*. Berkeley: University of California Press, 1968.

Levinas, Emmanuel. *Totality and Infinity: An Essay on Exteriority*. Trans. Alphonso Lingis. Pittsburgh, PA: Duquesne University Press, 1961.

Li Hongkuan. "Fu: Zhongguo xing jiaoyu de qianqu—Zhang Jingsheng" (Appendix: The pioneer of China's sex education—Zhang Jingsheng). In *Zhang Jing-*

sheng wenji (Zhang Jingsheng collection), 2 vols., 2 : 448 – 53. Guangzhou: Guangzhou chubanshe, 1998.

Li Jikai. *Minzu hun yu Zhongguo ren* (Racial spirit and the Chinese). Xi'an: Shanxi
renmin jiaoyu chubanshe, 1996.

Li Sizhen. "Kang Youwei yu *Datongshu*" (Kang Youwei and *The book of the great
union*). In Li Sizhen, ed., *Datongshu* (The book of the great union). Zhengzhou:
Zhongchuan guji chubanshe, 1998.

Li Yiyuan and Yang Guoshu, eds. *Zhongguo ren de xingge* (The character of the Chinese). Taibei: Institute of Ethnology, Academia Sinica, 1972.

Li Wai-yee. *Enchantment and Disenchantment: Love and Illusion in Chinese Literature*.
Princeton, NJ: Princeton University Press, 1993.

Liang Boqiang. "Yixue shangde Zhongguo minzu—hanzu—zhi yanjiu" (The
study of the Chinese race—the Han race—in medical science). *Dongfang zazhi*
13 (1926): 87–100.

Liang Qichao. *Liang Qichao quanji* (The complete works of Liang Qichao). Ed. Yang
Gang and Wang Xiangyi. 10 vols. Beijing: Beijing chubanshe, 1999.

———. *Yinbingshi heji* (Collated edition of ice drinking studio). 12 vols. Beijing:
Zhonghua shuju, 1989.

———. "Zhichi xuehui xu" (Preface to the Learning Society of Knowing Shame).
Shiwubao 40 (1897): 2705–7.

———. "Zhongguo renzhong zhi jianglai" (On the future of the Chinese race).
Qingyibao 19 (1899): 1183–92.

———. *Zhongguo zhi wushidao* (China's Bushido spirit). Shanghai: N.p., 1904.

Liang Xing. *Zhongguo biwang lun* (On China's inevitable death). Shanghai: Rixingyu
dixueshe, 1921.

Lieberman, Sally Taylor. *The Mother and Narrative Politics in Modern China*. Charlottesville and London: University Press of Virginia, 1998.

Lin Huixiang, ed. and trans. *Shijie renzhong zhi* (An encyclopedia of the world's
races). Shanghai: Shangwu yinshu guan, 1932.

Lin Jicheng. "Fuluoyide de xueshuo zai Zhongguo de chuanbo, 1914–1924"
(The dissemination of Freudian theory in China, 1914–1924). *Ershiyi shiji* 4
(April 1991): 20–31.

Lin Mohan and Wei Wei, eds. *Women tuoqi nazhong Zhongguo ren* (We spit on that
kind of Chinese). Lanzhou: Gansu renmin chubanshe, 1999.

Lin Shu. "'Yishuo yuyan' erti" (Two prefatory remarks on *Aesop's tales*). In A Ying,
ed., *Wanqing wenxue congchao: chengwai wenxue yiwen juan* (A collection of late Qing
literature: Fiction and drama), pp. 199–204. Beijing: Zhonghua shuju, 1960.

———, trans. *Minzhongxue* (Ethnology). 2 vols. Beijing: Beijing daxuetang guanshuju, 1903.

Lin Shu and Wei Yi, trans. *Heinu yu tian lu* (A record of the black slaves lamenting,
"Heaven!"). Beijing: Shangwu yinshu guan, 1981.

Lin Yongxuan. "Lun ershi shiji guoji jingzheng shengbai zhi zong yuanyin ji Zhongguo yu shijie shang zhi weizhi" (On the outcome of international competitions
in the twentieth century and China's position in the world). *Dongfang zazhi* 4.8
(1907): 39–51.

Lin Yusheng (Lin Yü-sheng). *The Crisis of Chinese Consciousness: Radical Anti-traditionalism in the May Fourth Era*. Madison: University of Wisconsin Press, 1979.

————. "Lu Xun geren zhuyi de xingzhi yu hanyi: jianlun 'guomingxing' wenti" (The nature and meaning of Lu Xun's individualism: Also on the question of "national character"). *Ershiyi shiji* 12 (August 1992): 83–91.

Lin Yutang. *My Country and My People.* New York: John Day, 1939.

Lindquist, Harvey M. "Arthur Henderson Smith: A Study in Ambivalence." MA thesis (Harvard University, 1962).

Ling Shi. "Du *Heinu yu tian lu*" (Reading *A record of the black slaves lamenting, "Heaven!"*). *Juemin* 7 (1904): 29–32.

Link, Perry. *Mandarin Ducks and Butterflies: Popular Fiction in Early Twentieth-Century Chinese Cities.* Berkeley: University of California Press, 1981.

"Lishi shang huangbai liangzhong zhi jingzheng" (The competition between the yellow and white races in history). *Dongfang zazhi* 13 (1906): 248–50.

Liu Delong. "Wanqing zhishi fenzi xintai de xiezhao" (A portrait of the mind-set of late Qing intellectuals). *Mingqing xiaoshuo yanjiu* (Study of Ming and Qing fiction) 32 (1994): 92–98.

Liu Kang and Tang Xiaobing, eds. *Politics, Ideology, and Literary Discourse in Modern China: Theoretical Interventions and Cultural Critique.* Durham, NC: Duke University Press, 1993.

Liu Maoling, Ye Guisheng, et al. *Guo Moruo xinlun* (A new perspective on Guo Moruo). Beijing: Shehui kexue wenxian chubanshe, 1992.

Liu Shipei. *Liu Shenshu xiansheng yishu* (The posthumous works of Lu Shipei). Nanjing: Jiangsu guji chubanshe, 1997.

————. *Zhongguo minzu zhi* (A survey of the Chinese race). Taibei: Zhongguo minzu xiehui, 1962.

Liu Xiong. *Yichuan yu yousheng* (Heredity and eugenics). Shanghai: Shangwu yinshu guan, 1924.

Liu, Lydia H. *The Clash of Empires: The Invention of China in Modern World Making.* Cambridge, MA: Harvard University Press, 2004.

————. *Translingual Practice: Literature, National Culture, and Translated Modernity.* Stanford: Stanford University Press, 1995.

London, Jack. *Jack London: Fantastic Tales.* Ed. Dale L. Walker. Lincoln and London: University of Nebraska Press, 1998.

Lü Bing. *Dongjing meng* (Tokyo dreams). Shanghai: Zuoxinshe, 1909.

Lu Pu and Zhang Zhenkun, eds. *"Huanghuo lun" lishi ziliao xuanji* (Selected historical documents on the history of the "yellow peril"). Beijing: Zhongguo shehui kexue chubanshe, 1979.

Lu Shoujing. "Chuanzhong gailiang xinxueshuo zhi yiban" (The school that propounds the new view of improving the inheritance of race). *Zhonghua xuesheng jie* 4 (1916): 1–8.

Lu Tonglin, ed. *Gender and Sexuality in Twentieth-Century Chinese Literature and Society.* Albany: State University of New York Press, 1993.

Lu Xun. *Lu Xun quanji* (The complete works of Lu Xun). 16 vols. Beijing: Renmin chubanshe, 1981.

————. *Lu Xun quanji* (The complete works of Lu Xun). 20 vols. Hong Kong: Wenxue yanjiu she, 1973.

————. *Lu Xun shuxin ji* (Lu Xun's correspondence). Ed. Renmin wenxue chubanshe. 2 vols. Beijing: Renmin wenxue chubanshe, 1976.

————, trans. *Kumen de xiangzheng* (Symbol of angst). Tianjin: Baihua wenyi chubanshe, 2000.

Lu Yin. *Lu Yin xiaoshuo quanji* (Complete fiction works of Lu Yin). Ed. Guo Junfeng and Wang Jinting. 2 vols. Chanchun: Shidao wenyi chubanshe, 1997.

"Lun baihuo" (On the white peril). *Jingzhong ribao* (05.05.1904).

"Lun baihuo" (On the white peril). *Waijiaobao* 122 (1905): 193–202.

"Lun datong pingdeng zhi shuo bu shiyong yu jingri zhi Zhongguo (On why principles of equality and great harmony are not appropriate when applied to China today). *Dongfang zazhi* 1.12 (1904): 301–2.

"Lun E De miyue" (On the secret Russo-German treaty). *Waijiaobao* 100 (1905): 127–28.

"Lun guafen zhina" (On partitioning China). *Xiangbao* 51 (1898): 429–30; 52 (1898): 441–42.

"Lun guafen Zhongguo zhi liuyan" (On the rumor of partitioning China). *Waijiaobao* 113 (1905): 116–18.

"Lun huanghuo" (On the yellow peril). *Dongfang zazhi* 1.2 (1904): 34–36.

"Lun huanghuo" (On the yellow peril). *Waijiaobao* 72 (1904): 487–94.

"Lun huanghuo" (On the yellow peril). *Waijiaobao* 80 (1904): 545–51.

"Lun huanghuo" (On the yellow peril). *Waijiaobao* 83 (1904): 567–80.

"Lun huanghuo" (On the yellow peril). *Waijiaobao* 90 (1904): 665–68.

"Lun huanghuo" (On the yellow peril). *Waijiaobao* 103 (1905): 27–29.

"Lun huanghuo shuo zhi bu zu xin" (On the lack of evidence for the warning of the "yellow peril"). *Jingzhong ribao* (07.21.1904).

"Lun huanghuo zhi shuo buhe yu xueli" (On the illogicality of the "yellow peril"). *Jingzhong ribao* (07.23.1904).

"Lun 'huanghuo' zhi shuyu huaren" (The "yellow peril" belongs to the Chinese). *Waijiaobao* 200 (1908): 401–5.

"Lun huangzhong jianglai zhi huo" (On the future peril of the yellow race). *Qingyibao* 13 (1899): 796.

"Lun huangzhong zhi jiang xing" (On the imminent rise of the yellow race). *Waijiaobao* 268 (1909): 319–36.

"Lun huangzhong zhi zhonghe" (On the yellow race's burden). *Waijiaobao* 157 (1906): 235–38.

"Lun Riben yan tangren wenhua" (On Japan's lineage from Tang culture). *Waijiaobao* 79 (1904): 463–66.

"Lun Riben yu De zhi jinqing" (On the recent relations between Japan and Germany). *Waijiaobao* 100 (1905): 129–31.

"Lun tianyan yu mingyun" (On evolution and fate). *Dongfang zazhi* 4.9 (1907): 168–72.

"Lun Yingelusaxun huo" (On the Anglo-Saxon peril). *Waijiaobao* 83 (1904): 659–60.

"Lun Zhongguo ren duiyu shijie zhi zeren" (On Chinese responsibility to the world). *Waijiaobao* 65 (1903): 391–94.

"Lun Zhongguo ren tianyan zhi shen" (On the advanced state of the evolution of the Chinese). *Dongfang zazhi* 2.1 (1905): 24–26.

"Lun Zhongguo renmin zhi yilaixing zhi qiyuan" (On the origins of the character of dependency of the Chinese). *Dongfang zazhi* 1.5 (1904): 93–99.

"Lun Zhongguo zeren zhi zhong" (On the weight of China's responsibility). *Dong-fang zazhi* 1.1 (1904): 3–5.

"Lun Zhongguo zhi qiantu" (On the future of China). *Waijiaobao* 125 (1905): 223–28.

"Lun Zhongguo zhi qiantu ji guomin yingjin zhi zeren" (On the future of China and the responsibilities its citizens should fulfill). *Hubei xuesheng jie* (Hubei students world) 3 (1903): 319–30.

Luo Binji. *Xiao Hong xiaozhuan* (Small biography of Xiao Hong). Shanghai: Jianwen shudian, 1947.

Luo Zhitian. "National Humiliation and National Assertion: The Chinese Response to the Twenty-one Demands." *Modern Asian Studies* 27.2 (1993): 297–319.

Ma Tailai. "Lin Wei fanyi yinyuan" (The coming about of Lin Shu and Wei Yi's collaboration in translation). In Wei Weiyi, ed., *Lin Shu Wei Yi heyi xiaoshuo quanji chongkan houji* (Afterword to the re-publication of The complete collection of fiction jointly translated by Lin Shu and Wei Yi), pp. 12–29. Taibei: Wei Weiyi, 1993.

Ma Zuyi. *Zhongguo fanyi jianshi: wusi yiqian bufen* (A short history of translation in China: Before the May Fourth period). Beijing: Zhongguo duiwai fanyi chuban gongsi, 1984.

MacKinnon, Catharine A. *Only Words.* Cambridge, MA: Harvard University Press, 1993.

Mao Dun. *Mao Dun quanji* (The complete works of Mao Dun). 33 vols. Beijing: Renmin wenxue chubanshe, 1984.

Marchetti, Gina. *Romance and the "Yellow Peril": Race, Sex, and Discursive Strategies in Hollywood Fiction.* Berkeley: University of California Press, 1993.

Marcuse, Herbert. *Eros and Civilization: A Philosophical Inquiry into Freud.* Boston: Beacon Press, 1966.

Marks, Joel, and Roger T. Ames. *Emotions in Asian Thought: A Dialogue in Comparative Philosophy.* Albany: State University of New York Press, 1995.

Martin, Brian G. *The Shanghai Green Gang: Politics and Organized Crime, 1919–1937.* Berkeley and Los Angeles: University of California Press, 1996.

Masini, Frederico. *The Formation of Modern Chinese Lexicon and Its Evolution Toward a National Language: The Period from 1840–1898.* Berkeley: Project on Linguistic Analysis, University of California, 1993.

Matsuda, Mari J., et al. *Words That Wound: Critical Race Theory, Assaultive Speech, and the First Amendment.* Boulder, CO: Westview Press, 1993.

McDougall, Bonnie. *The Introduction of Western Literary Theories into Modern China, 1919–1925.* Tokyo: Centre for East Asian Cultural Studies, 1971.

———, trans. *Love-Letters and Privacy in Modern China: The Intimate Lives of Lu Xun and Xu Guangping.* Oxford and New York: Oxford University Press, 2002.

McKewon, Adam. *Chinese Migrant Networks and Cultural Change: Peru, Chicago, Hawaii, 1900–1936.* Chicago: University of Chicago Press, 2001.

"Meibao lun zhinaren yizhu" (American newspaper on Chinese immigration). *Qingyibao* 22 (1899): 1408–9.

Meisner, Maurice. *Li Ta-Chao and the Origins of Chinese Marxism.* Cambridge, MA: Harvard University Press, 1967.

Meng Yu. "Wo suo zhidao de Zhang Jingsheng" (The Zhang Jingsheng I know) (11.20.1968) [Compilation of newspaper articles on file at Cornell University]. In

Zhang Jingsheng yu Xing Shi (Zhang Jingsheng and *Sexual histories*). Author and publication date unknown.

"Mianxue ge" (Song for encouraging learning). *Anhui suhuabao* 17 (1904): 2.

"Mingchi pian" (Understanding shame). *Jingye xunbao* 1 (1906): 15–18; 2(1906): 11–18.

Minow, Martha, ed. *Breaking The Cycles of Hatred*. Princeton, NJ: Princeton University Press, 2002.

Miyoshi, Masao, and H. D. Harootunian, eds. *Learning Places: The Afterlives of Area Studies*. Durham, NC: Duke University Press, 2002.

Mohanty, Chandra. *Third World Women and the Politics of Feminism*. Bloomington: Indiana University Press, 1991.

Morioka Kenji. *Kindai go no seiritsu: Meijiki go ihen* (The evolution of modern language: The vocabulary of the Meiji era). Tokyo: Meiji shoin, 1969.

Morris, Andrew D. *Marrow of the Nation: A History of Sport and Physical Culture in Republican China*. Berkeley: University of California Press, 2004.

Mosse, George. *Nationalism and Sexuality: Middle-Class Morality and Sexual Norms in Modern Europe*. Madison: University of Wisconsin Press, 1985.

Mu Chao. *Zhongguo minzuxing* (Chinese racial character). Nanjing: Zhongshan gongji yinshu guan, 1936.

Nairn, Tom. *The Break-Up of Britain: Crisis and Neonationalism*. London: NLB and Verso Editions, 1977.

———. *Faces of Nationalism: Janus Face Revisited*. London and New York: Verso, 1997.

Nancy, Jean-Luc. *The Inoperative Community*. Trans. Peter Conner. Minneapolis: University of Minnesota Press, 1991.

Nandy, Ashis. *The Intimate Enemy: Loss and Recovery of Self Under Colonialism*. Oxford and New York: Oxford University Press, 1983.

Nelson, Cary, and Lawrence Grossberg, eds. *Marxism and the Interpretation of Culture*. Urbana: University of Illinois Press, 1988.

Ng, Mau-sang. *The Russian Hero in Modern Chinese Fiction*. Hong Kong: Chinese University Press; New York: State University of New York Press, 1988.

Nietzsche, Friedrich. *The Birth of Tragedy and the Genealogy of Morals*. Trans. Francis Golffing. New York: Anchor Books, 1956.

Nussbaum, Martha C. *For Love of Country: Debating the Limits of Patriotism*. Ed. Josh Cohen. Boston: Beacon Press, 1996.

Ouyang Lun. *Zhongguo ren de xingge* (The Chinese character). Shanxi: Shanxi renmin jiaoyu chubanshe, 1989.

Pan Guangdan. "Feng Xiaoqing: Yijian yingnian zhi yanjiu" (Feng Xiaoqing: A study of narcissism). In Pan Naigu and Pan Naihe, eds., *Pan Guangdan xuanji* (Selected works of Pan Guangdan), 1:1–67. Beijing: Guangming ribao chubanshe, 1999.

———. "Funü jiefang xinlun: jieshao yingren Pushi shi de xueshuo" (New view on women's liberation: An introduction to the work of British scholar Meyrick Booth). *Yousheng yuekan* 3 (1931).

———. "Jingshen bing zhuanjia lai hua" (A specialist on psychopathology comes to China). *Huanian* 1 (1934): 2–3.

————. "Liangfeng qingshu" (Two love letters). *Huanian* 23 (1932): 445−46.

————. "Minzu yuanqi pian" (On the primary essence of race). *Yousheng yuekan* 5 (1931): 7−13.

————. *Pan Guangdan wenji* (Pan Guangdan collection). 14 vols. Beijing: Beijing daxue chubanshe, 1995.

————. *Pan Guangdan xuanji* (Selected works of Pan Guangdan). Ed. Pan Naigu and Pan Naihe. 4 vols. Beijing: Guangming ribao chubanshe, 1999.

————. "Wudu you ou de tongxingjian sha an" (Not an isolated case of same-sex homicide). *Huanian* 11 (1932): 205−6.

————. "'Xing boshi' bei kong" ("Dr. Sex" sued). *Huanian* 2.35 (1933): 682−83.

————. *Xunqiu Zhongguo ren weiyu zhi dao: Pan Guangdan wenxuan* (In search of the way of adaptation for the Chinese: Selected works of Pan Guangdan). Ed. Pan Naimu. 2 vols. Beijing: Guoji wenhua chuban gongsi. 1997.

————. *Yousheng yu kangzhan* (Eugenics and the War of Resistance). Chongqing: Shangwu yinshu guan, 1944.

————. "Zailun Tao Liu an de diaocha buzu" (Again on the insufficient investigation into the case of Tao and Liu). *Huanian* 26 (1932): 504−5.

————. "Zaiti Tao Liu dusha an" (Again on the Tao and Liu homicide case of jealousy). *Huanian* 5 (1932): 82−83.

————. "Zhi bujiangli" (Only being unreasonable). *Huanian* 18 (1932): 347−48.

Pan Quentin (Pan Guangdan). "Eugenics in China: A Preliminary Survey of the Background." *The Eugenical News* 11 (1923): 101−10.

Parekh, Bhikhu. *Rethinking Multiculturalism: Cultural Diversity and Political Theory.* Cambridge, MA: Harvard University Press, 2000.

Park, Graham, ed. *Heidegger and Asian Thought.* Honolulu: University of Hawaii Press, 1987.

Parker, Andrew, Mary Russo, Doris Sommer, and Patricia Yaeger, eds. *Nationalisms & Sexualities.* London: Routledge, 1992.

Pei Wei. "Jiefang de funü yu funü de jiefang" (Liberated women and women's liberation). *Funü zazhi* 5.11 (1919): 1−6.

Peng Xiaoling and Han Aili, eds. *A Q: qishi nian* (Ah Q: Seventy years). Beijing: Beijing shiyue wenyi chubanshe, 1993.

Peng Xiaoyan. *Chaoyue xieshi* (Transcending realism). Taibei: Lianjing, 1993.

"Pinglun Zhongguo" (Assessing China). *Lingxuebao* 1 (01.20.1898): 14−15.

Plaks, Andrew H., ed. *Chinese Narrative: Critical and Theoretical Essays.* Princeton, NJ: Princeton University Press, 1977.

Popenoe, Paul Bowman. *Applied Eugenics.* New York: Macmillan, 1918.

Pratt, Mary Louise. *Imperial Eyes: Travel Writing and Transculturation.* London and New York: Routledge, 1992.

Price, Don. *Russia and the Roots of the Chinese Revolution 1896−1911.* Cambridge, MA: Harvard University Press, 1974.

Proctor, Robert. *Racial Hygiene: Medicine Under the Nazis.* Cambridge, MA: Harvard University Press, 1988.

Prusek, Jaroslav. *The Lyrical and the Epic: Studies of Modern Chinese Literature.* Ed. Leo Ou-Fan Lee. Bloomington: University of Indiana Press, 1980.

Pryke, Sam. "Nationalism and Sexuality: What Are the Issues?" *Nations and Nationalisms* 4 (1998): 529–46.

Puett, Michael J. *To Become a God: Cosmology, Sacrifice, and Self-Divinization in Early China.* Cambridge, MA: Harvard University Asia Center, 2002.

Pusey, James Reeve. *China and Charles Darwin.* Cambridge, MA: Harvard University Press, 1983.

Qi Youzi. *Ku xuesheng* (The suffering student). In Wang Jiquan et al., eds., *Zhongguo jindai xiaoshuo daxi* (Compendium of China's early modern fiction). 80 vols., 54:127–75. Nanchang: Baihua Wenyi chubanshe, 1993.

Qian Qian. "A Study of the Third Kind of Fluid." *Xing zazhi* 2 (1927): 3–8.

Qian Xingcun. "*Dafu daibiao zuo houxu*" (Postscript to *Dafu's representative works*). In Chen Zishan and Wang Zili, eds., *Yu Dafu yanjiu ziliao* (Research Materials on Yu Dafu). Hong Kong: Sanlian, 1986.

Qian Zhixiu, trans. "Huanghuo lun" (On the yellow peril). *Dongfang zazhi* 9.2 (1912): 40–44.

Qin Yue, trans. *Zhongguo ren de suzhi* (Chinese characteristics). Shanghai: Xuelin chubanshe, 1999.

Qiu Jin. *Qiu Jin ji* (Collected works of Qiu Jin). Beijing: Zhonghua shuju, 1960.

Qiu Shan. "Ximeng pian" (On elucidating dreams). *Dongfang zazhi* 13.12 (1916): 6–14.

Rajchman, John. *Truth and Eros: Foucault, Lacan, and the Question of Ethics.* New York and London: Routledge, 1991.

Rankin, Mary Backus. *Early Chinese Revolutionaries: Radical Intellectuals in Shanghai and Chekiang, 1902–1911.* Cambridge, MA: Harvard University Press, 1971.

Rao Hongjing et al., eds. *Chuangzao she ziliao* (Research materials on Creation Society). 2 vols. Fuzhou: Fujian renmin chubanshe, 1985.

Reik, Theodor. *Masochism in Sex and Society.* Trans. Margaret H. Beigel and Gertrude M. Kurth. New York: New Grove Press, 1962.

Ren Jiantao. *Cong zizai dao zijue: Zhongguo guominxing tantao* (From self-ease to self-awareness: An inquiry into the Chinese national character). Xi'an: Shanxi renmin chubanshe, 1992.

Renan, Ernest. "What Is a Nation?" In Homi Bhabha, ed., *Nation and Narration.* New York: Routledge. 1990.

Rhoads, Edward. *Manchus & Han: Ethnics Relations and Political Power in Late Qing and Early Republican China, 1861–1928.* Seattle: University of Washington Press, 2000.

"Ri E kaizhan yu Zhongguo zhi guanxi" (The opening of the war between Russia and Japan and its relation to China). *Jiangsu* 8 (1904): 1377–83.

Riley, Denise. *"Am I That Name?" Feminism and the Category of "Women" in History.* Minneapolis: University of Minnesota Press, 1988.

Rogaski, Ruth. *Hygienic Modernity: Meanings of Health and Disease in Treaty-Port China.* Berkeley: University of California Press, 2004.

Ronell, Avital. *Finitude's Score: Essays for the End of the Millennium.* Lincoln: University of Nebraska Press, 1994.

Ropp, Paul S. *Banished Immortal: Searching for Shuangqing, China's Peasant Woman Poet.* Ann Arbor: University of Michigan Press, 2001.

Rose, Jacqueline. *Sexuality in the Field of Vision*. London and New York: Verso, 1986.

Ru Song. "Ping youshengxue yu huanjinglun de lunzheng—Pan Guangdan, Zhou Jianren, Sun Benwen zhuren yijian de qingsuan" (An assessment of the debates over eugenics and environmental determinism—taking stock of the opinions of Pan Guangdan, Zhou Jianren, Sun Benren, et al.). *Ershi shiji* 1 (February 1931): 57–124.

Ruo Nan. "Gao jiaomin" (Telling the people). *E shi jingwen* 21 (01.04.1904).

Rusch, Beate. *Kunst- und Literaturtheorie bei Yu Dafu (1896–1945)*. Dortmund, Germany: Projekt Verlag, 1994.

Russell, Bertrand. *The Problem of China*. New York: Century, 1922.

Said, Edward. *Culture and Imperialism*. New York: Vintage Books, 1994.

San Ai. "Wangguo pian" (A treatise on perished nations). *Anhui suhua bao* 8 (1904): 1–4; 9 (1904); 10 (1904): 1–4; 13 (1904): 1–4; 15 (1904); 17 (1904): 1–4; 19 (1904): 1–4.

Sanetō Keishū. *Zhongguo ren liuxue Riben shi* (History of Chinese students in Japan). Trans. Tan Ruqian and Lin Qiyan. Hong Kong: Zhongwen daxue chubanshe, 1982.

Sassen, Saskia. *Globalization and Its Discontents: Essays on the New Mobility of People and Money*. New York: The New Press, 1998.

Satō Saburō. "Nihonjin ga Chūgoku o *Shina* to yonda koto ni tsuite no kōsatsu" (A study of the Japanese use of *shina* for China). In *Kindai Nit-Chū kōshōshi no kenkyū* (Studies in the history of modern Sino-Japanese relations), pp. 25–66. Tokyo: Yoshikawa kōbunkan, 1984.

Saussy, Haun. *The Problem of a Chinese Aesthetic*. Stanford: Stanford University Press, 1993.

Scalapino, Robert A., and George T. Yu. *Modern China and Its Revolutionary Process: Recurrent Challenges to the Traditional Order, 1850–1920*. Berkeley: University of California Press, 1985.

Schiffrin, Harold Z. *Sun Yat-sen and the Origins of the Chinese Revolution*. Berkeley: University of California, 1970.

Schiller, F. C. S. *Social Decay and Eugenical Reform*. London, Constable, 1932.

Schoenhals, Michael. *Doing Things with Words in Chinese Politics: Five Studies*. Berkeley: Institute of East Asian Studies, University of California, 1992.

Schor, Naomi. *One Hundred Years of Melancholy*. Oxford: Clarendon Press, 1996.

Schwarcz, Vera. *The Chinese Enlightenment: Intellectuals and the Legacy of the May Fourth Movement of 1919*. Berkeley: University of California Press, 1986.

Schwartz, Benjamin. *In Search of Wealth and Power: Yen Fu and the West*. Cambridge, MA: Harvard University Press, 1964.

Scott, James C. *Domination and the Arts of Resistance: Hidden Transcripts*. New Haven, CT, and London: Yale University Press, 1990.

———. *Weapons of the Weak: Everyday Forms of Peasant Resistance*. New Haven, CT, and London: Yale University Press, 1985.

Se Lu. "Funü zhi jiefang yu gaizao" (The liberation and reconstruction of women). *Funü zazhi* 12 (1919): 3–7.

Seshadri-Crooks, Kalpana. *Desiring Whiteness: A Lacanian Analysis of Race.* London and New York: Routledge, 2000.

Sha Lianxiang, ed. *Zhongguo minzu xing* (The Chinese national character). 2 vols. Beijing: Zhongguo renmin daxue chubanshe, 1989.

Shah, Nayan. *Contagious Divides: Epidemics and Race in San Francisco's Chinatown.* Berkeley: University of California Press, 2001.

Shang, Wei. *Rulin waishi and Cultural Transformation in Late Imperial China.* Cambridge, MA: Harvard University Asia Center, 2003.

Shao Bozhou. *"A Q zhengzhuan" yanjiu zongheng tan* (A comprehensive discussion of the study of *The story of Ah Q*). Shanghai: Shanghai wenyi chubanshe, 1989.

Sheffield, Devello Z. *Xinlingxue* (Mind spirit study). Trans. Guan Guoquan. Beitongzhou: Gonglihui yinziguan, 1911.

Shen Songqiao. *Xueheng pai yu wusi shiqi de fan xin wenhua yundong* (The Critical Review group: A conservative alternative to the New Culture Movement in the May Fourth era). Taipei: Guoli Taiwan daxue chubanshe, 1984.

Shen Ying, ed. *Ershi shiji Zhongguo nüxing wenxue shi* (A literary history of women's writing in the twentieth century). Tianjin: Tianjin renmin chubanshe, 1995.

"Shi chouman" (Defining hatred against the Manchus). In Zhang Nan and Wang Yenzhi, eds., *Xinhai geming qian shinianjian shilun xuanji* (A selection of contemporary views in the ten years before the Revolution of 1911), 5 vols., 1.2:678–80. Beijing: Sanlian, 1960.

Shih Shu-mei. *The Lure of the Modern: Writing Modernism in Semicolonial China, 1917–1937.* Berkeley: University of California Press, 2001.

Shu Yang, Shu Ning, and Mu Ti, trans. *Wenming yu louxi: dianxing de Zhongguo ren* (Civilization and crude habits: The typical Chinese). Taiyuan: Shuhai chubanshe, 2004.

Silverman, Kaja. *Male Subjectivity at the Margins.* New York: Routledge, 1992.

Smith, Anthony D. *The Ethnic Origins of Nations.* Oxford and New York: Blackwell, 1986.

———. *Nations and Nationalism in a Global Era.* Cambridge, UK: Polity Press, 1995.

———. *Theories of Nationalism.* London: Duckworth, 1983.

Smith, Arthur H. *Chinese Characteristics.* New York: Fleming H. Revell, 1894.

Spivak, Gayatri Chakravorty. *Outside in the Teaching Machine.* New York and London: Routledge, 1993.

Stepan, Nancy Leys. *"The Hour of Eugenics": Race, Gender, and Nation in Latin America.* Ithaca, NY, and London: Cornell University Press, 1991.

Stolz, Christa. *Hermann Knackfuss: Monographie über e. im 19. Jahrhundert in Wissen geborenen Künstler.* Wissen, Germany: Verlag G. Nising, 1975.

Stowe, Harriet Beecher. *Uncle Tom's Cabin.* Ed. Elizabeth Ammons. New York: Norton, 1994.

Sun Benwen. *Wenhua yu shehui* (Culture and society). Shanghai: Donghai shudian, 1928.

Sun Jilin. "Lin Shu he Wei Yi" (Lin Shu and Wei Yi). In Wei Weiyi, ed., *Lin Shu Wei Yi heyi xiaoshuo quanji chongkan houji* (Afterword to the re-publication of The complete collection of fiction jointly translated by Lin Shu and Wei Yi). Taibei: Wei Weiyi, 1990.

Sun Lung-kee. "The Presence of the Fin-de-Siècle in the May Fourth Era." In Gail Hershatter et al., *Remapping China: Fissures in Historical Terrain*. Stanford: Stanford University Press, 1996.

Sun Naixiu. *Foluoyide yu ershi shiji Zhongguo zuojia* (Freud and twentieth-century Chinese writers). Taibei: Yeqiang chubanshe, 1999.

———. *Foluoyide yu Zhongguo xiandai zuojia* (Freud and modern Chinese writers). Taibei: Yeqiang chubanshe, 1995.

Sun Yu. "*He 'Zhongguo ren qizhi' chuban*" (Congratulating the publication of *Chinese Characteristics*): *Lu Xun yanjiu yuekan* 5 (1996): 51–55.

Sun Zhongshan (Sun Yat-sen). *Sanmin zhuyi* (Three people's principles). In Zhongyang dangshi shiliao bianzuan weiyuanhui, ed., *Guofu quanji* (The complete works of the nation's founding father), 6 vols., 1:1–284. Taibei: Zhongguo Guomingdang zhongyang weiyuanhui, 1973.

Sun Zhongtian and Zha Guohua, eds. *Mao Dun yanjiu ziliao* (Research materials on Mao Dun). 3 vols. Beijing: Zhongguo shehui kexue chubanshe, 1983.

Sutphen, Mary P., and Bridie Andrews, eds. *Medicine and Colonial Authority*. London and New York: Routledge, 2003.

Tambiah, S. J. *Leveling Crowds*. Berkeley: University of California Press, 1996.

Tan Zhengbi. *Zhongguo nüxing wenxue shihua* (A history of women's tradition in China). Tianjin: Baihua wenyi chubanshe, 1984.

Tang Caichang. *Tang Caichang nianpu changbian* (An expanded chronology of Tang Caichang). Ed. Chen Shanwei. 2 vols. Hong Kong: Zhongwen daxue chubanshe, 1990.

Tang Wenquan and Luo Fuhui. *Zhang Taiyan sixiang yanjiu* (A study of the thought of Zhang Taiyan). Wuchang: Huazhong shifan daxue chubanshe, 1986.

Tang Xiaobing. *Global Space and the Nationalist Discourse of Modernity*. Stanford: Stanford University Press, 1996.

Tang Zhijun. *Kang Youwei yu wuxu bianfa* (Kang Youwei and the Reform Movement of 1898). Beijing: Zhonghua shuju, 1984.

Tate, Claudia. *Psychoanalysis and Black Novels: Desire and the Protocols of Race*. New York and Oxford: Oxford University Press, 1998.

Taylor, Charles. *Multiculturalism: Examining the Politics of Recognition*. Princeton, NJ: Princeton University Press, 1994.

Tian Han. "Tan 'Heinu hen'" (About "The hatred of the black slaves"). In *Tian Han quanji* (The complete works of Tian Han), 20 vols., 16:477–92. Shijiazhuang: Huashan wenyi chubanshe, 2000.

———. "Xin luoman zhuyi ji qita" (New Romanticism and others). In *Tian Han quanji* (The complete works of Tian Han), 20 vols., 14:157–90. Shijiazhuang: Huashan wenyi chubanshe, 2000.

Tong Runzhi. "Zhongguo minzu de zhili" (The intelligence of the Chinese race). *Dongfang zazhi* 26.3 (1929): 67–76.

Treat, John Whittier. *Great Mirrors Shattered: Homosexuality, Orientalism, and Japan*. New York: Oxford University Press, 1999.

Trinh Minh-ha. *Woman, Native, Other: Writing Postcoloniality and Feminism*. Bloomington: Indiana University Press, 1989.

Tu Wei-ming. *Confucian Thought: Selfhood as Creative Transformation*. Albany: State University of New York Press, 1985.

————, ed. *The Living Tree: The Changing Meaning of Being Chinese Today*. Stanford: Stanford University Press, 1994.

Uppvall, Axel Johan. *August Strindberg: A Psychoanalytical Study with Special Reference to the Oedipus Complex*. Boston: Gorham Press, 1920.

Van der Veer, Peter. *Imperial Encounters: Religion and Modernity in India and Britain*. Princeton, NJ, and Oxford: Princeton University Press, 2001.

Varshney, Ashutosh. *Ethnic Conflict and Civic Life: Hindus and Muslims in India*. New Haven, CT, and London: Yale University Press, 2002.

Vattimo, Gianni. *The Transparent Society*. Trans. David Webb. Cambridge, UK: Polity, 1992.

Vico, Giambattista. *The New Science of Giambattista Vico*. Trans. Thomas Goddard Bergin and Max Harold Fisch. Ithaca, NY, and New York: Cornell University Press, 1968.

Viswanathan, Gauri. *Masks of Conquest*. New York: Columbia University Press, 1989.

Vizenor, Gerald. *Manifest Manners: Postindian Warriors of Survivance*. Hanover, NH: University Press of New England, 1994.

"Wairen qingwu Zhongguo duoyou Zhongguo zizhao shuo" (On how foreigners' contemptuous treatment of China is largely brought about by the Chinese themselves). *Dongfang zazhi* 1.8 (1904): 161–78.

"Waiwu pian" (An essay on humiliation from the outside). *Tongzi shijie* 32 (1903): 1–7.

Wakeman, Frederic. *Policing Shanghai, 1927–1937*. Berkeley: University of California Press, 1995.

Wang Ban. *Illuminations from the Past: Trauma, Memory, and History in Modern China*. Stanford: Stanford University Press, 2004.

Wang Gungwu. *The Chinese Overseas: From Earthbound China to the Quest for Autonomy*. Cambridge, MA: Harvard University Press, 2000.

Wang Hui. "'Sai xiansheng' zai Zhongguo de mingyun: Zhongguo jinxiandai sixiangzhong de kexue gainian jiqi shiyong" (The fate of Mr. Science in China: The concept of science and its applications in modern Chinese thought). *Xueren* 1 (1991): 49–123.

Wang Ling, Wei Kaifeng, and Wang Caimei. *Huanghe, Huangtudi, Yanhuang Zisun* (Yellow river, yellow earth, the children of Shennong). Beijing: Zhongguo shudian, 1991.

Wang Xiaoming, ed. *Wenxue yanjiu hui pinglun ziliao xuan* (A selection of discussions on Literary Research Association). Vol. 1. Shanghai: Huadong shifan daxue chubanshe, 1986.

Wang Xinming. *Yousheng wenti* (Havelock Ellis's *Problems in eugenics*). Shanghai: Shangwu yinshu guan, 1924.

Wang Xunzhao, Lu Zhengyan, and Ling Minghua, eds. *Guo Moruo yanjiu ziliao* (Research materials on Guo Moruo). 3 vols. Beijing: Zhongguo shehui kexue chubanshe, 1986.

Wang Yao. *Zhongguo xin wenxue shigao* (A draft of the history of New Literature in China). Shanghai: Kaiming shudian, 1951.

Wang, David Der-wei. *Fin-de-Siècle Splendor: Repressed Modernities of Late Qing Fiction, 1849–1911*. Stanford: Stanford University Press, 1997.

———. *The Monster That Is History: History, Violence, and Fictional Writing in Twentieth Century China*. Berkeley: University of California Press, 2004.

Wang, Q. Edward. *Inventing China Through History: The May Fourth Approach to Historiography*. Albany: State University of New York Press, 2001.

"Wangchi" (Forgetting shame). *Buren* 4 (1913): 1–7.

Wei Jian. "Chuangzaoshe xianxiang" (The phenomenon of Creation Society). In Zhongguo Guo Moruo yanjiu xuehui "Guo Moruo yanjiu" bianjibu (China's Guo Moruo research society "Guo Moruo" editorial department), ed., *Guo Moruo yanjiu* (Guo Moruo research), 12:248–63. Beijing: Wenhua yishu chubanshe, 1998.

Wei Shaochang, ed. *Yuanyang hudie pai yanjiu ziliao* (Research materials on Mandarin Duck and Butterfly fiction). 2 vols. Shanghai: Shanghai wenyi chubanshe, 1984.

———, ed. *Zhongguo jindai wenxue daxi: shiliao suoyin ji* (Great compendium of late imperial Chinese literature: An index of historical sources). 2 vols. Shanghai: Shanghai shudian, 1996.

Wei, C. X. George, and Liu Xiaoyuan. *Exploring Nationalisms of China: Themes and Conflicts*. Westport, CT: Greenwood Press, 2002.

Weindling, Paul. *Health, Race, and German Politics Between National Unification and Nazism, 1870–1945*. Cambridge: Cambridge University Press, 1989.

Weingart, Peter, Jürgen Kroll, and Kurt Bayertz. *Rasse, Blut, und Gene: Geschichte der Eugenik und Rassenhygiene in Deutschland*. Frankfurt am Main, Germany: Surkamp Verlag, 1988.

"Weisheng lun" (On hygiene). *Dongfang zazhi* 2.8 (1905): 156–57.

Wen Yiduo. *Wen Yiduo quanji* (The complete works of Wen Yiduo). Ed. Sun Dangbo and Yuan Jianzheng. 12 vols. Wuhan: Hubei renmin chubanshe, 1993.

———. *Wen Yiduo shuxin xuanji* (A selection of Wen Yiduo's letters). Beijing: Renmin wenxue chubanshe, 1986.

White, Hayden. *Tropics of Discourse: Essays in Cultural Criticism*. Baltimore and London: Johns Hopkins University Press, 1978.

Whitehead, P. J. P. "Darwin in Chinese: Some Additions." *Archives of Natural History* 15 (1988): 61–62.

Widmer, Ellen. "Xiaoqing's Literary Legacy and the Place of the Woman Writer in Late Imperial China." *Late Imperial China* 13 (June 1992): 111–53.

Widmer, Ellen, and David Der-wei Wang, eds. *From May Fourth to June Fourth: Fiction and Film in Twentieth-Century China*. Cambridge, MA: Harvard University Press, 1993.

Wilhelm, Richard. *The Soul of China*. Trans. John Holroyd Reese [from *Zhongguo jingshen*, 1926]. New York: Harcourt, Brace, 1928.

Williams, Patricia J. *The Alchemy of Race and Rights: Diary of a Law Professor.* Cambridge, MA: Harvard University Press, 1991.

Wong Young-tsu (Wang Rongzu). *Search for Modern Nationalism: Zhang Binglin and Revolutionary China, 1869–1936.* Oxford: Oxford University Press, 1989.

Wu Zelin. *Xiandai zhongzu* (Modern race). Shanghai: Xinyue shudian, 1931.

Wu Zhenzi. "Women wei shenmo yao yanjiu youshengxue?" (Why should we study eugenics?). *Xuesheng zazhi* 9 (1928): 27–33.

Wu, William F. *The Yellow Peril: Chinese Americans in American Fiction 1850–1940.* Hamden, CT: Archon, 1982.

Wulaisheng (Sir Bum). "Wo xianmin maoxian xingzhi zhi yiban" (About the trait of adventurousness in our forefathers). *Fubao* 5 (1906): 59–63.

"Xi boshi xinzhu Renwen yiben" (Regarding a new work, *The origin of species* by a Western scholar). *Shenbao* (08.21.1873).

Xiamin. "*Feiliebing waishi* zixu" (An unofficial history of the Philippines). In Chen Pingyuan and Xia Xiaohong, eds., *Ershi shiji Zhongguo xiaoshuo lilun ziliao 1897–1916* (Theoretical materials of Chinese novels in the twentieth century 1897–1916). Beijing: Beijing daxue chubanshe, 1989.

Xiang Tuijie. *Zhongguo ren xingge sumiao* (A sketch of the Chinese character). Harbin: Beifang wenyi chubanshe, 1988.

Xianxiansheng. "Lun Zhongguo jiang xing" (On China's imminent rise). *Waijiaobao* 114 (1905): 119–25.

Xiao Hong. *Xiao Hong wenji.* Ed. Zhang Yumao and Yan Zhihong. 3 vols. Hefei: Anhui wenyi chubanshe, 1997.

Xiao Hong yanjiu (Studies of Xiao Hong). Ed. Beifang Luncong bianjibu (Editorial department of discussion series of the North). Harbin: Harbin shifan daxue Beifang luncong, 1983.

Xiao Junhe. *Huahunlun* (Soul of China). 3 vols. Harbin: Heilongjiang jiaoyu chubanshe, 1995.

Xiao Meng and Lin Li, eds. and trans. *Sanzhi yanjing kan Zhongguo: Riben ren de pingshuo* (Looking at China through three lenses: Japanese assessments). Beijing: Zhongguo shehui chubanshe, 1997.

Xie Jinqing. *Riben minzuxing yanjiu* (A study of the Japanese racial character). Dongjing: Longxi xhushe, 1972.

"Xieleihen" (Traces of bloody tears). *Hubei xuesheng jie* 5 (1903): 1–9.

"Xingmengge" (A song for waking from a dream). *Anhui suhuabao* 8 (1904): 33–40.

Xingshi (Awakened lion). "Ti *Heinu yu tian lu* hou" (After *A record of the black slaves lamenting, "Heaven!"*). In A Ying, ed., *Wanqing wenxue congchao: xiaoshuo xiqu yanjiu juan* (A collection of late Qing literature: Fiction and drama), p. 591. Beijing: Zhonghua shuju, 1960.

"Xingshi ge" (Song of awakening the world). *Cuixinbao* 3 (1904): 1.

"Xinnian de mengxiang" (Dreams for the new year). *Dongfang zazhi* 1 (1933): 1–82.

Xiong Yuezhi. *Xixue dongjian yu wanqing shehui* (The rise of Western learning in the East and late Qing society). Shanghai: Renmin chubanshe, 1994.

Xu Qinwen. "Lu Xun he Tao Yuanqing" (Lu Xun and Tao Yuanqing). *Xin wenxue shiliao* (Historical documents on New Literature) 1 (1979): 70–85.

Xu Shiheng. "Jinhou funü yingyou de jingshen" (The spirit women should have from here on). *Funü zazhi* 6.8 (1920): 13–18.

Xu Shoushang. *Wang you Lu Xun yinxiang ji* (Reminiscences of my late friend Lu Xun). Beijing: Renmin wenxue chubanshe, 1947.

Xu Xing and Xun Bu, eds. *Fanxing Zhongguo ren* (Reflecting on the Chinese). Beijing: Zhongguo wenlian chuban gongsi, 1999.

Xu Zidong. *Yu Dafu xinlun* (A new interpretation of Yu Dafu). Hangzhou: Zhejiang wenyi chubanshe, 1984.

Xue Suizhi and Zhang Juncai, eds. *Lin Shu yanjiu ziliao* (Research materials on Lin Shu). Fujian: Fujian renmin chubanshe, 1983.

Xue Zhuo. "Lin Shu qianqi yishu sixiang guankui" (A glimpse into the thinking in Lin Shu's early translations). In Xue Suizhi and Zhang Juncai, eds., *Lin Shu yanjiu ziliao* (Research materials on Lin Shu), pp. 387–99. Fujian: Fujian renmin chubanshe, 1983.

"Xuwudang" (The Nihilist Party). In Zhang Nan and Wang Yenzhi, eds., *Xinhai geming qian shinianjian shilun xuanji* (A selection of contemporary views in the ten years before the Revolution of 1911). 5 vols., 1.2:696–98. Beijing: Sanlian, 1960.

Y (pseud.). "Foluote xinlixue zhi yiban" (The school of Freud's new psychology). *Dongfang zazhi* 22 (1920): 85–86.

Yamamoto Shūji. "Houji" (Postscript). In *Lu Xun yiwenji* (A collection of Lu Xun's translations), 17 vols., 3:90–91. Beijing: Renmin wenxue chubanshe, 1959.

Yan Fu. *Yan Fu ji* (Yan Fu collection). Ed. Wang Shi. 5 vols. Beijing: Zhonghua shuju, 1986.

Yan Guocai. *Zhongguo xinlixue shi* (A history of psychology in China). Hangzhou: Zhejiang jiaoyu chubanshe, 1998.

Yan Jinrong. "You tanxiangshan riji" (Diary from travels to Hawaii). *Qingyibao* 96 (1901): 6001–04; 97 (1901): 6063–68.

Yanbing. "Funü yundong de yiyi he yaoqiu" (The significance and demand of a women's movement). *Funü zazhi* 6.8 (1920): 1–6.

Yang Xinhui, ed. *Xinlixue tongshi* (A complete history of psychology). 5 vols. Jinnan: Shangdong jiaoyu chubanshe, 2000.

Yang Zhongming. *Xunzhao Zhongguo ren de zixin* (Searching for the confidence of the Chinese). Changsha shi: Hunan wenyi chubanshe, 1999.

Ye Haosheng. *Laoji fenti: Xinlixue yidai zongshi Gao Juefu* (Old steed galloping forth: The master of a generation of psychology, Gao Juefu). Nanjing: Nanjing daxue chubanshe, 2000.

Ye Shaojun. "Ye" (Night). In *Zhongguo xin wenxue daxi 1927–1937: xiaoshuo ji 1* (Compendium of modern Chinese literature: Short stories, vol. 1), pp. 104–13. Shanghai: Shanghai wenyi chubanshe, 1984.

Ye Weili. *Seeking Modernity in China's Name: Chinese Students in the United States, 1900–1927.* Stanford: Stanford University Press, 2001.

Ye Xiaoqing. "Shanghai Before Nationalism." *East Asian History* 3 (June 1992): 33–52.

Yeh Wen-hsin. *The Alienated Academy: Culture and Politics in Republican China, 1919–1937.* Cambridge, MA: Council on East Asian Studies, Harvard University, 1990.

————, ed. *Becoming Chinese: Passages to Modernity and Beyond.* Berkeley: University of California Press, 2000.

Yichi. "Shuo aiguo" (Talking about loving the nation). *Anhui suhuabao* 14 (1904): 1–4.

Yip Ka-Che. *Health and National Reconstruction in Nationalist China: The Development of Modern Health Services, 1928–1937.* Ann Arbor: University of Michigan, Association for Asian Studies, 1995.

Yong Li. "Lun paiwai buyi you xingji" (On how it is inappropriate to leave traces when rejecting the foreign). *Dongfang zazhi* 3.12 (1907): 227–29.

Youze pifu. *Zhongguo xianzai de bujiufa* (The present remedy for China). N.p., 1915.

Yu Dafu. *Yu Dafu wenji* (The works of Yu Dafu). 12 vols. Hong Kong: Sanlian shudian, 1982.

Yu Desun. "Minzhong zhi gailiang" (The improvement of race). *Yiyaoxue* 12 (1930): 7–12; 1 (1931): 39–46.

Yu Fenggao. *"Xinli fenxi" yu Zhongguo xiandai xiaoshuo* ("Psychoanalysis" and modern Chinese fiction). Beijing: Zhongguo shehui kexue chubanshe, 1987.

Yu Jingrang, ed. and trans. *Renzhong gailiang* (Racial improvement). Beijing: Zhengzhou shuju, 1936.

Yu Yi. "Minzu zhuyi lun" (On ethnonationalism). *Zhejiangchao* 1 (1903): 1–8; 2 (1903): 11–23; 5 (1903): 25–32.

Yuan Sun. "Luxiya xuwudang" (The Russian Nihilist Party). In Zhang Nan and Wang Yenzhi, eds., *Xinhai geming qian shinianjian shilun xuanji* (A selection of contemporary views in the ten years before the Revolution of 1911). 5 vols., 1.2: 565–70. Beijing: Sanlian, 1960.

Yue Aiguo and Zhang Huayu, trans. *Zhongguo ren de xingge* (The Chinese character). Hong Kong: Sanlian, 2000.

Yugong (Old fool). "Zhongguo zhongzu cunwang wenti" (The survival question for the Chinese race). *Zhenhua wuri dashiji* (Weekly report on major events in revitalizing China) 31 (1907): 1–8; 32 (1907): 1–10; 33 (1907): 1–8; 34 (1907): 1–10; 35 (1907): 1–10; 37 (1907): 1–11; 38 (1907): 1–8; 39 (1907): 1–8; 40 (1907): 1–9; 43 (1907): 1–10; 44 (1907): 1–8; 47 (1907): 1–9; 49 (1907): 1–8; 50 (1907): 1–8; 51 (1907): 6–13.

Yun Fang. " Xin Funü suo yinggai chanchude jizhong liegenxing" (Some negative characteristics that the "New Woman" should get rid of). *Funü zazhi* 9 (1920): 3–8.

Zang Guang'en. *Zhonghua minzu xinlun* (A new treatise on the Chinese race). Shanghai: Shangwu yinshu guan, 1946.

Zarrow, Peter. *Anarchism and Chinese Political Culture.* New York: Columbia University Press, 1990.

Zeitlin, Judith. *Historian of the Strange: Pu Songling and the Chinese Classical Tale.* Stanford: Stanford University Press, 1993.

Zeitlin, Judith, Ellen Widmer, and Lydia H. Liu, eds. *Writing and Materiality: Essays in Honor of Patrick Hanan.* Cambridge, MA: Harvard University Asia Center for the Harvard-Yenching Institute, 2003.

Zeng Shiqiang and Liu Junzheng. *Jiedu Zhongguo ren* (Decoding the Chinese). 3 vols. Beijing: Zhongguo gongren chubanshe, 2001.

Zhang Binglin. "Bo Kang Youwei shu" (A letter disputing Kang Youwei). In Zhang

Nan and Wang Yenzhi, eds., *Xinhai geming qian shinianjian shilun xuanji* (A selection of contemporary views in the ten years before the Revolution of 1911), 5 vols., 1.2:752–63. Beijing: Sanlian, 1960.

———. "Lun yazhou yi ziwei chunchi" (On how Asia would do well by maintaining the alliance between the teeth and lips). *Shiwubao* 18 (1897): 1177–79.

———. *Zhang Taiyan zhenglun xuanji* (A selection of Zhang Binglin's political views). Ed. Tang Zhijun. Beijing: Zhonghua shuju, 1977.

Zhang Dongsun, trans. *Chuanghualun* (Creative evolution). 2 vols. Shanghai: Shangwu yinshu guan, 1919).

Zhang Guangfu. *Lu Xun meishu lunji* (A collection of Lu Xun's views on art). Yunnan: Xinhua shudian, 1982.

Zhang Jinglu, ed. *Zhongguo jin xiandai chuban shiliao* (Historical materials on publications in modern China). 8 vols. Shanghai: Shanghai shudian, 2003.

Zhang Jingsheng. *Di sanzhong shui yu luanzhu ji shengji de dian he yousheng de guanxi—youming Meide xingyu* (The third kind of fluid and the relationship between eugenics and the electricity of vitality and the female egg—also titled Sexual desire based on beauty). Shanghai: N.p., 1927.

———. *Meide renshengguan* (A way of life based on beauty). In *Zhang Jingsheng wenji* (Collected works of Zhang Jingsheng), 2 vols., 1:24–138. Guangzhou: Guangzhou chubanshe, 1998.

———. *Meide shehui zuzhifa* (Organizational principles of a society based on beauty). In *Zhang Jingsheng wenji* (Collected works of Zhang Jingsheng), 2 vols., 1:139–264. Guangzhou: Guangzhou chubanshe, 1998.

———. *Zhang Jingsheng wenji* (Collected works of Zhang Jingsheng). 2 vols. Guangzhou: Guangzhou chubanshe, 1998.

———, trans. *Chanhuilu* (Confessions). Shanghai: Shijie shuju, 1931.

Zhang Jingsheng (K. S. Tchang). "Les Sources antiques des théories de J.-J. Rousseau sur l'éducation." Thèse de Doctorat d'Université (University of Lyon, 1919).

Zhang Jingsheng yu Xing shi (Zhang Jingsheng and *Sexual histories*). Hong Kong: Tao zhai shuwu, 1970.

Zhang Jingyuan. *Psychoanalysis in China: Literary Transformations, 1919–1949*. Ithaca, NY: Cornell East Asian Series, Cornell University Press, 1992.

Zhang Junjun. *Minzu suzhi zhi gaizao* (The improvement of racial essence). Shanghai: Zhonghua shuju, 1943.

———. *Zhongguo minzu zhi gaizao* (The reconstruction of the Chinese race). Shanghai: Zhonghua shuju, 1936.

———. *Zhongguo minzu zhi gaizao xubian* (Sequel to The reconstruction of the Chinese race). Shanghai: Zhonghua shuju, 1937.

Zhang Lisheng. *Zhongguo zhi minzu sixiang yu minzu qijie* (China's racial thinking and racial bearing). Chongqing: Qingnian shudian, 1940.

Zhang Mengyang. *A Q xinlun: A Q yu shijie wenxue zhongde jingsheng dianxing wenti* (A new interpretation of Ah Q: Ah Q and the problem of spiritual archetype in world literature). Shanxi: Shanxi renmin jiaoyu chubanshe, 1996.

———. "Lu Xun yu Shimisi de *Zhongguo ren qizhi*" (Lu Xun and Smith's *Chinese characteristics*). *Lu Xun yanjiu niankan* (Annual publication on Lu Xun studies) 2 (1980): 208–17.

Zhang Mengyang and Wang Lijuan, trans. *Zhongguo ren de qizhi* (Chinese characteristics). Lanzhou: Dunhuang wenyi chubanshe, 1995.

Zhang Nan and Wang Yenzhi, eds. *Xinhai geming qian shinianjian shilun xuanji* (A selection of contemporary views in the ten years before the Revolution of 1911), 5 vols. Beijing: Sanlian, 1960.

Zhang Pingzhi and Yang Jinglong. *Zhongguo ren de maobing* (The quirks of the Chinese). Beijing: Zhongguo shehui chubanshe, 1998.

Zhang Shizhao (Gutong). "Zaida Zhihui xiansheng" (Replying once more to Mr. Wu Zhihui). *Jiayin zazhi* 27 (1926): 6–12.

Zhang Taiyan. "Paiman pingyi" (An even assessment of ostracizing the Manchus). In Zhang Nan and Wang Yenzhi, eds., *Xinhai geming qian shinianjian shilun xuanji* (A selection of contemporary views in the ten years before the Revolution of 1911), 5 vols., 3:45–52. Beijing: Sanlian, 1960.

Zhang Xichen and Zhou Jianren, eds. *Xin xing daode taolunji* (Discussions on new sexual ethics). Shanghai: Kaiming shudian, 1936.

Zhang Xiruo. "Zhishi funü yu yousheng wenti" (Educated women and the problem of eugenics). *Huanian* 18 (1935): 346–48.

Zhang Xuanruo. *Zhongguo minzu zhi gaizao yu zijiu* (The reconstruction of the Chinese race). Shanghai: Shangwu yinshu guan, 1936.

Zhang Xudong. *Chinese Modernism in the Era of Reforms: Cultural Fever, Avant-Garde Fiction, and New Chinese Cinema.* Durham, NC: Duke University Press, 1997.

Zhang Ying. *Jingshen fenxixue shuping* (A narrative assessment of psychoanalysis). Shenyang: Liaoning daxue chubanshe, 1986.

Zhao Gonming. *Yichuanxue yu shehui* (The study of heredity and society). Shenyang: Liaoning renmin chubanshe, 1986.

Zhao Jiabi, ed. *Zhongguo xin wenxue daxi* (Compendium of modern Chinese literature). 10 vols. Shanghai: Liangyou, 1935–36.

Zhao Liru, Lin Fang, and Zhang Shiying, eds. *Xinli xueshi* (A history of psychology). Beijing: Tuanjie chubanshe, 1989.

"Zhen huanghuo lun" (On the real yellow peril). *Dongfang zazhi* 10.4 (1913): 15–22.

Zheng Boqi. *Zheng Boqi wenji* (Zheng Boqi collection). Ed. Zheng Boqi wenji bianwei hui. Xi'an: Shanxi renmin chubanshe, 1988.

Zheng Xinsen. *Wenhua pipan yu guominxing gaizao* (Cultural critique and the reconstruction of the national character). Shanxi: Shanxi renmin chubanshe, 1988.

Zhida. "Baoman yu paiman" (Protecting and discriminating against the Manchus). In Zhang Nan and Wang Yenzhi, eds., *Xinhai geming qian shinianjian shilun xuanji* (A selection of contemporary views in the ten years before the Revolution of 1911), 5 vols., 2.2:915–16. Beijing: Sanlian, 1960.

Zhong Xueping. *Masculinity Besieged? Issues of Modernity and Male Subjectivity in Chinese Literature of the Late Twentieth Century.* Durham, NC: Duke University Press, 2000.

Zhongguo Guo Moruo yanjiuhui, ed. *Guo Moruo yu dongxi wenhua* (Guo Moruo and Eastern and Western cultures). Beijing: Dangdai Zhongguo chubanshe, 1998.

"Zhongguo shuairuo fei Riben zhi fu shuo" (China's decline is not a blessing for Japan). *Dongfang zazhi* 1.10 (1904): 231–33.

Zhongguo shehui kexue yuan wenxue yanjiu suo xiandai wenxue yanjiushi (Chinese institute of social sciences literature division: Modern literary studies), ed. *"Geming wenxue" lunzheng ziliao xuanbian* (Selections of materials on the debates over "Revolutionary Literature"). 2 vols. Beijing: Renmin wenxue chubanshe, 1981.

Zhongguo xiandai zuojia zuopin yanjiu ziliao congshu bianji weiyuanhui, ed. *Guo Moruo zhuanji*. 2 vols. Chengdu: Sichuan renmin chubanshe, 1984.

Zhongyang jiji xuehui, ed. *Guoshu daquan* (Complete encyclopedia of martial arts). Shanghai: Shanghai quanshu yanjiu hui, 1929.

Zhongyang renmin guangbo diantai lilunbu (Central People's Broadcast Network Theory Division), ed. *Huashuo Zhongguo ren* (Talking about the Chinese). Beijing: Beijing gongye daxue chubanshe, 1992.

Zhou Jianren. "Funü yu shehui" (Women and society). *Funü zazhi* 9 (1921): 1–6.

———. "Geren yu zhongzu de shuailao" (The decrepitude of the individual body and race). *Dongfang zazhi* 19.10 (1922): 42–48.

———. "Jiating shenghuo de jinghua" (The evolution of family life). *Funü zazhi* 5 (1921): 1–5.

———. *Lun youshengxue yu zhongzu qishi* (On eugenics and racial discrimination). Shanghai: Sanlian, 1948.

———. "Shanzhongxue yu qi jianlizhe" (Eugenics and its founders). *Dongfang zazhi* 17.18 (1920): 69–76.

Zhou Zuoren. "Gouyan tongxing: Er" (Correspondence from *The studio of bitter rain gathering on the eaves: 2*). *Chenbao fukan* (08.27.1924).

———. *Zhou Zuoren jiwaiwen* (Uncollected works of Zhou Zuoren). Ed. Chen Zishan and Zhang Tierong. 2 vols. Haikou: Hainan guoji xinwen chuban zhongxin, 1995.

———. *Zhou Zuoren wenxuan* (Selected works of Zhou Zuoren). Ed. Zhong Shuhe. 4 vols. Guangzhou: Guangzhou chubanshe, 1996.

Zhu Guangqian. "Fulude de yinyishi shuo yu xinli" (Freud's theory of the unconscious and psychology). *Dongfang zazhi* 18.14 (1921): 41–50.

"Zhu huangzhong zhi jiangxing" (Well wishes for the imminent rise of the yellow race). *Dongfang zazhi* 1.1 (1904): 13–15.

Zhu Weizheng, ed. *Kang Youwei datonglun liang zhong* (Kang Youwei's view on the great union: Two kinds). Hong Kong: Sanlian shudian, 1998.

Zhuang You. "Guomin xin linghun" (The soul of the new citizen). *Jiangsu* 5 (1903): 1–9.

Zili guomin. "Meiguo nuedai huaren bugaowen" (A public notice on Americans' ill treatment of the Chinese). *Qingyibao* 99 (1901): 5657–65; 92 (1901): 5771–78; 93 (1901): 5831–32; 99 (1901): 6177–80.

Zito, Angela, and Tani Barlow, eds. *Body, Subject, & Power in China*. Chicago: University of Chicago Press, 1994.

Ziyouhua (Zhang Zhaotong). *Ziyou jiehun* (Freedom of marriage). In Wang Jiquan et al., eds. *Zhongguo jindai xiaoshuo daxi* (Compendium of China's early modern fiction). 80 vols., 25:103–286. Nanchang: Baihua wenyi chubanshe, 1991.

Zong Shishou. "Zhichi xuehui houxu" (Afterword to the Learning Society of Knowing Shame). *Shiwubao* 42 (1897): 2761–64.

Zou Rong. *Zou Rong ji qi gemingjun* (Zou Rong and his *The revolutionary army*). Ed. Sichuan congshu bianji weiyuanhui. Taibei: Zhongxi dazi fanyishe, 1978.

Zhuo Dai (Xu Zhuodai). "Fengehou zhi wuren" (Our people after the partition). *Jiangsu* 8 (1903): 19–20; 9–10 (1903): 1–16.

"Zoujin fei huanghuo shuo" (Against the report of "yellow peril"). *Jingzhong ribao* (07.31.1904).

"Zuijin zhi youlie tan" (Recent discussions on superiority and inferiority). *Dongfang zazhi* 1.8 (1904): 174–77.